29TH

DIVISIONAL ARTILLERY,

WAR RECORD

AND

HONOURS BOOK

1915–1918.

BY

LIEUT.-COLONEL R. M. JOHNSON, C.M.G., D.S.O.

The Naval & Military Press Ltd

published in association with

FIREPOWER
The Royal Artillery Museum
Woolwich

PREFACE.

The original intention of this book was to provide the recipients of honours with some record of the deeds for which such honours were bestowed. This intention owes its origin to the Honours Book kept by (then) Major-General Sir Beauvoir de Lisle and continued, after that officer left us on promotion to command an Army Corps, by Major-General D. S. Cayley. The Divisional Honours Book, however, did not include the text of the recommendations made in individual cases—in fact, could not possibly do so, as the necessary time and labour for the inclusion of so much detail would have been totally impracticable on active service. In the peaceful time, however, which reigned after the Division had settled down in its winter quarters after the march into Germany, an attempt was made to improve on the Divisional Book, as far as the Divisional Artillery was concerned, by the inclusion of the text of the recommendations. It was thought thereby to make the record more valuable to the recipients of honours, as, except in the case of immediate awards, no "story" appears in the gazette announcing such awards, whilst, even in the case of immediate ones, the volume of gazettes was so enormous during the war that many an individual may never have seen the text of his recommendation if he was not still present with his unit at the time the award was made.

Thanks, however, to the courtesy of the "A" Branch of the 29th Division, whose records were at my disposal, such a complete record was made of all the recommendations and awards, that it then seemed worth while to improve on the original idea and include a short history of the doings of the D.A., a list of casualties, and a record of officers' services.

The inclusion of these extra portions has unfortunately postponed publication very considerably. To take the case of casualties alone, although there was what purported to be a complete record of these in the D.A.H.Q. office and this was converted into alphabetical order by the strenuous efforts of the H.Q. clerks, yet when this list came to be checked by the Part II Orders of units, it was found to teem with omissions and inaccuracies, and the work of correction has been considerable and lengthy. Then again, some time elapsed before the opportunity presented itself of making many visits to the Historical Section of the Committee of Imperial Defence in order to extract the necessary information from the War Diaries of units for the compilation of the short history. The record of officers' services, on the other hand, was compiled with comparative ease, though from every conceivable source.

It was therefore not till the end of the year 1919 that the material had been collected, and even then it was obvious that, owing to the incompleteness of War Diaries and other records, the work would, without further information, fall far short of what it is desired to attain. Even at this period, an immense amount of rearranging and typing was necessary before going to press, and it was therefore thought that the best plan would be to get a considerable number of copies of the history portion in proof form, send a copy to every officer who would be likely to supply more information, and to get on with the preparation for the press of the rest of the work pending receipt of replies from the officers to whom the history had been sent.

Unfortunately, I have since been ordered to China, where distance from the U.K. precludes the above arrangement, and I must now adhere to the original plan which was explained to all ranks of the D.A. before the final break-up in Germany, viz:—to publish a first (cheap) edition of the work, and ask everyone to help in perfecting the final edition.

The history, as it stands at present, is in many cases incomplete, and is generally bald and comparatively uninteresting. Many officers and other ranks must have records, either in the form of diaries or letters to their relatives, recounting incidents which would be of great interest and historical value. I ask them to send them along. My address is given at the end of the preface.

It is not possible at the present moment to forcast what will be the price of the final edition, which it is thought should be a high class production, as far as printing, paper, and binding are concerned. Much will depend on the demand, and officers and others will assist materially by letting me know as soon as possible that they are willing to purchase a copy.

The question of maps to accompany the work has perplexed me considerably. The D.A. served in so many places in France and Belgium that the inclusion of maps to illustrate all their doings would make the price prohibitive. In the hope that purchasers are already in possession of maps of the theatre of operations in which they are particularly interested, I have omitted maps entirely!

In conclusion, I have to thank the following officers and others for their assistance:—

Sergeant-Major (Superintending Clerk) H. W. Adams, late chief clerk at D.A.H.Q., by whose untiring labour and excellent memory much of the spade work was accomplished.

Lance Bombr. H. P. Steel and Corporal D. J. Edwards, of the D.A.H.Q. clerical staff, for their labours with the Casualty Lists.

Major J. N. Thomson, D.S.O., M.C., late Brigade Major 29th D.A., for extracting entries from voluminous gazettes and for the entire work of proof reading and final editing of the book.

The Officer i/c R.H. and R.F.A. Records, for kindly placing all Part II Orders at my disposal.

Brig.-Genl. J. E. Edmonds, chief of the Historical Section of the C.I.D., for his assistance in placing the War Diaries at my disposal.

Major D. Daly, D.S.O., M.C., commanding the 26th Battery, for the excellent diary of the 26th Battery which had been kept up from start to finish.

Also many other officers who had served for long periods in the D.A. and were still therein when the work was started in Germany.

Commandant,
Shanghai Volunteer Corps,
Shanghai,
China.

LT.-COL., R.F.A.
(late Comdg. 29th Div. Arty).

CONTENTS.

The 29ᵗʰ Division

GALLIPOLI 1915-16   SOMME 1916-17

ARRAS 1917

YPRES 1917   CAMBRAI 1917

LYS 1918   GHELUVELT 1918   LEDEGHEM 1918

_____

_____

I HAVE·READ·WITH·MUCH PLEASURE·THE·REPORTS OF·YOUR·REGIMENTAL COMMANDER·AND BRIGADE·COMMANDER REGARDING·YOUR·GALLANT:CONDUCT·AND·DEVOTION·TO DUTY·IN·THE·FIELD·ON

_____

AND·HAVE·ORDERED·YOUR·NAME AND·DEED·TO·BE·ENTERED·IN·THE RECORD·OF·THE·29TH·DIVISION

Major-General
Commanding 29th Division

29TH DIVISIONAL ARTILLERY

WAR RECORD AND HONOURS BOOK

1915—1918.

PART I.

HONOURS.

(i) List of officers, in alphabetical order, who received honours for services in the 29th Divisional Artillery.

(ii) List of warrant officers, non-commissioned officers, and men, in alphabetical order, who received honours for services in the 29th Divisional Artillery.

(iii) List of honours, arranged according to units, in chronological order.

A

EXPLANATORY NOTES.

1.   The date given after the award in each case is the date of the London Gazette, or of the Supplement to a London Gazette, in which the particular award was published.

2.   The rank stated against the name of the individual is usually that held by him at the time of the action recorded.   As, however, official records almost invariably show the rank held at the time the *recommendation* for the award was submitted, it has been possible to give the correct rank in those cases only where the individual's record of service is sufficiently well known.

3.   The "story" recorded is, in the majority of cases, that which was submitted by the C.R.A. with his recommendation for award.   In some cases, however, e.g. of many actions performed in Gallipoli of which records are scanty, no guarantee can be given that the "story" is identical with that which accompanied the original recommendation.   There is, however, documentary evidence in every case that the story given here was submitted by a responsible officer at some time, and in no case is it probable that this story differs materially from the official version accompanying the recommendation.

4.   "Divisional Cards of Honour" were introduced by Major General Sir Beauvoir de Lisle, commanding the Division, about July 1917 when a Divisional Honours Book was instituted.   Thenceforward, anyone fortunate enough to have his name recorded in this book was granted a "Card of Honour", a parchment certificate of which a replica is given in the frontispiece, and was also entitled to wear the Divisional emblem of honour on the red triangle on the right shoulder.   The fact of being mentioned in despatches, or receiving an "immediate" or other award, entitled the recipient to a "Card of Honour".   In this work mention of these cards is made only in cases where the individual received no other award for that particular action.

(I) LIST OF OFFICERS, IN ALPHABETICAL ORDER, WHO RECEIVED HONOURS FOR SERVICES IN THE 29th DIVISION ARTILLERY.

Ashmore, E. B., c.m.g., m.v.o., Brevet-Col. (Temp. Br.-Genl.), HQ. 29th Div. Arty.
Somme, 1916-17.—For able command of the 29th Divisional Artillery during the period December 1916 to March 1917, with special reference to the operations on the Somme in January and February 1917. (Mention 15/15/17).

Bailey, G. H., Lieut. 460th Battery, R.F.A.
Gallipoli, 1915.—In the action of the 6th August, 1915, this officer was F.O.O. All communications with his battery were cut by the exceptionally heavy hostile shell fire. He came out into the open under the same shell fire, repaired the broken wire as he went, found his C.O., who was in another O.P., and then returned to his post. From May to August, 1915 this young officer showed exceptional coolness, initiative, resource and judgment on several occasions. (M.C. 2/2/16, Mention 28/6/16).

Bain, F. O., Temp. Lieut., D/17 Battery, R.F.A.
Somme, 1916-17.—For bravery and consistently good service between September 1916 and February 1917. He is an exceptionally gallant and successful observer. During December, 1916, when his C.O. was away, he commanded a battery with great success. (Mention 18/5/17).

Ball, C. J. P., 2nd Lieut., "B" Battery, R.H.A.
Gallipoli 1915.—After the actions of the 12th and 13th July, 1915, this officer volunteered to make a reconnaissance and forwarded an accurate report of great value. He was brought to notice on several other occasions in 1915 for energy and initiative in locating and pointing out targets for the infantry to fire at, and for reconnoitring forward positions for enfilading guns in localities exposed to fire. (M.C. 3/6/16, Mention 13/7/16).

"   "   Lieut. (actg. Major), 460th Battery, R.F.A.
Flanders and Cambrai, 1917.—Commanded his battery and fought with the greatest distinction in Flanders and before Cambrai during the period September, 1917, to February, 1918. Continually displayed remarkable bravery in the field, especially while in action with his battery at the battle of Cambrai. (D.S.O. 3/6/18 Mention 21/5/18).

Ball K. M., Captain 97th Battery, R.F.A.
Gallipoli, 1916.—For the successful evacuation of guns of the 97th and 368th batteries. On the 9th January, 1916, he was in charge of the last lighters to leave the shore and supervised the military arrangements as required by the Navy which resulted in the successful transfer of these guns to their ships in spite of a heavy swell. (Mention 13/7/16).

Barnett E. J., 2nd Lieut., 29th Divl. Sig. Co. (attd. HQ. 29th Div. Arty).
Gallipoli, 1915.—Was R.A. signalling officer in June, 1915. For excellent work in maintaining communications in the actions of the 4th and 28th June and in the French attack of 21st June. (Mention 5/11/15).

Bayley L. S., Major, 14th Siege Battery, R.G.A.
Gallipoli, 1915.—For excellent work when in command of his battery in the actions of the 4th and 28th June, 1915, and in support of the French attack of the 21st June. (Brevet Lt.-Col. 8/11/15, Mention 13/7/16).

Beaver R. H., Lieut., 92nd Battery, R.F.A.
Flanders, 1918.—Commanded his battery during operations before Menin from September 28th to October 1st, 1918. With great gallantry he took his guns forward and supported the infantry at very close range, thus enabling the latter to make a further advance. Although under heavy machine gun fire he kept his battery boldly in action until ammunition was exhausted. He was wounded but refused to leave his guns until ordered and until he had seen all his wounded safely away. He set a splendid example of courage and perseverance. (M.C. (immediate) 15/2/19).

Belcher H. B., Temp. Lieut. (actg. Capt.), 29th D.A.C.
    1917-18.—Did extraordinarily good and gallant service in a T.M. battery
in the Ypres and Cambrai operations of 1917 and up to the time when he
was seriously wounded in March, 1918, in the Passchendaele sector. Since
his return from convalescence he has been Adjutant of the D.A.C. and has
proved himself a most capable, hardworking and excellent adjutant.
(Divisional Card of Honour).

Blandy C. G. S., Captain, R.A.M.C. (attached 15th Brigade, R.H.A.)
    Gallipoli, 1915.—Attended French and British wounded without cessation
from 4 p.m. 1st May until midday on 2nd May, 1915, under rifle fire the
whole time. Also, in general, for energy, skill, and devotion to duty as
Medical Officer in charge of the 15th Brigade. R.H.A.   (M.C. 3/6/16,
Mention 13/7/16).

Booth P. D., Temp. Lieut., 26th Battery, R.F.A.
    Gallipoli, 1915.—For his enterprise, initiative and pluck, on 28th June,
1915, in pushing forward with his telephone and wires under heavy fire up
to the most advanced trench captured by our infantry, and establishing and
maintaining communication.   (M.C. 8/11/15, Mention 5/11/15).

  ,,   ,,   actg. Capt., Divisional Trench Mortar Officer.
    Cambrai, 1917.—On November 30th, near Cambrai, armed with a Lewis
gun, this officer with the help of a machine gunner held the ridge opposite
the 15th Brigade R.H.A. gun positions (north of the valley containing the
La Vacquerie-Masnieres road) for several hours against the attacking enemy.
He succeeded in holding the Germans back until such a time as an organised
defence could be made.
    About 4 p.m. on December 1st a party of the Guernsey Light Infantry was
sent across the bridge from the east side of the canal in Masnieres to clear
the enemy from Les Rues Vertes which they had just occupied.   Captain
Booth joined this party and led them along the street running south-west,
capturing 5 of the enemy and clearing all the north end of the village; he
then proceeded with his party to clear the southern portion.   On reaching
the main Cambrai road a party of at least 20 was encountered; as it was now
dark, Captain Booth went right up to within five yards of them to see who
they were.   On being challenged, they were found to be Germans armed with
bombs, which they threw, wounding Captain Booth.   The command of the
party then devolved on Captain Craib who, after ten minutes hard fighting,
drove the enemy back.   It was entirely due to the efforts of these two
officers that the enemy finally retained only that portion of Les Rues Vertes
which lies to the south of the main Cambrai road, and that the Advanced
Dressing Station in the brewery, from which a large number of our wounded
were finally evacuated, remained in our hands.   (D.S.O. (immediate) 4/2/18,
Mention 21/5/18).
    N.B.—Captain Booth unfortunately succumbed to his wounds.

Bright, F. Y., Temp. Lieut. (actg. Capt)), No. 1 Section, 29th D.A.C.
    Flanders, 1918.—For good work as a D.A.C. Section Commander.
(Mention 1/1/19).

Brooke, A. C., Captain, 26th Battery, R.F.A.
    Gallipoli, 1915.—(Chevalier, Legion of Honour 4/2/16, Mention 13/7/16).

Brooker, J. H., 2nd Lieut. (S.R.), 92nd Battery, R.F.A.
    1917-18.—For good work.   (Mention 21/5/18).
    Flanders, 1918.—In operations before Menin on September 28th, 1918,
this officer was instrumental in enabling his battery to get forward.   With
courage and perseverance he made a roadway for the guns under fire.
On October 1st he again got his guns forward and fired at close range over
open sights, thus materially assisting the rapid advance of the infantry.
His coolness, endurance and total disregard of danger were marked throughout
the operations.   (M.C. (immediate) 15/2/19).

Browne, V. F., Lieut. (actg. Capt.), Adjutant, 15th Brigade, R.H.A.
    Arras and Flanders, 1917.—For conspicuously good work in charge of
signal communications in the operations about Monchy in April. May and
June, 1917, and as Adjutant during the operations north of Ypres in July
and August, 1917.   (Mention 14/12/17).
    Flanders, 1918.—For good work as Adjutant throughout operations up to
September, 1918.   (Mention 23/12/18).
    Flanders, 1918.—For continuous good service as Adjutant, particularly
during the withdrawal from Passchendaele in April, 1918, and the successful
advance in October, 1918.   During these periods his devotion to duty,
frequently under heavy fire, was of material assistance to the support which
the brigade was able to render to the infantry.   (M.C. 3/6/19, Belgian Croix
de Guerre 4/9/19).

Burne, E. R., D.S.O., Lieut.-Col., HQ. 15th Brigade, R.H.A.
    1917-18.—For good work in command of his brigade, particularly in the operations near Cambrai in November-December, 1917. (Mention 21/5/18).

Burney, A. E. C., Capt., Adjt. 1/4th Highland Mountain Brigade, R.G.A. (T.F.).
    Gallipoli, 1915.—This officer was in command of the Highland Mountain Battery (organised from the Ross and Argyll Mountain Batteries) in the Gallipoli operations. He was indefatigable in reconnoitring forward positions for his guns, close to the front line trenches, placing his guns in them and superintending their fire. It is due to his initiative, resource and personal example that this Territorial battery has done such excellent work. During the first two months this battery had 3 officers killed and 4 wounded, and 54 N.C.O.'s and men killed and wounded. It never had a day's rest and yet its morale remained as good as ever, greatly due to Captain Burney's example. (M.C. 8/11/15, Mention 5/11/15).

Calvert, C. H., Temp., 2nd Lieut., Trench Mortar Group.
    Gallipoli, 1915.—For very good work with Trench Mortars in local attacks by the 52nd Lowland Division in November and December. (M.C. 3/6/16 Mention 13/7/16).

Calvert, J. H., 2nd Lieut, (S.R.), 13th Battery, R.F.A.
    Cambrai, 1917.—On 20th November he was in charge of a party preparing a road for the advance of his brigade. He displayed the greatest initiative and resource. In spite of heavy machine gun fire the work was carried out with the greatest speed, enabling the brigade to advance quickly and successfully. (Mention 21/5/18).

Campbell, N. StC., Major 13th Battery, R.F.A.
    Gallipoli, 1915.—This officer was in the battery from the landing onwards and worked extremely hard. He kept his battery in an extremely efficient condition throughout all difficulties. (D.S.O. 3/6/16, Mention 13/7/16).

Cattell, E. M., 2nd Lieut. (S.R.), 460th Battery, R.F.A.
    Somme, 1916-17.—For gallantry and excellent work between November, 1916, and February, 1917. On February 8th, 1917, when F.O.O. in an attack near Sailly Saillisel he took command of infantry who had lost their officers. He was wounded that day, whilst mending wires under shell fire. (Mention 18/5/17).

Chalkley, R., 2nd Lieut. (actg. Capt.), 26th Battery, R.F.A.
    Arras and Flanders, 1917.—For gallantry and devotion to duty throughout the operations in 1917 around Arras and Monchy and north of Ypres He has on several occasions by personal reconnaissance, though exposed to heavy shell fire, brought in valuable information. His personal courage and excellent work in the battery have been a fine example to all. (Mention 14/12/17).

Clare, H. T., 2nd Lieut., 460th Battery, R.F.A., and 13th Battery, R.F.A.
    Gallipoli, 1915.—For unvarying energy and ability in collecting and transmitting information and for directing the fire of his battery from exposed positions. (Mention 13/7/16).
    Gallipoli, 1915.—For good service throughout, often in very exposed positions as F.O.O. He accompanied his brigade when it went into action across the Suez Canal in February, 1916. (Order of Crown of Italy 2/11/18).

Clark, C. H., Major, Brigade Major 29th Divl. Arty.
    Gallipoli, 1915-16.—For excellent work as Brigade Major, showing marked zeal and ability in that appointment. His untiring energy and thoroughness in working out all details were very largely responsible for the successful completion of the evacuation of the Left Group. (D.S.O. 3/6/16, Mention 13/7/16).

    Somme, 1916-17.—For conspicuous good service and exceptional ability. Notably in the attack of January 27th, 1917, near Le Transloy he carried out the staff work in connection with a large force of artillery with marked success. (Mention 15/5/17).

Clarke, C., 2nd Lieut., "Y" Battery, R.H.A.
    Gallipoli, 1916.—For excellent work as F.O.O. on Jan 7th, 1916. He managed to repair his lines, in spite of the fact that the communication trench had been very heavily shelled and destroyed in many places. He was thus able to send in the most valuable report on the situation many hours ahead of information received from any other source. (M.C. 3/6/16, Mention 13/7/16).

Courage, M. R. F., Major (Temp. Lt.-Col.), 147th Brigade, R.F.A.
Somme, 1916.—As O.C. 370th Battery he worked with unremitting industry and skill during the preparation for the 1st July, 1916, in the Beaumont Hamel sector. During the battle he directed the fire of his battery with complete success. During the operations of 3rd September he commanded a group with energy and skill. (Mention 4/1/17).

Craib, W. H., Lieut. (S.R.), (actg. Capt.), V/29 Heavy Trench Mortar Battery.
Flanders, 1917.—During the period from 5/7/17 to 26/7/17, when commanding his battery at Boesinghe, he displayed the greatest gallantry under fire. He remained at the guns all the time refusing to be relieved, and showed consistent cheerfulness and disregard of personal danger. This officer has invariably shown himself an exceptionally capable, energetic and courageous battery commander. (M.C. 1/1/18).
Cambrai, 1917.—On December 1st, 1917, the Germans captured Les Rues Vertes (near Cambrai) and were advancing towards Masnieres. Captain Craib, with Captain Booth, organised a party of the Guernsey Light Infantry, and himself led a counter-attack which drove the enemy out of the northern part of the village, capturing several prisoners. Under the resolute leadership of these two officers, the party advanced on the southern portion of the village and in the dark encountered a party of Germans who were only recognised as very close quarters. The Germans threw bombs, wounding Captain Booth; Captain Craib maintained a determined resistance and succeeded in driving back the enemy and recovering Captain Booth. It was entirely due to the efforts of these two officers that the enemy finally retained only that portion of Les Rues Vertes which lies to the south of the main Cambrai road, and that the Advanced Dressing Station in the brewery, from which a large number of our wounded were finally evacuated, was captured by us. (Bar to M.C. (immediate) 4/2/18).

Cunnison, T. J., Temp. Lieut. (actg. Capt.), Staff Captain 29th Divl. Arty.
Somme, 1916-17.—For consistent good work as Staff Captain during the period December, 1916, to February, 1917, notably in connection with the supply of ammunition for a large force of artillery in the action of January 27th, 1917, near Le Transloy. (Mention 15/5/17).

Arras and Flanders, 1917.—For consistent good work as Staff Captain. He has shown the greatest care for the comfort and welfare of all ranks. The supply of ammunition has been invariably well maintained and on one or two occasions it was personally superintended by this officer under heavy shell fire. He has been a battery officer and Adjutant of a brigade through the Gallipoli campaign. He has worked most indefatigably in all his appointments. (M.C. 1/1/18).

„   „   13th Battery, R.F.A.
Flanders, 1918.—For general good work in 1918, with particular reference to the advance through Belgium in September and October, 1918. (Belgian Croix de Guerre 4/9/19).

Daly, D., Captain, 15th B.A.C. and Trench Mortar Group.
Gallipoli, 1915.—12th and 13th July. Fine work in charge of 12-pdr. gun in forward position exposed to heavy shell fire. 30th August to 27th November. Fine work while in charge of the Dumezil Trench Mortar Group. All minor operations during this period were very greatly aided by the fire of the Dumezils, which was largely due to the intrepidity and skill of Captain Daly. (M.C. 3/6/16, Mention 13/7/16).

„   Major, 26th Battery, R.F.A.
Cambrai, 1917, and Flanders, 1917-18.—Good work in command of his battery September, 1917, to February, 1918. (Mention 21/5/18).
Flanders, 1918.—For conspicuous ability in command of his battery in various operations, during the period under review (February to September, 1918), also whilst in temporary command of his brigade at various times. Proved himself to be an intrepid and brilliant leader who has set a splendid example by his cheerful demeanour under all forms of hostile fire and his utter disregard for danger and hardship. (D.S.O. 1/1/19, Mention 23/12/18).

d'Apice, J. E. F., Captain, Staff Captain 29th Divl. Arty.
Gallipoli, 1915.—For exceptional capacity and ability for organisation in connection with the ammunition supply for 110 guns of nine different calibres and with the administration of the artillery at Cape Helles comprising all branches, regulars, territorials, and Australian artillery. For untiring energy and zeal, good temper and tact. When Captain Walford, Brigade Major, was killed, this officer did the work of Brigade Major, as well as his own, from 26th April to the 5th May. Showed marked personal bravery and initiative in reconnaissance under heavy rifle fire. (D.S.O. 8/11/15, Mention 5/11/15, Mention 13/7/16).

Daubuz, C., Captain, Adjutant 15th Brigade, R.H.A.
Gallipoli, 1915.—On the night of the 1st/2nd May this officer displayed valuable initiative in going up to the firing line for information under heavy shrapnel fire, and gallantly helped to organise infantry who were retiring past the trenches. He was wounded in the cheek, but continued on duty after being attended to. (M.C. 8/11/15, Mention 5/11/15).

Denison, H., Captain, 97th Battery, R.F.A., and "B" Battery, R.H.A.
Gallipoli, 1915.—Commanded the 97th Battery, R.F.A., from the 29th April until appointed to command B" Battery, R.H.A., on the 3rd Spetember. Both batteries while under his command maintained a high standard of vigilance and fine efficiency in spite of constant changes among the junior officers. (D.S.O. 3/6/16, Mention 13/7/16).

Dixon, G. H. S., Lieut. (T.F.), 1/1st Warwickshire Battery, R.H.A. (T.F.).
Cambrai, 1917.—Displayed considerable dash and energy on 29th/30th November at the action in La Vacquerie valley. Superintended all night the digging out of men buried by gas shell, his own gas helmets having both been buried by gas shell. In the morning, this officer was the last to leave his battery, and carried away a breech block and a wounded man. (M.C. (immedite) 4/2/18).

Downs, J., 2nd Lieut. (S.R.), 460th Battery, R.F.A.
Flanders, 1918.—Commanded a section of guns ordered up to support the infantry at close range on September 29th near Kruiseecke. One gun was brought into action without difficulty, but the enemy then put down a heavy barrage. 2nd Lieut. Downs gallantly passed through this barrage three times in order to bring up the remaining guns and ammunition. Afterwards it became necessary to withdraw the guns. By this time the hostile fire had increased and had destroyed the road. It was not till the third attempt that the guns were got away. 2nd Lieut. Downs showed great coolness and courage in carrying his task to a successful conclusion. (M.C. (immediate) 15/2/19).

Duff, C. P., Temp. Lieut., 460th Battery, R.F.A., and H.Q. 15th Brigade R.H.A.
Gallipoli, 1915, and Somme, 1916-17.—For consistent good work from April, 1915, to February, 1917, in Gallipoli and France. On September 1st and 2nd, 1916, he was F.O.O. in Thiepval Wood, carried on his observation most carefully under constant shell fire and displayed great coolness. Since December, 1916, Lieut. Duff has been Orderly Officer to the 15th Brigade, R.H.A., and has done excellent work. Date of report, 6/3/17. (Mention 4/1/17, Mention 18/5/17).

Duncan-Wallace, T., Lieut. (T.F.), 1/4th Highland Mountain Brigade, R.G.A. (T.F.),
Gallipoli, 1915.—This officer showed great initiative and resource throughout. In the attack on the 28th June, he commanded with conspicuous gallantry a gun which had been placed close behind the firing line; and on the 12th July he commanded a section of guns similarly placed to enfilade the enemy's trenches. In the latter action he maintained the section in action throughout the whole day under heavy artillery fire, though four men were killed and four wounded during the first hour. (Mention 5/11/15).

Durell, T. C. V., Lieut. (S.R.), 26th Battery, R.F.A.
1917-18.—Has performed gallant and excellent service during the two years he has been in the battery. On one particular occasion he did a particularly fearless act in putting out a fire in an ammunition dump at a battery position under heavy shell fire, but, though this is the only specific instance that can be quoted, this officer has always displayed exemplary courage, coolness and resource in all the operations in which he has taken part. (Divisional Card of Honour).

Eden, Hon. R. E., Lieut. (T.F.), (actg. Major), 1/1st Warwickshire Battery, R.H.A. (T.F.).
Arras and Flanders, 1917.—For efficient and successful command of his battery. (Mention 14/12/17).
Flanders, 1917-18, and Cambrai, 1917.—Has commanded his battery with distinction during the period September, 1917, to February, 1918. Has served continuously as subaltern, captain, and commanding officer, in the same battery with which he came out to France in 1914, and during the past six months his personality and devotion to duty have maintained in his battery a very high level of efficiency and soldierly smartness. Report dated 5/3/18. (M.C. 3/6/18).

Eggleton, F., Temp. 2nd Lieut., 13th Battery, R.F.A.
Somme, 1916.—For continuous good work. Commanded a section of guns near Flers from 12th October till 27th November; constantly exposed to heavy shell fire, he kept his men cheerful and did excellent shooting. (Mention 18/5/17).
" actg. Major.
Arras and Flanders, 1917.—Commanded his battery throughout these operations with great ability; the high standard of efficiency maintained by the battery throughout these trying times is due to his energy and fine example. (Mention, 14/12/17).

Forman, D. E., Major, "B" Battery, R.H.A.
Gallipoli, 1915.—For fine work in command of his battery from 27th April to 5th May, especially during the night 1st/2nd May, in preventing the withdrawal of men from the trenches immediately in front of his battery whilst under heavy fire. For excellent work and accurate and effective fire of "B" Battery R.H.A. on the 4th June which contributed very largely to the successful advance of the infantry in the centre.
" Lieut.-Colonel, 147th Brigade, R.F.A.
Gallipoli, 1915.—For excellent work in command of the counter-battery group from 3rd November to 25th December, 1915. Showed the greatest energy and ability in this work. C.M.G. 2/5/16, Mention 5/8/15, Mention 5/5/16, Mention 13/7/16).

Fraser, A. A., Lieut., No. 4 Section, 29th D.A.C.
Gallipoli, 1915.—For good work in command of the detachment from the D.A.C. which landed on the peninsula. (Mention 13/7/16).

Gammell, J. A. H., Lieut., 460th Battery, R.F.A.
Gallipoli, 1915.—1st/2nd May. For good work when in charge of the guns, on the Turks breaking through the French line and getting within 200 yards of the battery. He maintained the fire of the battery at 800 yards range and inflicted very heavy casualties. He was slightly wounded twice (hand and chest). (Mention 5/11/15).

Gibbon, J. H., Major, 460th Battery, R.F.A.
Gallipoli, 1915.—For good work at the landing, and on 1st/2nd May when the Turks broke through the French line. (D.S.O. 2/5/16, Mention 5/5/16).

Grant, H. F. L., Major, Brigade Major 29th Divl. Arty.
Gallipoli, 1915.—Was Brigade Major from 5th May, 1915. The initiative, energy and hard work displayed by this officer were exceptional. Whatever success the artillery obtained during the actions of the 4th and 28th June were in a great measure due to this officer. (Mention 5/11/15).

Green, E. E., Lieut. (T.F.), (actg. Capt.), 29th Divl. Signal Co., R.E. (attached HQ. 29th Divl. Arty).
Arras and Flanders, 1917.—This officer has been responsible for the 29th D.A. Signals since March, 1917. In spite of every difficulty communications have been maintained, and this has been very largely due to Captain Green's personal work and supervision. His efforts have been invaluable. Report dated September, 1917. (Mention 14/12/17).
Flanders, 1917-18, and Cambrai, 1917.—This officer was responsible for the communications of the 29th D.A. during the period under review (September, 1917, to February, 1918). His power of organisation and the conscientious thoroughness of his work have ensured the maintenance of communications at critical times and in spite of every difficulty. (M.C. 3/6/18).

Grey, W. E., Lieut. (T.F.), (actg. Capt.), Y/29 Trench Mortar Battery.
Flanders and Cambrai, 1917.—For good and gallant work in command of his battery. (Mention 21/5/18).

Harris, F., Lieut., R.A.M.C. (attached 17th Baigade, R.F.A.).
Gallipoli, 1915.—For continuous good work since he landed with the 17th Brigade, R.F.A., on the 25th April. Has constantly attended men of other units in the Krithia nullah and has throughout shown great bravery and constant attention to his duties. (Mention 13/7/16).
" Temp. Capt., "
Flanders, 1917.—For conspicuous gallantry and devotion to duty. On the night 18/19th July the road forward from Elverdinghe was very heavily shelled for three hours and there were many casualties amongst men bringing up ammunition. During the whole time, Captain Harris was constantly working in the open amongst the killed and wounded in the worst of the fire. He succeeded in getting many of the wounded under cover and undoubtedly saved their lives. (M.C. (immediate) 26/9/17).

Haynes, A. E., Temp. Lieut., D/17 Battery, R.F.A.

Somme, 1916.—For excellent work in the Beaumont Hamel sector with a single detached howitzer, cutting wire at close range before the operations of September 3rd. The idea was entirely his own, and, after obtaining permission, he carried it out with complete success.

" actg. Capt., Divisional Trench Mortar Officer.

Somme 1916-17.—For continuous good service and gallant conduct. Commanded the Trench Mortars of the 29th D.A. with great ability from December, 1916, to February, 1917. (M.C. 4/6/17).

Hickes, L. D., Captain, Adjutant 17 Brigade, R.F.A., and Staff Captain 29th Divl. Arty.

Gallipoli, 1915. For excellent work as Adjutant 17th Brigade, R.F.A., and subsequently as Staff Captain. His energy was untiring and his supervision of details unfailing. He was responsible for the arrangements for horsing all R.A. guns and vehicles on the peninsula, and it speaks volumes for his organisation that the programme was correctly carried out night by night. (M.C. 3/6/16, Mention 13/7/16).

Hill, J. Shirley., 2nd Lieut. (S.R.), "B" Battery, R.H.A.

Arras, 1917.—On 17th June, the officers of the battery were endeavouring to form a smoke screen in front of the battery, with phosphorus bombs, to prevent balloon observation of the shelling of the battery by hostile 15'" howitzers. As the officers were all in the command post preparing a fresh supply of bombs, a shell dropped on the entrance, killing Major Merritt, badly wounding 2nd Lieut. Lunn, and wounding 2nd Lieut. Shirley Hill in five places. In spite of his wounds and of the very heavy shelling—so severe that each of the six guns received a direct hit—2nd Lieut. Hill, with the assistance of Bombardier Tristram, dug out 2nd Lieut. Lunn and the signallers who had been buried, and assisted to carry the former to the dressing station, across a heavily shelled area, before having his own wounds dressed. (M.C. (immediate) 17/9/17).

Holmes, H. O.. Temp. Capt. (actg. Major), D/147 (afterwards D/17) Battery, R.F.A.

Somme, 1916-17.—Commanded his battery with conspicuous ability between September, 1916, and February, 1917. The battery made excellent shooting. He is a very energetic and fearless officer. (Mention 18/5/17).

Arras and Flanders, 1917.—For great devotion to duty in these operations. Under severe fighting conditions he invariably handled his battery with conspicuous ability and courage, and set a noble example of endurance and cheerfulness. (M.C. 1/1/18).

Cambrai, 1917.—On November 30th. near Marcoing, the Germans broke through the sector to the right of that held by the 29th Division and approached to within close range of this officer's battery. To obtain good observation of the enemy he had to advance right through the retiring infantry and, ordering his guns to be swung round, opened a heavy fire, and so held the Germans until a counter-attack was organised. Although under heavy rifle fire all the time, he continued to direct the fire of his battery on the enemy as they retired. (Bar to M.C. 18/2/18).

" " actg. Brigade Major 29th Divl. Arty.

Flanders, 1918.—For excellent work when officiating as Brigade Major during the advance to Ploegsteert in August-September, 1918, and from Ypres in September-October, 1918. (Belgian Croix de Guerre 4/9/19).

Hunkin, Rev. J. W., Temp. Chaplain to the Forces (4th Class), attached HQ. 29th Divl. Arty.

Somme, 1916.—The C.R.A. drew attention to the excellent work done by this officer. "During the bombardment from June 4th to July 25th, the Rev. Hunkin lived in the dugouts of the front line batteries at his own request; his services amongst the batteries were welcomed by all ranks. On July 1st he spent the day at a dressing station in the communication trenches. He is always most indefatigable in his work and has done, and is doing, excellent service among men of the Artillery, by whom he is universally esteemed. On 3rd September he again went down voluntarily to the Mesnil valley and did excellent work assisting the wounded." Report dated 19/9/16. (Mention 4/1/17).

Arras, 1917.—For conspicuous bravery and devotion to duty. Throughout the operations in front of Arras from April 9th to the 24th, the Revd. Joseph Hunkin did excellent work in the most advanced dressing stations and among the gun lines. Notably near Monchy on the morning of the 23rd April, in his work among the wounded, he frequently went through heavy barrage fire, setting a fine example of personal disregard of danger. (M.C. (immediate) 16/8/17).

Cambrai, 1917.—For the great personal courage he displayed during the operations from November 30th to December 4th near Masnieres. He continually visited the aid posts and dressing stations in Marcoing and Masnieres, ministering to and assisting the wounded. His gallantry and utter disregard of danger in accompanying parties of stretcher-bearers on the most difficult and dangerous errands under intense shell and machine gun fire, was an example and encouragement to all who were working with him. He was the last person to leave Masnieres. (Bar to M.C. (immediate) 4/2/18).

Huttenbach, N. H., Lieut., "B" Battery, R.H.A.
Gallipoli, 1915.—For excellent work as F.O.O. in the action of the 28th June. A report by the O.C. 5th Battn. Royal Scots states:—"Huttenbach was simply splendid. He volunteered to place himself entirely at my disposal in the evening when I was left absolutely without an effective officer, and took charge of the fellows in the trench, organising the defence and looking after things. I am mentioning him also with others." (M.C. 8/11/15, Mention 5/11/15).

Ideson, A., 2nd Lieut. (Temp. Lieut.), 15th B.A.C., R.H.A., and HQ. 15th Brigade, R.H.A.
Gallipoli, 1915, and Somme, 1916-17.—For consistent good work in the line between April, 1915, and February, 1917. From September, 1916, as Adjutant of the 15th Brigade, R.H.A., his services were of the greatest value. (Mention 18/5/17).
" Actg. Capt., "L" Battery, R.H.A.
Arras, 1917.—Near Feuchy Chapelle, on April 20th, three men were buried in the gun line by a shell. The hostile bombardment was so heavy and accurate that the men of the battery had to be withdrawn to cover. In spite of this, Captain Ideson worked for an hour in the open in order to extricate the buried men. By his coolness and perseverance two of them were got out alive. (M.C. 18/6/17).

Johnson, R. Marr, Lieut.-Col. (Temp. Br.-Genl.), HQ. 29th Divl. Arty.
Flanders, 1918.—(C.M.G. 1/1/19, Mention 20/12/18).
Flanders, 1918.—For constant and conspicuous devotion to duty as C.R.A. since 12/12/17. The artillery under his able leadership and personal supervision has universally rendered valuable assistance to the infantry in all operations—notably in the recent operations commencing at Ypres, 28/9/18. (French Croix de Guerre 19/6/19).

Ker, S. H., 2nd Lieut. (S.R.), "B" Battery, R.H.A.
Flanders, 1918—On September 29th, near Gheluveldt, this officer was ordered to take his section up in close support of the infantry. As they came into action they were heavily fired upon by small parties of the enemy at 200 yards range and suffered casualties among the horses. 2nd Lieut. Ker immediately brought his Lewis gun into action and drove the enemy off. Later the guns came under heavy machine gun fire and 2nd Lieut. Ker showed great gallantry and power of command in keeping his guns in action and successfully maintaining their fire until the infantry were able to overcome all opposition and make good their objective. (M.C. (immediate) 2/4/19).

Kershaw, A. E. P., 2nd Lieut. (S.R.), 460th Battery, R.F.A.
Flanders, 1918.—On the night of the 7th/8th October, the battery wagon lines near Becelaere were heavily shelled, the first round bursting close to and riddling 2nd Lieut. Kershaw's tent. Despite the shock he immediately set to to care for the wounded and evacuate the rest of the men and the horses. The shelling went on for two hours but he remained the whole time and did splendid work, greatly encouraging all around him. He set a fine example of courage and devotion to duty. This is not the first occasion on which this officer has shown conspicuous gallantry. (M.C. 3/6/19).

King, A. J., Lieut., No. 1 Section, 29th D.A.C.
Flanders, 1918.—Has served in the 29th D.A. since Gallipoli. Has always done good work. He was one of the last to leave the peninsula. During the operations in 1918 he has frequently been in charge of ammunition dumps in the forward areas and has assisted largely in the supply of ammunition under very trying conditions. (Divisional Card of Honour).

Kinnersley, F. A., 2nd Lieut., 97th Battery, R.F.A.
Gallipoli, 1915.—In the action of the 28th June a 6-inch gun from the Asiatic shore suddenly opened fire in enfilade on the 97th battery. One gun was at once hit, all the detachment being killed or wounded. A few minutes later the wagon of this gun was hit and set on fire. This officer with two or three men at once rushed to the burning wagon to try and save

the ammunition which they knew to be very scarce.   Several rounds exploded but the rest were saved.   2nd Lieut. Kinnersley's hands were badly burnt. The ammunition in the pit under the wagon was also saved.   (M.C. 8/11/15, Mention 5/11/15).

Knatchbull-Huggessen, Hon. M. H. R., 2nd Lieut. "B" Battery, R.H.A. (attached Royal Naval Air Service).
  Gallipoli, 1915.—This officer was attached to the R.N.A.S.   Throughout the actions of the 4th and 28th June and the 12th and 13th July he spotted most accurately and was often under fire.   Ever since the landing on the peninsula this officer has renedered invaluable assistance to the Artillery as observer.   (Mention 5/11/15, M.C. 8/11/15).

Leach, R. S., Captain, 13th Battery, R.F.A.
  Gallipoli, 1915.—(Mention 13/7/16).
  Somme, 1916.—This officer commanded his battery during the operations from 24th June to 3rd September with conspicuous ability and cut a difficult piece of wire with remarkable success.   (M.C. 1/1/17).

Leadbetter, A. E. G., 2nd Lieut. (Temp. Lieut.), 92nd Battery, R.F.A., and HQ. 17th Brigade, R.F.A.
  Gallipoli, 1915.—For coolness, gallantry and hard work, often under heavy fire.   Showed capabilties far beyond his years.   (Mention 13/7/16).

  ,,   ,,   HQ. 17th Brigade, R.F.A.
  Somme, 1916.—For excellent work as Adjutant 17th Brigade, R.F.A., and Right Group during the whole of the operations in the Beaumont Hamel sector from July 1st to September 3rd.   Has been untiring in his work which has been performed in a most energetic and satisfactory manner. Although very young, he has carried out the arduous duties of Staff Officer to a large Group, sometimes consisting of nine or ten batteries, with marked success.   (Mention 4/1/17).

Lister, E. J. S., Lieut. (S.R.), "B" Battery, R.H.A.
  Flanders, 1918.—During the night operations of the 2nd/3rd June near the Nieppe Forest, this officer was out for 48 hours in or about the front trenches, registering before the operation and doing liaison work during the attack.   Amongst other things he maintained telephonic communication from the attacking platoons to their Company Headquarters, as well as communication by lamp back to the O.P. and battery H.Q. when all telephone lines were cut.   (Divisional Card of Honour).

  ,,   Captain   ,,
  Flanders, 1918.—On October 19th this officer was commanding "B" BatteryR.H.A., near Courtrai.   He was ordered into action to cover a withdrawal from a bridge-head during the evening.   Enemy shelling and gas were very heavy both on the position and its approaches, and, with the fall of darkness, confusion seemed inevitable.   Captain Lister, however, handled his battery most skillfully and, with exceptional gallantry and coolness, got his guns into action and his teams safely away although the ground was very bad and guns and vehicles had frequently to be extracted from shell-holes.   By his determined efforts fire was brought to bear on the enemy at the right time and place, thus enabling the operation to be successfully carried out.   (M.C. (immediate) 7/3/19).

Lloyd, C. H., Lieut., "L" Battery, R.H.A.
  Gallipoli, 1915.—Lieut. Lloyd was with the O.C. 1/10th Manchester Regiment during the operations of the night 18th/19th June as F.O.O. and was of the greatest assistance to that officer in rallying the men and getting them back again up the communication trench leading to H 11.   Major-General C. Douglas, commanding the 42nd Division, stated that Lieut. Lloyd went out of his way to assist in checking the retirement after the failure of an assaulting party, and was of the greatest help.   (M.C. 8/11/15, Mention 5/11/15).

Lowe, W., 2nd Lieut. (S.R.), "B" Battery, R.H.A.
  Flanders, 1918.—On the 22nd October, near Ooteghem, the battery was advancing in close support of the infantry when the latter were unexpectedly held up short of their objective.   There being no time to stop the battery it had to be brought into action in full view of the enemy and within 1,000 yards of his machine guns.   2nd Lieut. Lowe led the battery on through heavy shell fire with great coolness, remained till he had seen each team away safely and then went back and brought up ammunition.   Finally, when the battery was ordered to retire, he went back for the teams of each section in turn.   He displayed great courage and set a magnificent and inspiring example to the drivers.   (M.C. (immediate) 2/1/19).

Lush-Wilson, H. G., Captain, "Y" Battery, R.H.A.
    Gallipoli, 1915.—(Chevalier, Legion of Honour 30/3/16).

Lyon, K., 2nd Lieut. (actg. Capt.), Adjutant 17th Brigade, R.F.A.
    Arras and Flanders, 1917.—For conspicuous ability as Adjutant.   His
work has been beyond all praise.   (Mention 14/12/17).

MacDonald, A. H., Lieut. (T.F.), (Temp. Capt.), 1/4th Highland Mountain
Brigade, R.G.A. (T.F.).
    Gallipoli,1915.—On 28th June, when a wagon containing ammunition was
set on fire by a H.E. shell from the Asiatic shore, this officer, together with
one or two men, rushed to it and saved a number of rounds from the
burning wagon together with all the ammunition which was stored in the
pit beneath it.   Several of the rounds in the wagon exploded.   (M.C. 8/11/15,
Mention 5/11/15).

MacKelvie, T., Major (T.F.), 1/4th Highland Mountain Brigade, R.G.A. (T.F.).
    Gallipoli, 1915.—(C.M.G., Mention 5/11/15).

Maitland, R. C. F., D.S.O., Major (actg. Lt.-Col.), 15th Brigade, R.H.A.
    Flanders, 1918.—For skill and ability in the handling of the 17th
Brigade, R.F.A., during the successful operations of the Division in October.
(French Croix de Guerre 19/6/19).

Marshall, H. S., Major, 90th Heavy Battery, R.G.A. and 14th Siege Battery,
R.G.A.
        Gallipoli, 1915.—(D.S.O. 3/6/16, Mention 13/7/16).

Malby, H. F., 2nd Lieut. (S.R.), 1/1st Warwickshire Battery, R.H.A. (T.F.),
    Flanders, 1917.—On the evening of August 10th the Warwickshire Battery
in position on the canal bank at Boesinghe was being heavily shelled.   Two
guns were put out of action and their camouflage as well as that of one other
gun was set on fire, and the ammunition started exploding.   The detachments were cleared to a flank.   2nd Lieuts. Philip and Malby, with Sergeant
Kinman and Gunner Dixon, worked for 20 minutes under continuous shell
fire, with the ammunition continuing to explode, until all the fires were
extinguished and the guns recamouflaged.   By their prompt action a large
quantity of ammunition was saved and the guns preserved from further
damage.   (M.C. (immediate) 26/9/17).

Marx, R., 2nd Lieut. (Temp. Capt.), 92nd Battery, R.F.A.
    Somme, 1916.—On the night of the 6th/7th April this officer was F.O.O.
during a strong enemy raid on the "Mary" redan.   He behaved in a cool
and gallant manner and kept the fire of his battery up, and afterwards
assisted the commander of the troops in the front line trench.   As F.O.O.
this officer has consistently sent in good reports, and since his C.O. (Major
R. C. Williams, D.S.O.) was wounded he has commanded the 92nd Battery with
zeal and success.   (M.C. 1/1/17).
    ,,   Lieut. (actg. Major), D/17 Battery, R.F.A.
    Flanders, 1918.—For excellent work in command of his battery in the
operations from September to November.   (French Croix de Guerre 19/6/19).

McCracken, A. M., 2nd Lieut., 368th Battery, R.F.A.
    Gallipoli, 1915.—In the action of the 28th June the heather in front
of this battery was set alight by hostile shell fire.   This officer and four
men went to extinguish it.   Almost at once another shell burst killing one
man and seriously wounding two more of the above four men.   Lieut.
McCracken then ordered the only survivor back under cover and finally
succeeded in extinguishing the flames himself by means of wet sandbags.
The importance of doing so lay in the fact that the guns were so exposed
that the ammunition had to be kept in pits close to the guns, as no replenishment of ammunition during the action could have taken place.   If the fire
had reached the ammunition the battery would have been out of action all
day.   (M.C. 8/11/15, Mention 5/11/15).

McLachlan, E. M., Lieut., R.E. (T.F.), 29th Divl. Signal Company, R.E. (attached
H.Q. 29th Divl. Artillery).
    Somme, 1916-17.—For consistently good work as Signal Officer from
October, 1916, to February, 1917.   Notably during the attack of January
27th, 1917, near Le Transloy he organised and maintained the signal communications of a large force of artillery with great success.   Mention 18/5/17).

Medley, E. J., M.C., Captain (actg. Major), 13th Battery, R.F.A.
    Flanders, 1918.—Has commanded his battery since November, 1917.
His record as a Battery Commander is a brilliant one.   He is an exceptionally

good "gunner" and has handled his battery with the greatest skill, courage and determination. In the final stages of the fighting he showed particular enterprise in pushing his guns forward. His invariable cheerfulness and energy, even under the most adverse conditions, have been exceptional and have infused such a spirit into the personnel of the battery that it has been undoubtedly the most contented in the D.A. (Mention 7/7/19).

Milford, K. E., Major, "L" Battery, R.H.A.
Flanders, 1917-18, and Cambrai, 1917.—Commanded his battery during the operations from September, 1917, to February, 1918, with great ability, especially in the actions on the Steenbeek and before Cambrai when his resolute leadership inspired all ranks with a fine spirit in the face of every kind of difficulty. (D.S.O. 3/6/18, Mention 21/5/18).

Monkhouse, W. P., C.M.G., M.V.O., Lt.-Col., H.Q. 17th Brigade, R.F.A.
Gallipoli, 1915-16.—For the successful evacuation of the men and guns of Section A, Left Group, VIII Corps Artillery. Guns noted for demolition were duly destroyed. The fact that these operations were carried out with such complete success and punctuality is mainly due to Lt.-Col. Monkhouse's thorough organisation and supervision. (Mention, 13/7/16).
Somme, 1916.—For most successful command of the Right Group of the 29th D.A. from April 7th to July 13th. He was most energetic, has a thorough knowledge of detail, and the excellent shooting of his Group was in a great measure due to him. (Mention 4/1/17).

Morden-Wright, H., 2nd Lieut. (T.F.), X/29 Trench Mortar Battery.
Somme, 1916.—During the bombardment in the Beaumont Hamel sector from 24th to 30th June he was at his post continually observing the effects of our fire on the enemy's wire, notwithstanding the retaliatory fire which at times was extremely heavy. His O.P. was blown in three times, and once he was blown over by the blast of a shell. Nevertheless he continued to do his duty with extreme coolness. (M.C. (immediate) 22/9/16).

Morrice, J. S., Lieut. (S.R.), "L" Battery, R.H.A.
1915-18.—This officer has served in the 29th D.A. since October, 1915, with the exception of a period of seven months after he was wounded on 24th October, 1917. He has spent the great majority of this service in "L" Battery, R.H.A., and has done continuously good work. (Divisional Card of Honour).

Mulholland, A. E., 2nd Lieut., H.Q. 15th Brigade, R.H.A.
Cambrai, 1917.—On the 19th November Lieut. Mulholland with a small party put out a fire in a large dump of 4.5" howitzer shell at the quarry near Gouzeaucourt. The fire was caused by direct hits from 5.9" howitzers, had spread to the cartridges, and in a few minutes would have resulted in a considerable explosion. This officer acted quickly, with great presence of mind, and at great personal risk. (M.C. (immediate) 4/2/18).
„   Lieut.,   „.
Flanders, 1918.—For most efficient and gallant work as Brigade Signalling Officer and when acting as Signal Officer of the 29th D.A. Frequently during these operations he has unhesitatingly faced heavy shell fire in order to establish important communications. His devotion to duty and untiring efforts have been most marked. (French Croix de Guerre 19/6/19).

Mure, G. R. G., Lieut. (T.F.), (actg. Capt.), 1/1st Warwickshire Battery, R.H.A. (T.F.).
Arras and Flanders, 1917.—Has served continuously with his battery since 1915 and is most capable. Has frequently done good work as F.O.O. In August, 1917, he commanded, at a moment's notice, another battery most efficiently under trying conditions. (Mention 14/12/17).
Flanders, 1918.—For general good work as Captain of his battery and during periods of temporary command of the same. (Mention 23/12/18).
1915-18.—This officer has served in France with his battery since September, 1915. He served as a subaltern through the battle of the Somme and has commanded his battery on many occasions during the operations at Arras, in Flanders (1917), at Cambrai, and again in Flanders (September and October, 1918). He has always shown the greatest coolness under fire and has commmanded his battery with great ability. During his 3½ years in France, this officer has done a large amount of arduous and valuable work. (M.C. 3/6/19, Chevalier, Belgian Ordre de la Couronne and Croix de Guerre).

Murray, W. A., Major, 1/1st Warwickshire Battery, R.H.A. (T.F.).
Somme, 1916-17.—Has commanded his battery for over two years with conspicuous success. He brought the battery to a very high state of efficiency. (D.S.O. 4/6/17, Mention 18/5/17).

Murray, W. A., actg. Lt.-Col. H.Q. 17th Brigade, R.F.A.
    Arras and Flanders, 1917.—For great zeal and ability in command of his brigade and during the two months of his command of a group. (Brevet Lieut.-Col. 1/1/18, Mention 14/12/17).
    „   Brevet and actg. Lt.-Col.   „
    Flanders, 1918.—For skilful handling of his brigade in the operations of this year. A resourceful brigade commander, tactful in dealing with subordinates, he has proved an invaluable asset throughout his service with the D.A., and the smooth working of his brigade with the infantry it has supported from time to time merits the highest praise. (C.M.G. 3/6/19, Mention 7/7/19, French Croix de Guerre 19/6/19).

Peake, M., c.m.g., Colonel (Temp. Br.-Genl.), H.Q. 29th Divl. Arty.
    Somme, 1916.—For able command of the 29th Divisional Artillery. (Mention 4/6/17).

Peck, H. R., Major, "L" Battery, R.H.A.
    Gallipoli, 1915.—For excellent work and effective fire of his battery on 4th June which contributed largely to the success of the operations of that day. (C.M.G. 8/11/15, Mention 5/11/15).

Peel, E. J. R., d.s.o., Lieut.-Col., 15th Brigade, R.H.A.
    Gallipoli, 1915-16.—For the successful evacuation of Section B, Left Group, VIII Corps Artillery (31st December, 1915—9th January, 1916). Guns noted for demolition were duly destroyed. The fact that these operations were carried out with such complete success and punctuality is mainly due to Lt.-Col. Peel's thorough organisation and supervision. (Mention 13/7/16).

Peto, R. A., Lieut. (T.F.), 1/1st Warwickshire Battery, R.H.A. (T.F.).
    Somme, 1916-17.—Lieut. Peto did very good work on November 13th, 1916, during the operations near Beaumont Hamel, as F.O.O. He sent in most valuable information under heavy shell fire. He has served in France since October, 1914, and has always done extremely well. Report dated March, 1917. (Mention 18/5/17).

Philip, R. T., 2nd Lieut. (S.R.), 1/1st Warwickshire Battery, R.H.A. (T.F.)
    Flanders, 1917.—On the evening of the 10th August the Warwickshire Battery in position on the canal bank at Boesinghe was being heavily shelled. Two guns were put out of action and their camouflage as well as that of one other gun was set on fire, and the ammunition started exploding. The detachments were cleared to a flank. 2nd Lieuts. Philip and Malby, with Sergeant Kinman and Gunner Dixon, worked for twenty minutes under continuous shell fire, with the ammunition continuing to explode, until all fires were extinguished and the guns recamouflaged. By this prompt action a large quantity of ammunition was saved and the guns preserved from further damage. (M.C. (immediate) 26/9/17).

Phillips, A. S., Temp. Captain, 13th Battery, R.F.A.
    Somme, 1916-17.—For excellent work in charge of the battery wagon lines. Was indefatigable in looking after the welfare of men and horses under the terribly hard conditions in the winter of 1916-17. It was chiefly due to his energy and hard work that the ammunition supply was successfully carried out at all times. (Mention 14/12/17).
    „   „   No. 2 Section, 29th D.A.C.
    Flanders, 1918.—For excellent work in command of No. 2 Section, 29th D.A.C., since February, 1918. He has spared no pains in working for the efficiency of his men and horses. He has worked his section up to a very high standard of efficiency. (Divisional Card of Honour).

Price-Davis, S. D., Major (T.F.), (actg. Lt.-Col.), 29th Divl. Amm. Col.
    Flanders, 1917-18, and Cambrai, 1917.—For excellent work as Commander of the 29th D.A.C. under trying conditions. (Mention 21/5/18).

Ratsey, T. C., Temp. 2nd Lieut., H.Q. 17th Brigade, R.F.A.
    Somme, 1916-17.—For maintenance of communications of a large Group in circumstances of great difficulty and danger. Subsequently carried out the work of Staff Officer to a large Group with great ability. (Mention 18/5/17).
    „   Temp. Lieut. (actg. Capt.), H.Q. 17th Brigade, R.F.A., and 13th Battery, R.F.A.
    1915-18.—This young officer served continuously in the 29th Divl. Arty. from the Gallipoli operations to the armistice. During a considerable portion of that time he was Adjutant of the 17th Brigade, R.F.A. He was never sick or sorry and never shirked a dangerous duty. He has been recommended by his C.O. for award on several occasions, one of these being for good work at the evacuation of the peninsula. (Divisional Card of Honour).

Rawson, E. H., Temp. 2nd Lieut., D/17 Battery, R.F.A.
Cambrai, 1917.—On November 30th near Marcoing, when the enemy had broken through the division on our right and was approaching the battery from the flank, this officer showed great presence and skill in swinging his guns round and engaging the advancing troops. He commanded his guns with conspicuous courage all day under most trying circumstances and under heavy machine gun and shell fire, showing great devotion to duty and a fine example of courage and cheerfulness to his men. (M.C. (immediate) 4/2/18).

Sherbrooke, N. H. C., Major, D/132 Battery, R.F.A.
Somme, 1916.—For conspicuous ability and devotion to duty in command of D/132 Battery, R.F.A., in the Beaumont Hamel sector both prior to and during the operations of the 24th June—1st July. During these operations Major Sherbrooke controlled the fire of his battery with marked success from an O.P. in the front system of trenches often under heavy hostile fire. (Mention 4/1/17).

„ Actg. Lt.-Col., H.Q. 17th Brigade, R.F.A., and H.Q. 15th Brigade, R.H.A.
Somme, 1916-17.—For command of a brigade from July, 1916, to February, 1917, with conspicuous success. An officer of exceptional ability. (D.S.O. 4/6/17, Mention 18/5/17).

Simpson-Baikie, H. A. D., Lt.-Col. (Temp. Br. Genl.), H.Q. 29th Divl. Arty.
Gallipoli, 1915.—For good work at Cape Helles. To his arrangements for artillery support was due the success of the operations on the 28th June. (C.B. 8/11/15, Mention 5/11/15, Officier, Legion of Honour 24/2/16).

Spedding, E. W., c.m.g., Lt.-Col., 29th D.A.C.
Flanders, 1918.—This officer, in addition to the thorough performance of his normal duties, most unselfishly devoted himself to every scheme affecting economy and food supply. In the early spring the unit under his command ploughed and prepared for seed many acres of land. During the summer, while the Division was in the line near the Nieppe forest, he was responsible for the rescue of an immense quantity of agricultural machines and implements from farms in the forward area. Later, he was chiefly instrumental in the harvesting of the Centre Divisional Area of the XVth Corps. Without ever waiting to be ordered or asked, Colonel Spedding has tackled every one of these labours with an unflagging zeal that has been the admiration and envy of all connected with him. (O.B.E. 1/1/19, Mention 23/12/18).

Squire, B. B., Lieut. (actg. Capt.), 460th Battery, R.F.A.
Somme, 1916-17.—For gallantry and consistent good service, particularly whilst in command of his battery in February, 1917, and notably on January 27th, 1917, in the action near Le Transloy, when he did exceptionally gallant service as liaison officer with the attacking infantry. (Mention 18/5/17).

Stanford, A. W., 2nd Lieut. (S.R.), 26th Battery, R.F.A., and 370th Battery R.F.A.
Somme, 1916.—Has performed admirable service throughout. During the operations against Beaumont Hamel on the 1st July he was liaison officer with the 2nd Battalion S.W. Borderers and accompanied the last company of that battalion in the advance. He remained all day with the foremost men of the battalion, just outside the German wire. Both his telephonists were shot. (Mention 4/1/17).

„ „ 92nd Battery, R.F.A.
Somme, 1916.—This officer showed great courage and resource in moving a section of his battery to a forward position on the 29th October under circumstances of great difficulty. Finding it impossible to move the guns with horses, he took them to pieces and carried them on trollies up the valley running east of Eaucourt valley under heavy shell fire. Lieut. Stanford has been brought to notice on four previous occasions for gallantry and devotion to duty. (M.C. (immediate) 21/12/16).

„ Lieut. (S.R.), (actg. Major), „
Flanders, 1917-18, and Cambrai, 1917.—For good work in command of his battery from September 1917 to February 1918. (Mention 21/5/18).
Flanders, 1918.—This officer has commanded his battery with great gallantry and skill, and has inspired all serving under him with that spirit of loyalty and disregard for danger so essential to success in war. He has invariably displayed the greatest courage under fire and the state of efficiency to which he has brought his battery reflects the greatest credit on him. (D.S.O. 3/6/19, Mention 7/7/19, French Croix de Guerre 19/6/19).

Staveley, M., Lieut. (Temp. Capt.), 370th Battery, R.F.A.
Somme, 1916.—This young officer commanded the 370th Battery, R.F.A., in the Beaumont Hamel sector from 23rd July to 12th September. He has performed conspicuous good service and no experienced battery commander could have done better work than he did during the operations which culminated on the 3rd September. (Mention 4/1/17).

Stevenson, E. H., D.S.O., Brevet-Col. (Temp. Br. Genl.), H.Q. 29th Divl. Arty.
Flanders, 1917.—For splendid work as C.R.A. under trying conditions in September and October, also for previous good work in the operations round Zillebeke Lake when C.R.A. of the 30th Division. (Mention 11/12/17).
Flanders and Cambrai, 1917.—For conspicuous ability and devotion to duty. Notably during the operations at Ypres in the beginning of October and at Cambrai from the 29th to 30th November, in which the artillery rendered invaluable assistance to the troops of the Division and materially assisted in the success of the operations. (C.M.G. 3/6/18, Mention 20/5/18).

Stewart, J., Lieut. (actg. Capt.). 460th Battery, R.F.A.
Arras and Flanders, 1917.—He has served continuously with this battery in France since March, 1916. Has proved himself a very capable and reliable subaltern and took over command of his battery, owing to heavy casualties, for the operations north of Ypres in July and August, 1917. He commanded it with success under very trying circumstances. (Mention 14/12/17).
Cambrai, 1917.—Displayed great coolness and gallantry in the action at La Vacquerie valley on 30th November. This officer rallied some infantry who were retiring through the guns, and by his personal example stopped all traces of unsteadiness amongst the gunners which ensued. He continued to direct the fire from the centre of the battery for another hour and a quarter without taking any cover from rifle or machine gun fire and was the last to withdraw. By his personal disregard of danger or panic, he gave a great example to the men. (M.C. (immediate) 4/2/18).

Stocdkdale, H. E., D.S.O., Lieut.-Col., H.Q. 15th Brigade, R.H.A.
Gallipoli, 1915.—For good work at the landing on the peninsula. (Mention 5/8/15).

„ **Temp. Br.-Genl., H.Q. 29th Divl. Artillery.**
Gallipoli, 1915.—For good work as C.R.A. at Cape Helles. (C.M.G. 26/6/16, Mention 13/7/16.

Syers, T. S., Temp. Capt., 147th B.A.C. (attached Trench Mortar Group).
Gallipoli, 1915.—On the 9th August, 1915, this officer had Trench Mortars in action on the east of the Krithia nullah. Though heavily shelled by the Turks with some 200 or 300 shells, he stuck to his guns and bombarded G 11 a most effectually until the mortars were buried by the hostile shelling. Report by G.O.C. 42nd (E. Lancs.) Div. (M.C. 29/10/15, Mention 28/1/16).

Tasker, A. V. B., Lieut. (T.F.), (actg. Capt.), S.A.A. Section, 29th D.A.C.
1917-18.—For nearly two years this officer has commanded the S.A.A. Section and has always maintained it in a remarkable state of efficiency, even under the very adverse conditions that have prevailed at times. In fact, the smartness of the S.A.A. Section has always been a by-word in the division. This officer has not spared himself and has been of the greatest assistance to the "Q" staff in the multifarious tasks that have fallen to the lot of the S.A.A. Section which has very often been acting independently of the Divisional Artillery. He has been wounded once (April, 1916) when serving with a battery. (Divisional Card of Honour).

Terrell, C. R. àB., 2nd Lieut., 460th Battery, R.F.A.
Arras, 1917.—For conspicuous coolness and bravery. On 9th April, shortly after the opening of our barrage fire, the guns of which 2nd Lieut. Terrell was in charge were subjected to a very heavy shell fire. Five of the six detachments were disabled. He got the only two undamaged guns into action again and kept up the support of the infantry, his battery being under a very heavy fire the whole time. (M.C. (immediate) 18/7/17).

Thomson, A. F., Major, 368th Battery, R.F.A.
Gallipoli, 1915.—(D.S.O. 23/11/16, Mention 5/9/16).

Thomson, J. N., M.C., Captain, Brigade Major 29th Divl. Arty.
Arras and Flanders, 1917.—For excellent work as Brigade Major, May to September. He has shown the greatest keeness and ability in his work. His cheery disposition has overcome all difficulties and he has inspired all

ranks with the greatest confidence in very trying situations. As a Staff Officer he has been of the greatest assistance in the accurate and rapid grasp of the situation. (Mention 11/12/17).

Flanders, 1918.—For brilliant work as Brigade Major. Has, in the opinion of the C.R.A., contributed more towards the efficiency of the 29th Divisional Artillery than any other individual. His zeal, energy, tact and cheerfulness under fire and at all times, have been superb. He has many times assumed voluntarily the additional burden of duties beyond his normal province, and has made light of all difficulties. Words fail to express the loyal and gallant devotion to duty displayed by this officer. (D.S.O. 3/6/19, Mention 7/7/19, French Croix de Guerre 19/6/19).

Thorneycroft, G. E. M., Major, "L" Battery, R.H.A.

Somme, 1916.—Showed conspicuous ability and devotion to duty during the preliminary operations from 24th to 30th June. During that period he lived, often under shell fire, at his O.P. in the forward system of trenches, and carried out his wire-cutting task most successfully. He again did excellent work during the operations of the 3rd September. (Mention 4/1/17).

Tindal, C. H., 2nd Lieut. (S.R.), 460th Battery, R.F.A.

Flanders, 1917.—On the night of the 10th/11th August his battery was heavily shelled with 5·9 inch and 8 inch. When the shelling became severe he cleared the detachments to a flank, searching every dugout and remaining himself till the last. When the shelling abated he returned and then called up the detachments. A few minutes later the shelling recommenced. 2nd Lieut. Tindal again cleared the battery, remaining himself until every man was clear. As he was leaving, an enemy shell burst in a gun-pit, exploding a dump of gas shell and wounding him. He showed a fine example of coolness and courage. (M.C. (immediate) 26/9/17).

Trappes-Lomax, B. C., 2nd Lieut., "Y" Battery, R.H.A.

Gallipoli, 1915.—In the action of the 7th August, this officer received orders at 0070 to proceed to the firing line and report on the advance made from there by the 5th, 6th, 7th and 8th Battalions, Lancashire Fusiliers. He established his telephone there at 0830 and sent back constant and accurate reports of the infantry advance from 0940 onwards. At 1230 he went up the sap on the left of the vineyard, reconnoitred the whole of our front line there, visiting each barricade, and sent in an accurate report of the situation. During the afternoon and night he made constant reconnaissances under heavy rifle fire and sent back information. At 1000 on the 8th he made another detailed reconnaissance. At 2000 on the 8th his telephone wires were cut in several places by Turkish shells. As his constant efforts to repair it were unsuccessful he returned to the nearest point of unbroken communication and laid out a new line thence to his advanced post, re-establishing communication at 2330. He remained at his post until relieved at 0930 on the 9th continuing to reconnoitre the firing line and saps, and to send in reports. (M.C. 2/2/16, Mention 28/1/16).

Uniacke, C. D. W., Major "B" Battery, R.H.A.

Gallipoli, 1915, and Somme, 1916-17.—For consistent good service in command of his battery from July, 1915, to February, 1917. Under him "B" Battery, R.H.A., has maintained its high traditions. (Mention 18/5/17).

Vince, F. H., Lieut. (S.R.), "B" Battery, R.H.A.

Flanders, 1917-18, and Cambrai, 1917.—Served in "B" Battery, R.H.A., from 15/7/17 to 16/10/18, when he was wounded in the capture of the crossings of the Lys near Courtrai by a premature burst from a German 10·5" howitzer which he had turned round on the enemy. This officer was most reliable and was specially selected for the hazardous and important work of establishing an O.P. on the ridge at Passchendaele in February, 1918. He did gallant and valuable work on that occasion, as on many others. He is one of the reliable, scrupulously conscientious and hard-working type, who deserves recognition for his general good work. (Divisional Card of Honour).

Walford, G. N., Captain. Brigade Major 29th Divl. Arty.

Gallipoli, 1915.—"On 26th April, 1915, subsequent to a landing having been effected on the beach at a point on the Gallipoli peninsula, during which both Brigadier-General and Brigade-Major had been killed, Lieut.

B

Colonel Doughty-Wylie and Captain Walford organised and led an attack through and on both sides of the village of Sedd-el-Bahr on the Old Castle at the top of the hill inland. The enemy's position was very strongly held and entrenched, and defended with concealed machine guns and pom-poms. It was mainly due to the initiative, skill and great gallantry of these two officers that the attack was a complete success. Both were killed in the moment of victory." (Army Order 255, published on 26th June, 1915). (V.C., posthumous).

Walker, F. M., Temp. Capt., R.A.M.C., attached 15th Brigade, R.H.A.
Arras, 1917.—For conspicuous courage and devotion to duty during the operations between the 9th and 25th April. On several occasions he saved lives by his disregard of hostile shelling. Notably on the 20th April near Feuchy Chapelle he went through a heavy barrage to get to some injured men, and worked at them for an hour in the open under very heavy fire. (M.C. 18/6/17).

Watson, F. H. P., 2nd Lieut. (S.R.), 460th Battery, R.F.A.
Flanders, 1918.—During the night operations on the night 2nd/3rd June this officer was at the O.P. near Swartenbrouch and was blown from this position by a gas shell and slightly wounded. He continued at his post, though considerably shaken, and attended to the transmission of messages until relieved by another officer at 4-30 a.m. (Divisional Card of Honour).
     "   Captain,   "
Flanders, 1918.—It is understood that this officer was recommended for reward on several occasions when serving as a Sergeant in C/61 Battery, R.F.A. (afterwards became D/76 Battery, R.F.A.), i.e., he was recommended for the D.C.M. first at the battle of Loos, and twice again during the Somme operations for gallant and heroic conduct as signalling sergeant. He is a very gallant and first-class officer who has done extraordinarily good work since he came to the 29th D.A. in October, 1917. He has proved himself a born leader of men and has not spared himself in carrying out his duty or in attending to the welfare and training of his men. (Mention 7/7/19).

Wells, P., 2nd Lieut. (S.R.), "L" Battery, R.H.A.
Flanders, 1918.—This officer was F.O.O. for the 15th Brigade, R.H.A., during the attack on Outtersteene on 18th August. Finding observation impossible on account of the dust and smoke raised by the hostile barrage he made his way forward alone, passed through the barrage on into the village which at the time was being heavily shelled. He succeeded in obtaining valuable information as to the infantry situation and returned through the barrage in order to pass it on. By his quick appreciation of the situation and determined courage in getting the information through he was instrumental in enabling our guns to ward off a counter-attack. (M.C. immediate) 7/11/18).

Williams, R. C., Major, 92nd Battery, R.F.A.
Gallipoli, 1915.—For great ability, energy and zeal in command of his battery since 26th April, 1915. The battery maintained a high standard of vigilance and fine efficiency throughout in spite of constant changes in the junior officers. This officer was specially brought to notice for the good work of his battery on 4th June and 12th July. (D.S.O. 3/6/16, Mention 13/7/16).

Winter, O. deL'E., Major, 10th Battery, R.F.A.
Gallipoli, 1915.—This officer commanded the 10th Battery, R.F.A., which was always the one selected by his Group Commander for any exceptionally difficult work on account of the skill, untiring energy and resource of its commander, in all of which qualities the latter is far above the normal. This officer did exceptional work and spent the little leisure he got in taking up the Naval 12-pdr. to the forward trenches and harassing the enemy. (D.S.O. 8/11/15, Mention 5/11/15).

Wright, J., 2nd Lieut., 368th Battery, R.F.A.
Gallipoli, 1915.—(Mention 13/7/16).

Wylie, A. L., Temp. 2nd Lieut., Y/29 Trench Mortar Battery.
Somme, 1916.—For good work whilst in command of Y/29 Battery in the Beaumont Hamel sector on September 1st and 2nd and previously. One of his gun-pits having been blown in by hostile fire, he took the guns out into the open under fire and completely cut the enemy wire which had been allotted to him. (Mention 4/1/17).
Somme, 1916.—For great courage and resource, during the period October 22nd to 30th when the medium T. M. Batteries of the Division

had four guns in a forward position at the sunken road north of Geudicourt. 2nd Lieut. Wylie was in command of these guns five days out of the nine. He maintained his guns in action in an open position under most difficult conditions and successfully accomplished a very difficult and dangerous task. (M.C. 10/1/17).

Wynter, F. A., D.S.O., Major (Temp. Lt.-Col.), H.Q. 1/4th Highland Mountain Brigade, R.G.A. (T.F.).

Gallipoli, 1915.—4th and 28th June.   This officer was in charge of Group III comprising 30 guns.   He handled his command with great ability during these operations.   He is zealous and energetic beyond the normal.   He was indefatigable and never spared himself to ensure the success of the operations.   (Brevet Lieut.-Colonel 8/11/15).

(II) LIST OF WARRANT OFFICERS, NON-COMMISSIONED OFFICERS AND MEN, WHO RECEIVED HONOURS FOR SERVICES IN THE 29th DIVISIONAL ARTILLERY.

Adams, H. W., 9623, Actg. S.M., H.Q. 29th D.A.
Gallipoli, 1915.—For exceptionally good work in the field for the past four months. This N.C.O. is the Artillery Clerk in charge of the 29th D.A.H.Q. office and landed with the 29th D.A. on 25th April, and has performed his duties to the entire satisfaction of the C.R.A., often under shell fire. He has not spared himself and has laboured day and night to ensure the prompt duplication and despatch of artillery orders, returns, and general correspondence, which have been sometimes very heavy. Since the formation of the VIIIth Corps and the withdrawal of the 29th D.A. from the 29th Division for administrative purposes, this N.C.O. has carried out, with the machinery of the 29th D.A.H.Q., the clerical work of the whole of the artillery of the VIIIth Corps on the peninsula, which up till recently comprised 30 batteries of all natures, together with the Ammunition Columns for the same. He is in possession of the medal for Long Service and Good Conduct. (Report dated 28/8/15). (Mention 28/1/16, M.S.M. 11/11/16).
Somme, 1916.—For efficiency and high sense of duty. His work has necessitated long hours and constant application and has always merited high praise. (Russian medal of St. George 2nd Class 15/2/17).
Arras and Flanders, 1917.—(Mention 14/12/17).

Akerman, A. V., 614005, Sergt., 1/1st Warwickshire Battery, R.H.A. (T.F.).
Somme, 1916-17.—For great gallantry and coolness in charge of battery signals, notably in the action of January 27th, 1917 near Le Transloy, when he repaired lines in the open under heavy shell fire. (Mention 18/5/17).

Alcock, T., 39003, Cpl./S.S., "B" Battery, R.H.A.
Flanders, 1918.—During the operations from September 28th to October 22nd between Ypres and Courtrai, this N.C.O. showed great gallantry and skill in handling men and horses under fire. He has frequently taken teams and ammunition over heavily shelled roads, and on one occasion when horses were stampeded by shell fire did splendid work in restoring order, caring for the wounded and inspiring the men with confidence. On another occasion near Kruiseecke he displayed great courage and powers of command when the wagon lines of which he was in charge came under heavy machine gun fire. (M.M. (immediate) 17/6/18).

Allen, F., 60741, B.S.M., 13th Battery, R.F.A.
Somme, 1916-17.—For gallantry and consistent good work. Notably on the 22nd/23rd October, 1916 near Flers, when he brought up ammunition on pack animals to an advanced section under very heavy shell fire. (D.C.M. 3/6/17, Regular Commission 19/3/17).

Allpress, F. C., 35237, Corpl., "B" Battery, R.H.A.
Gallipoli, 1915.—For gallantry and devotion to duty in maintaining his position in a forward trench and observation post when the trenches had been evacuated by the infantry on the night 1st/2nd May and maintaining communication with his brigade and batteries. (D.C.M. 6/9/15).

Almond, C. P. P., 102465, Bombr. H.Q. 29th D.A.C.
Flanders, 1918.— On 26th September he was on patrol duty near Zillebeke, reconnoitring forward roads for the advance of the D.A.C. He came to the assistance of another N.C.O. who had discovered and held up a dug-out containing eight Germans. Between them they disarmed and captured all and marched them back to Vlamertinghe. (M.M. (immediate) 14/5/19).

Almond, J. H., 12161, Corpl., 92nd Battery, R.F.A.
Flanders, 1917.—On the night of July 18th the road forward of Elverdinghe was heavily shelled. Corpl. Almond, who was in charge of wagons bringing up ammunition, was severely wounded; in spite of this and always under a heavy fire, he extricated a team which had been partly

knocked out, delivered his ammunition at the gun line and got his wagons away before he went to have his wounds dressed. He showed a fine example of steadfastness. (M.M., immediate, 17/9/17).

Amos, C. L., 68745, Bombr., "B" Battery, R.H.A.
Flanders, 1918.—On 22nd October near Ooteghem, when the battery moved up in close support of the infantry, there was found to be a gap of 1,000 yards between two battalions. Bombr. Amos ran out a telephone line under heavy machine gun fire to a farm whence observation of this gap could be obtained. He and another N.C.O. remained at the farm for 18 hours establishing a post of three Lewis gunners, four riflemen and bombers. He sent most valuable reports and frequently went out to repair the line. The enemy artillery made four direct hits on the farm but the admirable dispositions of Bombr. Amos effectually prevented counter-attacks developing. His courage and resource proved invaluable. (D.C.M. (immediate) 12/3/19).

Andrews, F. E., 253549, Pioneer, 29th Divl. Sig. Co., R.E. (attached 15th Brigade, R.H.A.).
Flanders, 1917.—On the night of 21st/22nd October, he acted as half-way house repairer of a line laid by a party under Sergt. Nightingale. His position was shelled throughout the night, calling for constant repairs under fire, which were carried out with great promptness and courage. (Divisional Card of Honour No. 2783).

Anthony, C. H. G., 107815, Gunner, 26th Battery, R.F.A.
Arras and Flanders, 1917.—For continuous good service and conspicuous gallantry during the operations at Monchy le Preux and north of Ypres. He has always shown the greatest courage whenever the battery has been under fire. His high reputation among his comrades and his demeanour under fire have been a splendid example. This man finally went to hospital suffering from gas after serving his gun under a heavy gas bombardment. (D.C.M. 1/1/18).

Archbold, J., 34447, A/Bombr., 97th Battery, R.F.A.
Gallipoli, 1915.—For gallantry under fire as under:—
(a) On 27th June he went out under fire and brought in two wounded men of the 7th Battn. Royal Scots from in front of the Battery Commander's O.P.;
(b) On 14th July he brought in a wounded man at night under heavy rifle fire;
(c) For repeatedly repairing telephone wires under heavy shell and rifle fire. (D.C.M. 16/11/15, Mention 5/11/15).

Armitage, A., 52654 or 58654, Corpl., 97th Battery, R.F.A.
Gallipoli, 1915.—For conspicuous gallantry during the attacks of the 2nd May, 4th and 28th June, 6th and 7th August, in repeatedly repairing telephone wires under heavy shell and rifle fire. (M.M. 11/11/16).

Ashley, P., 745423, Driver, 1/1st Warwickshire Battery, R.H.A. (T.F.).
Flanders, 1918.—On the night 5th/6th September the battery wagon lines near Le Veau were subjected to a concentrated gas bombardment, many shells bursting close enough to splash the horses with liquid. This driver was one of a party who most gallantly managed to move from the shelled area all the 39 horses that were there and to put nose-bags on them filled with damp grass. This prompt action saved many horses from serious consequences and set a fine example to the other men. (M.M. (immediate) 11/2/19).

Atkins, W. E., 40517, B.S.M., S.A.A. Section, 29th D.A.C.
Flanders, 1917-18, and Cambrai, 1917.—For great devotion to duty and to the welfare of his section . On many occasions and in trying circumstances his energy and proved reliability have set a fine example and have ensured thoroughness and efficiency in the work of men under his charge. (M.S.M. 17/6/18).
Flanders, 1918.—For general good work. (Belgian Croix de Guerre).

Austing, A., B.S.M., "L" Battery, R.H.A.
Regular Commission August 1918.

Baddeley, G., 80139, Driver, 26th Battery, R.F.A.
Flanders, 1918.—On September 29th near Gheluveldt he was taking up ammunition to the guns which had advanced in close support of the infantry. On arrival, the gun position was found to be under heavy fire and the detachments withdrawn to cover. Although told to abandon his wagon and save

himself and his horses, Driver Baddeley displayed great courage and devotion to duty in delivering his ammunition before withdrawing and getting the wagon safely away. (M.M. (immediate) 14/5/19).

Baggaley, C. H., 46927, Bombr., No. 2 Section 29th D.A.C.
Flanders, 1918.—On March 18th at Wieltje an enemy shell struck an ammunition dump. Flames at once sprang up through the tarpaulin covering the ammunition. Corpl. Roberts and Bombr. Baggaley tried to approach but were driven off by six successive explosions. Finally, however, at great personal risk they succeeded in throwing the end of the tarpaulin over the fire and continued to pour on water till the fire was extinguished. By their prompt and gallant action they undoubtedly prevented a great deal of damage and saved a large amount of ammunition from being destroyed. (M.M., immediate, 12/6/18).

Baker, C., 54288, Sergt., "B" Battery, R.H.A.
Flanders, 1917.—On 9th October Sergt. Baker's gun was in action near the Steenbeek. The whole of his detachment was wounded by a direct hit on the gun. He himself received a severe shock and was stained yellow with the fumes. He took the wounded men to the dressing station but returned himself without seeing the medical officer, reporting for duty at another gun.
On 21st October he was in charge of two guns approaching the Steenbeek positions. Under a barrage of 5.9″ shell one driver was killed, two others badly wounded, and seven horses wounded. He himself was badly wounded but managed to bandage up the man who had a leg blown off and to bandage roughly the other. He unhooked the teams and temporarily withdrew them and the men until he himself collapsed. (M.M., immediate, 28/1/18).

Baker, W. J., 18757, Farrier-Sergt., 92nd Battery, R.F.A.
Flanders, 1918.—Has served in the battery for over three years. Thoroughly hard-working, efficient and painstaking, he has carried out his work in a most efficient manner. By his zealous efforts, personal example, and keen supervision, he has imbued those under him with energy and enthusiasm. He has constantly taken up ammunition to the gun line and has never failed to complete his duty. (M.S.M. 18/1/19, French Croix de Guerre 19/6/19).

Barker, A. G. Clayton, 88917, 10th Battery, R.F.A.
Gallipoli, 1915.—Brought to notice for very useful work at his O.P. on the nights 1st/2nd, 2nd/3rd, and 3rd/4th May. (Temporary Commission Nov. 1915).

Barrett, T. N., 558173, Sapper, 29th Divl. Sig. Co., R.E. (attached H.Q. 29th D.A.).
1915-18.—Has been with the Division since its formation. He took part in the landing on the peninsula, served throughout the Gallipoli campaign and was in the evacuation both of Sulva Bay and of Cape Helles. He came to France with the Division and has served continuously with it till the armistice. He has done good work as an operator and as signal clerk with Divisional Headquarters and Infantry Brigade Signal Sections. Since June, 1917, he has been attached to D.A.H.Q. as telegraphist and exchange operator. (Divisional Card of Honour).

Barry, J., 80519, Corpl., X/29th Trench Mortar Battery.
Flanders, 1918.—In the operations near Outtersteene on 18th August this N.C.O. succeeded in establishing his trench mortar in an advanced and very exposed position in order to support the infantry advance. He worked for 36 hours with skill and energy—finally keeping his mortar in action for two hours under a heavy fire. The fine example of courage and enthusiasm shown by Corpl. Barry was materiaaly responsible for the success of the detachment in its task. (M.M. (immediate) 24/1/19).

Batt, J. H., 68013, Bombr., 26th Battery, R.F.A.
Gallipoli, 1915.—For exceptionally good work in laying out wires and keeping communications open on June 28th in very difficult circumstances. (M.M. 11/11/16).

Beardmore, W., 29925, Driver, 460th Battery, R.F.A.
Flanders, 1918.—As lead driver near Gheluveldt on September 29th this man set a very fine example of courage and devotion to duty. He drove his gun into action under heavy fire and then volunteered to go back through the barrage for ammunition. (M.M. (immediate) 14/5/19).

Beardsle,y, W. T., Sergt., "B" Battery, R.H.A.
Regular Commission 18/8/16.

Beecham, D., 87799, Corpl., "L" Battery, R.H.A.
Flanders, 1918.—At about 7 a.m. on the 8th June, the battery position near Grand Sec Bois began to be considerably shelled with 10·5″ howitzers. A direct hit was obtained on a gun-pit setting alight the camouflage which fell over one of the ammunition recesses and set fire to the sand-bags. In spite of the shelling and the explosion of a dump of S.A. Ammn., this N.C.O., with three others, with great gallantry came out of safety to put out the fire and managed to do so before a single round exploded. (Divisional Card of Honour No. 2788).

Bell, J. G., B.Q.M.S., 97th Battery, R.F.A.
Regular Commission 23/6/16.

Bell, W., 15389, Sergt., 1/4th Highland Mountain Brigade, R.G.A. (T.F.).
Gallipoli, 1915—This N.C.O. took charge of 2nd Lieut. Mackenzie's section when the latter was killed early in the action of the 28th June. This section was detached in action close behind the forward trenches. He did excellent work and showed exceptional coolness and resource. Since the landing this N.C.O. has shown marked ability and initiative. (D.C.M 16/11/15, Mention 5/11/15, Mention 28/1/16).

Bendon, J. W., 210611, Driver, 92nd Battery, R.F.A.
Flanders, 1918.—On September 28th Driver Bendon was one of a party taking ammunition up to the guns after an advance near Gheluveldt. The party encountered such intense shell fire that it appeared impossible to get the ammunition through. Nevertheless with admirable courage and determination they pressed on and succeeded in their task. They then immediately returned for a second load, thus enabling the guns to support a further advance (M.M. (immediate) 14/5/19).

Bennett, G., 88483, Farrier Q.M.S., 10th Battery, R.F.A.
Gallipoli, 1915.—26th May. For very good work in cutting horses loose from picket lines under heavy H.E. and shrapnel fire. Many horses were saved. (M.M. 11/11/16).

Bennett, P., 80613, Sergt., 92nd Battery, R.F.A.
1915-18.—This N.C.O. has been in the battery since the 29th D.A. was first formed. He took part in the landing and evacuation of the peninsula, and came to France with the battery in March, 1916. Practically all his service has been gun-line work in France and he has commanded a sub-section in all the big battles in which his battery has taken part. He always showed great coolness under shell fire and could be thoroughly relied upon at all times. His example of personal energy whenever a new position had to be made had a great effect on his men and he has maintained a high state of discipline in his sub-section which has always been the best in the battery. (Divisional Card of Honour).

Bennett, R. B., 64632, Driver, 92nd Battery, R.F.A.
Arras, 1917.—For gallantry and devotion to duty. On April 14th, when his battery was being heavily shelled he brought up the rations that were urgently required with a total disregard to fire. His good example helped to keep the battery steady in trying circumstances. (M.M. (immediate) 9/7/17).

Berry, W. B., 34655, Sergt., 26th Battery, R.F.A.
Gallipoli, 1915.—(Medaille Militaire 24/2/16).

Bird, D., 2782, B.S.M., 10th Battery, R.F.A.
Gallipoli, 1915.—On the 1st June he formed part of a volunteer gun detachment for a Naval 12-pdr. gun which was in action in an open position under heavy shell fire, and remained in action for 49 minutes while firing 30 rounds at a range of 700 yards from the enemy trenches. This N.C.O. and a Gunner were in the most dangerous positions of the gun detachment. (D.C.M. 16/11/15, Mention 5/11/15, Regular Commission 10/11/15).

Bishop, F. H., Corpl., "L" Battery, R.H.A.
Regular Commission 19/6/16.

Bishop, J., 604281, Driver, 1/1st Warwickshire Battery, R.H.A. (T.F.).
Flanders, 1918.—On the 29th April the limber lines were heavily shelled and the men were ordered to withdraw. After some time, while the shelling was continuing, Driver Bishop was seen tying up horses, and explained that being stableman on duty, he thought he ought to remain and not take cover with the rest of the men. (Divisional Card of Honour No 2785).

Bishop, R. J., 444, Arm. S.-Sergt., A.O.C., attached 147th Brigade, R.F.A.
    Gallipoli, 1915, and Somme, 1916.—For conspicuous ability and devotion
to duty, in Gallipoli and France, notably during the operations of 24th June
to 1st July, 1916, in the Beaumont Hamel sector, where he constantly had
to ride his bicycle under shell fire to attend to damaged guns and equipment.
(Mention 4/1/17).

Blake, B. W., 77271, Gunner, "B" Battery, R.H.A.
    Gallipoli, 1915.—For excellent work in giving first aid to wounded whilst
employed as stretcher-bearer, under heavy fire all day on the 28th April,
1915.   (Mention 5/11/15, M.M. 11/11/16).

Bohmer, A., 1610, Gunner, 371st Battery, R.F.A.
    Somme, 1916.—In the Engelbelmer sector on the 3rd and 22nd August
Gunner Bohmer showed great resource and intrepidity in dealing with
wounded under shell fire.   After they had been attended to, he went on his
own initiative for an ambulance, under very heavy fire, the detachments
having been withdrawn from the battery position.   (6th Division
"Gallantry Card").

Bonny, R. G., 27914, Sergt., "L" Battery, R.H.A.
    Cambrai, 1917.—Displayed great gallantry at La Vacquerie valley on
29th/30th November.   Took the place of the layer at his gun who had
been killed and laid over open sights with great steadiness.   Encouraged
his men by being cool and good-humoured throughout and finally was the last
to leave carrying a dial sight and a wounded man under heavy rifle and
machine gun fire.   (M.M. (immediate) 2/4/18).

Boost, T. W., 65749, Bombr., 10th Battery. R.F.A
    Gallipoli, 1915.—For excellent work mending and relaying telephone wires
at all times, especially on the night of the 1st/2nd May under heavy rifle
fire.   (M.M. 11/11/16).

Bowles, F. W., 65311, Sergt., "L" Battery, R.H.A.
    Somme, 1917.—On February 10th the battery in action behind Morval
was heavily shelled by 5.9's.   Two guns were destroyed and the ammunition
in the pits caught fire.   This N.C.O. immediately entered the pits and tried
to get the fire under control by removing some of the ammunition.   He was,
however, unable to effect this and was driven away by some of the ammunition starting to explode.   He then went round the dug-outs which were
under the burning pits to make sure that all the men had left the position.
All this was done under heavy shell fire.   (M.M. (immediate) 26/3/17, Regular
Commission March 1917).

Bowman, D., B.Q.M.S., 147th B.A.C.
    Regular Commission 15/6/15.

Brand, G., B.S.M., "L" Battery, R.H.A.
    Regular Commission February 1917.

Bridges, H. G., 64224, Sergt., "B" Battery, R.H.A.
    Arras and Flanders, 1917.—A most excellent and trustworthy N.C.O. who
has been of great use to his battery.   Cool and steady under fire, he keeps his
men together and sets a most excellent example.   He has been on active
service since 1914, including the retreat from Mons, Gallipoli, Somme, Arras,
and Ypres (1917).   (D.C.M. 1/1/18).

Broad, C. E., 745281, Sergt., 92nd Battery, R.F.A.
    Flanders, 1918.—For general good work.   (Belgian Croix de Guerre
4/9/19).

Brodie, J., 82549, Driver, 92nd Battery, R.F.A.
    Flanders, 1918.—On September 28th Driver Brodie was one of a party
taking ammunition up to the guns after an advance near Gheluveldt.   The
party encountered such intense shell fire that it appeared impossible to get
the ammunition through.   Nevertheless, with admirable courage and determination they pressed on and succeeded in their task.   They then immediately returned for a second load, thus enabling the guns to support a
further advance.   (M.M. (immediate) 14/5/19).

Brook, E., L/29301, Gunner, 13th Battery, R.F.A.
    Flanders, 1917-18, and Cambrai, 1917.—Has repeatedly shown great
courage.   As linesman he has frequently maintained communications in

spite of heavy shelling and the difficulties of darkness and heavy ground. His spirit of self-sacrifice and ready resource have constantly been of the highest military value; on one occasion he continued patrolling his line though wounded, but this is but one instance of his fine spirit and continuous good work. (D.C.M. 3/6/18).

Brooker, E. H., 59032, Sergt., 13th Battery, R.F.A.
Flanders, 1918.—This N.C.O. repeatedly displayed great gallantry and devotion to duty. On more than one occasion, when ammunition wagons were overturned or damaged by shell fire, he promptly effected repairs or salvage. He displayed particular gallantry on an occasion when a hut in which 25 men were sleeping was destroyed by shell fire, by caring for the wounded regardless of danger. (D.C.M. 3/6/18).

Brooks, L. C. D., 144571, Gunner, 13th Battery, R.F.A.
Flanders, 1918.—For good work. (Mention 23/12/18).

Brooks, W. J., 14675, R.S.M., H.Q. 15th Brigade, R.H.A.
· Gallipoli, 1915, and Somme, 1916.—For general good work throughout. (Serbian Cross of Kara George 2nd Class with swords 14/2/17, Regular Commission February 1917).

Brough, W., 40495, Sergt. (a/B.S.M.), 26th Battery, R.F.A.
Gallipoli, 1915.—For exceedingly good work whilst in charge of battery communications after June 2nd, often under shell fire. (M.M. 11/11/16).

Brown, H., 554, B.S.M., 90th Heavy Battery, R.G.A.
Gallipoli, 1915.—In the action of the 28th June, a six-inch gun from the Asiatic shore suddenly fired in enfilade on the 90th Heavy Battery. Sergeant-Major Brown displayed great coolness in encouraging the men at the guns. He was twice knocked down by the blast of shells bursting near him but refused to take cover in order to devote himself to the wounded. (D.C.M. 6/9/15).

Bruce, A. J., 58390, a/Bombr., H.Q. 15th Brigade, R.H.A.
Gallipoli, 1915.—For continual good work as telephonist and linesman from 27th April, and especially on the night of the 28th June when he assisted in repairing wires under very heavy fire. (M.M. 11/11/16).

Bull, C., 614009, a/B.S.M., 1/1st Warwickshire Battery, R.H.A. (T.F.).
Flanders, 1917.—B.S.M. Bull was in charge of the party bringing up ammunition on the night of the 27th/28th July to the battery position near White Hope corner. All the road east of Elverdinghe was under heavy fire from 5·9 inch and gas shell. B.S.M. Bull kept his party together with courage and coolness and succeeded in delivering his ammunition and getting his party back safely; he also managed to extricate and bring back a wagon which had been hit and overturned. (M.M. (immediate) 18/10/17, French Croix de Guerre 17/12/17).

Bunning, A. H., 90th Heavy Battery, R.G.A.
Regular Commission 14/10/15.

Bunter, W. H., 91570, Corpl., Y/29 Trench Mortar Battery.
Flanders, 1918.—From February to June in the Passchendaele and Vieux Berquin sectors this N.C.O. has constantly shown gallantry and coolness, whether in charge of his mortar during local raids or in command of carrying parties bringing bombs to the gun positions. His battery was often short of officers and to his courage and energy was largely due the effective assistance given by his mortars to raiding parties. (M.M. 13/3/18).

Burbridge, W., 253192, Sapper, 29th Divl. Sig. Co., R.E. (attached 15th Brigade, R.H.A.).
Flanders, 1918.—For general good work. (Belgian Croix de Guerre 4/9/19).

Burford, J. P.,123596, a/Bombr., No. 1 Section, 29th D.A.C.
Flanders, 1917.—On the night of the 18th/19th September near Boesinghe this N.C.O. was in charge of a wagon bringing ammunition to the guns. He and the lead driver were wounded by a shell which killed several horses of his own and two other wagons. The two latter were unable to proceed but actg. Bombr. Burford, although wounded in two places, took the place of the wounded lead driver of his own team, drove on, delivered the ammunition to the guns, and brought the empty wagon back four miles to camp. (D.C.M. (immediate) 19/11/17).

Bush, F. G., 68200, Corpl., 13th Battery, R.F.A.
    Gallipoli, 1915.—For consistent good work as telephonist to his battery;
he has repeatedly repaired wires under heavy fire.   (M.M. 21/9/16).
    Somme, 1916.—This N.C.O. was in charge of the telephonists of the 13th
Battery, R.F.A. throughout the preliminary operations and by his example of
fearlessness and devotion to duty has set and maintained a very high standard
amongst the men under him.   On July 1st at about 7-20 a.m. he went out
to repair a break in the line to the F.O.O. in Praed Street.   Afterwards he
voluntarily patrolled an extension to the front line trench for the use of the
party going forward to the attack with the Hampshire Regiment and owing
to the congestion in the trenches was obliged to get out of the trench and
proceed across the open under heavy machine gun fire.   On arriving there
he tested the line, found all correct and returned the same way that he went
out.   (Bar to M.M. 16/8/17).

Butler, E., 64208, Driver, D/17th Battery, R.F.A.
    1916-18.—Served with his battery throughout all operations since 1916
(inclusive).   Has always distinguished himself by great devotion to duty
under all conditions.   On one occasion, when the advanced wagon lines near
Ypres were being heavily shelled, he displayed great coolness in removing
wounded to a place of safety.   He has frequently shown the same coolness
and determination in taking ammunition up to the guns in very trying
circumstances.   (Divisional Card of Honour).

Cage, H. N., 197300, Lance Bombr., 92nd Battery, R.F.A.
    Flanders, 1918.—On his way to deliver rations in the mess-cart on May
20th, was wounded in the head by hostile shell fire.   He then led on the
horse which also was wounded, but both he and the horse collapsed when
about fifty yards from the battery position.   (Divisional Card of Honour).

Cann, F. W., 106887, Driver, D/17th Battery, R.F.A.
    Flanders, 1917.—On the 20th July, on the Elverdinghe-Boesinghe road,
Driver Cann was wheel driver of a wagon taking up ammunition to his battery
under heavy shell fire and gas barrage.   A shell killed the off-leader and
wounded the N.C.O. in charge of the wagon.   Though himself wounded subsequently by another shell he assisted the lead driver to deliver the ammunition to the guns with four horses, and returned with the empty wagon to the
wagon line.   (M.M. (immediate) 28/9/17).

Cayless, A. W., 223104, Gunner, 26th Battery, R.F.A.
    Flanders, 1918.—During the operations on the night 2nd/3rd June this
man was one of the signallers with the F.O.O.   The wires having been cut
in several places by hostile shell fire, he immediately volunteered to go out
and mend them in spite of the heavy bombardment that was going on at the
time.   Having restored communication he rejoined his party.   A few
minutes later the wires were cut again, and although the bombardment was,
if anything, heavier than before, he at once volunteered to go out again.   He
restored communication and enabled the F.O.O. to get his information
through.   His prompt action and utter disregard of danger merit the highest
praise.   (M.M. (immediate) 17/10/18).

Checkley, E., 614036, Sert., 1/1st Warwickshire Battery, R.H.A. (T.F.).
    Flanders, 1918.—For general good work.   (Mention 23/12/18).

Churchman, W. F., L/46907, Driver, "L" Battery, R.H.A.
    Flanders, 1918.—On the night of the 29th/30th September near Ghelu-
veldt was one of a team which displayed great gallantry in delivering their gun
into action over extremely bad roads under very heavy shell fire.   Their
coolness and skill in handling their horses under the worst conditions were
worthy of the highest praise.   (M.M. (immediate) 14/5/19).

Clarke, H., 63376, Gunner, "Y" Battery, R.H.A.
    Gallipoli, 1915.—Was one of the detachment manning the 12-pdr. Naval
gun on the 13th July.   Owing to the firing gear breaking down it was
necessary to cock the lock with a drag-rope.   This was done by Gunner Clarke
who had to stand in a very exposed position under heavy fire.   He continued
to fire the gun until he received orders to get under cover.   (D.C.M. 16/11/15,
Mention 5/11/15).

Cleall, E. H., 14th Siege Battery, R.G.A.
    Commission October 1915.

Coates, C. H., 19776, B.S.M., 460th Battery, R.F.A.
    Somme, 1916.—For conspicuous good work and devotion to duty. This W.O.

has the single idea of keeping up a high standard of efficiency among both men and horses, with excellent results. (Mention 4/1/17, Regular Commission 21/12/16).

Collingridge, A., 614126, Sergt., 1/1st Warwickshire Battery, R.H.A. (T.F.).
Flanders, 1918.—On the night of the 5th/6th September the battery wagon lines near Le Veau were subjected to a concentrated gas bombardment, many shells bursting close enough to splash the horses with liquid. This Sergeant, with the assistance of two other men, gallantly managed to remove from the shelled area all the 39 horses that were there and to put nose-bags on them filled with damp grass. This prompt action saved many horses from serious consequences and set a fine example to the other men. (M.M. (immediate) 11/2/19).

Cook, C. W., 43325, Bombr., 368th Battery, R.F.A.
Gallipoli, 1915.—During the action of the 28th June a high explosive shell from the Asiatic shore hit one of the guns of the 97th Battery and killed or wounded all the detachment. A few minutes later the wagon of this gun was hit and set on fire. This N.C.O. at once rushed to the burning wagon to try and save the ammunition which he knew to be scarce. Several rounds exploded but the rest were saved, also that from the pit under the wagon. (D.C.M. 16/11/15, Mention 5/11/15).

Corfield, H., 85564, Gunner, 26th Battery, R.F.A.
Somme, 1916.—As battery linesman during the operations in the Beaumont Hamel sector on September 3rd he repaired his lines several times under heavy shell fire after they had been cut during the hostile bombardment. (M.M. (immediate) 9/12/16).

Coulling, H. J., 74754, Bombr., "L" Battery, R.H.A.
Gallipoli, 1915, and Somme, 1916-17.—For gallantry and devotion to duty. Notably at Gueudecourt in November, 1916, he showed great bravery while working in the front line with trench mortars. On this occasion he was thrice buried by shell fire. (Mention 18/5/17).

Crossley, R., 66495, Gunner, 10th Battery, R.F.A.
Gallipoli, 1915.—On the 1st May was one of a volunteer 12-pdr. gun detachment in action in the open under heavy shell fire for 40 minutes, firing 30 rounds at 700 yards from the enemy trenches. (M.M. 11/11/16).

Croucher, J., 82918, Lance Bombr., 26th Battery R.F.A.
Cambrai, 1917, and Flanders, 1917-18.—Has been responsible for the delivery of rations to the battery. Has continually displayed initiative, resource, and great courage throughout this period. In spite of being frequently exposed to shelling and gas, especially during the operations in Flanders, he has never failed to deliver water and rations to the battery. His resourcefulness and invariable stoutheartedness have set a fine example. (M.S.M. 17/6/18).

Cutts, F. W., Sergt., "B" Battery, R.H.A.
Regular Commission February 1917.

Dadd, R. C., 68728, Gunner, "L" Battery, R.H.A.
Flanders, 1917.—On the night of the 17th/18th August "L" Battery in action near Boesinghe was shelled with 5·9's. One shell set fire to the camouflage. The whole battery turned out like one man to put it out, the lead being specially taken by Gunner Dadd and Bombr. Duffill and Gunners Turk and Wilkins. But for their prompt action and disregard of danger it is extremely probable that all the guns and ammunition, not only of the battery but of the adjoining one, would have been destroyed. On the afternoon of the 19th August "L" Battery was heavily shelled with 8 inch or 11 inch shell and the detachments were ordered by the officer on duty to evacuate the position. Gunner Dadd went straight back to the position under very heavy shell fire to fetch a stretcher. (D.C.M. (immediate) 22/10/17, Belgian Croix de Guerre 15/4/18).

Dannatt, A., M.M., Sergt., "B" Battery, R.H.A.
Regular Commission April 1918.

Davis, A. J., 67089, Corpl., 92nd Battery, R.F.A.
Arras, 1917.—On the night of the 2nd/3rd May near Monchy the battery was heavily shelled when an S.O.S. signal was received. Corporal Davis continued to serve his gun alone, after the rest of the detachment had been put out of action, and kept up the fire, though many gas shells fell within a few feet of him. (M.M. (immediate) 9/7/17).

Deag, A. J., 68564, Driver, "L" Battery, R.H.A.
    Arras and Flanders, 1917.—Has served continuously in "L" Battery,
R.H.A., since the beginning of the war, including the retreat from Mons and
the Gallipoli campaign.   His work in the wagon line has been exceptionally
good.   Latterly he has brought up ammunition in very trying circumstances,
frequently under fire, and his demeanour throughout has been excellent.
(Mention 14/12/17).

Dawson, W. J., 47659, Corpl., H.Q. 29th Divl. Artillery.
    Gallipoli, 1915.—This N.C.O. landed at Helles on the 25th April as
signaller to the H.Q. 29th D.A. and was successful. in maintaining visual
signal communication between the beach and the ships landing troops during
the first three days of the landing.   On the night of the 25th April when
the infantry were being heavily attacked he performed good work by carrying
up ammunition under heavy fire.   (M.M. 11/11/16).
    Flanders, 1918.—During operations from the 14th to the 22nd October
near Dadizeele and St. Louis Corporal Dawson has displayed great gallantry
in laying and repairing telephone lines under fire.   On October 14th he
established important communications, prior to a successful attack, despite
intense shell fire and gas.   On the night of the 22nd/23rd October he was
in charge of a forward exchange and, although subjected to a very heavy
fire, maintained his communications throughout, frequently going out to
repair them.   This N.C.O.'s devotion to duty and cool courage have at all
times been a splendid example to his comrades.   (Bar to M.M. (immediate)
17/6/19).

Deal, A. T., 82901, Gunner, 460th Battery, R.F.A.
    Flanders, 1917.—On July 31st, Gunner Deal was a signaller with the
F.O.O. party during the attack near Boesinghe.   He performed valuable
service in maintaining wires, which he repaired continually under heavy fire,
thereby maintaining communication to the rear.   When finally it became
impossible to keep wires through, he was of great value in assisting to establish visual signalling.   (Divisional Card of Honour No. 231).

Dingley, A., 34723, Corpl., V/29th Heavy Trench Mortar Battery.
    Somme, 1916.—For good work with the Heavy Trench Mortar Battery
prior to and during the bombardment from 24th June to the 1st July, constantly under shell fire.   (Mention 4/1/17).

Disley, H., B.S.M., 370th Battery, R.F.A.
    Regular Commission 30/4/16.

Dixon, H. J., 172365, Gunner, 1/1st Warwickshire Battery, R.H.A. (T.F.).
    Flanders, 1917.—On the evening of the 10th August the battery in
position on the canal bank at Boesinghe was being heavily shelled.   Two
guns were put out of action, and their camouflage as well as that of one other
gun was set on fire, and the ammunition started exploding.   The detachments
were cleared to a flank.   2nd Lieuts. Philip and Malby with Sergeant Kinman
and Gunner Dixon worked for 20 minutes under continuous shell fire, with
the ammunition continuing to explode, until all fires were extinguished and
the guns recamouflaged.   By their prompt action, a large quantity of ammunition was saved and the guns preserved from further damage.   (M.M.
(immediate) 18/10/17).

Donkin, A., L/11582, Sergt., Y/29th Trench Mortar Battery.
    Cambrai, 1917.—At Masnieres on November 30th and December 1st this
Sergeant was the senior N.C.O. in charge of a six-inch Newton Trench
Mortar Battery.   Under the heavy enemy barrage he fired his guns at the
advancing infantry until the former had been put out of action by enemy
shell fire.   He then collected all available men with rifles and revolvers and
assisted the infantry to hold back the Germans.   After the enemy had been
repulsed he organised his men for the conveyance of wounded to safety.   He
displayed great courage and resourcefulness throughout, his behaviour being
exemplary.   (M.M. (immediate) 19/3/18).

Downs, S. G., 46836, Corpl., 13th Battery, R.F.A.
    Gallipoli, 1915.—For consistently good work as telephonist since the
landing on April 26th.   Frequently mended lines under heavy fire and was
wounded in doing so.   Has done a great deal in maintaining the communications of his battery in an efficient condition.   (D.C.M. 3/6/16, Mention
13/7/16).

Drew, J. E., 3934, B.S.M., D/17th Battery, R.F.A.
    Flanders, 1917-18, and Cambrai, 1917.—Has continually displayed cool-
ness, determination, and initiative.   On several occasions he has had to take

action on his own judgment when no officer was present and by his resource and devotion to duty has set a fine soldierly example to the battery. (M.S.M. 17/6/18).

Dubois, O. C., 78293, Bombr., 460th Battery, R.F.A.
Gallipoli, 1915.—On August 6th this N.C.O. spent four hours repairing telephone lines under exceptionally heavy shell fire, doing his work quietly, carefully and well. Also on April 28th when sent with a message to the French firing line he picked up a wounded Frenchman on his back and carried him to the nearest dressing station, the whole action being performed under very heavy rifle fire. He has been distinguished throughout the operations for his coolness under fire. (D.C.M. 16/11/15, Mention 28/1/16).

Duffill, W., 87801, Bombr., "L" Battery, R.H.A.
Flanders, 1917.—On the night of August 17th/18th "L" Battery, R.H.A., in action near Boesinghe was shelled with 5·9's. One shell set fire to the camouflage covering four of the six guns and ammunition. The whole battery turned out like one man to put out the fire, the lead being specially taken by Gnr. Dadd, Bombr. Duffill, and Gunners Turk and Wilkins. But for their prompt action and disregard of danger there is no doubt that all the guns and ammunition of both "L" and the adjoining battery would have been destroyed. (Divisional Card of Honour No. 223).

Dyer, H., 66764, Sergt., 13th Battery, R.F.A.
Flanders, 1918.—This N.C.O. did exceptionally good work during the operations in Belgium from September to November. On many occasions he displayed great courage and resource in bringing up ammunition under conditions of danger and difficulty. (Belgian Croix de Guerre 4/9/19, Mention 7/7/19).

Edwards, R., 201132, a/Fitter Staff Sergt., H.Q. 17th Brigade, R.F.A.
1916-18.—This N.C.O. has been with the H.Q. 17th Brigade, R.F.A., since the latter landed in France, and has carried out his duties throughout in a manner which deserves the highest praise. Absolutely fearless and ready to endure any hardship, he has been able by his work and endurance to keep the guns of the brigade in first-class order, often under most distressing conditions. (M.S.M. 18/1/19).

Ellen, H. F., 558235, Sergt., 29th Divl. Sig. Co., R.E. (attached H.Q. 29th Divl. Artillery).
Flanders, 1917.—For conspicuous gallantry and devotion to duty. From the 17th to the 20th October in the sector north-east of Ypres this N.C.O. as Sergeant in charge of the Signal Section, H.Q. 29th D.A., displayed the greatest gallantry and coolness in laying and repairing telephone lines continuously under heavy shell fire. On the 20th October, after his fellow linesman had been wounded, he worked on single-handed under heavy fire and was successful in maintaining communications throughout the day. (M.M. (immediate) 28/1/19).
1915-18.—Sergeant Ellen has served continuously in the 29th Division since 1915, was in the original landing and in the subsequent operations at Gallipoli, and came to France with the Division in 1916. He has been in charge of the 29th D.A.H.Q. Signal Section since its formation in 1917 and has been in every action in which the D.A. has taken part, showing great gallantry on many occasions, notably during the battles in October, 1917, at Langemarck, and at Ploegsteert in September, 1918. His initiative at critical times and devotion to duty under the most trying conditions have contributed most materially to the successful maintenance of the artillery communications. (Belgian "Decoration Militaire,"2nd Class, and Croix de Guerre, 24/10/19).

Ewen, C. B. (or D.), 38092, Bombr., 92nd Battery, R.F.A.
Gallipoli, 1915.—For indefatigable work as telephonist. Frequently laying out telephone wires under fire. (M.M. 11/11/16).

Fellows, G F., 83893, Corpl., D/17th Battery, R.F.A.
Flanders, 1917.—For gallantry and devotion to duty on October 21st at Langemarck when in charge of a party with pack animals bringing up ammunition to the battery position. Though the road was heavily shelled he returned and brought up a second load. He remained with some wounded horses on the road under heavy fire and by his own exertions brought them safely back to the wagon lines, after delivering the ammunition. (M.M. (immediate) 28/1/18).

Fells, A., L/1625, Driver, 26th Battery, R.F.A.
Flanders, 1918.—On September 29th, near Gheluveldt, he was taking

ammunition up to the guns which had advanced in close support of the infantry. On arrival it was discovered that the gun position was under heavy fire and the detachments had been withdrawn to cover. Although told to abandon his wagon and save himself and his horses, Driver Fells displayed great courage and devotion to duty in delivering his ammunition before withdrawing and getting his wagon safely away. (M.M. (immediate) 14/5/19).

Fisher, B., 68889, Bombr., "B" Battery, R.H.A.
Gallipoli, 1915.—For conspicuous good work as look-out man for his battery during the whole time the battery was in action, often under heavy fire, from 27th April to 15th June. (M.M. 11/11/16).

Fisher, F. S., 66765, Corpl., V/29th Heavy Trench Mortar Battery.
Arras and Flanders, 1917.—His services when in action before Arras were of a very high order. It was largely due to his efforts that the battery was in position for fire at the appointed hour. Subsequently during the operations north of Ypres he constructed a bridge and carried up heavy T.M. bombs under heavy fire and continuously showed a fine example of steadfastness. (D.C.M. 1/1/18).

Franklin, F. W., 614048, Sergt., 1/1st Warwickshire Battery, R.H.A. (T.F.).
Flanders, 1918—.From 16th September till the cessation of hostilities this N.C.O. acted as B.S.M. He showed persistent gallantry and devotion to duty. His fine example in the most trying circumstances was a constant encouragement to the men, and his ability and leadership contributed greatly to the way in which the battery adapted itself to the conditions of moving warfare. (M.S.M. 3/6/19).

Fraser, D., 1105, Corpl., 1/4th Highland Mountain Brigade, R.G.A. (T.F.).
Gallipoli, 1915.—(Mention 5/11/15).

Frost, E., 51694, a/Bombr., 97th Battery, R.F.A.
Gallipoli, 1915.—In the attacks of 2nd May, 4th June, 28th June, 6th and 7th August, this N.C.O. showed conspicuous bravery in repeatedly repairing telephone lines under heavy shell and rifle fire. No work, however hazardous, was too great for him, and he showed the greatest devotion to duty. (D.C.M. 16/11/15, Mention 5/11/15).

Fryer, T. H., 40929, Gunner, Y/29th Trench Mortar Battery.
Somme, 1916.—During the operations on the night 7th/8th May, Y/29 Trench Mortar Battery was heavily shelled. Shortly before midnight No. 1 emplacement was wrecked, the mortar smashed, the Sergeant in charge was killed, and a badly-wounded Corporal was buried beneath the debris. Gunner Fryer, though badly shaken, proceeded unaided to dig out the Corporal whilst the bombardment was in progress and got him safely under cover. (M.M. (immediate) 10/8/16).

Gadsby, J., 91427, Corpl., 13th Battery, R.F.A.
1917-18.—Was in charge of signals of the battery for eighteen months. Has always shown himself indefatigable in the maintenance of communications and, whenever a difficult job was to be done, he did it himself, showing complete disregard of his personal safety. He did particularly good work during the Ypres offensive in 1917, on one occasion being buried twice whilst maintaining communications. Throughout he has set an example of cheerfulness and hard work; and has been most valuable to his battery commander. He has served in the B.E.F. since 1915. (Divisional Card of Honour).

Gazzard, F. J., 558123, Corpl., 29th Divl. Sig. Co., R.E. (attached H.Q. 29th Divl. Artillery).
1915-18.—Served with the Signal Company in Gallipoli and came to France with the Division in 1916. Has been with the H.Q. 29th D.A. Signal Section since its formation in 1917. He did excellent work at Arras and in the third battle of Ypres in 1917, and was in charge of the lines from the forward exchange on Welsh Ridge in the battle of Cambrai, keeping these lines working up to the last during the German attack of November 30th. He rendered splendid service in maintaining communications during the retirement from the Ypres salient in 1918 and throughout the whole operations of that year. (Divisional Card of Honour).

Glass, D. K., 1031, Armt. Staff-Sergt., A.O.C., attached 132nd Brigade, R.F.A.
Somme, 1916.—For devotion to duty during the bombardment from the 24th June to the 1st July. Unremitting in his attention to material during the heavy fighting, he worked day and night at the gun-pits effecting repairs to guns and trench mortars. (D.C.M. 1/1/17).

Glaysher, W. F., 47232, Fitter, 10th Battery, R.F.A.
Gallipoli, 1915.—Formed one of a 12-pdr. gun detachment in action in the open on May 1st under heavy shell fire, and remained in action for forty minutes, firing 30 rounds at a range of 700 yards from the enemy trenches. (M.M. 11/11/16).

Glazier, P., 48567, Sergt., 368th Battery, R.F.A.
Gallipoli, 1915.—For valuable services, gallantry and devotion to duty, as senior telephonist with the battery, frequently attending to lines under heavy fire, especially on 4th June, 18th June, and 28th June. (M.M. 11/11/16).

Glew, H., 47989, B.Q.M.S., 460th Battery, R.F.A.
Cambrai, 1917.—For great coolness and gallantry in the back areas on November 30th. He assisted in rallying some infantry who were retiring through the wagon lines near Gouzeaucourt and supplied them with S.A.A. by taking a party on bicycles to fetch it up, and also continued to send up S.A.A. to the front line where it was urgently required. This N.C.O., who has a knowledge of steam vehicles, found one of these abandoned on a road and drove it back for further supplies of S.A.A. for the front. After making two journeys he drove it back to a place of safety. Altogether he set a fine example to all near him. (M.M. (immediate) 13/3/18).

Gobbett, J., 13347, R.S.M., H.Q. 17th Brigade, R.F.A.
Flanders 1917-18, and Cambrai, 1917.—For excellent work. He has carried out his duties in a most efficient manner, and by his example has set up a very high standard of efficiency. (M.S.M. 17/6/18).

Godfrey, R. B., 102475, Gunner, "Y" Battery, R.H.A.
Somme, 1916.—Was one of the Left Group linesman up to and including 1st, 2nd and 3rd September. Did excellent work during this period and was to a large extent responsible for maintaining the wire from the Left Group H.Q. to Thiepval Wood, and on the 3rd September maintained communication between Battalion H.Q. in Hamel and the advanced Battalion H.Q. This wire was cut on seven occasions but the Artillery Liaison Officer was never out of touch for more than ten minutes. (M.M. (immediate) 9/12/16).

Gooch, S., 56818, Sergt., "B" Battery, R.H.A.
Flanders, 1917-18, and Cambrai, 1917.—This N.C.O. has invariably shown a high sense of duty and devotion to his battery. His continuous good work has resulted in a very high standard of efficiency and smartness in his sub-section. His work has been beyond all praise. (M.S.M. 17/6/18).

Gough, D., 4972, Driver, D/147th Battery, R.F.A.
Somme, 1916.—For devotion to duty and excellent work in establishing and maintaining permanent communications in the Beaumont Hamel sector during the operations of July and September under heavy shell fire. (Serbian Silver Medal 14/2/17).

Gourley, H., 253552, Sapper, 29th Divl. Sig. Co., R.E. (attached H.Q. 15th Brigade, R.H.A.).
Flanders, 1918.—For gallantry and devotion to duty on the night of 13th/14th October near Dadizeele in maintaining communications between the infantry and the guns prior to the attack. He went frequently out under heavy barrages to repair his lines (French Medaille Militaire 21/8/19).

Granados, F. A., 10019, B.Q.M.S., 368th Battery, R.F.A.
Gallipoli, 1915.—For excellent work in charge of the wagon line, supplying ammunition and looking after the horses. (M.M. 11/11/16).

Green, A. T., 106055, B.S.M., 371st Battery, R.F.A.
Somme, 1916.—For excellent work in the wagon line and for keeping his battery constantly and punctually supplied with ammunition. Both horses and wagon lines have been maintained in good condition in spite of hard work and adverse conditions. (Mention 4/1/17).

Greig, A. W., M.2/082643, Private, 29th M.T. Co., A.S.C. (attached H.Q. 29th Divl. Artillery).
Flanders, 1918.—For continued exemplary service as driver of the R.A. car. Has shown a high degree of skill and nerve, and persistent devotion to duty. In the most trying circumstances he has never failed in coolness and courage, whilst the care he has bestowed on his car is proved by the fact of its immunity from trouble after more than three years continuous work at the front. (M.S.M. 18/1/19, Belgian Croix de Guerre 4/9/19).

Griffiths, W. H., 90th Heavy Battery, R.G.A.
    Regular Commission 14/10/15).

Guiver, H. S., 52850, Sergt., "L" Battery, R.H.A.
    Flanders, 1917.—On August 9th a working party was preparing a forward position for the battery near Boesinghe. They came under heavy shell fire which caused some casualties. The working party received orders to clear to a flank. Sergt. Guiver and Gunner Rea remained to bandage and carry the wounded off on a stretcher and then returned under heavy shell fire to bandage and remove a wounded infantryman. M.M. (immediate) 18/10/17, Regular Commission 23/3/18).

Gullick, L., 745326, Gunner, Z/29 Trench Mortar Battery.
    Cambrai, 1917.—At Masnieres on November 30th, as runner, he carried reports of the situation to and from the 86th Infantry Brigade and the Trench Mortar positions, under continual shell fire, thus enabling the T.M.'s to be used to the best advantage. (Divisional Card of Honour No. 1022).

Hale, S., 49201, Corpl., B" Battery, R.H.A.
    Flanders, 1918.—This N.C.O. has shown particular dash and gallantry. He has always taken pains to secure for himself dangerous employment, frequently extricating guns and wagons from difficulties under heavy fire. He has been twice seriously wounded. (D.C.M. 3/6/19).

Hall, C. W., 12073, B.S.M., 97th Battery, R.F.A.
    Gallipoli, 1915.—For taking up men with ammunition to the firing line on the night 1st/2nd May at the request of the 86th Infantry Brigade. He collected a party of unwilling stragglers and compelled them by sheer force of character to follow him back to the firing line, carrying up S.A.A. He repeated this act twice during the night, having volunteered to do so. (D.C.M. 6/9/15, Regular Commission 4/10/15).

Hall, S., 49201, Corpl., "B" Battery, R.H.A.
    Flanders, 1918.—For continuous gallantry during the advance, between the 29th September and 25th October. In action with his gun and on the move with his sub-section this N.C.O. has given a splendid example to his men. He has constantly been under all sorts of fire and has always been eager to do more than his share of the forward work. (Divisional Card of Honour No. 2790).

Hambley, P., 38101, Sergt., 26th Battery, R.F.A.
    Gallipoli, 1915.—For great zeal in maintenance of telephone communications, especially on the night of the 29th June when, during a strong counter-attack by the Turks, he ran out a telephone line under heavy fire to the forward line. (D.C.M. 3/6/16, Mention 13/7/16).

Hammond, F. W., 52589, Driver, "B" Battery, R.H.A.
    Flanders, 1917.—On August 1st "B" Battery, R.H.A. was advancing across the canal and found the road completely blocked at White Hope Corner. The road was then heavily shelled and there was a tendency among the horses to stampede. This driver rallied the young drivers in his team, unhooked the wheelers, and removed the team steadily off the road out of the line of fire, thereby avoiding casualties to men and horses, and setting a good example to the rest of the drivers of the battery. (Divisional Card of Honour No. 220).

Harbord, E. M., 99646, B.Q.M.S., S.A.A. Section, 29th D.A.C.
    1915-18.—Has served continuously with the 29th D.A. from and including the Gallipoli campaign to the armistice in November, 1918. His devotion to duty and excellent work merit the highest praise. (Mention 7/7/19).

Hardy, A. J., 86688, Bombr., S/29 Trench Mortar Battery.
    Somme, 1916.—For devotion on the 1st July. Whilst acting as No. 1 of his gun, he continued to fire after an enemy shell had caused a premature in the gun-pit and wounded him in the face and arm. After being sent to the dressing station by his C.O. he returned and voluntarily worked his gun again. (M.M. (immediate) 21/9/16).

Harling, W. J., 940003, B.S.M., 460th Battery, R.F.A.
    Flanders, 1918.—For continuous good service and executive ability as Sergeant-Major of his battery. His personal keenness and example have maintained a high standard of general efficiency in the battery. (M.S.M. 18/1/19).
    Flanders, 1918.—This W.O. displayed the most praiseworthy courage on two separate occasions when his battery wagon lines near Becelaere were

shelled. On the night 4th/5th October when a dug-out was hit he extricated four men under fire, bandaged the wounded and got them safely away. On the night 7th/8th October the lines were again heavily shelled and he spent two hours attending to wounded men and horses. Furthermore, three ammunition wagons caught fire; realising the danger of an explosion, he immediately organised a party and put the fire out. (D.C.M. (immediate) 12/3/19).

Hart, W., 78560, Gunner, "L" Battery, R.H.A.
Somme, 1916.—For gallantry and devotion to duty. During the bombardment on the 27th and 28th June he three times mended the telephone wire under heavy shell fire where the trenches had been blown in on Redan Ridge, thus enabling the wire-cutting of his battery to be continued. (M.M. (immediate) 21/9/16).

Hayes, F., 614412, B.Q.M.S., 1/1st Warwickshire Battery, R.H.A. (T.F.).
Flanders, 1917-18, and Cambrai, 1917.—For exemplary conduct, courage and cheerfulness. His hard and conscientious work has materially contributed to the welfare and efficiency of his battery in which he has served in France since 1914. (M.S.M. 17/6/18).

Haylock, G., 85584, Gunner, 460th Battery, R.F.A.
Flanders, 1917.—On the night 10th/11th August the 460th Battery, R.F.A., in action near Boesinghe was heavily shelled with 5·9 shell. Gunner Haylock was battery cook, and when the detachments were ordered to evacuate the position, would not leave the cook-house where the men's evening meal was being prepared until personally ordered to do so. When a gun-pit was subsequently blown up he was first on the spot to render assistance to officers and men injured by the explosion which set off some gas shell and partially buried some of the injured men. Although slightly gassed himself he was the foremost in extricating these men, under continuous shell fire, until all had been removed to the dressing station. (M.M. (immediate) 18/10/17).

Hedges, W., 52554, Corpl., "L" Battery, R.H.A.
Flanders, 1917.—On October 7th, when the battery was advancing into action over the Steenbeek and near Langemarck, it came under heavy fire. The officer leading the battery had his horse shot under him and the horses of the leading teams were getting out of hand. Corporal Hedges with great coolness picked up the officer and then led forward the teams until the officer came up and took over command. He then extricated the wounded men from among the teams and carried them out of the shelled zone. (Divisional Card of Honour No. 2782).

"   Sergt.,   "
Flanders, 1918.—At about 7 a.m. on June 8th the battery position near Grand Sec Bois began to be considerably shelled with 10·5" howitzers. A direct hit was obtained on a gun-pit setting alight the camouflage which fell over one of the ammunition recesses and set fire to the sand-bags. In spite of the shelling and the explosion of a dump of S.A. Ammunition, this N.C.O. with three others with great gallantry came out of safety to put the fire out and managed to do so before a single round exploded. (Divisional Card of Honour No. 2786).
Flanders, 1918.—On the night of 4th/5th October Sergeant Hedges was taking his gun into action with Bombr. Merrill as lead driver. Near Dadizeele the heavy fire alarmed the horses and the team became entangled in the barbed wire. Both N.C.O.'s showed marked courage and coolness in disentangling the frightened animals, finally getting the gun into action. They were under shell fire the whole time. (M.M. (immediate) 14/5/19).

Henny, J. H., 24091, Driver, 13th Battery, R.F.A.
Somme, 1916.—For conspicuous gallantry in the Auchonvillers sector on August 17th. Whilst his battery was being accurately and consistently bombarded with 21" shells the men were ordered to clear to a flank for protection. Driver Henny was leaving his dug-out for this purpose when one of his comrades was buried by the trench being blown in. Driver Henny at once stopped and started digging him out unaided. He was indefatigable in his efforts, the whole time under shell fire, until the man was finally dug out. By his prompt action he undoubtedly saved his comrade from suffocation. (M.M. (immediate) 21/9/16).

Heppell, S., 46885, Corpl., 97th Battery, R.F.A.
Gallipoli, 1915.—For conspicuous gallantry during the attacks of the 2nd May, 4th and 28th June, 6th and 7th August, in repeatedly repairing telephone wires under heavy shell and rifle fire. (M.M. 11/11/16).

C

Hewitt, W. V., 108356, Gunner, "L" Battery, R.H.A.
Cambrai, 1917.—Acted as runner to the F.O.O. during the advance on Masnieres on November 20th/21st. He carried several messages from our front line through heavy machine gun barrage, including one which enabled a local counter-attack to be dealt with. (Divisional Card of Honour No. 2784).

Hill, R. W., L/44290, Sergt., 92nd Battery, R.F.A.
Flanders, 1918.—On September 29th this N.C.O. was in charge of a gun in an advanced section closely supporting the infantry near Gheluveldt. The section came under heavy machine gun and rifle fire and the officer in command was wounded. Sergeant Hill carried on alone, showing great coolness and disregard for danger. He kept his gun in action and undoubtedly was of great assistance in maintaining the advance. (D.C.M. (immediate) 12/3/19).

Hilton, A. H., 60328, Sergt., 97th Battery, R.F.A.
Gallipoli, 1915.—In the action on June 28th a six-inch gun from the Asiatic shore suddenly opened fire in enfilade on the 97th Battery. One gun was at once hit, all the detachment being killed or wounded. A few minutes later the wagon of this gun was hit and set on fire. Sergeant Hilton was one of those who at once rushed to the burning wagon to try and save the ammunition which they knew to be very scarce. Several rounds exploded but the rest was saved. They also saved the ammunition in the pit under the wagon. (D.C.M. 6/9/15).

Hobdell, F. J., 128823, Driver, "B" Battery, R.H.A.
Flanders, 1917.—Driver Hobdell was on duty as linesman on July 31st and August 1st with the F.O.O. party during the attack, for 36 hours continuously. He carried a heavy reel of wire alone through a barrage and was indefatigable during the whole period in mending his wires and endeavouring to maintain communication, under frequent fire and in most inclement weather. All the time he was suffering from physical disability for which he refused to go sick until his duty was completed. (M.M. (immediate) 18/10/17).

Hollister, H., 49206, Gunner, H.Q. 17th Brigade, R.F.A.
Arras, 1917.—For conspicuous bravery on April 9th when the enemy's bombardment continually cut the artillery telephone wire. He went out many times and carried out repairs in the open under the heaviest fire, thus maintaining the communication on which depended the effective support of the infantry by the guns. (M.M. (immediate) 9/7/17).

Hughes, D. L., 745274, Driver, 26th Battery, R.F.A.
Flanders, 1918.—On September 29th near Gheluveldt Driver Hughes was lead driver of a team taking ammunition to the guns in close support of the advancing infantry. On arrival at the gun position it was seen to be under heavy shell fire and the detachments to have been withdrawn under cover. With great gallantry and coolness Driver Hughes led on and succeeded in delivering his ammunition and in withdrawing his wagon safely despite the fact that he had been told to abandon it and save his horses and himself. (M.M. (immediate) 14/5/19).

Hughes, J. E., 52057, Corpl., 368th Battery, R.F.A.
Gallipoli, 1915.—For excellent work as linesman, repairing and relaying telephone wires often under heavy fire. (M.M. 11/11/16).

Hurst, F. R., 13346, Corpl., D/17th Battery, R.F.A.
Cambrai, 1917.—On November 30th this N.C.O. was in charge of No. 1 gun of his battery. He showed great skill and courage in turning his gun about and firing it on the enemy who was advancing at close range on the flank and rear. Though his gun was exposed to heavy machine gun fire he fought it throughout, laying himself when the layer had been hit by rifle fire. (M.M. (immediate) 19/3/18).

Hyde, E. C., a/R.S.M., 1/4th Highland Mountain Brigade, R.G.A. (T.F.).
Regular Commission 14/10/15.

Ideson, A., 31891, "B" Battery, R.H.A.   (See also under "Officers").
Regular Commission October 1915.

Ivill, J., 177180, Driver, "B" Battery, R.H.A.
Cambrai, 1917.—For gallantry and devotion to duty. On November 25th Driver Ivill was lead driver of a team carrying ammunition to the guns in a valley beyond La Vacquerie. A shell burst on the team wounding two drivers and two horses. Driver Ivill with considerable courage and presence of mind changed the horses, shot the wounded ones, and drove on up to the guns with the ammunition wagon with one pair of horses under heavy shell fire. (M.M. (immediate) 19/3/18).

Jackson, E. W., 53472, Driver, 460th Battery, R.F.A.
Flanders, 1917.—Near Woesten on the night 15th/16th July the guns of the 460th Battery were being brought into action. When passing De Wippe Cabaret they were heavily shelled. One shell wounded all the horses and the other drivers of the team of which Driver Jackson was wheel driver, he himself being badly shaken. In the subsequent confusion he showed great coolness and presence of mind. He at once started to extricate the two wounded drivers from the mangled mass of harness and horses; he then stood to his own two horses, quieted them down and prevented the gun from being overturned into the ditch. By his coolness the gun was enabled to be brought on into action with a fresh team the same night. (M.M. (immediate) 18/10/17).

Jackson, F. A., 140173, Gunner, "L" Battery, R.H.A.
Flanders, 1918.—On October 19th near Courtrai Gunner Jackson went forward to an O.P. as signaller with his battery commander. Shell fire was very heavy and the wires were frequently cut. On every occasion Gunner Jackson went out without hesitation and effected repairs. Although accompanied by another signaller he refused to allow him to go out, on the grounds of his youth and inexperience. Gunner Jackson carried on until he was badly wounded in the leg but nevertheless succeeded in maintaining communication long enough for his B.C. to register the battery at a critical time. (D.C.M., (immediate) 12/3/19).

Jefferson, J., 11909, Gunner, D/17th Battery R.F.A.
Somme, 1916-17.—For consistent good work and gallantry. Notably in October, 1916, during attacks on Delville Wood, he served his gun alone under a very heavy fire. (Mention 18/5/17).
Flanders, 1918.—This man has served in the battery since its arrival in France in March, 1916, and has invariably shown cool courage on critical occasions. As an instance of his gallantry may be quoted an incident on the night of October 20th/21st, 1918, at Kapart in Belgium when the battery suddenly came under heavy shell fire whilst night firing. Gunner Jefferson continued to serve his gun single-handed and carried out the allotted task with supreme contempt for the inferno raging about him. (Divisional Card of Honour).

Jefford, J. W., 49124, Corpl., "B" Battery, R.H.A.
Flanders, 1917.—About 0045 on the 23rd August eight light horse teams arrived at the battery position near Boesinghe to move the guns forward. While the guns were being limbered up a heavy barrage of gas shell was opened on the battery position. Corpl. Jefford was hit by a piece of shell in the face which also smashed his box respirator. In spite of his wound and of having no gas mask he continued to cheer on the drivers and get the teams unhooked and away as ordered. He refused to go to the dressing station until all the horses were clear and then only when given a direct order to do so. By his coolness and courage he materially helped to get the horses away without casualties. (M.M. (immediate) 2/11/17).

Jewell, F., 32501, Corpl. S/Smith, 26th Battery, R.F.A.
Flanders, 1918.—During the operations of September and October he was almost nightly employed in bringing up ammunition and, in spite of frequent shelling and gassing, never failed to carry out his duties. He came with the battery to France in 1916. A thoroughly efficient and conscientious workman, he has imbued those under him with the same spirit. (M.S.M. 3/6/19).

Johnson, J. T., 52736, Bombr., "B" Battery, R.H.A.
Flanders, 1917.—Bombr. Johnson was in entire charge of the battery communications between July 15th and August 17th. Throughout the whole of the 1st, 2nd and 3rd August he was out continuously in incessant rain and continual shell fire laying wires between the battery position in Boesinghe and the O.Ps. on the Pilckem ridge. It was entirely owing to his untiring efforts that the battery, having advanced as far forward as the inclement weather permitted, was able to register and maintain its fire. He has proved himself a splendid example of courage and perseverance to the rest of the battery signallers. (Divisional Card of Honour No. 217).

Jolly, C., 42887, Bombr., "Y" Battery, R.H.A.
Gallipoli, 1915.—For excellent work since the landing. He did very good work as No. 1 of a 12-pdr. in a forward position. (M.M. 11/11/16).

Jones, A. C. E., 54318, a/Bombr., "B" Battery, R.H.A.
Arras, 1917.—For conspicuous bravery near Monchy on May 4th when the battery was being heavily shelled. A 5·9 inch shell hit an ammunition pit and set fire to the ammunition. Bombr. Jones left his shelter at great risk and got the fire down. He thus saved the gun and a large quantity of ammunition. (M.M. (immediate) 9/7/17).

Jones, F. J., 25287, Corpl., 92nd Battery, R.F.A.
    Flanders, 1918.—On September 28th near Gheluveldt this N.C.O. was in
charge of a party taking ammunition to the guns after they had advanced.
Intense shell fire was encountered and it appeared impossible to get the ammunition through.   With a splendid display of courage and coolness Corporal
Jones urged his party on, delivered the ammunition, then immediately returned
for a second load.   (M.M. (immediate) 14/5/19).

Jones, J., 101726, Farrier Q.M.S., "L" Battery, R.H.A.
    1915-17.—This N.C.O. is 44 years old and has served in "L" Battery,
R.H.A., continuously since 1915.   He has always shown himself invincible
under the most difficult circumstances and through his devotion to duty he
has at many times at Boesinghe during the period July to September, 1917,
brought ammunition up to the guns under very heavy shell fire.   His care
of the horses during the very cold months of February and March, 1917, near
Montauban was beyond reproach, and by his untiring energy he has
undoubtedly saved the lives of many horses.   (Mention 14/12/17).

Judd, H, 65810, Sergt., "L" Battery, R.H.A.
    Flanders, 1918.—At about 7 a.m. on the 8th June the battery position near
Grand Sec Bois began to be considerably shelled with 10·5″ howitzers.   A
direct hit was obtained on a gun-pit, setting alight the camouflage which fell
over one of the ammunition recesses and set fire to the sand-bags.   In spite
of the shelling and the explosion of a dump of S.A.A., this N.C.O. and three
others with great gallantry came out of safety to put out the fire and managed
to do so before a single round exploded.   (Divisional Card of Honour No.
2787).
    Flanders, 1918.—This N.C.O. by continuous gallantry of a very high
standard and total contempt of danger, as well as by never-failing energy and
keenness, has set the finest example to all ranks.   On one occasion, during
the Passchendaele operations (April, 1918), he particularly distinguished himself by putting out burning camouflage under fire, and conducted the supply
of ammunition through heavy hostile barrages.   (D.C.M. 1/1/19).

Kearney. H., 881838, Gunner, 92nd Battery, R.F.A.
    Flanders, 1918.—On October 1st Gunner Kearney was acting as signaller
to the artillery liaison officer with an infantry brigade near Gheluveldt.   The
Infantry Brigade communications with one of their battalions were destroyed by
the heavy shell fire and, realising the urgency o fthe matter, Gunner Kearney
volunteered to go out and repair the line.   With great gallantry he went
out under extremely heavy machine gun and shell fire and succeeded in restoring the line on several occasions.   (M.M. (immediate) 14/5/19).

Keen, G. H. M., 614060, Corpl., 1/1st Warwickshire Battery, R.H.A. (T.F.).
    Cambrai, 1917.—At the quarry near Gouzeaucourt on November 19th,
under hostile shell fire, Corporal Keen and Gunner Perks assisted Lieut.
Mulholland to put out a fire in a large dump of 4·5 inch howitzer ammunition.   These two men acted quickly and fearlessly, and the party undoubtedly
prevented by a few minutes an explosion which would have affected the
Infantry Battalion Headquarters located in the quarry.   (M.M. (immediate)
19/3/18).

King, C. W., 19364, Sergt., 460th Battery, R.F.A.
    Gallipoli, 1915, and Somme, 1916-17.—For consistently good service.
Sergeant King has always performed his duties with gallantry and coolness,
frequently under heavy shell fire.   (Mention 18/5/17).
    Arras, 1917.—On April 9th the battery in action on the railway bank was
heavily shelled by a high velocity gun.   All the ammunition had been piled
up under a road bridge over the railway.   A shell hit this dump and the
bridge was blown up, large pieces falling on the battery and putting four guns
out of action, killing 2nd Lieut. Nowell and causing several other casualties.
Sergeant King collected the survivors and kept the remaining guns firing on
their barrage lines till more officers arrived.   (M.M. (immediate) 9/7/17).

King, W. F., 558215, 2nd Corpl. (a/Corpl.), 29th Divl. Sig. Co., R.E. (attached
H.Q. 29th Divl. Artillery).
    Flanders, 1918.—This N.C.O. has shown consistent gallantry and devotion
to duty.   On October 14th near Dadizeele he was in charge of the cable
section and maintained communication with forward brigades throughout the
advance in the most efficient manner, despite heavy shell fire.   Again, near
St Louis on October 22nd, he performed his duties under similar conditions.
His gallantry and coolness under fire have undoubtedly encouraged his detachment to persevere and succeed in their difficult and frequently dangerous work.
(M.M. (immediate) 17/6/19).

Kinman, W. N., 614376, Corpl., 1/1st Warwickshire Battery, R.H.A. (T.F.).
Arras, 1917.—On April 9th this N.C.O. under heavy enemy fire and without any regard to his own personal safety continued to serve his gun, notwithstanding that the next gun had received a direct hit, killing 10 and wounding 5. (M.M. (immediate) 9/7/17).

" Sergt., "
Flanders, 1917.—On the evening of August 10th the battery in action on the canal bank at Boesinghe was being heavily shelled. Two guns were put out of action and their camouflage as well as that of one other gun was set alight; the ammunition started exploding. 2nd Lieut. Philip at once collected a party, the detachments having been cleared to a flank, consisting of 2nd Lieut. Malby, Sergeant Kinman and Gunner Dixon, which worked for 20 minutes under continuous shell fire, with the ammunition continuing to explode, until all fires were extinguished and the guns recamouflaged. By their prompt action, a large quantity of ammunition was saved and the guns preserved from further damage. (Bar to M.M. (immediate) 18/10/17).

Kirby, R., 114482, Driver, 13th Battery, R.F.A.
Arras, 1917.—Near Feuchy Chapelle during the night 20th/21st April the enemy's gun and machine gun fire made the supply of ammunition to the forward gun positions a matter of great danger and difficulty. Driver Kirby set a good example of coolness and bravery, and was instrumental in getting a large amount of ammunition through under a very heavy and continuous fire. (M.M. (immediate) 9/7/17).

Knight, C. J., 88195, Bombr., X/29th Trench Mortar Battery.
Somme, 1916.—Showed greatest pluck and resource both previous to and during the bombardment from June 24th to July 1st. After his gun-pit had been knocked in by a shell he repaired it under fire and made it fit for use again. When the telephone broke down he acted as runner between the O.P. and the guns, having to use a trench which was being heavily shelled and in some places having to come out into the open, where the trench was completely demolished. (M.M. (immediate) 21/9/16).

Knight, F. A. J., 38628, a/R.S.M., H.Q. 29th D.A.C.
Arras and Flanders, 1917.—This W.O. has continually rendered valuable and efficient services as R.S.M. of his unit and has greatly assisted in the work of the D.A.C. and the supply of ammunition. (D.C.M. 1/1/18).
1915-18.—This W.O. has served continuously with the 29th D.A., including the Gallipoli campaign, during which his services were invaluable. His constant devotion to duty and gallantry are unquestionable, and he has always been first in undertaking any difficult or dangerous task. His example and persistent efforts have contributed to the attainment and maintenance of the high standard of efficiency of his unit. (French Medaille d'Honneur avec glaives en vermeil, 29/1/19).

Lane, F., 55713, a/Bombr., 97th Battery, R.F.A.
Gallipoli, 1915.—In the attacks of the 2nd May, 4th and 28th June, 6th and 7th August, this N.C.O. showed conspicuous gallantry in repeatedly repairing telephone lines under heavy shell and rifle fire. No work was too hazardous for him to undertake and he showed throughout the greatest devotion to duty. (D.C.M. 16/11/15, Mention 5/11/15).

Laslett, L. W., 33089, Sergt., "B" Battery, R.H.A.
1915-17.—During this period (Gallipoli and France) this N.C.O. has shown a fine example of gallantry and coolness, often under very heavy shell fire. (Mention 18/5/17, Regular Commission May 1917).

Lawrence, S. E., 5772, Corpl., H.Q. 17th Brigade, R.F.A.
Somme, 1916.—For splendid work with the telephone system of the Right Group, 29th D.A., in front of Beaumont Hamel. It was largely due to his devotion to duty that the system never failed and that the Group Commander was able to direct the fire of batteries, during the bombardment from June 24th to July 1st, with the utmost speed on to any desired target. (D.C.M. 1/1/17).

Leedham. G., 41515, Driver, No. 1 Section, 29th D.A.C.
Flanders, 1918.—Has been employed as an orderly on many occasions and has shown considerable gallantry and initiative on many occasions under shell fire during the final operations. He had a horse shot under him on one occasion. (Divisional Card of Honour).

Leslie, J., 5101, Bombr., Y/29th Trench Mortar Battery.
    Flanders, 1918.—On the night of October 13/14th near Ledeghem this
N.C.O. did magnificent work in getting up ammunition under continual
harassing fire.   At 0530 on the 14th he manned his mortar, and in spite
of coming directly under the enemy's barrage successfully fired the allotted
number of rounds in support of our attack.   (M.M. (immediate) 20/8/19).

Levi, F. E., Sergt., "L" Battery, R.H.A.
    Regular Commission April 1918.

Lindop, A. J., 253198, Pioneer, 29th Divl. Sig. Co., R.E. (attached 17th Brigade,
R.F.A.).
    1915-17.—This man has been lineman to 17th Brigade H.Q. throughout
the operations in Gallipoli and France.   He has throughout done excellent
work and has never hesitated to go out on the line, no matter what the conditions were.   He is a very gallant man and has always displayed great
devotion to duty.   (Mention 14/12/17).

Lindsay, H. V., 56855, a/Sergt., R.G.A. Clerks' Section (attached H.Q. 29th D.A.).
    Gallipoli, 1915.—For excellence of work and devotion to duty during the
whole period of the occupation.   (M.S.M. 11/11/16).

Llewellyn, T. E., 44630, Sergt., 10th Battery, R.F.A.
    Gallipoli, 1915.—1st May.   This N.C.O. formed one of a .12-pdr. gun
detachment in action in the open under heavy shell fire, remaining in action
for forty minutes firing 30 rounds at a range of 700 yards from the enemy
trenches.   (M.M. 11/11/16).

Lock, F., 59358, Driver, "L" Battery, R.H.A.
    Flanders, 1918.—This driver was one of a team which displayed great
gallantry on the night of 29th/30th September near Gheluveldt, in driving
their gun into action over extremely bad roads under heavy shell fire.
Their coolness and skill in handling their horses under the worst conditions
was worthy of the highest praise.   (M.M. (immediate) 14/5/19).

Longfoot, R., 40374, Driver, 92nd Battery, R.F.A.
    Arras and Flanders, 1917.—This driver has invariably displayed great
coolness in bringing up ammunition under fire and gas.   On one occasion
when gas masks were being worn an aeroplane dropped a bomb close to his
team wounding one of his horses.   He helped to unload his wagon and on
return to the wagon lines spent the remainder of the night looking after
his wounded horse.   For two years this driver has kept his horses in the
best condition and his harness clean under all weather conditions.
(Mention 14/12/17).

Lott, P. H., 70366, Corpl., H.Q. 147th Brigade, R.F.A.
    Gallipoli, 1915.—For excellent work as telephonist and lineman, often
under fire, repairing and relaying telephone wires.   (M.M. 11/11/16).

Lorne, G. W., 62917, Sergt. and B.S.M., No. 2 Section, 29th D.A.C.
    1915-18.—For continuous hard work and devotion to duty.   He landed
with the 29th Division at Gallipoli on April 25th, 1915, and remained with
the Division till it reached the Rhine in December, 1918.   (Mention 21/5/18,
M.S.M. 18/1/19).

Lynch, J. P., 42542, Gunner, 26th Battery, R.F.A.
    Gallipoli, 1915.—(Mention 13/7/16).

Marks, J. H., 614144, a/Bombr., 1/1st Warwickshire Battery, R.H.A. (T.F.).
    Flanders, 1917.—Displayed great courage and coolness when taking ammu-
nition to the guns on various occasions under heavy shell fire between the
20th and 27th July.   (Divisional Card of Honour No. 218).

Marsh, N. E., 50405, Bombr., "Y" Battery, R.H.A.
    Somme, 1916.—For gallantry on October 22nd when his battery in Delville
valley was heavily shelled with 15" shell.   One shelled killed or wounded 19
men of the battery, and, although wounded himself, he rendered great
assistance in helping to collect the other wounded and carry them on stretchers
under shell fire to the dressing station before reporting his own wound.   (M.M.
(immediate) 22/1/17).

Matheson, A., 4259, Sergt., 1/4th Highland Mountain Brigade, R.G.A. (T.F.).
    Gallipoli, 1915.—This N.C.O. acted as No. 1 at one of the guns in the
action of July 12th and, though the guns were heavily shelled, gallantly served
his gun and kept up his fire.   (D.C.M. 2/2/16. Mention 28/1/16).

Mayo, S. J., 15010, Gunner, 13th Battery, R.F.A.
Gallipoli, 1915, and Somme, 1916.—Has done exceptionally good work during the whole preiod he has been with the battery (August, 1915, to September, 1916). The entire responsibility of laying and maintaining telephone wires has been his since July, 1916, and the work has been particularly well carried out, often under trying circumstances. (Serbian Gold Medal 14/2/17).

McCrory, H., B.Q.M.S., 17th B.A.C.
Regular Commission 10/6/15.

McCubbin, K., 956139, Corpl., 460th Battery, R.F.A.
Flanders, 1918.—On the night 7th/8th October the battery wagon lines near Becelaere were heavily shelled. One shell burst in the tent where this N.C.O. was sleeping, killing four men and wounding him in two places. Disregarding his wounds, he rendered first aid to the survivors, then reported himself to the B.S.M. and assisted other wounded men. He next saw his sub-section horses safely away and then was one of the foremost in extinguishing some burning ammunition wagons. He did not report his wounds till all the foregoing had been accomplished and everything was quiet again. His steady courage and devotion to duty were magnificent. (D.C.M. (immediate) 12/3/19).

McCully, W., 4866, B.S.M.,1/4th Highland Mountain Brigade, R.G.A. (T.F.).
Gallipoli, 1915.—(Mention 28/1/16).

McGuire, P., 45358, Corpl., " Y " Battery, R.H.A.
Gallipoli, 1915.—For particularly good work after landing and as senior telephonist from July, often under fire. (M.M. 11/11/16).

McKenzie, H., 48332, Sergt., 368th Battery, R.F.A.
Gallipoli, 1915.—For conspicuous gallantry during the attacks of May 2nd, June 4th and 28th, August 6th and 7th, in repeatedly repairing telephone wires under heavy shell and rifle fire. (M.M. 11/11/16).

McLaughlan, J., 5039, Gunner, 1/4th Highland Mountain Brigade, R.G.A. (T.F.).
Gallipoli, 1915.—June 28th. On a wagon containing ammunition being set on fire by a high explosive shell from the Asiatic shore, this man formed one of a party which rushed to the burning wagon and saved a number of rounds from it, together with all the ammunition which was stored in the pit beneath it. Several rounds in the wagon exploded in the process. (Mention 5/11/15, M.M. 11/11/16).

MacPhee, D., 42324, Sergt., 10th Battery, R.F.A.
Somme, 1916.—For conspicuous gallantry. On August 13th the 10th Battery position near Engelbelmer was heavily shelled and Sergeant MacPhee's gun was knocked out by two direct hits; another direct hit on the control station wounded Sergeant Holland and three other men. After the detachments had been withdrawn to a safe distance Sergeant MacPhee left his cover and, though the shell fire was too intense for stretcher-bearers to reach the wounded, returned to the battery and carried Sergeant Holland away to a neighbouring battery position that was not being shelled. (M.M. (immediate) 21/9/16).

McPherson, H., 340, Gunner, 1/4th Highland Mountain Brigade, R.G.A. (T.F.).
Gallipoli, 1915.—On July 12th, while acting as one of a detachment serving a gun in a forward position enfilading the enemy's trenches, this man showed great bravery in assisting at the service of the gun, helping to remove the wounded from the gun platform, and passing orders to the guns under heavy rifle and shell fire. (Mention 28/1/16).

Merrell, W. H., 53970, Driver, " B " Battery, R.H.A.
Flanders, 1917.—On August 1st " B " Battery, R.H.A., was advancing to cross the canal and found the road completely blocked at White Hope Corner. The road was then heavily shelled and there was a tendency among the horses to stampede. This driver rallied the young drivers in his team, unhooked the wheelers, and removed the team steadily off the road out of the line of fire, thereby avoiding many casualties to men and horses, and setting a good example to the rest of the drivers in the battery. (Divisional Card of Honour No. 219).
"   "   Bombr., " L " Battery, R.H.A.
" Flanders, 1918.—On the night 4th/5th October Sergeant Hedges was taking his gun into action with Bombr. Merrill as lead driver. Near Dadizeele the heavy shell fire alarmed the horses and the team became entangled in barbed wire. Both N.C.Os. showed marked courage and coolness in disentanglin·· the frightened animals, finally getting the gun into action. They were und·· · shell fire all the time. (M.M. (immediate) 14/5/19).

Messenger, L. W., 55583, Corpl., "L" Battery, R.H.A.
    Gallipoli, 1915-16.—For devotion to duty, laying and repairing telephone
wires constantly under heavy shell fire, especially on June 28th, July 5th and
12th, August 6th and 7th.   On January 7th, 1916, he went across the open
through a shell-swept zone and succeeded in re-establishing communication
when it was of the utmost importance.   (M.M. 11/11/16).

Millar, J. Y., S.E./12872, Sergt., A.V.C. attached 460th Battery, R.F.A.
    Flanders, 1918.—By his devotion to duty and self-sacrificing love of horses,
this N.C.O. has won for himself a great reputation in the battery to which
he is attached.   During the final operations in Belgium wagon lines were
frequently heavily shelled.   Sergeant Millar was invariably in the lines,
soothing the horses, caring for the wounded, and inspiring confidence.   He
has been invaluable in keeping the battery mobile and efficient.   (M.S.M.
3/6/19), Belgian Croix de Guerre 4/9/19).

Mitson, D., 5900, Sergt., "Y" Battery, R.H.A.
    Gallipoli, 1915.—For conspicuous good work and devotion to duty during
the occupation of the peninsula.   (M.M. 11/11/16).

Moore, J., 3811, Gunner, 10th Battery, R.F.A.
    Gallipoli, 1915.—On June 1st he formed part of a volunteer gun detach-
ment for a Naval 12-pdr. gun in action in an open position under heavy shell
fire, and remained in action for forty minutes while firing 30 rounds at a
range of 700 yards from the enemy trenches.   This gunner and B.S.M. Bird
were in the most dangerous positions of the detachment.   (Mention 5/11/15).

Moreland, T., 55652, Corpl., 10th Battery, R.F.A.
    Gallipoli, 1915.—For excellent work laying and mending telephone wires
at all times, especially on the night May 1st/2nd, under heavy rifle fire.
(M.M. 11/11/16).

Morgan, C. S. S., Sergt., 26th Battery, R.F.A.
    Regular Commission 25/1/16.

Morissey, T., 38443, Sergt., 371st Battery, R.F.A.
    Somme, 1916.—In the Engelbelmer sector on Aug. 3rd this N.C.O. showed
great coolness and courage under heavy shell fire   After the detachments
had been ordered to withdraw to safety, he remained in the telephone pit,
and during the height of the shelling went out and mended the telephone
wire on four occasions.   Again, on May 22nd, he assisted in dressing and
carrying wounded to the dressing station under shell fire.   On his way back
he collapsed from shell shock and was removed to hospital unconscious.   M.M.
(immediate) 21/10/16).

Morraghan, F. B., 34863, Sergt., "B" Battery, R.H.A.
    Gallipoli, 1915.—This N.C.O. did exceptionally good work with a gun of
"B" Battery, R.H.A., dug in, in a forward position in December.   (M.M.
11/11/16).

Morton, G. A., 255321, Fitter, 26th Battery, R.F.A.
    Flanders, 1918.—On October 18th near Heule the enemy commenced a
heavy bombardment of and around the battery wagon lines.   An orderly
bringing a message was seen to be severely wounded and Fitter Morton and
Gunner Priestley at once went to his assistance and succeeded in getting
him in.   They faced and remained under very heavy fire.   In doing this
Fitter Morton was wounded, Gunner Priestley eventually bringing him in.
Both displayed conspicuous bravery and set a fine example. (M.M. (immediate)
20/8/19).

Mullins, A. J., 971320, Corpl., D/17 Battery, R.F.A.
    Flanders, 1918.—On the morning of March 11th, near Wurst Farm (West
of Passchendaele), this N.C.O. was in charge of No. 1 gun of his battery when
fire was opened in answer to an S.O.S. signal.   The battery was being heavily
shelled at the time by 77″ guns and 10·5″ howitzers.   During the forty-
five minutes that the firing was kept up the battery was shelled continuously.
Several shells' fell within a few feet of No. 1 gun, and one of these set the
camouflage on fire.   Corporal Mullins kept up the correct rate of fire throughout and put out the camouflage when it caught fire.   Finally the pit received
a direct hit wounding Corporal Mullins and two men.   In spite of the shell
fire, Corporal Mullins handled his detachment with great coolness, and owing
to his gallant example and conduct his gun was never out of action nor
failed to keep up its fire.   (M.M. (immediate) 12/6/18).

Musgrove, W., 64203, Sergt., "L" Battery, R.H.A.
Flanders, 1918.—This N.C.O. has done excellent work throughout the war, especially during the last operations in Flanders. He has shown exceptional gallantry and complete disregard of danger on many occasions. Continually serving his gun under fire, he has handled his sub-section admirably under difficult conditions. (D.C.M. 3/6/19).

Myers, G. D., 26077, Bombr., "B" Battery, R.H.A.
Cambrai, 1917.—Displayed great gallantry on the 29th/30th November at La Vacquerie valley in maintaining wire communication to the Brigade under heavy gas shelling for several hours and at very vital moments. Later on, when the action developed into close "open sights" work, this N.C.O. took his place in serving the guns and withdrew finally with a wounded Gunner under close rifle fire. (M.M. (immediate) 2/4/18).

Nally, P., 67884, Driver, 460th Battery, R.F.A.
Flanders, 1918.—On the night 7th/8th October the battery wagon lines near Becelaere were heavily shelled for two hours. Driver Nally was of the greatest assistance to his Section Commander, bringing water and bandages to the wounded under fire and getting them away to safety. He also formed one of a party which volunteered to extinguish some burning ammunition wagons, and successfully averted an explosion. His courage and calmness set a splendid example. (M.M. (immediate) 14/5/19).

Nelson, J. L., 4888, Bombr., 1/4th Highland Mountain Brigade, R.G.A. (T.F.).
Gallipoli, 1915.—For conspicuous bravery on August 9th. All the other gun numbers having been wounded, he was left alone to work his gun under the accurate fire of the enemy's guns at close range. With the greatest courage and devotion to duty he kept up his fire single-handed and rendered inestimable service at a critical period. (D.C.M. 16/11/15, Mention 28/1/16).

Nelson, T. H., Sergt., D/17th Battery, R.F.A.
Regular Commission 7/11/17.

Newman, C. V., 62688, Corpl., 26th Battery, R.F.A.
Flanders, 1918.—On September 29th this N.C.O. was taking up ammunition to his battery at Niewe Kruiseecke after an advance. Heavy fire was encountered and the lead driver was wounded. Corporal Newman immediately took his place and drove on to the battery position, where, owing to the heavy fire, it was found that the gun detachments had been temporarily withdrawn. Although ordered to leave his wagon and get away, he displayed splendid devotion to duty and complete disregard for danger in delivering his ammunition before withdrawing his wagon (M.M. (immediate) 14/5/19).

Nightingale, W. H., 558029, Sergt., 29th Divl. Sig. Co., R.E. (attached 15th Brigade, R.H.A.).
Flanders, 1917.—For conspicuous courage and personal example. This N.C.O. was in charge of a party which successfully maintained a very long line during the operations at Langemarck on the night 21st/22nd October, personally repairing it several times under hostile barrage fire. (M.M. (immediate) 28-1-18).

Noble, H., 32443, Bombr., 13 Battery, R.F.A.
Flanders, 1917.—For gallantry. On the night 17th/18th July, in charge of the ration party, he was held up on his way to the battery in action by a block in the traffic and subjected to continual shelling and gas, being forced to wear his gas mask. He managed to overcome all difficulties and deliver his rations at the guns. Again on the 22nd/23rd and 26th/27th he and Driver Pollock brought up rations through a heavy gas barrage. It was owing to his coolness and courage that the rations were safely delivered on every occasion. (M.M. (immediate) 26/9/17).

Norwood, W. S., 915281, Driver, D/17th Battery, R.F.A.
Flanders, 1917.—For gallantry. On the night of 20th July on the Elverdinghe-Boesinghe road he was lead driver of a wagon taking ammunition up to his battery under heavy shell fire and gas barrage. A shell killed his off horse and severely wounded the centre driver and the N.C.O. in charge of the wagon. Driver Norwood dismounted, tied his riding horse to a tree and mounting the centres helped the wheel driver to bring the ammunition up to the guns and the empty wagon back to the wagon lines, though himself wounded by another shell subsequently. He picked up his riding horse on the return journey. (M.M. (immediate) 28/9/17).

Ogden, S. J. B., 35259, Corpl., "Y" Battery, R.H.A.
  Gallipoli, 1915.—For particularly good work as senior telephonist of the battery from the date of landing until he was wounded in July, often under fire. (M.M. 11/11/16).

Officer, H. L., 96877, Corpl., No. 2 Section, 29th D.A.C.
  Flanders, 1918.—This N.C.O. has done extraordinarily good service in taking ammunition up to the guns on many occasions. Two examples may be quoted:—(i) During the operations in June near Nieppe Forest he was mainly instrumental in extricating a convoy of ammunition from a difficult situation caused by gas shelling; (ii) on October 25th near Harlebeke he led a convoy of ammunition with much skill and nerve through a heavily shelled area. He showed considerable determination and self-reliance on both these occasions, as on many others. (Divisional Card of Honour).

Opie, F., 74570, a/B.S.M., 13th Battery, R.F.A.
  Flanders, 1917-18, and Cambrai, 1917.—Has proved himself most capable and has carried out the duties of B.S.M. in a most efficient manner. Under most trying circumstances both in Flanders and at Cambrai he has set a most excellent example of cheerfulness, and the fighting efficiency of the battery has been maintained through his unremitting good work and his tried capacity for handling horses and men in times of great strain and difficulties. (M.S.M. 17/6/18).

Orton, R. G., H/45431, Driver, 26th Battery, R.F.A.
  Flanders, 1918.—During the attack on Outtersteene, on August 18th, this man was on signalling duty with the F.O.O.'s party, which established itself in a house in an advanced and very exposed position. Heavy shell fire was endured throughout the afternoon, including six direct hits on the house. Driver Orton was indefatigable in his efforts to establish visual communication. The party was driven out of the house several times, but on every occasion Driver Orton refused to leave until he had removed his signalling gear to a place of safety. His cheerfulness and utter disregard of danger set a magnificent example and greatly facilitated the task of the F.O.O. (M.M. (immediate) 24/1/19).

Packham, G., 121001, Driver, "B" Battery, R.H.A.
  Flanders, 1917.—On August 1st "B" Battery, R.H.A., was advancing to cross the canal and found the road completely blocked at White Hope Corner. The road was then heavily shelled and there was a tendency amongst the horses to stampede. This driver rallied the young drivers in his team, unhooked the wheelers and removed the team steadily off the road out of the line of fire, thereby avoiding many casualties to men and horses, and setting a good example to the rest of the drivers in the battery. (Divisional Card of Honour No. 221).

Paramor, W., 36717, Sergt., 97th Battery, R.F.A.
  Gallipoli, 1915.—In action on June 28th a six-inch gun from the Asiatic shore suddenly opened fire in enfilade on the 97th Battery. One gun was at once hit, all the detachment being killed or wounded. A few minutes later the wagon of this gun was hit and set on fire. This N.C.O. was one of a party which at once rushed to the burning wagon to try and save the ammunition which they knew to be scarce. Several rounds exploded but the rest was saved. They also saved the ammunition in the pit under the wagon. (D.C.M. 6/9/15).

Parker, A., 5955, B.S.M., 460th Battery, R.F.A.
  Arras and Flanders, 1917.—A most efficient and capable W.O. with an admirable knowledge of how to handle N.C.O.'s and men. During August at Boesinghe, when his battery lost three officers and eight Nos. 1 in a week, he took over the entire duties of a subaltern officer, and did excellent work in reorganising the gun detachments. Not content with this, while in charge of the working party in the forward position behind Abri Wood, although frequently interfered with by shell fire, he built four gun-pits and the necessary dug-outs for the men in record time. (D.C.M. 1/1/18; Regular Commission).

Parker, J. A., 40678, Sergt., "B" Battery, R.H.A.
  Flanders, 1917.—For conspicuous gallantry and resource. He conducted two guns which were urgently required from the workshops into action on the Steenbeek on October 21st under heavy shell fire. A 5·9" shell had killed one driver, wounded the N.C.O. in charge, two other drivers, and seven horses. Sergeant Parker grasped the situation, stripped both guns, shot the badly wounded horses, cleared the road, and sent the wounded to the dressing station, all under heavy fire of 5·9" shell. Subsequently the guns were brought up into action in time to relieve the others during barrage fire on the final objective line. (M.M. (immediate) 28/1/18, Regular Commission 15/4/18).

Parry, R. F., 83054, Bombr., Z/29 Trench Mortar Battery.
Cambrai, 1917.—On November 30th at Masnieres on the approach of the enemy to the village and whilst under heavy shell fire, he reversed his mortar bed and fired about twenty rounds into the enemy who had penetrated Les Rues Vertes, the whole operation being carried out by him with rapidity and coolness. He behaved splendidly throughout the whole action. (M.M. (immediate) 2/4/18).

Patterson, A., 38083, Bombr., 13th Battery, R.F.A.
Gallipoli, 1915.—For consistent good work as look-out man, and as lineman has frequently mended wires under heavy fire. (M.M. 11/11/16).

Pavey, R. G., 78393, a/Bombr., Y/29 Trench Mortar Battery.
Somme, 1916.—For devotion to duty during the bombardment in the Beaumont Hamel sector between the 24th June and the 1st July under the most trying circumstances. This N.C.O. under heavy shell fire kept one gun in action throughout almost the whole period of the bombardment. The gun-pits of the battery suffered seven direct hits on them by enemy H.E. shells. After firing was over, he volunteered and brought up water for the detachment under heavy shell fire. (D.C.M. 1/1/17).

Pawley, C. E., 52839, Bombr., "B" Battery, R.H.A.
Gallipoli, 1915.—May 1st/2nd. For good work as signaller in maintaining his position at the O.P. when the Turks broke through. He was shot in the neck by a Turk who put his rifle through the sangar. (Mention 5/11/15).

Peach, B. A., 59544, Lance Bombr., "L" Battery, R.H.A.
Flanders, 1918.—This N.C.O. has shown very exceptional courage and coolness while acting in charge of the Brigade medical station. He has often been left in sole charge and has never failed under the heaviest fire in his skilful attention to the wounded of R.H.A., R.G.A., and Infantry units. M.S.M. 18/1/19).

Perks, J. C., 614069, Gunner, 1/1st Warwickshire Battery, R.H.A. (T.F.).
Cambrai, 1917.—At the quarry near Gouzeaucourt on November 19th under hostile shell fire Corporal Keen and Gunner Perks assisted Lieut. Mulholland to put out a fire in a large dump of 4·5" howitzer ammunition. These two men acted quickly and fearlessly, and the party undoubtedly prevented by a few minutes an explosion which would have affected two Infantry Battalion headquarters located in the quarry. (M.M. (immediate) 19/3/18).

Perrins, L. G., 614394, Lance Bombr., 1/1st Warwickshire Battery, R.H.A. (T.F.).
Flanders, 1918.—This N.C.O. was in charge of signal communications of the 15th Brigade, R.H.A., during the attack and capture of Outtersteene on August 18th. Throughout the day, by untiring effort and unfailing courage, he maintained his communications intact, displaying marked coolness in effecting repairs under heavy fire, and setting a splendid example to all working under him. It was largely due to his efforts that information vital to the success of the operations was got back to both the artillery and infantry commanders. (M.M. (immediate) 24/1/19).

Pilkington, J., 88197, Driver, "L" Battery, R.H.A.
Flanders, 1918.—On the night of 29th/30th September, near Gheluveldt, he was one of a team which displayed great gallantry in driving their gun into action over extremely bad roads under heavy shell fire. Their coolness and skill in handling their horses under the worst conditions were worthy of the highest praise. (M.M. (immediate) 14/5/19).

Pitts, T., L/47423, a/Sergt., 10th Battery, R.F.A.
Gallipoli, 1915.—Was brought to notice by the O.C. 10th Battery, R.F.A. on three occasions for the excellence of his work as the senior telephonist of that battery—especially on the night 1st/2nd May when the work of mending and relaying the wire was carried out under heavy rifle fire. (M.M. 11/11/16).

Pleece, A. V., 86987, Corpl., 92nd Battery, R.F.A.
Flanders, 1918.—On October 19th, near Cappel St. Catherine, he was the only N.C.O. at the battery wagon lines which were shelled at intervals during the day. He displayed great courage and coolness in moving the animals to places of safety and in attending to wounded horses under fire. He set a splendid example to the men and assisted materially in keeping the situation in hand. On many occasions this N.C.O. has shown great initiative and has displayed marked devotion to duty. (Belgian "Decoration Militaire" (2nd Class) and Croix de Guerre 24/10/19).

Pollock, J., 101219, Driver, 13th Battery, R.F.A.
Flanders, 1917.—For gallantry. He was lead driver of a wagon bringing ammunition to the guns on the night 17th/18th July, when there was continual gas and shelling. The party was held up by an overturned wagon for an hour and had to wear respirators all the time. They delivered their ammunition in spite of all difficulties. On each succeeding night up to August 1st, knowing the risk he ran, he volunteered to accompany Bombr. Noble in bringing up rations to the gun position, as lead driver in the cooks' cart. On the nights 22nd/23rd and 26th/27th July the gas was again very bad, but Bombr. Noble and Driver Pollock came through it and delivered the rations. It was due to the coolness and good work of these two men that on neither of these occasions did the water and rations fail to reach the battery. (M.M. (immediate) 26/9/17).

Poole, L. R., 614101, Gunner, 1/1st Warwickshire Battery, R.H.A. (T.F.).
Flanders, 1917.—For conspicuous courage and good work during operations on the night 22nd/23rd October at Langemarck. This man was sent on the forward end of the F.O.O.'s telephone wire. He acted as runner and repaired the wire under heavy shell fire continuously throughout the night. On one occasion during a breakdown he covered one-and-a-half miles with an important message, displaying considerable courage and energy. (M.M. (immediate) 28/1/18).

Powell, S., 32228, Gunner, "B" Battery, R.H.A.
Flanders, 1918.—This man was in the furthest and most exposed portion of the wire during the operations of June 2nd/3rd near Vieux Berquin and kept it going throughout; this included a double line from the F.O.O. back to the infantry company and was used by the latter when all other wires and means of communication had gone. He showed great coolness under fire and gas, and successfully repaired his portion of the line in a gas helmet. (M.M., (immediate) 7/10/18).

Powrie, H., 44209, Sergt., 92nd Battery, R.F.A.
Gallipoli, 1915.—Superintended the communications of his battery with the greatest skill and devotion to duty, frequently laying and mending telephone wires under fire and in face of great difficulties. (M.M. 11/11/16).

Preston, I. E., 198692, Bombr., 460th Battery, R.F.A.
Flanders, 1918.—On the night of October 7th/8th this N.C.O. was in charge of the wagon lines picquet near Becelaere. The lines were heavily shelled for two hours. He showed great coolness and presence of mind in the face of danger, rallying his picquet, going round the horses and getting the unwounded ones away. He also volunteered without hesitation to put out some burning ammunition wagons and was generally of the greatest assistance at a very difficult and dangerous time. (M.M. (immediate) 14/5/19).

Priestley, S., 26656, Gunner, 26th Battery, R.F.A.
Flanders, 1918.—On October 18th, near Heule, the enemy heavily bombarded the battery wagon lines and surroundings. Fitter Morton and Gunner Priestley went to assist an orderly bringing a message who was seen to be severely wounded and succeeded in getting him in. They faced and remained under a very heavy fire in doing this. Fitter Morton was wounded and was brought in by Gunner Priestley. Both displayed conspicuous bravery and set a fine example. (M.M. (immediate) 20/8/19).

Pritchard, A. B., 253196, Lance Corpl., 29th Divl. Sig. Co., R.E. (attached 15th Brigade, R.H.A.).
Cambrai, 1917.—Near Masnieres, on November 20th, he laid a line to the advanced infantry battalion under heavy rifle and machine gun fire; this wire was the only means of communication at the time between the infantry and the artillery and was maintained throughout the night. (Divisional Card of Honour No. 780).
Flanders, 1917-18, and Cambrai, 1917.—This N.C.O. has distinguished himself by gerat personal bravery, constant good work, and untiring devotion to duty. As Corporal of the Brigade signallers he has always displayed the greatest courage, initiative and resource, often under heavy shell fire; and on many occasions during the battles of Flanders and Cambrai his prompt and courageous action under shell and machine gun fire has succeeded in maintaining communications in the most adverse circumstances. (D.C.M.).

Pye, W. H., B.S.M., 92nd Battery, R.F.A.
Regular Commission 15/3/18.

Pyrah, S., 34479, Driver, S.A.A. Section, 29th D.A.C.
Flanders, 1917.—On the night of 17th/18th August, whilst a convoy of thirty pack horses and mules was off-loading ammunition at Widgendrift cross-roads, they came under heavy shell fire, Sergt. Maton and Driver Platt being wounded. There was considerable confusion owing to a number of animals stampeding, but Driver Pyrah immediately handed on his mule to another man and proceeded alone along the Widgendrift road, which was then under fire, for about 200 yards to obtain a stretcher. When he returned the convoy had moved away, but he remained with the two wounded men, giving them such aid as he was able to by himself, until bearer parties could be obtained, when he assisted to carry Sergt. Maton to the dressing station. Driver Platt had meanwhile died. Driver Pyrah showed considerable coolness and presence of mind in going to fetch a stretcher on his own initiative, in spite of the confusion prevailing at the time. (M.M. (immediate) 18/10/17).

Randall, H., 14873, Corpl., X/29 Trench Mortar Battery.
Flanders, 1917.—On July 27th, during an infantry attack opposite Boesinghe, a party of men of X/29 Trench Mortar Battery under an officer went out to inspect the results of their fire. On returning Corporal Randall was fired upon by a German officer. He returned the fire with his revolver, and after an interchange of shots succeeded in shooting the officer and in taking five men prisoner. These he brought back, and, knowing that there were more Germans left, returned to the attack while a party including Driver Rowland moved round to a flank. This party bombed the German dug-out, and Rowland, borrowing a revolver, rushed up to it. The Germans ran down the trench a short way but eventually surrendered. Thus mainly owing to the conduct of Corporal Randall and Driver Rowland one German officer was shot, and one officer and twenty-one other ranks were captured. (D.C.M. (immediate) 17/9/17).

Rayner, W., 50718, Bombr., 368th Battery, R.F.A.
Gallipoli, 1915.—A battery telephonist who has done excellent and consistent work in mending telephone wires under fire and in keeping the communications in order. (M.M. 11/11/16).
Somme, 1916.—For conspicuous good work and devotion to duty in the period June—September in charge of signals and telephonic communications of his battery in the Beaumont Hamel sector. (D.C.M. 13/2/17).

Rea, A. F., 61772, Gunner, "L" Battery, R.H.A.
Flanders, 1917.—On August 9th a working party was preparing a forward position for "L" Battery, R.H.A., near Boesinghe. They came under heavy shell fire which caused some casualties. The working party received orders to clear to a flank. Sergeant Guiver and Gunner Rea remained to bandage and carry off on a stretcher the wounded and then returned under heavy shell fire to bandage and remove a wounded infantryman. (M.M. (immediate) 18/10/17).

Redigan, J. L., 66203, B.S.M., D/17 Battery, R.F.A.
Flanders, 1918.—For good work in the final operations in Belgium, September to November. (Belgian Croix de Guerre 4/9/19).

Richardson, W. J., 76176, Corpl., 15th B.A.C.
Gallipoli, 1915.—For the efficient manner in which he commanded a 12-pdr. in a forward position, especially during the attack of August 12th-14th. (M.M. 11/11/16).

Riley, F. W., 63398, Lance Bombr., "B" Battery, R.H.A.
Flanders, 1918.—On October 15th, near Ledeghem, this N.C.O. was getting his gun on to its line of fire preparatory to firing a barrage. Five minutes before the commencement of the barrage he was shot through the left wrist. Hastily binding up his wound he carried on with his work and served his gun throughout the barrage which lasted two hours. The position was very advanced and had been shelled throughout the night. Lance Bombardier Riley set a splendid example of courage and devotion to duty. (M.M., immediate).

Roberts, E., 745034, Corpl., No. 1 Section, 29th D.A.C.
Flanders, 1918.—On March 18th at Wieltje an enemy shell struck an ammunition dump. Flames at once sprang up through the tarpaulin covering the ammunition. Corporal Roberts and Bombardier Baggaley tried to approach but were driven off by six successive explosions. Finally, however, at great personal risk, they succeeded in throwing the end of the tarpaulin over the fire and continued to pour on water till the fire was extinguished. By their prompt and gallant action they undoubtedly prevented a great deal of damage and saved a large amount of ammunition from being destroyed. (M.M. (immediate) 12/6/18).

Roberts, W., 558447, 2nd Corpl., 29th Divl. Sig. Co., R.E. (attached 17th Brigade, R.F.A.).
    Cambrai, 1917.—At Marcoing, on November 30th, during the German attack, this N.C.O. was in charge of the linemen throughout the day and night. The lines were considerably broken and on every occasion he led a party out under heavy shell fire and mended the breaks. It was due to his energy, courage and pertinacity that communications were kept up. (Divisional Card of Honour No. 1019).
    ,,   Corpl.,   ,,
    Flanders, 1918.—This N.C.O. has been responsible for the maintenance of his brigade's communications and has carried out his duties in the most exemplary manner under conditions calling for great courage and skill. He has repeatedly shown conspicuous gallantry and devotion to duty. (French Croix de Guerre 19/6/19).

Rodger, R. C., 2214, Corpl., 1/4th Highland Mountain Brigade, R.G.A. (T.F.).
    Gallipoli, 1915.—June 28th. On a wagon containing ammunition being set on fire by a H.E. shell from the Asiatic shore, this N.C.O. formed one of a party which rushed to the burning wagon and saved a number of rounds from it, together with all the ammunition which was stored in the pit beneath it. Several rounds in the wagon exploded in the process. (D.C.M. 6/9/15).

Rowland, A. J., 82645, Driver, X/29 Trench Mortar Battery.
    Flanders, 1917.—On July 27th, during an infantry attack opposite Boesinghe, a party of men of X/29 Trench Mortar Battery under an officer went out to inspect the results of their fire. On returning Corporal Randall was fired upon by a German officer. He returned the fire with his revolver, and after an interchange of shots succeeded in shooting the officer and in taking five men prisoners. These he brought back and, knowing that there were more Germans left, returned to the attack while a party including Driver Rowland moved round to a flank. This party bombed the German dug-out and Rowland, borrowing a revolver, rushed up to it. The Germans ran down the trench a short way but eventually surrendered. Thus mainly owing to the conduct of Corporal Randall and Driver Rowland one German officer was shot, and one officer and twenty-one other ranks were captured. (M.M. (immediate) 26/9/17).

Roxburgh, W. E., 614014, Sergt., 1/1st Warwickshire Battery, R.H.A. (T.F.).
    Arras, 1917.—On April 9th Sergeant Roxburgh was in charge of a gun in action. Although the gun next to his was knocked out and his own detachment had many casualties, he maintained his gun in action under very heavy shelling, and carried out his programme of fire all day. (M.M. (immediate) 9/7/17).

Rushbrooke, G. W., 56368, Bombr., 92nd Battery, R.F.A.
    Somme, 1916.—For consistent good work and devotion to duty, especially during the period prior to and during the bombardment in the Beaumont Hamel sector, June 24th—July 1st. (Mention 4/1/17).

Sansum, W., 60342, Gunner, 97th Battery, R.F.A.
    Gallipoli, 1915.—In the attacks of May 2nd, June 4th and 28th, August 6th and 7th, this man showed conspicuous gallantry in repeatedly repairing telephone lines under heavy shell and rifle fire. No work was too hazardous for him to undertake and he showed throughout the greatest devotion to duty. (D.C.M. 16/11/15, Mention 5/11/15).

Saunders, J., 52182, Bombr., "B" Battery, R.H.A.
    Gallipoli, 1915.—For excellent work repairing telephone wires whilst in action, often under shell fire. (M.M. 11/11/16).
    Gallipoli, 1915, and Somme, 1916.—For good work throughout the Gallipoli campaign and on the Somme. (Serbian Gold Medal 15/2/17).

Savage, E. A., 16288 or 86057, Gunner, "L" Battery, R.H.A.
    Flanders, 1917.—On July 31st he was one of the F.O.O. signallers during the attack. While crossing the Yser canal under a heavy hostile barrage one heavy reel of telephone wire was dropped into the canal by one of the party. Gunner Savage volunteered to go back through the barrage and succeeded in rescuing the wire which was of vital importance to the communications. Throughout the remainder of the day he was indefatigable in patrolling and mending wires under continual shell fire, and at the same time keeping touch with and periodically rejoining his party which was continually advancing. He finally after rejoining his party established visual communication back. (M.M. (immediate) 18/10/17).

Savage, J., 85851, Bombr., 460th Battery, R.F.A.
Flanders, 1917-18, and Cambrai, 1917.—For general good work. (Mention 21/5/18).

" " Corpl., " "
Flanders, 1918.—On the night June 2nd/3rd in minor operations this N.C.O. maintained visual communication by lamp under difficult circumstances with the F.O.O. accompanying the attack, after all wires had gone. Messages were thus transmitted as to the progress of the operations all night. When the F.O.O. was put out of action by a gas shell, this N.C.O., though temporarily blinded by the same shell, carried on in a most gallant manner. (Divisional Card of Honour).

Sayer, R. H., 46082, Sergt., 26th Battery, R.F.A.
Somme, 1916-17.—For gallantry and consistent good work. His devotion showed great courage and coolness. (D.C.M. 3/6/17, Regular Commission 16/3/17).

Sayers, F., 97552, Gunner, 26th Battery, R.F.A.
Cambrai, 1917.—Brought to notice for good work as runner near Marcoing on November 30th and December 1st. He carried messages day and night always under heavy shell fire, and was largely responsible for the close touch maintained between the infantry and the artillery. (Divisional Card of Honour No. 1017).

" Bombr., "
Flanders, 1917-18, and Cambrai, 1917.—Has acted with the greatest devotion to duty during the operations in Flanders and at Cambrai. His continuous good work as signaller and the fine soldierly spirit he has displayed throughout the most trying circumstances have set a high standard of efficiency and duty to the battery and merit every praise. (M.S.M. 17/6/18).

Scurrah, A. E., 32638, Driver, 460th Battery, R.F.A.
Flanders, 1918.—On the night of October 2nd/3rd the battery wagon lines near Becelaere were heavily shelled. One shell actually burst in the shelter where Driver Scurrah and two other men were lying, wounding both the latter. In spite of the shock and continued shelling Driver Scurrah displayed great gallantry and presence of mind in bandaging his wounded comrades and going out immediately afterwards to attend to the wounded horses. His splendid example greatly encouraged the other drivers. (M.M. (immediate) 14/5/19).

Shadgett, J. H., L/40465, Corpl., No. 2 Section, 29th D.A.C.
Flanders, 1918.—This N.C.O. was sent out on September 26th on patrol duty from the D.A.C. to reconnoitre forward roads prior to operations. Near Zillebeke he came across a concrete dug-out containing 8 Germans. Though only armed with a revolver he had no hesitation in calling on them to surrender and, with the assistance of Bombardier Almond, disarmed and searched the lot, finally marching them back to Vlamertinghe. (D.C.M., (immediate) 18/2/19).

Shanahan, E., 76885, Driver, 13th Battery, R.F.A.
1915-17.—For over two years this driver has set an example of what a driver should be. He always considers his horses before himself and, no matter what the conditions are, his horses are in the best condition and his harness clean. By his example he sets a high standard to the drivers in the battery. (Mention 14/12/17).

Ship, G., 177008, Driver, "B" Battery, R.H.A.
Flanders, 1917.—For conspicuous gallantry and resource. This driver had one of the leading pairs of a convoy of pack animals to deliver ammunition at the Steenbeek positions. All this time there was very heavy shelling and all the regular routes were blocked for hours with wagons, dead and wounded horses, etc. This driver pushed on by all sorts of devious routes and led his convoy, eventually delivering all the ammunition at the guns after a twelve hours' struggle. The pluck and example shown by this man had the effect of causing many of the units which had been ordered or were going back to press forward across country instead, and so relieve the congestion on the roads. This gallant conduct was reported by the Military Police. (M.M. (immediate) 28/1/18).

Shirley, G., 614018, Staff Sergt. Farrier, 1/1st Warwickshire Battery, R.H.A. (T.F.).
1916-18.—This N.C.O. has served with the battery since it came out to France in 1914. His hard work and skill as Farrier and his inspiring example of vigour and resourcefulness have largely contributed to the general efficiency of the battery. (M.S.M. 17/6/18).

Shrubsole, P. A., 49692, Corpl, H.Q. 15th Brigade, R.H.A.
Somme, 1916.—For conspicuous good work and devotion to duty in the Left Group 29th D.A. telephone exchange during the bombardment from June 24th to July 1st in the Beaumont Hamel sector. (D.C.M. 1/1/17).

Shultz, J. H., 103105, Gunner, "L" Battery, R.H.A.
Flanders, 1917.—For devotion to duty with the F.O.O.'s party on July 31st. Having had, with other men, the difficult and fatiguing work of carrying cable to the front line, he was despatched as runner with an important message from Artillery Wood to a signal station on the further side of the canal. He got safely and quickly through the enemy's barrage, and wihtout a guide managed to rejoin the F.O.O. before the capture of the "Green Line." He later ably assisted Signaller Savage in the difficult task of establishing visual communication, which was only effected at 10 p.m. the following night. (Divisional Card of Honour No. 230).

Smith, A. G., 614411, Sergt., 1/1st Warwickshire Battery, R.H.A. (T.F.).
Flanders, 1918.—This N.C.O. has proved himself a first-rate No. 1. His bravery, coolness under fire, and cheerfulness contributed greatly to the high moral of the battery during the final operations in Belgium. (Mention 7/7/19).

Smith, H. S., 32445, Driver, "B" Battery, R.H.A.
Flanders, 1917.—For conspicuous gallantry and resource. This driver had one of the leading pairs of a convoy of pack animals to deliver ammunition at the Steenbeek positions. All this time there was very heavy shelling and all the regular routes were blocked for hours with wagons, dead and wounded horses, etc. This driver pushed on by all sorts of devious routes and led his convoy, eventually delivering all the ammunition at the guns after a twelve hours' struggle. The pluck and example shown by this man had the effect of causing many of the units which had been ordered or were going back to press forward across country instead, and so relieve the congestion on the road. This gallant conduct was reported by the Military Police. (M.M. (immediate) 28/1/18).

Snowden, J., L/1688, Driver, "L" Battery, R.H.A.
Flanders, 1917.—On August 1st, near Boesinghe, when the Battery was advancing into action and was being heavily shelled, the team in which Driver Snowden was driving had two horses killed, and two more were down. Unassisted, he pulled the wheel driver from under his horses, which were struggling under the limber, and carried him to a place of safety. He then returned and, still under shell fire, disentangled his own horses and led them to a place of safety. (Divisional Card of Honour No. 587).

Sparrow, H., 28370, Gunner, H.Q. 15th Brigade, R.F.A.
Flanders, 1918.—For general good work. (Belgian Croix de Guerre 4/9/19).

Spray, A. C., 745024, Sergt., 92nd Battery, R.F.A.
Flanders, 1918.—This N.C.O. was No. 1 of a gun forming part of an advanced section on September 29th near Gheluveldt supporting the infantry at close range. The section came under heavy machine gun fire and the officer in charge was wounded. Nevertheless, Sergeant Spray kept his gun in action and displayed great gallantry in maintaining fire, enabling the advance to be successfully continued. (D.C.M. (immediate) 12/3/19).

Stace, H. J., 51661, Sergt., "B" Battery, R.H.A.
Flanders, 1918.—A very fine No. 1, whether in or out of action. He has shown splendid devotion to duty, zeal and gallantry, particularly during the operation in Flanders from April to November. (Mention 7/7/19).

Stagg, A., 26605, B.S.M., "L" Battery, R.H.A.
1917-18.—This W.O. has served continuously in France since the commencement of the war. He has been B.S.M. of "L" Battery, R.H.A., since October, 1917, and has served throughout the operations in which his battery has taken part since that date. His quiet force of character and gallant behaviour on the most trying occasions have been a pattern to all ranks. Though the majority of his work has been at the wagon lines he has often taken upon himself to supervise personally the bringing up of ammunition to the guns when the difficulties likely to be encountered were considerable. He has fully justified the unbounded confidence placed in him by his superiors. (French Croix de Guerre 19/6/19).

Staples, C., 41830, Sergt., No. 2 Section, 29th D.A.C.
Arras and Flanders, 1917.—For valuable and distinguished service in the field. (Mention 14/12/17)
    „   B.Q.M.S., No. 1 Section, 29th D.A.C.
Flanders, 1917-18, and Cambrai, 1917.—Has served with distinction. Has proved himself invariably trustworthy and conscientious and has taken the greatest care of and interest in the equipment and welfare of his section. (M.S.M. 17/6/18).

Stewart, L., 51021, Sergt., 26th Battery, R.F.A.
Arras and Flanders, 1917.—For excellent work as acting B.S.M. at the gun line. This N.C.O. has fourteen years service, and throughout the operations in which his battery has taken part has shown complete indifference to danger. By his devotion to duty he has earned a high reputation among all ranks. (D.C.M. 1/1/18).

Stone, A. A., 29701, Corpl., 15th B.A.C.
Gallipoli, 1915.—For devotion to duty in helping to move 12-pdr. forward guns and taking up wagons of ammunition under difficult circumstances at various times, often under shell fire. (M.M. 11/11/16).

Stone, H. S., Driver, 614458, Driver, 1/1st Warwickshire Battery, R.H.A. (T.F.).
Cambrai, 1917.—For gallantry and devotion to duty. On November 20th Driver Stone was leading pack horses up to supply ammunition during the advance in the valley beyond La Vacquerie. A shell wounded him threw him down and scattered his horses. He went after his horses, caught them, delivered the ammunition to the guns, and watered his horses at a shell hole; he then fainted from his wounds. (M.M. (immediate) 19/3/18).

Street, E. F., Sergt., X/29 Trench Mortar Battery.
Regular Commission 10/12/16.

Stroud, A. E., 36943, Bombr., H.Q. 15th Brigade, R.H.A.
Gallipoli, 1915.—During the action of June 28th this N.C.O. was constantly at work repairing telephone lines under heavy rifle and shell fire from 10 a.m. till 4 p.m., when he was at last severely wounded. Throughout the action the telephonic communication of all the artillery never failed in spite of the hostile gun fire. This was due to the coolness and self-sacrifice of the linemen. As it was impossible to recommend all these men for reward, this N.C.O. was selected from amongst them. (D.C.M. 16/11/15, Mention 5/11/15).

„ a/Sergt., "B" Battery, R.H.A.
Flanders, 1918.—On January 2nd, near Passchendaele, while "B" battery, R.H.A., was being shelled, this N.C.O.'s gun was blown out of its pit by a direct hit which set fire to the ammunition. He immediately came out of his dug-out and in spite of heavy shelling succeeded, unaided, in putting out the fire. He displayed great courage and devotion to duty. (M.M. (immediate) 2/4/18).

Sumner, G. H., 46308, Farrier Sergt., 26th Battery, R.F.A.
Flanders, 1918.—A first-class workman and full of perseverance, this N.C.O. has carried out his duties in a highly efficient manner. He has almost invariably come up in charge of wagons at night and in spite of frequent shelling has never failed to deliver his ammunition. He has served in the 17th Brigade, R.F.A., throughout the Gallipoli campaign and since then in France. (M.S.M. 18/1/19).

Sutcliffe, S., 19530, Driver, 370th Battery, R.F.A.
Somme, 1916.—Did exceptionally good work from April 5th to July 1st supplying ammunition in the Beaumont Hamel sector. Under fire his bearing was faultless. (Mention 4/1/17).

Sykes, T., 253187, Corpl., 29th Divl. Sig. Co., R.E. (attached 15th Brigade, R.H.A.).
Arras and Flanders, 1917.—In the battle of Arras, as Corporal in charge of Brigade H.Q. signals, he did exceptionally good work in maintaining communications with the batteries under the heaviest shell fire, when the Brigade was in action near Monchy. On most occasions he repaired the wires himself, and by his general devotion to duty and absolute fearlessness set an admirable example to the linemen in his charge. He also did good work in the battles of the Somme and Flanders. (Mention 14/12/17).

Swift, G. T., L/9442, Sergt., D/17 Battery, R.F.A.
Arras, 1917.—For conspicuous gallantry near Monchy on April 24th. A shell wounded all the men of his detachment and set fire to an ammunition dump fifteen yards away. He continued to serve his gun in support of the infantry although he well knew the ammunition would probably blow up. (M.M. (immediate) 9/7/17).

Talbot, A. J., 51794, Staff Sergt. Artificer, A.O.C. (attached 460th Battery, R.F.A.).
Flanders, 1917-18, and Cambrai, 1917.—This N.C.O. has displayed the greatest devotion to duty. His thorough and conscientious work have contributed very largely to the efficiency of the battery, in which he has served since the landing at Gallipoli. (M.S.M. 17/6/19).

D.

Taylor, A., 51720, Staff Sergeant Fitter, "L" Battery, R.H.A.

Somme, 1917.—On February 10th the battery in action behind Morval was heavily shelled by 5˙9s. Two guns were destroyed, and the ammunition in both pits caught fire. This N.C.O. immediately went into the burning pits and tried to get the fire under control until driven away by the ammunition starting to explode. All this was under heavy 15″ shell fire. (M.M. (immediate) 26/3/17).

Taylor, C. K., 59520, Driver, "B" Battery, R.H.A.

Flanders, 1918.—During operations between Ypres and Courtrai from September 28th to October 18th Driver Taylor has continuously been employed as a mounted orderly and as a horse-holder. On many occasions he has carried messages through the heaviest fire, never failing to deliver them correctly. As a horse-holder he has handled his horses most skilfully under fire, always being ready at the right moment. (M.M. (immediate) 17/6/19).

Taylor, F., 63111, Bombr., "Y" Battery, R.H.A.

Gallipoli, 1915.—For gallantry and devotion to duty during the bombardment of our line. He was acting as telephonist to the F.O.O. of his battery. In spite of the fact that the wire had been broken in many places he managed to re-establish communication with his battery by 1630 at the time when it was most needed. He was one of the party of signallers of the 15th Brigade, R.H.A., which landed with the Lancashire Fusiliers on April 25th and assisted Regimental Headquarters in maintaining communication with the Beach. (D.C.M. 3/6/16, Mention 13/7/16).

Gallipoli, 1916.—For gallantry and devotion to duty on the day prior to the evacuation of Cape Helles, when telephonist to the F.O.O. during a heavy Turkish bombardment.

Note.—The Battery Commander reported as follows:—"On January 7th this N.C.O. was telephonist to 2nd Lieut. Clark, the F.O.O., in the section of our trenches opposite to J 12 c. This section of the trenches was very heavily bombarded all the afternoon between 1200 and 1630. Many of the support trenches through which out wires ran were filled in in parts and our telephone wires were cut and burnt in many places. At 1630, however, Bombr. Taylor and Lieut. Clark managed to mend the wires and send in their report to the Group Commander. This was of particular value as it was the only report which got in before 2000, and up to then there was a certain amount of uncertainty as to the result of the Turks' attack." (M.M. 11/11/16).

Taylor, H., W/5602, Gunner, "L" Battery, R.H.A.

Flanders, 1918.—At about 7 a.m. on June 8th the battery position near Grand Sec Bois began to be considerably shelled by 10˙5″ howitzers. A direct hit was obtained on a gun pit setting alight the camouflage which fell over one of the ammunition recesses and set fire to the sand-bags. In spite of the shelling and the explosion of a dump of S.A.A. this man, with three N.C.Os., with great gallantry came out of safety to put out the fire and managed to do so before a single round exploded. (Divisional Card of Honour No. 2789).

Thomason, B., 614111, Lance Bombr., 1/1st Warwickshire Battery, R.H.A. (T.F.).

Flanders, 1918.—On the night of September 5th/6th the wagon lines of the battery near Le Veau were subjected to a concentrated gas bombardment, many shells bursting close enough to splash the horses with liquid. This man was one of three who gallantly managed to remove from the shelled area all the 39 horses that were there, and to put nosebags on them filled with damp grass. This prompt action saved many horses from serious consequences and set a fine example to the other men. (M.M. (immediate) 11/2/19).

Thornton, J., 88186, Lance Bombr., "L" Battery, R.H.A.

Flanders, 1918.—Near Gravenstafel on March 21st, about 4 a.m., during a four hours' gas shelling of the gun position, an ammunition recess was set on fire by a H.E. shell. This N.C.O. with great promptness ran up and extinguished the fire at great risk to himself, as the dump was in flames and rounds were exploding. He then served his gun during two shoots. During the whole period he had to wear his box respirator. (M.M. (immediate) 12/6/18).

Timms, F. J., 68431, Bombr., "Y" Battery, R.H.A.

Somme, 1916.—For gallantry displayed on October 22nd when his battery in Delville valley was heavily shelled with 15″ shell. One shell killed or wounded 19 men of the battery, and although he himself had several wounds in both legs from shell fragments he helped to collect the other wounded and carry them on stretchers under shell fire to the dressing station before reporting his own wounds. (M.M. (immediate) 22/1/17).

Tobin, J., 55901, Sergt., 460th Battery, R.F.A.
Gallipoli, 1915.—Throughout the occupation this N.C.O. was in charge of the communications of his battery and as such displayed great gallantry and coolness on several occasions when attending to his wires under heavy fire. (M.M. 11/11/16).

Toomer, S. E., 4901, Gunner, 1/4th Highland Mountain Brigade, R.G.A. (T.F.).
Gallipoli, 1915.—On a wagon containing ammunition being set on fire by a H.E. shell from the Asiatic shore, this gunner formed one of a party which rushed to the burning wagon and saved a number of rounds from it, together with all the ammunition which was stored in the pit beneath it. Several rounds exploded in the process. (Mention 5/11/15).

Toone, H. E. V., 10d893, Corpl., "L" Battery, R.H.A.
Flanders, 1917-18, and Cambrai, 1917.—For continuous good service. He has been responsible for the battery signals. His conscientious and hard work throughout has been of invaluable service to the battery and has merited all praise. (M.S.M. 17/6/18).
Flanders, 1918.—During the night operations of June 2nd/3rd near Nieppe Forest he restored telephone communication under heavy fire, including gas, repairing breaks in five places, thus enabling messages to come through from the most advanced infantry up to the time of their gaining their objectives. His assistants being temporarily out of action from gas he carried on single-handed. (Divisional Card of Honour).

Tosney, J., 11565, Lance Bombr., D/17th Battery, R.F.A.
Flanders, 1917-18, and Cambrai, 1917.—For general good work. (Mention 21/5/18).

Tristram, W., 68884, Bombr., "B" Battery, R.H.A.
Arras, 1917.—On June 17th heavy fire was opened on the battery in action behind the crest at Monchy village, killing Lieut (acting Major) F. C. Merritt and wounding 2nd Lieut. R. W. Lunn, 2nd Lieut. J. Shirley Hill, and Signaller Shepperton. 2nd Lieut. Shirley Hill, in spite of his wounds, at once rushed to the assistance of 2nd Lieut. Lunn and the signaller, who were buried, closely followed by Bombr. Tristram. With one stretcher-bearer Bombr. Tristram then carried the two wounded to the dressing station, making the double journey under continuous and heavy shell fire. (M.M. (immediate) 16/8/17).

Tubb, W., 80909, Gunner, 26th Battery, R.F.A.
Gallipoli, 1915.—(Mention 13/7/16).

Turk, C., 128959, Gunner, "L" Battery, R.H.A.
Flanders, 1917.—On the night of August 17th/18th "L" Battery, R.H.A., in action near Boesinghe was shelled with 5˙9s. One shell set fire to the camouflage covering four of the six guns and ammunition. The whole battery turned out like one man to put out the fire, the lead being specially taken by Gunner Dadd, Bombardier Duffill, and Gunners Turk and Wilkins. But for their prompt action and disregard of danger there is no doubt that all the guns and ammunition of both "L" and the adjoining battery would have been destroyed. (Divisional Card of Honour No. 224).

Uzzell, J. N., 745218, Sergt., No. 2 Section, 29th D.A.C.
Flanders, 1918.—This N.C.O. has rendered valuable service, especially during the operations in Flanders in 1918, when he repeatedly delivered ammunition to the guns under conditions of great danger and difficulty, setting a fine example of devotion to duty. (Mention 7/719).

Wakelin, S., 90497, Bombr., H.Q. 15th Brigade, R.H.A.
Cambrai, 1917.—On November 30th, in La Vacquerie valley, this N.C.O. acted as orderly to the Brigade Commander after the enemy had taken the guns. He assisted to man a trench and inflicted casualties on the enemy. He brought up ammunition twice and displayed the greatest coolness and gallantry in a small action to recapture the wireless station and tear up and burn all maps, papers and codes. (M.M. (immediate) 2/4/18).

Walker, H., 91887, Gunner, Y/29 Trench Mortar Battery.
Somme, 1916.—For conspicuous good work with his battery in the Beaumont Hamel sector. Under constant shell fire he kept the telephone wire between the guns and the O.P. in a state of repair. (M.M. (immediate) 9/12/16).

Walker, J. W., 12185, Sergt., "L" Battery, R.H.A.
   1915-17.—For consistently good work in "B" and "L" Batteries in Gallipoli and France up to February, 1917. He always set to those under him a high example of cheerfulness and energy.   (D.C.M. 3/6/17).

Walton, J. W. H., 98581, Sergt., 460th Battery, R.F.A.
   Flanders, 1918.—A very reliable and resourceful N.C.O. who has frequently distinguished himself by his devotion to duty and gallantry.   (Mention 7/7/19).

Warburton, W., 14th Siege Battery, R.G.A.
   Regular Commission 18/10/15.

Warr, H. F. D., 15144, Sergt., 460th Battery, R.F.A.
   Arras, 1917.—On April 9th, when our barrage to cover the attack commenced, the 460th Battery came under very heavy hostile shell fire and suffered severely. Four guns were put out of action (see story under Sergeant C. W. King of the same battery), one officer and some twenty other ranks being killed or wounded. Sergeant Warr kept his guns in action till the end of the barrage, though himself twice wounded. (French Medaille Militaire 14/7/17).

Warren, G. O., 119142, Driver, 460th Battery, R.F.A.
   Flanders, 1918.—On September 29th, near Gheluveldt, he was lead driver of a team sent up to withdraw a howitzer. The position was under such heavy shell fire that three attempts had to be made before this could be done. His example of cheerful courage and determination undoubtedly inspired his fellow drivers to persevere and succeed in their difficult task. (M.M., (immediate) 14/5/19).

Waterson, R. F., 54625, Corpl., 92nd Battery, R.F.A.
   Gallipoli, 1915.—For exceedingly good work as look-out man for the battery throughout the occupation; of immense value to his Battery Commander as such.   (M.M. 11/11/16).

Watkinson, H. N., 42133, Driver, No. 1 Section, 29th D.A.C.
   Flanders, 1918.—On the night of June 1st/2nd near Grand Sec Bois he was lead driver of one of two teams taking up battery ammunition. On approaching their destination both teams were knocked down by a heavy burst of hostile shelling and most of the horses killed. This driver and his horses were twice knocked down, and the latter wounded. He stuck to his horses, removed a little distance from the danger spot, and then though severely shaken returned voluntarily to assist 2nd Lieut. Watson and a party of the 460th Battery in the clearance of the wounded men and horses. He displayed great courage and devotion to duty. (M.M. (immediate) 21/10/18).

Watterson, G., L/18506, Gunner, 92nd Battery, R.F.A.
   1916-18.—This man has served in every action in which his battery has participated in France, displaying constant devotion to duty, unfailing courage and cheerfulness in the face of danger. On one occasion, near Ingoyghem, he laid his gun throughout a barrage under direct enemy observation and set a splendid example to the rest of the detachment.   (D.C.M. 3/6/19).

Watts, R. H., 34219, Sergt., "L" Battery, R.H.A.
   Somme, 1917.—On February 10th, during heavy shelling of the battery near Morval, two guns were destroyed and the ammunition set alight. After collecting his detachment and getting them away to safety, this N.C.O. returned to his gun-pit and tried to get the fire under control. He continued until driven away by the ammunition starting to explode. All this was done under heavy 15″ shell fire.   (M.M. (immediate) 26/3/17).

White, G. E., 99377, Gunner, "B" Battery, R.H.A.
   Somme, 1916.—For continuously mending wire in the Beaumont Hamel sector from 5 a.m. to 5 p.m. on September 3rd (between 12 noon and 2 p.m. under heavy shell fire).   (M.M. (immediate) 9/12/16).

Whitley, A., 34462, Corpl., Y/29 Trench Mortar Battery.
   Flanders, 1918.—For general good work. (Belgian Croix de Gueere 4/9/19).

Wilders, S., 43341, Bombr., "B" Battery, R.H.A.

Flanders, 1918.—On September 29th, near Gheluveldt and on subsequent occasions near Courtrai, Bombardier Wilders was in charge of three Lewis guns moving with advanced sections of the battery. He boldly brought his Lewis guns into action at short range and dislodged small parties of the enemy who were preventing the guns from getting into action, and then explored several dug-outs to make certain that the ground was clear of the enemy. Whenever the guns of the battery have been in advanced positions Bombardier Wilders has gone forward with his Lewis guns to protect them from the action of enemy infantry. His resolute courage and admirable dispositions have instilled confidence into officers and men, enabling the battery to push boldly forward at times when its close support has been invaluable to our advancing infantry. (M.M. (immediate) 23/1/19).

Wilkins, E., 126482, Gunner, "L" Battery, R.H.A.

Flanders, 1917.—On the night of August 17th/18th "L" Battery, R.H.A., in action near Boesinghe was shelled with 5·9's. One shell set fire to the camouflage covering four of the six guns and ammunition. The whole battery turned out like one man to put out the fire, the lead being specially taken by Gunner Dadd, Bombardier Duffill, and Gunners Turk and Wilkins. But for their prompt action and disregard of danger there is no doubt that all the guns and ammunition of both "L" and the adjoining battery would have been destroyed. (Divisional Card of Honour No. 225).

Wilson, F., 174555, Bombr., Y/29 Trench Mortar Battery.

Flanders, 1918.—On the night of October 13th/14th, near Ledeghem, this N.C.O. did magnificent work in getting up ammunition under continual harassing fire. At 5-30 a.m. on the 14th he manned his mortars and, in spite of coming directly under the enemy's barrage, successfully fired the allotted number of rounds, materially assisting in the success of the operations. (M.M. 20/8/19).

Woodhall, B. G., L/33279, Driver, 26th Battery, R.F.A.

Flanders, 1918.—This man has frequently faced heavy shell fire and brought his ammunition up with resolute courage. Particularly on October 14th when ammunition wagons came under heavy fire and suffered severe casualties, did he display courage, attending to the wounded men and reorganising the survivors of the shattered teams. (D.C.M. 3/6/19).

Woodham (or Woodman), A., 39590, a/Bombr., 460th Battery, R.F.A.

Somme, 1917—On February 8th this N.C.O. was signaller with 2nd Lieut. E. M. Cattell. He laid the wire from our trenches at Sailly Saillisel across No Man's Land and mended it several times under heavy shell fire. On finding it impossible to establish communication he occupied himself in supplying grenades to the infantry. He was cool and determined throughout. (M.M. (immediate) 26/3/17).

Yearsley, E., 91469, Gunner, D/17 Battery, R.F.A.

1917-18.—Has served with his battery throughout the operations of 1917 and 1918 and has always shown great gallantry and devotion to duty. On one occasion, near Ledeghem, on October 15th, 1918, when layer of his gun, he coolly carried on with serving the piece, undisturbed by the fact that the majority of his detachment had been put out of action by a very sharp bombardment, including gas shells. (Divisional Card of Honour).

(III) LIST OF HONOURS, ARRANGED ACCORDING TO UNITS, IN CHRONOLOGICAL ORDER.

NOTES.—Awards of commissions are not shown in this list.

No award is entered more than once. In cases, therefore, of awards given for a period during which the individual served in more than one unit, the entry is made under the unit in which he served for the major portion of such period.

CONTENTS.

(a) Headquarters 29th Divisional Artillery.

(b) 15th Brigade, R.H.A.
> (i) Brigade Headquarters.
> (ii) " B " Battery, R.H.A.
> (iii) " L " Battery, R.H.A.
> (iv) "Y" Battery, R.H.A.
> (v) 1/1st Warwickshire Battery, R.H.A. (T.F.).
> (vi) 460th (Howitzer) Battery, R.F.A.

(c) 17th Brigade, R.F.A.
> (i) Brigade Headquarters.
> (ii) 13th Battery, R.F.A.
> (iii) 26th Battery, R.F.A.
> (iv) 92nd Battery, R.F.A.
> (v) D/17 (Howitzer) Battery, R.F.A. (including all batteries which originally had other titles but eventually were merged into D/17).

(d) 147th Brigade, R.F.A.
> (i) Brigade Headquarters.
> (ii) 10th Battery, R.F.A.
> (iii) 97th Battery, R.F.A.
> (iv) 368th Battery, R.F.A.

(e) 132nd Brigade, R.F.A.
> (i) Brigade Headquarters.
> (ii) 370th Battery, R.F.A.
> (iii) 371st Battery, R.F.A.

(f) Trench Mortar Batteries.

(g) 29th Divisional Ammunition Column (including the Brigade Ammunition Columns which were transferred to the D.A.C. in May 1916).

(h) 14th Siege Battery, R.G.A.

(j) 90th Heavy Battery, R.G.A.

(k) 1/4th Highland Mountain Brigade, R.G.A. (T.F.`

(a) Headquarters, 29th Divisional Artillery.

Date of Action.	Rank and Name.	Award.
Gallipoli, 1915.		
April 25 — 47659	Dawson, Corpl. W. J.	M.M.
April 26	Walford, Capt. G. N.	V.C.
June 28	Simpson-Baikie, Brig.-Genl. H. A. D.	C.B., Mention, Legion of Honour.
June	Barnett, 2nd Lieut. E. J. (R.E.)	Mention.
	Grant, Major H. F. L.	Mention.
	Clark, Major C.H.	D.S.O. and Mention.
	D'Apice, Capt. J. E. F.	D.S.O. and 2 Mentions.
	Hickes, Capt. L. D.	M.C. and Mention.
	Stockdale, Brig.-Genl. H. E., D.S.O.	C.M.G. and Mention.
9623	Adams, A/S.M. H. W.	M.S.M. and Mention.
56855	Lindsay, A/Sergt. H. V.	M.S.M.
Somme, 1916-17.		
June—Sept.	Hunkin, Revd. J. W.	Mention.
	Peake, Brig.-Genl. M., C.M.G.	Mention.
	Ashmore, Brig.-Genl. E. B., C.M.G., M.V.O.	Mention.
Jan. 27	Clark, Major C. H., D.S.O.	Mention.
	Cunnison, A/Capt. T. J.	Mention.
	McLachlan, Lieut. E. M. (R.E.)	Mention.
9623	Adams, S.M., H. W., M.S.M.	Russian Medal of St. George.
Arras, 1917.		
Apr. 9—24	Hunkin, Revd. J. W.	M.C.
Flanders, 1917.		
Oct. 17—20 — 558235	Ellen, Sergt. H. F. (R.E.)	M.M.
	Stevenson, Brig.-Genl. E. H., D.S.O.	Mention.
	Thomson, Capt. J. N., M.C.	Mention.
	Cunnison, A/Capt. T. J.	M.C.
	Green, A/Capt. E. E. (R.E.)	Mention.
Arras & Flanders, 1917.		
9623	Adams, R.S.M., H. W., M.S.M.	Mention.

Campaign / Date	Number	Name	Award
Cambrai, 1917. Nov. 30—Dec. 4		Hunkin, Revd. J. W., M.C.	Bar to M.C.
Flanders 1917-18 & Cambrai 1917.		Stevenson, Brig.-Genl. E. H., D.S.O.	C.M.G. and Mention.
		Green, A/Capt. E. E. (R.E.)	M.C.
Flanders, 1918. July—Oct.		Holmes, A/Major H. O., M.C.	Belgian Croix de Guerre.
Oct. 14—22	47659	Dawson, Corpl. W. J., M.M.	Bar to M.M.
,,	558215	King, A/Corpl. W. F.	M.M.
		Johnson, Brig.-Genl. R. Marr, D.S.O.	C.M.G., Mention, French Croix de Guerre.
	M 2/082643	Greig, Private A. W. (A.S.C.)	M.S.M. & Belgian Croix de Guerre.
	558235	Ellen, Sergt. H. F., M.M. (R.E.)	Belgian Décoration Militaire & Croix de Guerre.
		Thomson, Capt. J. N., M.C.	D.S.O., Mention, French Croix de Guerre.
1915-1917.	558123	Gazzard, Corpl. F. J. (R.E.)	Card of Honour.
	558173	Barrett, Sapper T. N. (R.E.)	Card of Honour.

(b) 15th Brigade, R.H.A.

(i) Brigade Headquarters.

Campaign / Date	Number	Name	Award
Gallipoli, 1915. April		Stockdale, Lieut.-Col. H. E., D.S.O.	Mention.
May 1/2		Daubuz, Capt. C.	M.C. and Mention.
		Blandy, Capt. C. G. S. (R.A.M.C.)	M.C. and Mention.
		Stroud, Bombr. A. E.	D.C.M. and Mention.
,, 28	36943	Bruce, A/Bombr. A. J.	M.M.
Dec.—Jan.	58390	Peel, Lieut.-Col. E. J. R., D.S.O.	Mention.

Date of Action.	Rank and Name.	Award.
Somme, 1916-17.		
June 24—July 1	49692 Shrubsole, Corpl. P. A.	D.C.M.
July—Feb.	Sherbrooke, A/Lieut.-Col. N. H. C.	D.S.O. and Mention.
	Duff, T/Lieut. C. P.	Mention.
	Ideson, 2nd Lieut. A.	Mention.
Gallipoli 1915 & Somme 1916.		
	14675 Brooks, R.S.M., W. J.	Serbian Cross of Kara George.
Arras, 1917.		
April 19/20	Walker, T/Capt. F. M. (R.A.M.C.)	M.C.
Flanders, 1917.		
Oct. 21/22	558029 Nightingale, Sergt. W. H. (R.E.)	M.M.
	253549 Andrews, Pioneer F. E. (R.E.)	Card of Honour.
Arras & Flanders, 1917.		
	Browne, A/Capt. V. F.	Mention.
	253187 Sykes, Corpl. T. (R.E.)	Mention.
Cambrai, 1917.		
Nov. 19	Mulholland, 2nd Lieut. A. E.	M.C.
Nov. 30	90497 Wakelin, Bombr. S.	M.M.
	253196 Pritchard, L/Corpl. A. B. (R.E.)	Card of Honour.
Flanders 1917-18 & Cambrai 1917.		
	Burne, Lieut.-Col. E. R., D.S.O.	Mention.
	253196 Pritchard, Corpl. A. B. (R.E.)	D.C.M.
	Browne, A/Capt. V. F.	Mention.
Flanders, 1918.		
Oct. 13/14	253552 Gourley, Sapper H. (R.E.)	French Medaille Militaire.
	Maitland, A/Lieut.-Col. R. C. F., D.S.O.	French Croix de Guerre.
	Mulholland, Lieut. A. E., M.C.	French Croix de Guerre.
	28370 Sparrow, Gunner H.	Belgian Croix de Guerre.
	253192 Burbridge, Sapper W. (R.E.)	Belgian Croix de Guerre.
	Browne, A/Capt. V. F.	M.C. and Belgian Croix de Guerre.

(ii) "B" Battery, R.H.A.

Forman, Major D. E. — C.M.G. and Mention.
(see also under H.Q. 147th Brigade).

Gallipoli, 1915.

April 28	77271	Denison, Capt. H.	D.S.O. and Mention.
May 1/2	35237	Blake, Gunner B. W.	M.M. and Mention.
	52839	Allpress, Corpl. F. C.	D.C.M.
	68889	Pawley, Bombr. C. E.	Mention.
April—June		Fisher, Bombr. B.	M.M.
June 28		Huttenbach, Lieut. N. H.	M.C. and Mention.
July 12/13		Ball, 2nd Lieut. C. J. P.	M.C. and Mention.
June—July		Knatchbull-Hugessen, 2/Lt. Hon. M. H. R.	M.C. and Mention.
December	34863	Morraghan, Sergt. F. B.	M.M.
	52182	Saunders, Bombr. J.	M.M.

Somme, 1916. Sept. 3

	99377	White, Gunner G. E.	M.M.

Gallipoli 1915 & Somme 1916.

	33089	Uniacke, Major C. D. W.	Mention.
	52182	Laslett, Sergt. L. W.	Mention.
		Saunders, Bombr. J., M.M.	Serbian Gold Medal.

Arras, 1917.

May 4	54318	Jones, A/Bombr. A. C. E.	M.M.
June 17		Shirley Hill, 2nd Lieut. J.	M.C.
	68884	Tristram, Bombr. W.	M.M.

Flanders, 1917.

July—Aug.	52736	Johnson, Bombr. J. T.	Card of Honour.
July 31—Aug 1	128823	Hobdell, Driver F. J.	M.M.
Aug. 1	53970	Merrill, Driver W. H.	Card of Honour.
„	52589	Hammond, Driver F. W.	Card of Honour.
„	121001	Packham, Driver G.	Card of Honour.

Date of Action.		Rank and Name.	Award.
Flanders, 1917.			
Aug. 23	49124	Jefford, Corpl. J. W.	M.M.
Oct. 9—21	54288	Baker, Sergt. C.	M.M.
Oct. 21	40678	Parker, Sergt. J. A.	M.M.
Oct. 22	177008	Ship, Driver G.	M.M.
,,	32445	Smith, Driver H. S.	M.M.
Arras & Flanders, 1917.			
	64224	Bridges, Sergt. H. G.	D.C.M.
Cambrai, 1917.			
Nov. 25	177180	Ivill, Driver J.	M.M.
Nov. 29—30	26077	Myers, Bombr. G. D.	M.M.
Flanders 1917-18 & Cambrai 1917.			
	56818	Gooch, Sergt. S.	M.S.M.
Flanders, 1918.			
Jan. 2	36943	Stroud, A/Sergt. A. E., D.C.M.	M.M.
June 2—3		Lister, Lieut. E. J. S.	Card of Honour.
	32228	Powell, Gunner S.	M.M.
Sept. 28—Oct. 22	39003	Alcock, Corpl. S.S., T.	M.M.
,,	59520	Taylor, Driver C. K.	M.M.
,,	43341	Wilders, Bombr. S.	M.M.
,,	49201	Hall, Corpl. S.	Card of Honour.
Sept. 29		Ker, 2nd Lieut. S. H.	M.C.
Oct. 15	63398	Riley, L/Bombr. F. W.	M.M.
Oct. 19		Lister, A/Capt. E. J. S.	M.C.
Oct. 22		Lowe, 2nd Lieut. W.	M.C.
,,	68745	Amos, Bombr. C. L.	D.C.M.
	49201	Hale, Corpl. S.	D.C.M.
		Vince, Lieut. F. H.	Card of Honour.
	51661	Stace, Sergt. H. J.	Mention.

(iii) "L" Battery, R.H.A.

Gallipoli, 1915.

Date	No.	Name	Award
June 4		Peck, Major H. R.	C.M.G. and Mention.
June 18/19		Lloyd, Lieut. C. H.	M.C. and Mention.
June—Jan.	55583	Messenger, Corpl. L. W.	M.M.

Somme, 1916-17.

Date	No.	Name	Award
June—Sept.	78560	Thorneycroft, Major G. E. M.	Mention.
June 27/28	51720	Hart, Gunner W.	M.M.
Feb. 10	34219	Taylor, S.Sergt. Fitter A.	M.M.
"	65311	Watts, Sergt. R. H.	M.M.
"	12185	Bowles, Sergt. P. W.	M.M.
	74754	Walker, Sergt. J. W.	D.C.M.
		Coulling, Bombr. H. J.	Mention.

Arras, 1917. April 20

Date	No.	Name	Award
		Ideson, A/Capt. A.	M.C.

Flanders, 1917.

Date	No.	Name	Award
July 31	16288	Savage, Gunner E. A.	M.M.
"	103105	Shultz, Gunner J. H.	Card of Honour.
Aug 1	L/1688	Snowden, Driver J.	Card of Honour.
Aug. 9	52850	Guiver, Sergt. H. S.	M.M.
	61772	Rea, Gunner A. F.	M.M.
Aug. 17/18	68728	Dadd, Gunner, R. C.	D.C.M. & Belgian Croix de Guerre.
"	87801	Duffill, Bombr. W.	Card of Honour.
"	128959	Turk, Gunner C.	Card of Honour.
	126482	Wilkins, Gunner E.	Card of Honour.
Oct. 7	52554	Hedges, Corpl. W.	Card of Honour.

Arras & Flanders, 1917.

Date	No.	Name	Award
	101726	Jones, Farrier Q.M.S., J.	Mention.
	68564	Deag, Driver A. J.	Mention.

Date of Action.		Rank and Name.	Award.
Cambrai, 1917.			
Nov. 20/21	108356	Hewitt, Gunner W. V.	Card of Honour.
Nov. 29/30	27914	Bonny, Sergt. R. G.	M.M.
Flanders 1917-18 & Cambrai 1917.			
	101893	Milford, Major K. E.	D.S.O. and Mention.
		Toone, Corpl. H. E. V.	M.S.M.
Flanders, 1918.			
March 21	88186	Thornton, L/Bombr. J.	M.M.
June 2/3	101893	Toone, Corpl. H. E. V.	Card of Honour.
June 8	52554	Hedges, Sergt. W.	Card of Honour.
”	65810	Judd, Sergt. H.	Card of Honour.
”	87799	Beecham, Corpl. D.	Card of Honour.
	W/5602	Taylor, Gunner H.	Card of Honour.
Aug. 18		Wells, 2nd Lieut. P.	M.C.
Sept. 29/30	L/46907	Churchman, Driver W. F.	M.M.
”	59358	Lock, Driver F.	M.M.
”	88197	Pilkington, Driver J.	M.M.
Oct. 4/5	32554	Hedges, Sergt. W.	M.M.
	53970	Merrill, Bombr. W. H.	M.M.
Oct. 19	140173	Jackson, Gunner F. A.	D.C.M.
	26605	Stagg, B.S.M., A.	French Croix de Guerre.
	59544	Peach, L/Bombr. B. A.	M.S.M.
	65810	Judd, Sergt. H.	D.C.M.
	64203	Musgrove, Sergt. W.	D.C.M.
1917-1918.			
		Morrice, Lieut. J. S.	Card of Honour.

(iv) "Y" Battery, R.H.A.

Gallipoli, 1915.

June 28	63111	Taylor, Bombr. F.	D.C.M. and Mention.
July 13	63376	Clarke, Gunner H.	D.C.M. and Mention.
April—July	35259	Ogden, Corpl. S. J. B.	M.M.
Aug. 7/8		Trappes-Lomax, 2nd Lieut. B. C.	M.C. and Mention.
	42887	Jolly, Bombr. C.	M.M.
	45358	McGuire, Corpl. P.	M.M.
	5900	Mitson, Sergt. D.	M.M.
		Lush-Wilson, Capt. H. G.	Legion of Honour.
Jan. 7		Clarke, 2nd Lieut. C.	M.C. and Mention.
	63111	Taylor, Bombr. F., D.C.M.	M.M.

Somme, 1916.

Sept. 1/3	102475	Godfrey, Gunner R. B.	M.M.
Oct. 22	50405	Marsh, Bombr. N. E.	M.M.
,,	68431	Timms, Bombr. F. J.	M.M.

NOTE.—On or about the 25th November, 1916, "Y" Battery left the 15th Brigade, R.H.A., on transfer from the 29th Divisional Artillery to the 1st Cavalry Division. The 1/1st Warwickshire Battery, R.H.A. (T.F.) joined the 15th Brigade, R.H.A. on the same date from the 1st Cavalry Division and served for the remainder of the war in that brigade in the 29th Divisional Artillery.

(v) 1/1st Warwickshire Battery, R.H.A. (T.F.)

Somme, 1916-17.

Nov. 13		Murray, Major W. A.	D.S.O. and Mention.
Jan. 27		Peto, Lieut. R. A.	Mention.
Arras, 1917.	614005	Akerman, Sergt. A. V.	Mention.
April 9	614014	Roxburgh, Sergt. W. E.	M.M.
,,	614376	Kinman, Corpl. W. N.	M.M.

Date of Action.		Rank and Name.	Award.
Flanders, 1917.			
July 20/27	614144	Marks, A/Bombr. J. H.	Card of Honour.
July 27/28	614009	Bull, A/B.S.M., C.	M.M. and French Croix de Guerre.
Aug. 10		Philip, 2nd Lieut. R. T.	M.C.
,,		Malby, 2nd Lieut. H. F.	M.C.
,,	614376	Kinman, Sergt. W. N., M.M.	Bar to M.M.
,,	172365	Dixon, Gunner H. J.	M.M.
Oct. 22/23	614101	Poole, Gunner L. R.	M.M.
Arras & Flanders, 1917.		Eden, A/Major Hon. R. E.	Mention.
		Mure, A/Capt. G. R. G.	Mention.
Cambrai, 1917.			
Nov. 19	614060	Keen, Corpl. G. H. M.	M.M.
,,	614069	Perks, Gunner J. C.	M.M.
Nov. 20	614458	Stone, Driver H. S.	M.M.
Nov. 29/30		Dixon, Lieut. G. H. S.	M.C.
Flanders 1917-18 & Cambrai 1917.		Eden, A/Major Hon. R. E.	M.C.
	614412	Hayes, B.Q.M.S., F.	M.S.M.
	614018	Shirley, S.Sergt. Farrier G.	M.S.M.
Flanders, 1918.			
April 29	604281	Bishop, Driver J.	Card of Honour.
Aug. 18	614394	Perrins, L/Bombr. L. G.	M.M.
Sept. 5/6	614126	Collingridge, Sergt. A.	M.M.
,,	614111	Thomason, L/Bombr. B.	M.M.
,,	745423	Ashley, Driver P.	M.M.
		Mure, A/Capt. G. R. G.	M.C., Mention, Belgian Ordre de la Couronne and Croix de Guerre.
	614036	Checkley, Sergt. E.	Mention.
	614048	Franklin, Sergt. F. W.	M.S.M.
	614411	Smith, Sergt. A. G.	Mention.

(vi) 460th (Howitzer) Battery, R.F.A.

NOTE.—This battery was unbrigaded in Gallipoli; formed part of the 132nd Brigade, R.F.A., and was nominally entitled "A/132", from Feb. to May 1916; formed part of the 17th Brigade, R.F.A. from May to Sept. 1916; and finally joined the 15th Brigade, R.H.A. in Sept. 1916.

Date	Number	Name	Award
Gallipoli, 1915.			
April 25—May 1/2		Gibbon, Major J. H.	D.S.O. and Mention.
May 1/2		Gammell, Lieut. J. A. H.	Mention.
April 28—Aug. 6	78293	Dubois, Bombr. O. C.	D.C.M. and Mention.
Aug. 6		Bailey, Lieut. G. H.	M.C. and Mention.
	55901	Tobin, Sergt. J.	M.M.
		Clare, 2nd Lieut. H. T.	(see under 13th Battery, R.F.A.)
Somme, 1916-17.			
Jan./Feb.	19776	Coates, B.S.M. C. H.	Mention.
Feb. 8	39590	Squire, A/Capt. B. B.	Mention.
„		Woodham, (or Woodman) A/Bombr. A.	M.M.
		Cattell, 2nd Lieut. E. M.	Mention.
		Leadbetter 2nd Lieut. A. E. G.	(see under H.Q. 17th Brigade, R.F.A.)
Gallipoli 1915 & Somme 1916.			
	19364	Duff, T/Lieut. C. P.	Mention.
		King, Sergt. C. W.	Mention.
Arras, 1917.			
April 9	19364	Terrell, A/Capt. C. R. a'B.	M.C.
„	15144	King, Sergt. C. W.	M.M.
		Warr, Sergt. H. F. D.	French Médaille Militaire.
Flanders, 1917.			
July 15/16	53472	Jackson, Driver E. W.	M.M.
July 31	82901	Deal, Gunner A. T.	Card of Honour.
Aug. 10/11		Tindal, 2nd Lieut. C. H.	M.C.
„	85584	Haylock, Gunner G.	M.M.

E.

Date of Action.		Rank and Name.	Award.
Arras & Flanders, 1917.			
Aug.	5955	Parker, B.S.M., A.	D.C.M.
		Stewart, A/Capt. J.	Mention.
Cambrai, 1917.			
Nov. 30	47989	Stewart, A/Capt. J.	M.C.
”		Glew, B.Q.M.S. H.	M.M.
Flanders 1917-18 & Cambrai 1917.			
	51794	Ball, A/Major C. J. P., M.C.	D.S.O. and Mention.
		Talbot, S.Sergt. Artificer A. J.	M.S.M.
	85851	Savage, Bombr. J.	Mention.
Flanders, 1918.			
June 2/3	85851	Watson, 2nd Lieut. F. H. P.	Card of Honour.
		Savage, Corpl. J.	Card of Honour.
Sept. 29		Downs, 2nd Lieut. J.	M.C.
”	29925	Beardmore, Driver W.	M.M.
”	119142	Warren, Driver G. O.	M.M.
Oct. 2/3	32638	Scurrah, Driver A. E.	M.M.
Oct. 4/8	940003	Harling, B.S.M., W. J.	D.C.M.
Oct. 7/8		Kershaw, 2nd Lieut. A. E. P.	M.C.
	956139	McCubbin, Corpl. K.	D.C.M.
”	198692	Preston, Bombr. I. E.	M.M.
”	67884	Nally, Driver P.	M.M.
”	940003	Harling, B.S.M., W. J., D.C.M.	M.S.M.
	SE/12872	Millar, Sergt. J. Y. (A.V.C.)	M.S.M. & Belgian Croix de Guerre.
	98581	Walton, Sergt. J. W. H.	Mention.
1915-1917.			
		Watson, A/Capt. F. H. P.	Card of Honour.

(c) 17th Brigade, R.F.A.

(i) Brigade Headquarters.

Gallipoli, 1915.

Monkhouse, Lt.-Col. W. P., C.M.G., M.V.O. — Mention.
Leadbetter, 2nd Lieut. A. E. G. — Mention.
Harris, Lieut. F. (R.A.M.C.) — Mention.
Hickes, Capt. L. D. (see under Headquarters 29th Divl. Artillery).

Somme, 1916-17.

Monkhouse, Lt.-Col. W. P., C.M.G., M.V.O. — Mention.
Sherbrooke, A/Lieut.-Col. N. H. C. (see under Headquarters 15th Brigade, R.H.A
Leadbetter, 2nd Lieut. A. E. G. — Mention.
Ratsey, T/2nd Lieut. T. C. — Mention.
5772 Lawrence, Corpl. S. E. — D.C.M.

Arras, 1917.
April 9
49206 Hollister, Gunner H. — M.M.

Flanders, 1917.
July 18/19
Harris, T/Capt. F. (R.A.M.C.) — M.C.

Arras & Flanders, 1917.

Murray, A/Lieut.-Col. W. A., D.S.O. — Bt. Lieut.-Col. and Mention.
Lyon, A/Capt. K. — Mention.
253198 Lindop, Pioneer A. J. (R.E.) — Mention.

Cambrai, 1917.
558447 Roberts, 2nd Corpl. (R.E.) — Card of Honour.

Flanders 1917-18 & Cambrai 1917.
13347 Gobbett, R.S.M., J. — M.S.M.

Date of Action.		Rank and Name.	Award.
Flanders, 1918.	201132	Edwards, A/Fitter S.Sergt. R.	M.S.M.
		Murray, Bt. Lt.-Col. W. A., D.S.O.	C.M.G., Mention, French Croix de Guerre.
	558447	Roberts, Corpl. W. (R.E.)	French Croix de Guerre.
		Ratsey, A/Capt. T. C.	Card of Honour.
		(ii) 13th Battery, R.F.A.	
Gallipoli, 1915.		Campbell, Major N. St. C.	D.S.O. and Mention.
		Leach, Capt. R. S.	Mention.
		Clare, 2nd Lieut. H. T.	Mention & Order of Crown of Italy.
	46836	Downs, Corporal S. G.	D.C.M. and Mention.
	68200	Bush, Corpl. F. G.	M.M.
	38083	Patterson, Bombr. A.	M.M.
Somme, 1916-17.			
June—Sept.	68200	Leach, Capt. R. S.	M.C.
July 1		Bush, Corpl. F. G., M.M.	Bar to M.M.
Aug. 17	24091	Henny, Driver J. H.	M.M.
Oct. 22/23	60741	Allen, B.S.M., F.	D.C.M.
Oct.—Nov.		Eggleton, T/2nd Lieut. F.	Mention.
		Phillips, T/Capt. A. S.	Mention.
Gallipoli 1915 & Somme 1916.	15010	Mayo, Gunner S. J.	Serbian Gold Medal.
Arras, 1917.			
April 20/21	114482	Kirby, Driver R.	M.M.
Flanders, 1917.			
July 17/27	32443	Noble, Bombr. H.	M.M.
„	101219	Pollock, Driver J.	M.M.

Arras & Flanders, 1917.

Eggleton, A/Major F. — Mention.

Cambrai, 1917.
Nov. 20

Calvert, 2nd Lieut. J. H. — Mention.

Flanders 1917-18 & Cambrai 1917.

| 29301 | Brook, Gunner E. | D.C.M. |
| 74570 | Opie, A/B.S.M. F. | M.S.M. |

1915-1917.

| 76885 | Shanahan, Driver E. | Mention. |

1915-1917.

144571	Brooks, Gunner L. C. D.	Mention.
	Cunnison, A/Capt. T. J., M.C.	Belgian Croix de Guerre.
66764	Dyer, Sergt. H.	Mention & Belgian Croix de Guerre.
	Ratsey, T/Lieut. T. C. (see under Headquarters 17th Brigade, R.F.A.)	
59032	Brooker, Sergt. E. H.	D.C.M.
91427	Gadsby, Corpl. J.	Card of Honour.

(iii) 26th Battery, R.F.A.

Gallipoli, 1915.
June 28
,, June 29

	Booth, Lieut. P. D.	M.C. and Mention.
68013	Batt, Bombr. J. H.	M.M.
38101	Hambley, Sergt. P.	D.C.M. and Mention.
	Brooke, Capt. A. C.	Mention and Legion of Honour.
34655	Berry, Sergt. W. B.	French Médaille Militaire.
40495	Brough, A/B.S.M., W.	M.M.
42542	Lynch, Gunner, J. P.	Mention.
80909	Tubb, Gunner W.	Mention.

Date of Action.	Rank and Name.	Award.
Somme, 1916-17.		
Sept. 3	85564 Corfield, Gunner H.	M.M.
	46082 Sayer, Sergt. R. H.	D.C.M.
Arras & Flanders, 1917.		
	51021 Chalkley, A/Capt. R.	Mention.
	Stewart, Sergt. L.	D.C.M.
	107815 Anthony, Gunner C. H. G.	D.C.M.
Cambrai, 1917.		
Nov. 30—Dec. 1	97552 Sayers, Gunner F.	Card of Honour.
Flanders 1917-18 & Cambrai 1917.		
Sept.—Feb.	Daly, Major D., M.C.	Mention.
	97552 Sayers, Bombr. F.	M.S.M.
	82918 Croucher, L/Bombr. J.	M.S.M.
Flanders, 1918.		
June 2/3	223104 Cayless, Gunner A. W.	M.M.
Aug. 18	45431 Orton, Driver R. G.	M.M.
Sept. 29	62688 Newman, Corpl. C. V.	M.M.
„	80139 Baddeley, Driver G.	M.M.
„	L/1625 Fells, Driver A.	M.M.
„	745274 Hughes, Driver D. L.	M.M.
Oct. 18	255231 Morton, Fitter G. A.	M.M.
„	26656 Priestley, Gunner S.	M.M.
„	Daly, Major D., M.C.	D.S.O. and Mention.
	46308 Summer, Farrier Sergt. G. H.	M.S.M.
	32501 Jewell, Corpl. S.Smith F.	M.S.M.
	L/33279 Woodhall, Driver B. G.	D.C.M.
	Durell, Lieut. T. C. V.	Card of Honour.

(iv) 92nd Battery, R.F.A.

Gallipoli, 1915.

	Name	Award
	Williams, Major R. C.	D.S.O. and Mention.
44209	Powrie, Sergt. H.	M.M.
54625	Waterson, Corpl. R. F.	M.M.
38092	Ewen, Bombr. C. B.	M.M.
	Leadbetter, 2nd Lieut. A. E. G.	(see under Headquarters 17th Brigade, R.F.A.)

Somme, 1916-17.

		Name	Award
April 6/7		Marx, T/Capt. R.	M.C.
June 24—July 1	56368	Rushbrooke, Bombr. G. W.	Mention.
Oct. 29		Stanford, 2nd Lieut. A. W.	M.C.

Arras, 1917.

		Name	Award
April 14	64632	Bennett, Driver R. B.	M.M.
May 2/3	67089	Davis, Corpl. A. J.	M.M.

Flanders, 1917.

		Name	Award
July 18	12161	Almond, Corpl. J. H.	M.M.

Arras & Flanders, 1917.

	Name	Award
40374	Longfoot, Driver R.	Mention.

Flanders 1917-18 & Cambrai 1917.

Name	Award
Stanford, A/Major A. W., M.C.	Mention.
Brooker, 2nd Lieut. J. H.	Mention.

Flanders, 1918.

		Name	Award
May 20	197300	Cage, L/Bombr. H. N.	Card of Honour.
Sept. 28	25287	Jones, Corpl. F. J.	M.M.
"	210611	Bendon, Driver J. W.	M.M.
"	82549	Brodie, Driver J.	M.M.
Sept. 28—Oct. 1		Beaver, Lieut. R. H.	M.C.
		Brooker, 2nd Lieut. J. H.	M.C.
Sept. 29	L/44290	Hill, Sergt. R. W.	D.C.M.
"	745024	Spray, Sergt. A. C.	D.C.M.
Oct. 1	881838	Kearney, Gunner H.	M.M.

Date of Action.	Rank and Name.	Award.
Flanders, 1918—(*Continued*).		
Oct. 19	86987 Pleece, Corpl. A. V.	Belgian Decoration Militaire and Croix de Guerre.
	18757 Baker, Farrier Sergt. W. J.	M.S.M. and French Croix de Guerre.
	745281 Broad, Sergt. C. E.	Belgian Croix de Guerre.
	Stanford, A/Major A. W., M.C.	D.S.O., Mention, French Croix de Guerre.
	80613 Bennett, Sergt. P.	Card of Honour.
	L/18506 Watterson, Gunner G.	D.C.M.

(v) D/17 (Howitzer) Battery, R.F.A.

NOTE.—The two batteries which were thus entitled at certain times were originally formed from the 181st Battery of the 57th Brigade, R.F.A., which started life at the Curragh in Sept. 1914, and were called A/57 and D/57. After serving in Gallipoli these two batteries came to the 29th Divisional Artillery in February 1916 and formed part of the newly formed 132nd Brigade, R.F.A. as B/132 and C/132 respectively.

On the reorganization of the 132nd Brigade in May 1916, B/132 (late A/57) became D/147, whilst C/132 (late D/57) became D/132. The 460th Battery at the same time became the Howitzer battery of the 17th Brigade but never took the title of D/17.

When the 132nd Brigade was broken up on Sept. 12th 1916, D/132 (late C/132 and originally D/57) became D/17, whilst the 460th Battery was transferred from the 17th Brigade to the 15th Brigade, R.H.A.

Finally, on February 1st 1917, D/147 (late B/132 and originally A/57) which had hitherto been on a four howitzer basis was transferred to the 17th Brigade and became D/17, whilst the then D/17 (late D/132 and C/132—originally D/57) was broken up and sent one section to the new D/17 and the other to the 460th Battery in order to make these batteries up to six howitzers apiece.

Hence honours awarded to individuals in B/132, C/132, D/132, and D/147 batteries are included under the heading of "D/17 (Howitzer) Battery, R.F.A."

Somme, 1916-17.

June—July			
July—Sept.			
Sept.	4972	Sherbrooke, Major N. H. C.	Mention.
		Gough, Driver D.	Serbian Silver Medal.
Sept.—Feb.		Haynes, T/Lieut. A. E.	(see under Trench Mortar Batteries).
		Holmes, A/Major H. O.	Mention.
		Bain, T/Lieut. F. O.	Mention.
,, Oct.	11909	Jefferson, Gunner J.	Mention.

Arras, 1917.

April 24	L/9442	Swift, Sergt. G. T.	M.M.

Flanders, 1917.

July 20	106887	Cann, Driver F. W.	M.M.
	915281	Norwood, Driver W. S.	M.M.
,, Oct. 21	83893	Fellows, Corpl. G. F.	M.M.

Arras & Flanders, 1917.

		Holmes, A/Major H. O.	M.C.

Cambrai, 1917.

Nov. 30		Holmes, A/Major H. O., M.C.	Bar to M.C.
		Rawson, T/2nd Lieut. E. H.	M.C.
,,	13346	Hurst, Corpl. F. R.	M.M.

Flanders 1917-18 & Cambrai 1917.

	3934	Drew, B.S.M., J. E.	M.S.M.
	11565	Tosney, L/Bombr, J.	Mention.

Date of Action.	Rank and Name.	Award.
Flanders, 1918.		
March 11	971320 Mullins, Corpl. A. J.	M.M.
July—Nov.	Marx, A/Major R., M.C.	French Croix de Guerre.
	66203 Redigan, B.S.M., J. L.	Belgian Croix de Guerre.
	64208 Butler, Driver E.	Card of Honour.
	11909 Jefferson, Gunner J.	Card of Honour.
	91469 Yearsley, Gunner E.	Card of Honour.
	Holmes, A/Major H. O.	(see under Headquarters 29th Divl. Artillery).

(d) 147th Brigade, R.F.A.

NOTE.—This brigade formed part of the 29th Divisional Artillery up to 19th January 1917, when it became an "Army Field Artillery Brigade".

Honours awarded to individuals in D/147 Battery, which existed under that title from May 1916 to February 1st 1917, will be found under "D/17 (Howitzer) Battery, R.F.A." which was the battery's final designation.

The 368th Battery was broken up on 12th September 1916 in order to make the 10th and 97th batteries up to a six-gun basis.

(i) Brigade Headquarters.

Date of Action.	Rank and Name.	Award.
Gallipoli, 1915.	Forman, Lieut.-Col. D. E., C.M.G.	Twice Mentioned.
	(see also under "B" Battery, R.H.A.)	
Somme, 1916.	70366 Lott, Corpl. P. H.	M.M.
	Courage, T/Lieut.-Col. M. R. F.	Mention.
Gallipoli 1915 & Somme 1916.	444 Bishop, Armament S.Sergt. R. J. (A.O.C.)	Mention.

(ii) 10th Battery, R.F.A.

Gallipoli, 1915.

Date	Number	Name	Award
May 1		Winter, Major O. de L'E.	D.S.O. and Mention.
,,	44630	Llewellyn, Sergt. T. E.	M.M.
,,	66495	Crossley, Gunner R.	M.M.
May 1/2	47232	Glaysher, Gunner W. F.	M.M.
,,	55652	Moreland, Corpl. T.	M.M.
,,	65749	Boost, Corpl. T. W.	M.M.
May 26	L/47423	Pitts, A/Sergt. T.	M.M.
June 1	88483	Bennett, Farrier Q.M.S., G.	M.M.
,,	2782	Bird, B.S.M., D.	D.C.M. and Mention.
	3811	Moore, Gunner J.	M.M.

Somme, 1916.

Date	Number	Name	Award
Aug. 13	42324	MacPhee, Sergt. D.	M.M.

(iii) 97th Battery, R.F.A. (see under "B" Battery, R.H.A.)

Gallipoli, 1915.

Date	Number	Name	Award
May 1/2	12073	Denison, Capt. H.	D.C.M.
June 28		Hall, B.S.M., C. W.	M.C. and Mention.
,,	60328	Kinnersley, 2nd Lieut. F. A.	D.C.M.
,,	36717	Hilton, Sergt. A. H.	D.C.M.
June 27 & July 14	34447	Paramor, Sergt. W.	D.C.M. and Mention.
May—Aug.	51694	Archbold, A/Bombr. J.	D.C.M. and Mention.
,,	55713	Frost, A/Bombr. E.	D.C.M. and Mention.
,,	60342	Lane, A/Bombr. F.	D.C.M. and Mention.
,,	52654	Sansum, Gunner W.	M.M.
Jan. 9	46885	Armitage, Corpl. A.	M.M.
		Heppell, Corpl. S.	M.M.
		Ball, Capt. K. M.	Mention.

(iv) 368th Battery, R.F.A.

Date of Action.		Rank and Name.	Award.
Gallipoli, 1915.			
June 4/28		Thomson, Major A. F.	D.S.O. and Mention.
June 28	48567	Glazier, Sergt. P.	M.M.
		McCracken, 2nd Lieut. A. M.	M.C. and Mention.
May—Aug.	43325	Cook, Bombr. C. W.	D.C.M. and Mention.
	48332	McKenzie, Sergt. H.	M.M.
	10019	Granados, B.Q.M.S., F.A.	M.M.
	52057	Hughes, Corpl. J. E.	M.M.
	50718	Rayner, Bombr. W.	Mention.
		Wright, 2nd Lieut. J.	
Somme, 1916.	50718	Rayner, Bombr. W., M.M.	D.C.M.

(e) 132nd Brigade, R.F.A.

NOTE.—This brigade was formed in Egypt in February 1916 as a Howitzer Brigade of three batteries:—(i) 460th Battery, hitherto unbrigaded, which was nominally entitled A/132, (ii) A/57 which now joined the D.A. and became B/132, and (iii) D/57 which also joined the D.A. at this period and became C/132.

Between the 18th & 20th May 1916 the brigade was reorganized and ceased to be a Howitzer Brigade. The 460th Battery was transferred to the 17th Brigade, and B/132 became the howitzer battery of the 147th Brigade changing its title to D/147. The 132nd Brigade then consisted of the four following batteries:—

(i) 369th Battery which had joined the D.A. 19.3.16 and been attached to the 15th Brigade, R.H.A.

(ii) 370th Battery which had joined the D.A. 19.3.16 and been attached to the 17th Brigade, R.F.A.

(iii) 371st Battery which had joined the D.A. 19.3.16 and been attached to the 147th Brigade, R.F.A.

(iv) C/132 Howitzer Battery (late D/57) which now became D/132.

On September 12th 1916, the 132nd Brigade was broken up and ceased to exist. The batteries hitherto composing it were disposed of as under:—

The 369th Battery sent its right section to the 92nd and its left section to "Y".

The 370th Battery sent its right section to the 26th and its left section to 13th.

The 371st Battery sent its right section to the "B" and its left section to "L"

whilst D/132 (late C/132 and originally D/57) became the howitzer battery of the 17th Brigade, with the title "D/17", in place of the 460th Battery which was transferred to the 15th Brigade, R.H.A.

Honours awarded to individuals in the 460th Battery will be found under the heading of that battery in the 15th Brigade R.H.A., whilst those awarded to B/132, C/132 and D/132 will be found under the heading "D/17 (Howitzer) Battery R.F.A." in the 17th Brigade, R.F.A.

(i) Brigade Headquarters.

1031 Glass, S.Sergt. D. K. (A.O.C.)   D.C.M.

(ii) 370th Battery, R.F.A.

19530 Sutcliffe, Driver S.   Mention.
Staveley, T/Capt. M.   Mention.
Stanford, 2nd Lieut. A. W.   Mention.
Courage, T/Major M. R. F.   (see under Headquarters 147th Brigade, R.F.A.)

Somme, 1916.
June—July
Somme, 1916.
April—July
July—Sept.
July 1

(iii) 371st Battery, R.F.A.

Date of Action.		Rank and Name.	Award.
Somme, 1916.			
Aug. 3/22	38443	Morissey, Sergt. T.	M.M.
,,	1610	Bohmer, Gunner A.	6th Division "gallantry card."
	106055	Green, B.S.M., A. T.	Mention.

(f) Trench Mortar Batteries.

NOTE.—Trench Mortar Batteries were not on a permantnt basis till the summer of 1916, but a "Trench Mortar Group" was temporarily organized during the Gallipoli campaign, and honours awarded to individuals serving in that group are included here.

During the summer of 1916 S/29, X/29, Y/29, Z/29, and V/29 (heavy), batteries were formed. S/29 T.M.B. was broken up in September of the same year. The remaining batteries continued in existence till 4th February 1918, when V/29 Heavy T.M.B. was broken up on Heavy T.M.B's becoming part of the Army Corps organization, and Z/29 T.M.B. was merged into X/29 and Y/29 which henceforward consisted of six 6-inch Newton Trench Mortars each.

Date of Action.		Rank and Name.		Award.
Gallipoli, 1915.				
Aug. 9		Syers, T/Capt. T. S.		M.C. and Mention.
Aug.—Nov.		Daly, Capt. D.		M.C. and Mention.
		Calvert, T/2nd Lieut. C. H.		M.C. and Mention.
Somme, 1916-17.				
May 7/8	40929	Fryer, Gunner T. H.	Y/29	M.M.
June 24—July 1	78393	Pavey, A/Bombr. R. G.	Y/29	D.C.M.
,,	88195	Knight, Bombr. C. J.	X/29	M.M.
,,	34723	Dingley, Corporal A.	V/29 (H)	Mention.
,,		Morden-Wright, 2nd Lieut. H.	X/29	M.C.

Somme, 1916-17.—(Continued).

July	91887	Walker, Gunner H.	Y/29	M.M.
	86688	Hardy, Bombr. A. J.	S/29	M.M.
Sept. 1/2		Wylie, T/2nd Lieut. A. L.	Y/29	Mention
Oct. 22/30		Wylie, T/2nd Lieut. A. L.	do	M.C.
Dec.—Feb.		Haynes, A/Capt. A. E.	D.T.M.O.	M.C.

Flanders, 1917

July 27	14873	Randall, Corpl. H.	X/29	D.C.M.
" July	82645	Rowland, Driver A. J.	X/29	M.M.
		Craib, A/Capt. W. H.	V/29 (H)	M.C.

Arras & Flanders, 1917.

	66765	Fisher, Corpl. F. S.	V/29 (H)	D.C.M.

Cambrai, 1917.

Nov. 30	745326	Gullick, Gunner L.	Z/29	Card of Honour.
	83054	Parry, Bombr. R. F.	Z/29	M.M.
" Nov. 30—Dec 1		Booth, A/Capt. P. D.	D.T.M.O.	D.S.O. and Mention.
Dec 1	L/11582	Donkin, Sergt. A.	Y/29	M.M.
		Craib, A/Capt. W. H., M.C.	V/29 (H)	Bar to M.C.

Flanders 1917-18 & Cambrai 1917.

		Grey, A/Capt. W. E.	Y/29	Mention.

Flanders, 1918.

Feb—June	19570	Bunter, Corpl. W. H.	Y/29	M.M.
Aug. 18	80519	Barry, Corpl. J.	X/29	M.M.
Oct. 13/14	5101	Leslie, Bombr. J.	Y/29	M.M.
	174555	Wilson, Bombr. F.	Y/29	M.M.
	34462	Whitley, Corpl. A.	Y/29	Belgian Croix de Guerre.

(g) 29th Divisional Ammunition Column.

NOTE.—Of the original D.A.C. which went out from England with the 29th Division in March 1916, only a detachment served on the Gallipoli peninsula, and the only honour which appears to have been gained was that awarded to Lieut. A. A. Fraser which is included in Egypt in Feb./March 1916. On arrival of the Division in France, the 53rd (Welsh) Divisional Ammunition Column became the 29th D.A.C., its actual date of joining the Division being April 10th, 1916.

On May 13th 1916 Brigade Ammunition Columns were abolished and the D.A.C. was reorganized as follows:—

The 15th B.A.C. (R.H.A.) became No. 1 Section, 29th D.A.C.
The 17th B.A.C. became No. 2 Section, 29th D.A.C.
The 147th B.A.C. became No. 3 Section, 29th D.A.C.
The 132nd B.A.C. ceased to exist, the personnel being transferred to various sections of the D.A.C.
No. 4 Section, 29th D.A.C. was formed from the old sections of the D.A.C.

The only honours awarded to individuals in the old B.A.C's appear to be those marked with a * below, and both of these N.C.O's were then serving in the 15th B.A.C. (R.H.A.).

When the 147th Brigade R.F.A. became an Army Field Artillery Brigade on Jan. 19th, 1917, and left the 29th D.A., No. 3 Section of the D.A.C. reassumed its former title of " 147th B.A.C." and left with its brigade.

No. 4 Section of the D.A.C. was renamed later the "S.A.A. Section".

			Mention.
	Fraser, Lieut. A. A.	No. 4	Mention.
76176	Richardson, Corpl. W. J.	*	M.M.
29701	Stone, Corpl. A. A.	*	M.M.

Gallipoli, 1915.
Aug. 12/14

Date of Action.		Rank and Name.		Award.
Flanders, 1917.				
Aug. 17/18	34479	Pyrah, Driver S.	S.A.A.	M.M.
Sept. 18/19	123596	Burford, A/Bombr. J. P.	No. 1	D.C.M.
Arras & Flanders, 1917.				
	38628	Knight, A/R.S.M., F. A. J.	H.Q.	D.C.M.
	41830	Staples, Sergt. C.	No. 2	Mention.
Flanders 1917-18 & Cambrai 1917.				
		Price-Davies, A/Lieut.-Col. S. D.	H.Q.	Mention.
	40517	Atkins, B.S.M., W. E.	S.A.A.	M.S.M.
	41830	Staples, B.Q.M.S., C.	No. 1	M.S.M.
	62917	Lorne, Sergt. G. W.	No. 2	Mention.
Flanders, 1918.				
March 18	745034	Roberts, Corpl. E.	No. 1	M.M.
	46827	Baggaley, Bombr. G. H.	No. 2	M.M.
	42133	Watkinson, Driver H. N.	No. 1	M.M.
June 1/2	L/40465	Shadgett, Corpl. J. H.	No. 2	D.C.M.
Sept. 26	102465	Almond, Bombr. C. P. P.	H.Q.	M.M.
		Spedding, Lieut.-Col. E. W., C.M.G.	H.Q.	O.B.E.
		Bright, A/Capt. F. Y.	No. 1	Mention.
	38628	Knight, A/R.S.M., F. A., D.C.M.	H.Q.	French Médaille d'Honneur.
	62917	Lorne, B.S.M., W. E., M.S.M.	No. 2	M.S.M.
	40517	Atkins, B.S.M., W. E, M.S.M.	S.A.A.	Belgian Croix de Guerre.
	745218	Uzzell, Sergt. J. N.	No. 2	Mention.
	96877	Officer, Corpl. H. L.	No. 1	Card of Honour.
	41515	Leedham, Driver G.	No. 2	Card of Honour.
1917-1918.				
		Phillips, T/Capt. A. S.	H.Q.	Card of Honour.
		Belcher, A/Capt. H. B.	S.A.A.	Card of Honour.
		Tasker, A/Capt. A. V. B.	No. 1	Card of Honour.
		King, Lieut. A. J.		Card of Honour.

F

Date of Action. 1915-1918.	S.A.A.	Rank and Name.	Award.
	99646	Harbord, B.Q.M.S., E. M.	Mention.

(h) 14th Siege Battery, R.G.A.
(formed part of the 29th Divisional Artillery during the Gallipoli Campaign).

Date of Action. 1915-1918.	S.A.A.	Rank and Name.	Award.
Gallipoli, 1915. June		Bayley, Major L. S.	Bt. Lieut.-Col. and Mention.
		Marshall, Major H. S.	D.S.O. and Mention.

(j) 90th Heavy Battery, R.G.A.
(formed part of the 29th Divisional Artillery during the Gallipoli Campaign).

Date of Action. 1915-1918.	S.A.A.	Rank and Name.	Award.
Gallipoli, 1915. June 28	554	Brown, B.S.M., H.	D.C.M.
		Marshall, Capt. H. S.	(see under 14th Siege Battery, R.G.A.)

(k) 1/4th Highland Mountain Brigade R.G.A. (T.F.)
(formed part of the 29th Divisional Artillery during the Gallipoli Campaign).

Date of Action. 1915-1918.	S.A.A.	Rank and Name.	Award.
Gallipoli, 1915. June 4 & 28		Wynter, T/Lieut.-Col. F. A., D.S.O.	Brevet Lieut.-Colonel.
June 28		MacDonald, T/Capt. A. H.	M.C. and Mention.
,,	15389	Bell, Sergt. W.	D.C.M. and twice Mentioned.
,,	2214	Rodger, Corpl. R. C.	D.C.M.
,,	5039	McLaughlan, Gunner S.	M.M. and Mention.
	4901	Toomer, Gunner S. E.	Mention.
,, June 28 & July 12		Duncan-Wallace, Lieut. T.	Mention.
July 12	4259	Matheson, Sergt. A.	D.C.M. and Mention.
	340	McPherson, Gunner H.	Mention
,, Aug. 9	4888	Nelson, Bombr. J. L.	D.C.M. and Mention
		MacKelvie, Major T.	C.M.G. and Mention
		Burney, Capt. A. E. C.	M.C. and Mention.
	4866	McCully, B.S.M. W.	Mention.
	1105	Fraser, Corpl. D.	Mention.

Part II.

LIST OF ALL THOSE WHO WERE KILLED, WOUNDED, OR MISSING, WHILST SERVING IN THE 29th DIVISIONAL ARTILLERY.

(a) Officers, in alphabetical order.

(b) Other Ranks, in alphabetical order.

Explanation of abbreviations used in the lists.

a/	=	Acting.
acc.	=	Accidentally—i.e., through cause not directly attributable to enemy action.
A.M.	=	Air Mechanic (Royal Flying Corps or Royal Air Force).
att'd.	=	Attached.
B.A.C.	=	Brigade Ammunition Column.
Bde.	=	Brigade.
Bdr.	=	Bombardier.
B.Q.M.S.	=	Battery Quartermaster Sergeant.
B.S.M.	=	Battery Sergeant Major.
Bty.	=	Battery.
Cpl.	=	Corporal.
2/Cpl.	=	2nd Corporal (Royal Engineers—Signal Service).
D.A.	=	Divisional Artillery.
D.A.C.	=	Divisional Ammunition Column.
D.T.M.O.	=	Divisional Trench Mortar Officer.
Dvr.	=	Driver.
Farr.	=	Farrier.
Ftr.	=	Fitter.
Gnr.	=	Gunner.
H.B.	=	Heavy Battery.
4th H. M. Bde., R.G.A.	=	1/4th Highland Mountain Brigade, Royal Garrison Artillery (Territorial Force).
H.Q.	=	Headquarters.
Pnr.	=	Pioneer (Royal Engineers—Signal Service).
R.E.	=	Royal Engineers.
R.F.A.	=	Royal Field Artillery.
R.G.A.	=	Royal Garrison Artillery.
R.H.A.	=	Royal Horse Artillery.
R.S.M.	=	Regimental Sergeant-Major.
S.B.	=	Siege Battery.
Sdlr.	=	Saddler.
Sgt.	=	Sergeant.
Sig.	=	Signaller.
Spr.	=	Sapper (Royal Engineers—Signal Service).
S.S.	=	Shoeing-Smith.
S.Sgt.	=	Staff Sergeant.
T.M. Bty.	=	Trench Mortar Battery.
Tpr.	=	Trumpeter.
War. Bty., R.H.A.	=	1/1st Warwickshire Battery, Royal Horse Artillery (Territorial Force).

NOTE.—When one date only is given in the last column, followed by the words "died of wounds," this means that, so far as the author has been able to ascertain, the individual concerned died of wounds received the same day. When both date of wounding and of death therefrom are known to be different, both dates are given.

(a) Officers.

Name & Rank.	Unit.	Date.	Casualty.
Aschwanden, Lt.-Col. S. W. L.,	17 Bde. R.F.A.	10-11-17	Wounded (Gas)
Bailey, Major G. H., M.C.,	"L" Bty. R.H.A.	28-2-17	Killed
Bain, Lieut. F. C.,	D/17 Bty. R.F.A.	6-5-17	Wounded (Gas)
Ball, Capt. C. J. P., M.C.,	"B" Bty. R.H.A.	19-5-17	Wounded
„ Major „	„ „	22-8-17	„
		22-10-17	„
Bankes-Williams, Capt. I. M.,	"26 Bty. R.F.A.	19-7-18	Wounded
Beaver, 2/Lieut. R. H.,	13 Bty. R.F.A.	23-10-16	Wounded
„ „	„ „	22-4-17	„
„ Lieut. „	92 „	30-9-18	„
Beckett, Lieut. C. T.,	368 Bty. R.F.A.	4-6-15	Wounded
Bedford-Pim, Lieut. E. W.,	D/17 Bty. R.F.A.	{ 14-10-17	Wounded
		{ 26-4-18	„
Belcher, Lieut. H. B.,	X/29 T.M. Bty.	28-3-18	Wounded
Blunt, 2/Lieut. J. S.	War. Bty. R.H.A.	21-11-17	Wounded
Booth, Lieut. P. D.,	{ 26 Bty. R.F.A.	28-4-15	Wounded
	{ D.T.M.O.	1-12-17	Wounded
			(Dd. of Wds. 2-12-17)
Bradshaw, 2/Lieut. G. R.,	"B" Bty. R.H.A.	20-9-17	Wounded
Brooke, 2/Lieut. P. A.,	26 Bty. R.F.A.	12-5-15	Wounded
Brooker, 2/Lieut. J. H.,	92 Bty. R.F.A.	30-9-18	Wounded
Brown, 2/Lieut. M. F.,	29 D.A.C.	20-4-17	Wounded
Brown, 2/Lieut. T. S. W.	460 Bty. R.F.A.	16-8-17	Wounded
Burne, Lt.-Col. E. R., D.S.O.,	15 Bde. R.H.A.	1-10-18	Killed
Butler, 2/Lieut. E. A.,	370 Bty. R.F.A.	31-8-16	Wounded
Caiger, 2/Lieut. F. H. S.,	92 Bty. R.F.A.	11-11-16	Killed
Cameron, 2/Lieut. J. M.,	368 Bty. R.F.A.	7-5-15	Killed
Carter, 2/Lieut. W. B.,	"Y" Bty. R.H.A.	4-6-15	Wounded
Cattell, Lieut. E. E.,	V/29 T.M. Bty.	1-8-16	Wounded
Cattell, 2/Lieut. E. M.,	460 Bty. R.F.A.	{ 8-2-17	Wounded
		{ 21-8-17	„
Cazeaux, 2/Lieut. R. J.,	13 Bty. R.F.A.	29-9-17	Wounded (Gas)
Chapman, Capt. A. C.,	V/29 T.M. Bty.	20-8-16	Killed
Chisholm-Batten, Capt. J. de H.	10 Bty. R.F.A.	13-8-16	Wounded
Clare, Lieut. H. T.,	"L" Bty. R.H.A.	14-6-17	Wounded
Clempson, 2/Lieut. L.,	14 S.B. R.G.A.	3-7-15	Wounded
Clutterbuck, 2/Lieut. B. V.,	Z/29 T.M. Bty.	13-7-17	Killed
Cooper, 2/Lieut. C. D.,	D/17 Bty. R.F.A.	5-4-17	Wounded
Cowley, 2/Lieut. R. E.,	T.M. Group	28-12-15	Wounded
Crawford, 2/Lieut. S. W. K.	26 Bty. R.F.A.	21-10-16	Wounded
Daubuz, Capt. C.,	15 Bde. R.H.A.	2-5-15	Wounded
Davidson, Lt.-Col. N. R.,	"L" Bty. R.H.A.	22-7-17	Wounded (Gas)
Davies, Lieut. T. L.,	26 Bty. R.F.A.	22-10-18	Wounded
Davis, 2/Lieut. D. F.,	26 Bty. R.F.A.	1-7-16	Wounded
Deams, Capt. W. W., (R.A.M.C.)	att'd 147 Bde. R.F.A.	3-1-16	Died of Wounds
Denison, Major H., D.S.O.,	368 Bty. R.F.A.	1-7-16	Wounded
Dolphin, Major V .O.,	26 Bty. R.F.A.	7-6-17	Killed
Donnally, 2/Lieut. R. C.,	147 B.A.C.	3-8-15	Wounded
„ Lieut. „	97 Bty. R.F.A.	21-10-16	Killed
Drake, 2/Lieut. W.,	"Y" Bty. R.H.A.	26-6-16	Killed
Duckworth, 2/Lieut. P. B.,	War. Bty. R.H.A.	9-4-17	Killed
Duff, Lieut. C. P.,	H.Q. 15 Bde. R.H.A.	23-5-17	Wounded
Eden, Capt. Hon. R. E.,	War. Bty. R.H.A.	22-7-17	Wounded (Gas)
Edgar, Lieut. G. H. S.,	"L" Bty. R.H.A.	4-9-18	Wounded
Eggleton, Major F.,	13 Bty. R.F.A.	21-10-17	Killed
Elliot, 2/Lieut. J.,	26 Bty. R.F.A.	9-8-15	Wounded
Ely, 2/Lieut. D. M.,	13 Bty. R.F.A.	{ 25-12-15	Wounded
		{ 5-10-17	„
Enright, 2/Lieut. A. B.,	D/17 Bty. R.F.A.	21-4-17	Wounded
			(Dd. of Wds. 11-5-17)

Name & Rank.	Unit.	Date.	Casualty.
Ferdinando, Lieut. G. H. F.,	368 Bty. R.F.A.	4-6-15	Wounded
Fifield, 2/Lieut. L. R.,	26 Bty. R.F.A.	10-4-17	Wounded
Forman, Major D. E.,	" B " Bty R.H.A.	10-8-15	Wounded
Fulford-Brown, 2/Lieut. C.,	D/17 Bty. R.F.A.	28-1-17	Wounded
Furze-Morrish, 2/Lt. L. S. R. B.,	13 Bty. R.F.A.	22-4-17	Wounded
		3-5-17	"
Gaisford, 2/Lieut. J. W.,	" 15 B.A.C.	6-5-15	Wounded
	" B " Bty. R.H.A.	14-7-15	"
Gammell, 2/Lieut. J. A. H.,	460 Bty. R.F.A.	23-4-15	Wounded
Gascoyne-Cecil, Lieut. R. W.,	{ X/29 T.M. Bty.	15-7-17	Wounded
	{ V/29 T.M. Bty.	30-11-17	Killed
Gibson, 2/Lieut. A.,	T.M. Bty.	5-7-17	Wounded
			Dd of Wds
Giffard, Lieut. S.,	26 Bty. R.F.A.	2-5-15	Wounded
			(Dd. of Wds. 3-5-15)
Godwin, 2/Lieut. G.,	26 Bty. R.F.A.	28-9-18	Killed
Gough, 2/Lieut. J. N.,	Y/29 T.M. Bty.	8-3-18	Killed
Grant Suttie, 2/Lieut. A. R.,	" L " Bty. R.H.A.	22-7-17	Wounded
			(Dd. of Wds. 23-7-17)
Gray, 2/Lieut. C. E. P.,	" L " Bty. R.H.A.	9-10-17	Wounded
			Dd of Wds
Grey, Lieut. W. E.,	Y/29 T.M. Bty.	7-2-18	Wounded
Gye, Capt. D. A.,	" L " Bty. R.H.A.	28-2-17	Killed
Hancocks, Lieut. A. C.,	10 Bty. R.F.A.	2-7-15	Wounded
Harris, Capt. F. (R.A.M.C.) att'd 17 Bde. R.F.A.		{ 6-5-17	Wounded (Gas)
		{ 17-8-17	Wounded
Hart, 2/Lieut. W. L. D'A.,	13 Bty. R.F.A.	23-10-16	Wounded
" " "	26 Bty. R.F.A.	3-5-17	" (Gas)
		4-10-17	"
Haswell, 2/Lieut. G. D.,	460 Bty. R.F.A.	21-8-17	Wounded
Haynes, Capt. A. E.,	D/17 Bty. R.F.A.	26-9-17	Wounded
Hayward, 2/Lieut. B. R.,	26 Bty. R.F.A.	6-6-15	Killed
Heath, 2/Lieut. H. N.,	" L " Bty. R.H.A.	9-4-17	Wounded
Henny, 2/Lieut. H. N.,	26 Bty. R.F.A.	{ 24-10-16	Wounded
		{ 25-4-17	Killed
Hetherington, Capt. C. G.,	371, Bty. R.F.A.	26-6-16	Wounded
Hilary, 2/Lieut. H. J.,	92 Bty. R.F.A.	3-6-17	Died of Wounds
Hill, 2/Lieut. J. S.,	" B " Bty. R.H.A.	17-6-17	Wounded
Hindle, 2/Lieut. A. H.,	26 Bty. R.F.A.	12-5-18	Killed
Holmes, Capt. H. O.,	D/147 Bty. R.F.A.	28-10-16	Wounded
Hook, 2/Lieut. S. R.,	Y/29 T.M. Bty.	27-9-18	Wounded
Howells, 2/Lieut. J. H.	460 Bty. R.F.A.	9-10-17	Killed
Hulbert, 2/Lieut. B. W.,	Y/29 T.M. Bty.	30-4-18	Wounded
Hutton, 2/Lieut. J.,	D/147 Bty. R.F.A.	23-10-16	Wounded
" Lieut. "	D/17 Bty. R.FA.	12-8-17	"
Ideson, Capt. A.,	" L " Bty. R.H.A.	23-4-17	Wounded
		16-7-17	"
Jennings, 2/Lieut. A.,	10 Bty. R.F.A.	28-10-15	Wounded
Johnson, 2/Lieut. C. E.,	" B " Bty. R.H.A.	30-11-17	Wounded
Johnson, Lt. S.G. (R.A.M.C.) att'd 17 Bde R.F.A.		10-11-17	Wounded
Jordan, 2/Lieut. H. R.,	92 Bty. R.F.A.	1-10-17	Wounded
Kay, Lieut. N. R. W.,	" L " Bty. R.H.A.	30-6-18	Wounded
			(Dd. of Wds. 3-7-18)
Keane, Capt. J. S.,	A.V.C.	30-11-17	Wounded
Kellock, Lieut. H.P. (N.I.H.),	13 Bty. R.F.A.	28-9-18	Wounded
			Dd of Wds
Lake, 2/Lieut. A. H.,	92 Bty. R.F.A.	7-3-17	Wounded
Lane-Mullins, 2/Lieut. J. B.,	War. Bty. R.H.A.	14-6-17	Killed
Leach, Major R. S., M.C.,	13 Bty. R.F.A.	23-4-17	Wounded
Leadbetter, 2/Lieut. A. E. G.,	460 Bty. R.F.A.	14-11-16	Wounded
.. Capt.	" L " Bty. R.H.A.	4-8-17	Killed
Lefeaux, 2/Lieut. J. F.,	War. Bty. R.H.A.	15-10-18	Wounded
			Dd of Wds
Lister, 2/Lieut. J. C.,	92 Bty. R.F.A.	20-5-17	Killed
Lockwood, 2/Lieut. F. G.,	D/147 Bty. R.F.A.	21-10-16	Wounded
Lunn, 2/Lieut. R. W.,	" B " Bty. R.H.A.	17-6-17	Wounded
			Dd of Wds
Lush-Wilson, Major H. G.,	" Y " Bty. R.H.A.	21-7-16	Killed
MacLean, 2/Lieut. W. I.,	D/17 Bty. R.F.A.	24-11-17	Wounded
MacKelvie, Major T.,	4th H.M. Bde. R.G.A.	(?)	Twice W'ded
MacKenzie. 2/Lieut. M. J.,	4th H.M. Bde. R.G.A.	28-6-15	Killed
Martin, 2/Lieut. S. G.,	13 Bty. R.F.A.	18-4-17	Killed

Name & Rank.	Unit.	Date.	Casualty.
Marx, 2/Lieut. R.	13 Bty. R.F.A.	22-5-15	Wounded
„ Capt. „	92 Bty. R.F.A.	25-9-16	,,
„ Major „ M.C.	„ „	29-5-17	,,
„ „ „		23-7-17	,,
Matthew, 2/Lieut. P. M.,	"L" Bty. R.H.A.	9-5-17	Wounded
McCrory, 2/Lieut. H.,	92 Bty. R.F.A.	1-7-16	Wounded
McLeod, Lieut. A. R.,	"Y" Bty. R.H.A.	25-4-15	Killed
Meeson, 2/Lieut. F. R.,	13 Bty. R.F.A.	14-10-18	Wounded
			Dd of Wds
Merritt, Capt. F. C.,	"B" Bty. R.H.A.	19-5-17	Wounded
„ Major „		17-6-17	Killed
Middleton, 2/Lieut. A. A.,	97 Bty. R.F.A.	25-4-15	Wounded
Morgan, 2/Lieut C. S. S.	17 B.A.C.	26-4-16	Wounded
Morgan, Capt. F. H. L.,	17 Bde. R.F.A.	2-5-15	Killed
Morrice, 2/Lieut. J.,	D/132 Bty. R.F.A.	19-8-16	Wounded
Morrice, Lieut. J. S.,	"L" Bty. R.H.A.	17-10-17	Wounded
Morrison, Lieut. A. D.,	4th H.M. Bde. R.G.A.	25-7-15	Dd of Wds
Morrison, Lt. A. J. McC. C. (R.A.M.C.)	147 Bde. R.F.A.	{ 16-6-15 ⎰ 4-7-15	Wounded ,,
Mulholland, 2/Lieut. A. E., H.Q.	15 Bde. R.H.A.	30-11-17	Wounded
Murray, Major W. A.,	War. Bty. R.H.A.	4-12-16	Wounded
„ Lt.-Col. „	17 Bde. R.F.A.	30-9-17	,, (Gas)
Nicholls, 2/Lieut. G. A.,	War. Bty. R.H.A.	9-4-17	Killed
Nicoll, 2/Lieut. D. A.,	92 Bty. R.F.A.	16-5-15	Wounded
Nicolson, Capt. T.,	4th H.M. Bde. R.G.A.	12-7-15	Wounded
Nowell, 2/Lieut. W. J.,	460 Bty. R.F.A.	9-4-17	Killed
Oswald, 2/Lieut. J. C.,	26 Bty. R.F.A.	30-7-17	Wounded (Gas)
Palethorpe, 2/Lieut. E. D.,	War. Bty. R.H.A.	9-10-17	Killed
Park, 2/Lieut. K. R.,	10 Bty. R.F.A.	21-10-16	Wounded
Parkinson, 2/Lt. F. W. L., H.Q.	15 Bde. R.H.A.	20-8-17	Wounded
„ „ „	460 Bty. R.F.A.	20-9-17	,,
Pattison, Major J. H.,	26 Bty. R.F.A.	28-4-15	Killed
Peppé 2/Lieut. W. T. H.,	26 Bty. R.F.A.	7-6-15	Wounded
Pierson, 2/Lieut. K. L. M. K.	10 Bty. R.F.A.	8-16	Wounded
Pilgrim, 2/Lieut. H. St. C.,	92 Bty. R.F.A.	30-6-17	Wounded (Gas)
Pilling, 2/Lieut. E.,	460 Bty. R.F.A.	23-4-17	Killed
Pirkis, Lieut. F. C .L.,	10 Bty. R. F.A.	19-11-15	Wounded
Prior, 2/Lieut. G. W.,	14 S.B. R.G.A.	20-6-15	Wounded
Redgate, 2/Lieut. B. A.,	"B" Bty. R.H.A.	29-4-18	Killed
Reynolds, Capt. H.,	26 Bty. R.F.A.	5-12-17	Wounded
Richardson, 2/Lieut. S. G.,	26 Bty. R.F.A.	5-12-17	Wounded
Robinson, 2/Lieut. W. C. E.,	97 Bty. R.F.A.	4-9-16	Wounded (Gas)
Russell, 2/Lieut. W. E.,	Z/29 T.M. Bty.	13-7-17	Killed
Saggers, 2/Lieut. W.,	92 Bty. R.F.A.	3-12-17	Wounded
Salberg, 2/Lieut. E. T.,	26 Bty. R.F.A.	3-5-17	Wounded (Gas)
Sherbrooke, Lt.-Col. N.H.C., D.S.O.,	15 Bde. R.H.A.	11-5-17	Wounded
Shone, Capt. G. G., M.C.,	H.Q. 29 D.A.	31-7-18	Wounded
Shorney, 2/Lieut. F. C.,	War. Bty. R.H.A.	30-11-17	Wounded
Skitt, 2/Lieut. M.,	92 Bty. R.F.A.	{ 1-5-15 ⎰ 30-11-15	Wounded ,,
Smith, Colonel E. P.,	17 Bde. R.F.A.	2-5-15	Killed
Smith, Lt.-Col. H. R. W. M.,	132 Bde. R.F.A.	3-8-16	Wounded
Smith, 2/Lieut. J. W.,	92 Bty. R.F.A.	{ 10-17 ⎰ 11-3-18	Wounded (Gas) Wounded
Snowball, 2/Lieut. W.,	V/29 T.M. Bty.	13-7-17	Wounded
Squire, Capt. B. B.,	460 Bty. R.F.A.	23-4-17	Killed
Stanford, Capt. A. W., M.C.,	92 Bty. R.F.A.	27-5-17	Wounded
Stephenson, 2/Lieut. N. A.,	Y/29 T.M. Bty. (att'd. 92 Bty. R.F.A.)	19-5-17	Wounded
Stevenson, Brig-Genl. E. H., D.S.O.,	H.Q. 29 D.A.	30-11-17	Wounded
Swan, 2/Lieut. D. B.,	War. Bty. R.H.A.	7-3-17	Killed
Syers, Capt. T. S.,	147 B.A.C.	18-7-15	Wounded
Tarrant, 2/Lieut. S.,	D/17 Bty. R.F.A.	22-9-17	Wounded
Taylor, 2/Lieut. E. D.,	"Y" Bty. R.H.A.	28-4-15	Killed
Terrell, Capt. C. R. a'B., M.C.,	460 Bty. R.F.A.	8-6-17	Wounded (Dd. of Wds. 10-6-17)
Thompson, Lieut. H. B.,	H.Q. 29 D.A.	2-10-17	Killed
Thoneman, 2/Lieut. H. E.,	13 Bty. R.F.A.	3-5-17	Missing
Todd, Capt. W.,	4th H.M. Bde. R.G.A.	29-6-15	Dd of Wds
Touzel, 2/Lieut. F. G.,	"L" Bty. R.H.A.	22-7-17	Wounded (Gas)
Uniacke, Major C. D. W.,	"B" Bty. R.H.A.	{ 7-8-16 ⎰ 23-4-17	Wounded ,,

Name & Rank.	Unit.	Date.	Casualty.
Vince, 2/Lieut. F. H.,	"B" Bty. R.H.A.	15-10-18	Wounded
Walford, Capt. G. N., **C**,	H.Q. 29 D.A.	26-4-15	Killed
Walker, Lieut. D. S. H.,	Z/29 T.M. Bty.	18-4-17	Wounded
Walker, Capt. F. M. (R.A.M.C.),	15 Bde. R.H.A.	30-11-17	Missing P'ner of War
Walker, 2/Lieut. R.,	92 Bty. R.F.A.	19-9-17	Wounded
Watson, 2/Lieut. F. H. P.,	460 Bty. R.F.A.	3-6-18	Wounded
Wells, 2/Lieut. P.,	"L" Bty. R.H.A.	15-6-17	Wounded
Whiteside, 2/Lieut. W. L.,	26 Bty. R.F.A.	5-7-15	Killed
Whitley, 2/Lieut. J.,	92 Bty. R.F.A.	29-9-18	Wounded
Williams, Major R. C.,	92 Bty. R.F.A.	26-6-15 / 27-6-16	Wounded ,,
Wright, 2/Lieut. J. W.,	368 Bty. R.F.A.	12-12-15	Wounded

(b) Other Ranks.

57947	Abbott, Gnr. S.,	"L" Bty. R.H.A.	30-11-17	W'ded & Missing
98614	Abel, Dvr. F. W.,	460 Bty. R.F.A.	10-4-18	Wounded
90734	Abley, a/Bdr. J.,	10 Bty. R.F.A.	22-10-15	Dd of Wds
26393	Acocks, Sgt. H.,	26 Bty. R.F.A.	6-10-18	Wounded
38332	Adams, Gnr. D.,	92 Bty. R.F.A.	11-5-15	Wounded
9623	Adams, S.M. (AC) H. W.,	HQ. 29 D.A.	30-11-17	Wounded
147020	Adams, Gnr. E.,	29 D.A.C.	14-8-17	Wounded
194862	Adams, Gnr. W. G.,	"B" Bty. R.H.A.	9-8-17	Wounded
558100	Adams, L/Cpl. W. R.,	(R.E.) 15 Bde. R.H.A.	7-10-18	Wounded
16529	Aimson, Gnr. W.,	26 Bty. R.F.A.	6-8-15	Wounded
20716	Ainsworth, Gnr. G.,	D/17 Bty. R.F.A.	15-6-17	Wounded
40599	Aitken, Dvr. A. D.,	13 Bty. R.F.A.	14-5-15	Wounded
601005	Akerman, Sgt. A. V.,	War. Bty. R.H.A.	23-4-17	Wounded
L/10792	Alcock, Gnr. L.,	13 Bty. R.F.A.	30-9-17 / 1-10-17	Wounded (Gas) ,, ,,
L/34458	Aldred, Gnr. W.,	"Y" Bty. R.H.A.	22-10-16	Wounded
67698	Alexander, Gnr. A.,	26 Bty. R.F.A.	29-4-15	Wounded
	,, a/Bdr.	,, ,,	29-6-15	Wounded
65790	Alexander, Cpl. J. G.,	92 Bty. R.F.A.	18-4-17	Wounded
196606	Alford, L/Bdr. S.,	War. Bty. R.H.A.	30-11-17	Killed
42257	Allen, Gnr. G. H.,	370 Bty. R.F.A.	21-7-16	Wounded
50307	Allen, Dvr. J.,	10 Bty. R.F.A.	9-5-15	Wounded
61754	Allen, a/Bdr. J.,	D/147 Bty. R.F.A.	3-9-16	Wounded
	,, Bdr.	D/17 Bty. R.F.A.	24-4-17	Wounded
745327	Allen, Gnr. R. J.,	Z/29 T.M. Bty.	15-7-17	Wounded
40208	Allen, a/Bdr. W.,	15 B.A.C.	28-6-15	Wounded
12161	Almond, Cpl. J. H., m.m.,	92 Bty. R.F.A.	18-7-17	Wounded
94707	Ambridge, Gnr. W.,	D/17 Bty. R.F.A.	15-10-18	Wounded
76277	Ames, Bdr. E.,	460 Bty. R.F.A.	7-10-18	Wounded
81348	Amiot, Sgt. C. T. C.,	13 Bty. R.F.A.	24-4-17	Killed
68715	Amos, Gnr. C. L.,	"B" Bty. R.H.A.	9-4-17	Wounded
152771	Anderson, Gnr. G.,	26 Bty. R.F.A.	30-11-17	Wounded
374	Anderson, Gnr. J.,	4th H.M.Bde. R.G.A.	1-5-15	Wounded
111259	Anderson, Dvr. T.,	D/147 Bty. R.F.A.	16-11-16	Killed
184124	Anderson, a/Bdr. W. G.,	92 Bty. R.F.A.	20-9-17	Killed
82904	Andrews, Dvr. W.,	26 Bty. R.F.A.	29-6-16	Wounded
72795	Annison, a/Bdr. A. T.,	460 Bty. R.F.A.	4-10-15	Wounded (Dd. of Wds. 8-10-15)
17934	Ansell, Sgt. G. W.	(R.H.A.) 460 Bty. R.F.A.	27-1-18	Wounded Dd of Wds
107815	Anthony, Gnr. C. H.,	26 Bty. R.F.A.	23-7-17	Wounded (Gas)
60167	Appleby, Gnr. W.,	10 Bty. R.F.A.	2-7-16	Wounded
35708	Arbuckle, Dvr. A.,	147 Bde. R.F.A.	17-6-15	Wounded
34447	Archbold, Bdr. J., d.c.m.,	HQ. 29 D.A.	22-10-17	Wounded
91667	Archer, Dvr. E.,	26 Bty. R.F.A.	13-8-15	Wounded
24030	Arnold, Cpl. G. F.,	14 S.B. R.G.A.	9-5-15	Wounded
45808	Arrowsmith, Dvr. A.,	13 Bty. R.F.A.	23-11-17	Wounded
87488	Artell, Gnr. G.,	26 Bty. R.F.A.	12-4-17	Wounded
38438	Ashley, Dvr. H.,	13 Bty. R.F.A.	25-9-17	Wounded
558335	Ashton, Dvr.,	(R.E.) HQ. 29 D.A.	29-9-18	Wounded
153614	Ashton, Gnr. C.,	460 Bty. R.F.A.	17-11-17	Wounded (Gas)
221972	Ashworth, Gnr. H.,	13 Bty. R.F.A.	22-7-17	Wounded
138645	Aspden, Dvr. F.,	29 D.A.C.	20-9-18	Wounded

	Name & Rank.	Unit.	Date.	Casualty.
25484	Aspinall, Cpl. J.,	V/29 T.M. Bty.	25-7-17	Wounded
65281	Asson, a/Bdr. B.,	"L" Bty. R.H.A.	24-7-17	Wounded
529	Astbury, Dvr. A.,	29 D.A.C.	17-12-16	Wounded
70550	Astley, Dvr. S.,	29 D.A.C.	6-12-17	Dd of Wds
810042	Aston, Sgt. R.,	92 Bty. R.F.A.	29-4-17	Killed
47171	Atkins, Sgt. E. C.,	460 Bty. R.F.A.	9-4-17	Wounded
618031	Atkins, Gnr. F.,	War. Bty. R.H.A.	24-3-18	Wounded (Gas)
54280	Atkins, Sgt. W. H.	D/147 Bty. R.F.A.	21-9-16	Wounded
116367	Atkins, Gnr. W. H.,	D/147 Bty. R.F.A.	14-11-16	Wounded
68820	Austin, Gnr. A.,	"B" Bty. R.H.A.	20-6-15	Killed
63709	Austin, Dvr. E.,	"B" Bty. R.H.A.	16-11-16	Wounded
98574	Austin, Gnr. R.,	D/147 Bty. R.F.A.	29-6-16	Wounded
42444	Avis, Cpl. F.,	13 Bty. R.F.A.	29-10-17	Wounded (Gas)
14883	Ayling, Bdr. B. A.,	460 Bty. R.F.A.	30-6-16	Wounded
89936	Bacon, Gnr. G.,	"Y" Bty. R.H.A.	5-9-16	Wounded
80139	Baddeley, Dvr. G., M.M.,	26 Bty. R.F.A.	14-10-18	Wounded
620355	Badger, Gnr. E. L.,	War. Bty. R.H.A.	26-11-17	Missing
614360	Bailey, Gnr. A. W.,	War. Bty. R.H.A.	25-7-17	Wounded
96004	Bailey, Dvr. R. C.,	368 Bty. R.H.A.	14-4-16	Killed (Acc.)
80890	Bailey, Dvr. W.,	"Y" Bty. R.H.A.	2-11-15	Wounded
614550	Bain, Gnr. D.,	War. Bty. R.H.A.	9-4-17	Killed
111	Bain, Gnr. J., 4th H. M. Bde. R.G.A.		28-4-15	Wounded
34163	Bain, Gnr. M.,	90 H.B. R.G.A.	27-12-15	Wounded
15790	Baines, Dvr. J. W.,	26 Bty. R.F.A.	9-6-15	Wounded
54288	Baker, a/Cpl. C.,	"B" Bty. R.H.A.	18-4-17	Wounded
"	" Sgt. M.M.,	" "	9-10-17	Wounded
			21-10-17	Wounded
73615	Baker, Gnr. E. H.,	370 Bty. R.F.A.	16-8-16	Wounded
87710	Baker, Gnr. F. S.,	"L" Bty. R.H.A.	8-6-15	Wounded
222640	Baker, Gnr. G. V.,	92 Bty. R.F.A.	1-6-18	Wounded
32584	Baker, Gnr. J.,	X/29 T.M. Bty.	19-6-16	Wounded
45002	Baker, Gnr. R. J.,	13 Bty. R.F.A.	23-4-17	Wounded
74724	Baker, Gnr. W. H.,	"B" Bty. R.H.A.	18-4-17	Wounded (Dd. of Wds. 19-4-17)
118417	Bakewell, Gnr. R. (or H.),	460 Bty. R.F.A.	8-10-18	Wounded
158919	Balcombe, Gnr. E.,	"B" Bty. R.H.A.	1-4-17	Wounded
616505	Baldwin, Gnr. F.,	War. Bty. R.H.A.	2-4-18	Wounded (Gas)
188240	Baldwin, Gnr. J.,	D/17 Bty. R.F.A.	24-4-17	Dd of Wds
2095	Baldwin, Bdr. T.,	26 Bty. R.F.A.	16-6-17	Wounded
153572	Ball, Gnr. A. C.,	29 D.A.C.	31-5-18	Wounded
99344	Ball, Gnr. H. D.,	"L" Bty. R.H.A.	7-10-17	Wounded
78283	Bampton, a/Bdr. H.,	460 Bty. R.F.A.	28-6-15	Wounded
"	" Sgt.	"	11-8-17	Wounded (Gas)
23252	Bancroft, Dvr. R.,	97 Bty. R.F.A.	16-4-15	Drowned
29883	Banks, Gnr. G.,	14 S.B. R.G.A.	12-7-15	Wounded
53555	Banning, Gnr. H.,	29 D.A.C.	26-7-15	Killed
2987	Bannister, Sgt. O. P.,	D/17 Bty. R.F.A.	7-8-17	Killed
75813	Barber, Dvr. A.,	"B" Bty. R.H.A.	13-8-17	Wounded
68415	Barden, Gnr. F.,	29 D.A.C.	23-10-15	Drowned
442	Barford, Arm. Staff-Sgt. W. J., (A.O.C.) 15 Bde. R.H.A.		10-5-15	Killed
31997	Barker, Sgt. A. E.,	"Y" Bty. R.H.A.	2-5-15	Wounded (Dd. of Wds. 3-5-15)
88917	Barker, a/Bdr. A. G. C.,	10 Bty. R.F.A.	4-5-15	Wounded
224105	Barker, Gnr. F.,	"B" Bty. R.H.A.	29-5-18	Wounded
182017	Barlow, Gnr. G.,	26 Bty. R.F.A.	6-5-17	Wounded (Gas)
38182	Barlow, Sgt. H.,	D/132 Bde. R.F.A.	19-8-16	Wounded
66447	Barnes, Gnr. A. L.,	13 Bty. R.F.A.	22-10-16	Wounded
170467	Barnes, Dvr. C.,	92 Bty. R.F.A.	10-10-17	Wounded
73520	Barnes, Bdr. G.,	13 Bty. R.F.A.	22-4-17	Wounded (Gas)
34274	Barnes, Gnr. G.,	29 D.A.C.	14-8-18	Wounded
102514	Barnes, Gnr. H.,	"Y" Bty. R.H.A.	22-10-16	Wounded
56064	Barnes, Gnr. J.,	97 Bty. R.F.A.	16-4-15	Drowned
91911	Barnes, Gnr. O.,	92 Bty. R.F.A.	9-4-17	Wounded
73893	Barnes, Gnr. W. P.,	26 Bty. R.F.A.	12-5-15	Wounded
"	" a/Bdr.	"	4-6-17	Wounded (Gas)
480689	Barnett, Spr. E., (R.E.) 17 Bde. R.F.A.		30-9-17	Wounded (Gas)
224046	Barnett, Gnr. J. C.,	"B" Bty. R.H.A.	14-10-18	Wounded
127659	Barnett, Gnr. T.,	26 Bty. R.F.A.	24-7-17	Wounded (Gas)
80179	Barraclough, Gnr. S.,	13 Bty. R.F.A.	{ 29-6-15	Wounded
			23-4-17	"

Name & Rank.		Unit.	Date.	Casualty.	
68900	Barrett, Gnr. A.,	"B" Bty. R.H.A.	26-1-18	Wounded Dd of Wds	
70586	Barrington, Dvr. G. E.	"L" Bty. R.H.A.	{ 11-6-15 { 27-7-15	Wounded ,,	
26688	Barry, Bdr. T.,	90 H.B. R.G.A.	19-12-15	Wounded	
658220	Barter, Spr. G. W., (R.E.)	HQ. 29 D.A.	22-10-18	Wounded	Dd of Wds.
L/22653	Bartlett, Gnr. A.,	"B" Bty. R.H.A.	19-9-17	Wounded	
84645	Bartlett, Gnr. W.,	92 Bty. R.F.A.	6-8-15	Wounded	
71140	Barton, Dvr. G.,	460 Bty. R.F.A.	19-12-15	Wounded	
49190	Barton, Gnr. H.,	"Y" Bty. R.H.A.	29-5-15	Wounded	
46870	Bashford, Dvr. E. C.,	29 D.A.C.	14-10-18	Wounded	
840337	Bason, Sgt. J.,	D/17 Bty. R.F.A.	8-5-18	Wounded	
110863	Batchelor, Dvr. C.,	371 Bty. R.F.A.	22-8-16	Wounded	
L/3214	Bate, Dvr. A. C.,	26 Bty. R.F.A.	28-9-18	Wounded	
83664	Bateman, Gnr. G.,	"B" Bty. R.H.A.	22-7-17	Wounded	(Gas)
14951	Bates, Gnr. A.,	90 H.B. R.G.A.	28-6-15	Wounded	
52857	Bates, Gnr. G. F.,	"B" Bty. R.H.A.	10-5-15	Wounded	
,,	,, Cpl.	,, ,,	22-7-17	Wounded	(Gas)
72507	Bath, Dvr. H.,	460 Bty. R.F.A.	3-6-15	Wounded	
38106	Batt, Bdr. E.,	26 Bty. R.F.A.	23-4-17	Wounded	
68269	Batt, a/Bdr. F. G.,	26 Bty. R.F.A.	1-5-15	Wounded	
,,	,, Bdr.	,, ,,	27-6-16	Wounded	
,,	,, Sgt.		19-9-17	Killed	
36720	Batt, Sgt. G.,	370 Bty. R.F.A.	27-6-16	Wounded	
44944	Batt, Gnr. J.,	10 Bty. R.F.A.	5-6-15	Wounded	
152348	Batty, Gnr. T.,	13 Bty. R.F.A.	23-7-17	Wounded	(Gas)
126668	Baxter, Dvr. T.,	War. Bty. R.H.A.	20-4-18	Wounded	
67127	Bayley, Gnr. H.,	26 Bty. R.F.A	27-4-17	Wounded	
25160	Bayne, Gnr. J. G.,	97 Bty. R.F.A.	16-4-15	Drowned	
44961	Beadle, 2nd/A.M. W. C., (R.F.C.)	H.Q. 17 Bde. R.H.A.	23-4-19	Wounded	(Gas)
43956	Beardsley, Bdr. R. O.,	"Y" Bty. R.H.A.	22-10-16	Wounded	
66738	Beasley, a/Bdr. M.,	92 Bty. R.F.A.	10-5-15	Wounded	
,,	,, Bdr.		24-7-17	Wounded	(Gas)
308	Beddoe, Dvr. T.,	"29 D.A.C.	24-12-16	Wounded	
53615	Beeching Gnr. W. G.,	368 Bty. R.F.A.	12-7-15	Dd of Wds	
122977	Belcher, Gnr. O. T.,	"B" Bty. R.H.A.	3-5-17	Wounded	(Gas)
94058	Beldham, Dvr. P. A.,	460 Bty. R.F.A.	15-7-17	Wounded	
645743	Bell, Sig. E.,	29 D.A.C.	14-10-18	Wounded Dd of Wds	
111777	Bell, Cpl. H. S.,	26 Bty. R.F.A.	3-10-17	Wounded	
47336	Bell, Gnr. J.,	460 Bty. R.F.A.	24-7-17	Wounded	(Gas)
154393	Bell, Gnr. R. E.,	D/17 Bty. R.F.A.	18-4-17	Wounded	
56618	Bell, Bdr. S.,	10 Bty. R.F.A.	20-6-15	Wounded	
91161	Bell, Sgt. W.,	Z/29 T.M. Bty.	19-12-16	Wounded	(Gas)
50740	Bennett, Sgt. B. C.,	92 Bty. R.F.A.	14-10-17	Wounded	
64632	Bennett, Dvr. R. B.,	92 Bty. R.F.A.	8-5-15	Wounded	
618478	Bennett, Gnr. R. G.,	War. Bty. R.H.A.	15-10-18	Wounded	
100780	Bennett, Dvr. S.,	460 Bty. R.F.A.	23-4-17	Wounded	
57802	Benning, Gnr. J.,	368 Bty. R.F.A.	9-5-15	Wounded	
614086	Bentley, Dvr. W.,	War. Bty. R.H.A.	18-10-17	Wounded	
560298	Bernard, Spr. J. C., (R.E.)	15 Bde. R.H.A.	23-1-18	Wounded	
129031	Berry, Gnr. A.,	"L" Bty. R.H.A.	24-7-17	Wounded	
34655	Berry, Sgt. W. B.,	13 Bty. R.F.A.	{ 17-8-16 { 4-2-17 { 24-9-17	Wounded ,, ,,	(Gas)
24557	Berryman, Sgt. H. C.,	26 Bty. R.F.A.	28-11-17	Wounded	
36050	Best, Dvr. A.,	"Y" Bty. R.H.A.	23-10-16	Killed	
80371	Bettle Cpl. J. S.,	Y/29 T. M. Bty. (attcd. 460 Bty. R.F.A.)	26-10-18	Wounded	
61511	Bevan, a/Bdr. C. J.,	"L" Bty. R.H.A.	8-5-15	Wounded	
433037	Bex, Pte. G. (R.A.M.C.)	15 Bde. R.H.A.	25-7-17	Wounded	
4869	Bexon, Gnr. M., 4th	H.M. Bde. R.G.A.	?-7-15	Wounded	
88181	Bickley, Dvr. W. A.,	"L" Bty. R.H.A.	4-9-18	Killed	
85435	Billyald. Dvr.,	368 Bty. R.F.A.	4-8-15	Missing	
73525	Bingham, Sgt. G.,	460 Bty. R.F.A.	30-11-17	Missing	P of W
176893	Birch, Gnr. W.,	"B" Bty. R.H.A.	19-9-17	Wounded	
172220	Bird, Gnr. A.,	War. Bty. R.H.A.	30-8-17	Wounded	
2782	Bird, B.S.M., D.C.M.,	10 Bty. R.F.A.	12-7-15	Wounded	
69645	Bird, L/Bdr. E. C., HQ.	15 Bde. R.H.A.	30-11-17	Missing	P of W
175114	Bird, Gnr. J., HQ.	15 Bde. R.H.A.	30-11-17	Killed	

Name & Rank.	Unit.	Date.	Casualty.
98477 Bird, Gnr. W.,	D/17 Bty. R.F.A.	18-4-17	Wounded
158907 Birkinshaw, Gnr. H. W., "L" Bty. R.H.A.		3-5-17	Wounded (Dd. of Wds. 8-5-17)
64946 Birrell, Dvr. A.,	26 Bty. R.F.A.	4-6-15	Wounded
113203 Bishop, Gnr. E. J.,	"B" Bty. R.H.A.	3-5-17	Wounded (Gas)
92687 Bishop, Dvr. T.,	92 Bty. R.F.A.	14-4-17	Wounded (Gas)
139959 Bispham, Gnr. F.W.,	"B" Bty. R.H.A.	8-10-17	Killed
102745 Bixby, Dvr. T.,	13 Bty. R.F.A.	15-10-18	Wounded
5045 Black, Gnr. N.	4th H.M. Bde. R.G.A.	?-6-15	Wounded
614333 Blackburn, Dvr. E.,	War. Bty. R.H.A.	21-4-17	Wounded
115041 Blackburn, Dvr. N.,	29 D.A.C.	9-10-17	Wounded
91905 Blackwell, Gnr. F. A.,	HQ. 17 Bde. R.F.A.	18-9-17	Wounded
28918 Blair, Gnr. G.,	13 Bty. R.F.A.	15-5-17	Wounded
47000 Blake, Gnr. H. S.,	29 D.A.C.	?-7-15	Wounded
„ „ Bdr. „	92 Bty. R.F.A.	20-10-17	Wounded (Gas)
„ „ Cpl. „	„ „	6-4-18	Wounded
6653 Blaney, Dvr. J.,	26 Bty. R.F.A.	1-7-15	Dd of Wds
234192 Blount, Gnr. E. C.,	460 Bty. R.F.A.	24-11-17	Wounded
210235 Boatman, Dvr. A. J.,	D/17 Bty. R.F.A.	3-12-17	Wounded
164799 Bobby, Gnr. J. T.	460 Bty. R.F.A.	22-8-17	Wounded
65976 Bolton, Gnr. H.,	26 Bty. R.F.A.	4-6-15	Wounded
102431 Boltwood, Dvr. T. F.,	"B" Bty. R.H.A.	18-10-16	Wounded
83883 Bond a/Bdr. C. A.,	D/17 Bty. R.F.A.	23-4-17	Wounded
196611 Bond, Gnr. F.,	War. Bty. R.H.A.	13-8-17	Wounded
253207 Bone, Spr. G. E. (R.E.)	HQ. 29 D.A.	30-11-17	Wounded
176935 Booth, Dvr. J. F.,	"L" Bty. R.H.A.	29-7-17	Wounded (Gas)
2199 Borley, Sgt. F.,	29 D.A.C.	27-12-15	Killed
31533 Boss, Gnr. A. E.,	"L" Bty. R.H.A.	{ 5-5-17 / 30-11-17	Wounded (Gas) / Missing
90462 Boss, Gnr. G.,	"Y" Bty. R.H.A.	22-10-16	Wounded
205281 Bossom, Gnr. P.,	26 Bty. R.F.A.	14-10-17	Wounded
42537 Bostock, Dvr. E.,	29 D.A.C.	5-12-17	Wounded
50218 Botterill, Dvr. E.,	92 Bty. R.F.A.	1-4-17	Wounded
78686 Bottle, Dvr. E.,	460 Bty. R.F.A.	12-7-15	Wounded
50659 Bottle, Bdr. C. E.,	97 Bty. R.F.A.	{ 20-10-16 / 14-11-16	Wounded / „
184186 Bowden, Dvr. H.,	92 Bty. R.F.A.	30-9-18	Wounded
9828 Bowen, Dvr. H.,	460 Bty. R.F.A.	5-6-15	Wounded
630684 Bowen, Gnr. R.,	13 Bty. R.F.A.	23-4-17	Wounded
87837 Bowen, Dvr. W.,	13 Bty. R.F.A.	25-9-17	Wounded
44518 Bowring, Cpl. J. H.,	92 Bty. R.F.A.	30-12-15	Wounded
51565 Bowyer, Smith-Sgt. W.,	14 S.B. R.G.A.	5-6-15	Wounded
45470 Bowyer, Dvr. W. E.,	17 B.A.C.	26-4-16	Wounded
39082 Boyce, Gnr. T. W.,	92 Bty. R.F.A.	14-9-15	Wounded
77940 Boyle, Dvr. W.,	10 Bty. R.F.A.	{ 28-5-15 / 15-10-16	Wounded / Wounded (Dd. of Wds. 20-10-16)
604337 Boylin, a/Bdr. H. P.,	War. Bty. R.H.A.	{ 9-10-17 / 13-10-17	Wounded / „
614571 Braddy, Dvr. W.,	War. Bty. R.H.A.	25-4-17	Wounded
14675 Bradford, Bdr.,	Y/29 T.M. Bty.	28-6-16	Wounded
42492 Bradford, Gnr. J. W.,	13 Bty. R.F.A.	8-12-17	Wounded
36495 Bradley, Sgt. E. A.,	29 D.A.C.	?-8-15	Wounded
32979 Bradley, a/Bdr. G.,	460 Bty. R.F.A.	20-5-15	Wounded
215845 Bradley, Cpl. O. (R.E.)	17 Bde. R.F.A.	29-9-17	Wounded (Gas)
99836 Brain, Bdr. H.,	10 Bty. R.F.A. (att'd. Y/29 T.M. Bty.)	19-7-16	Wounded
76302 Bramwell, Bdr. H.,	29 D.A.C.	6-9-17	Wounded (Gas)
20163 Branch, Bdr. G. W.,	D/17 Bty. R.F.A.	4-3-17	Wounded
10361 Brassington, Ftr. A.,	13 Bty. R.F.A.	9-11-16	Wounded
L/34353 Brav, Gnr. E. W.,	26 Bty. R.F.A.	12-4-17	Killed
745261 Brazell, Gnr. T. H.	29 D.A.C.	7-9-17	Killed
194882 Brenchley, Gnr. H. J.,	"L" Bty. R.H.A.	28-7-17	Wounded
76997 Brett, Gnr. J.,	"B" Bty. R.H.A.	18-10-16	Wounded (Dd. of Wds. 19-10-16)
36538 Brewer, Dvr. J. H.,	D/17 Bty. R.F.A.	18-10-17	Wounded
89458 Brewerton, Dvr. S.,	368 Bty. R.F.A.	14-6-15	Wounded
32074 Brice, Sgt. F.,	10 Bty. R.F.A.	27-5-15	Wounded
49072 Briggs. Dvr. C.,	92 Bty. R.F.A.	?-5-15	Wounded
147377 Brightmore, Dvr. V.,	29 D.A.C.	11-9-17	Wounded
51149 Britton, Gnr. W.,	"B" Bty. R.H.A.	?-6-15	Wounded
28018 Broad, Bdr. W. H.,	"B" Bty. R.H.A.	22-7-17	Wounded (Gas)
77917 Broadfield, Dvr. R.,	92 Bty. R.F.A.	18-6-15	Wounded

Name & Rank.	Unit.	Date.	Casualty.
90736 Broadhurst, Gnr. D.,	10 Bty. R.F.A.	22-10-15	Wounded (Dd. of Wds. 23-10-15)
87044 Broadway, Dvr. J.,	29 D.A.C.	8-10-17	Wounded
53518 Brockett, a/Bdr. H. J.,	"B" Bty. R.H.A.	1-7-16	Killed
51980 Brockhouse, a/Bdr., T.,	HQ., 15 Bde. R.H.A.	25-4-15	Wounded
32444 Brocklesby, Gnr. E.,	13 Bty. R.F.A.	17-8-16	Wounded
14711 Brockman, B.S.M., J.,	"B" Bty. R.H.A.	5-7-15	Wounded
42664 Bromhead, Cpl. J.,	460 Bty. R.F.A.	15-7-17	Wounded
70795 Brook, Bdr. W. H,	D/17 Bty. R.F.A.	28-8-17	Wounded
62718 Brooker, Dvr. L.,	92 Bty. R.F.A.	10-6-15	Wounded
„ „ a/Bdr.	„ „	18-9-17	Wounded
27931 Brooks, a/Bdr. C. S.,	'14 S.B. R.G.A.	22-6-15	Wounded
144571 Brooks, Gnr. L. C. D.,	13 Bty. R.F.A.	6-12-17	Wounded
66283 Brooks, Dvr. W.,	368 Bty. R.F.A.	13-5-15	Wounded
14675 Brooks, a/R.S.M. W. J.,	HQ. 15 Bde. R.H.A.	5-7-15	Wounded
8933 Broome, Gnr. W. E.,	X/29 T.M. Bty.	18-3-18	Wounded
805848 Brough, Dvr. W.,	29 D.A.C.	9-10-17	Wounded
6974 Brown, Sgt. A. G.,	Y/29 T.M. Bty.	8-10-17	Wounded (Dd. of Wds. 11-10-17)
15371 Brown, Dvr. C. C.,	D/17 Bty. R.F.A.	28-4-18	Killed
43709 Brown, a/R.S.M. F. D.,	HQ. 15 Bde. R.H.A.	30-11-17	Wounded
42470 Brown, Gnr. G. R.,	"L" Bty. R.H.A.	25-4-17	Wounded
79119 Brown, Dvr. H.,	26 Bty. R.F.A.	{28-5-15	Wounded
		{21-5-16	Wounded (Dd. of Wds. 29-6-16)
38105 Brown, Gnr. J.,	HQ. 17 Bde. R.F.A.	25-4-17	Wounded
55847 Brown, Dvr. J.,	147 B.A.C.	16-4-15	Drowned
66357 Brown, Gnr. J.,	97 Bty. R.F.A.	24-6-16	Wounded
36077 Brown, Gnr. J. N. (R.G.A.),	368 Bty. R.F.A.	22-5-15	Wounded
223153 Brown, Gnr. M.,	26 Bty. R.F.A.	{17-8-17	Wounded
		{28-11-17	„
6823 Brown, Dvr. T.,	92 Bty. R.F.A.	18-6-15	Wounded
87877 Brown Bdr. T.,	"B" Bty. R.H.A.	2-4-17	Wounded
45914 Brown, Cpl. W.,	92 Bty. R.F.A.	14-10-17	Wounded
7479 Brown, Cpl. W. A.,	HQ. 17 Bde. R.F.A.	14-8-15	Wounded
25137 Brown, Sgt. W. F.,	460 Bty. R.F.A.	21-6-17	Wounded
33167 Brown, Gnr. W. H.,	29 D.A.C.	27-12-15	Killed
614555 Browne, Gnr. J.,	War. Bty. R.H.A.	27-5-17	Wounded
58390 Bruce, Gnr. A. J.,	HQ. 15 Bde. R.H.A.	24-5-15	Wounded
„ „ Cpl. „	"B" Bty. R.H.A.	26-1-17	Killed
558590 Bruce, Spr. E. W. (R.E.),	HQ. 29 D.A.	30-11-17	Wounded
6752 Bryan, Dvr. W.,	147 B.A.C.	16-4-15	Drowned
93220 Bryden, Bdr. G.,	29 D.A.C.	19-9-17	Wounded
28775 Buck, Bdr. A.,	D/147 Bty. R.F.A.	21-10-16	Wounded
222591 Buck, Gnr. J., .	26 Bty. R.F.A.	29-11-17	Killed
223150 Buckle, Gnr. W.,	26 Bty. R.F.A.	24-7-17	Wounded (Gas)
45968 Buffie, Gnr. F. G.,	29 D.A.C.	8-10-17	Wounded
51043 Bulford, Cpl. W.,	10 Bty. R.F.A.	5-11-16	Wounded
614009 Bull, Sgt. C.,	War. Bty. R.H.A.	21-5-17	Wounded
50771 Bull, Dvr. L.,	92 Bty. R.F.A.	13-8-15	Wounded
614511 Bull, Gnr. T.,	War. Bty. R.H.A.	5-5-17	Killed
1340 Bullen, a/Bdr. W.,	460 Bty. R.F.A.	27-9-15	Wounded
70073 Bullock, Gnr. J. R.,	"Y" Bty. R.H.A.	22-10-16	Wounded
56478 Bunch, Gnr. W. H.,	14 S.B. R.G.A.	13-5-15	Wounded
67963 Bundock, Gnr. E. J.,	"Y" Bty. R.H.A.	{9-1-16	Wounded
		{13-11-16	„
1005 Bunter, Gnr. W. H.,	Z/29 T.M. Bty.	29-10-16	Wounded
(afterwards 91570)			
205981 Burch, Gnr. S. G.,	"B" Bty, R.H.A.	{20-9-17	Wounded
		{10-10-17	„
69368 Burd, Gnr. G. A. J.,	13 Bty. R.F.A.	19-4-17	Dd of Wds
123596 Burford, a/Bdr. J. P., D.C.M.	29 D.A.C.	19-9-17	Wounded
32313 Burgess, Bdr. A. J.,	26 Bty. R.F.A.	24-4-17	Wounded
45171 Burgess, Sgt. H.,	368 Bty. R.F.A.	15-9-15	Wounded
39766 Burgess, a/Sgt. W.,	10 Bty. R.F.A.	19-11-15	Wounded (Dd. 28-11-15)
5799 Burgin, Gnr. J. T.,	460 Bty. R.F.A.	31-7-16	Wounded
56329 Burke, Cpl. F.,	17 B.A.C.	16-6-15	Wounded

Name & Rank.	Unit.	Date.	Casualty.
40548 Burnett, Dvr. A.,	26 Bty. R.F.A.	18-6-15	Wounded
96715 Burnley, Bdr. H.,	26 Bty. R.F.A.	31-5-15	Wounded
382355 Burr, Gnr. W., (late 685)	V/29 T.M. Bty.	1-5-17	Wounded
170022 Burrill, Gnr. W.,	460 Bty. R.F.A.	5-2-18	Wounded
32689 Burrows, Dvr. B.,	"B" Bty. R.H.A.	16-11-16	Wounded
48735 Burrows, Gnr. E.,	13 Bty. R.H.A.	25-9-17	Wounded .
155180 Burton, Dvr. A. E.,	29 D.A.C.	13-7-17	Wounded
45710 Burton, Gnr. A. J.,	13 Bty. R.F.A.	{ 7-8-17 {25-9-17	Wounded ,,
223156 Burton, Gnr. D.,	26 Bty. R.F.A.	29-11-17	Dd of Wds
44466 Burton, Bdr. H. R.,	13 Bty. R.F.A.	{ 7-8-17 {19-1-18	Wounded ,,
68200 Bush, Bdr. F. G.,	13 Bty. R.F.A.	22-5-15	Wounded
,, Cpl. ,, M.M.	,,	3-9-16	Wounded
48744 Bushnell, Sig. W. C.,	"L" Bty. R.H.A.	23-10-18	Wounded
745049 Butler, Dvr. E. L.,	29 D.A.C.	15-7-17	Killed
15024 Butterworth, Dvr. E.,	13 Bty. R.H.A.	6-8-15	Wounded
78294 Buxton, Dvr. D.,	460 Bty. R.F.A.	6-11-15	Wounded (Dd. of Wds. 11-12-15)
85612 Bygrave, Dvr. R. G.,	26 Bty. R.F.A.	23-4-17	Wounded
211113 Byham, Dvr. L. C.,	13 Bty. R.F.A.	25-9-17	Killed
63144 Byham, Gnr. W.,	"Y" Bty. R.H.A.	17-5-15	Wounded
15353 Byrne, Gnr. J.,	17 Bde. R.F.A.	5-6-16	Wounded
59543 Byrne, Dvr. L.,	15 B.A.C.	19-6-15	Wounded
38161 Byrne, Bdr. P.,	26 Bty. R.F.A.	14-8-17	Wounded
L/47270 Byrnes, Dvr. H.,	29 D.A.C.	1-12-17	Wounded
197300 Cage, L/Bdr. H. N.,	92 Bty. R.F.A.	21-5-18	Wounded
88363 Cage, S/S J.,	"L" Bty. R.H.A.	25-3-18	Wounded
12301 Cahill, Gnr. J.,	14 S.B. R.G.A.	4-5-15	Dd of Wds
5135 Cain, Gnr. F.,	92 Bty. R.F.A.	5-8-17	Wounded (Gas)
614034 Caldicott, Gnr. F. W.,	War. Bty. R.H.A.	9-4-17	Killed
77016 Callaghan, Gnr. T.,	13 Bty. R.F.A.	13-10-18	Wounded
55185 Callam. Gnr. C.,	13 Bty. R.F.A.	23-5-17	Wounded
32355 Calvert, Gnr. F.,	Z/29 T.M. Bty.	31-7-17	Wounded
966062 Cameron, Gnr. A.,	460 Bty. R.F.A.	21-3-18	Wounded
205988 Camp, Gnr. H.,	"L" Bty. R.H.A.	30-11-17	Killed
59532 Campbell, Dvr. A.,	"Y" Bty. R.H.A.	29-6-15	Wounded
146962 Campbell, Dvr. H. A.,	29 D.A.C.	19-7-17	Wounded (Dd. of Wds. 23-7-17)
4288 Campbell, Gnr. N.	4th H.M.Bde. R.G.A.	9-8-15	Dd of Wds
128850 Canham, Gnr. O.,	"L" Bty. R.H.A.	28-2-17	Wounded (Dd. of Wds. 5-3-17)
78641 Cann, Gnr. R.,	92 Bty. R.F.A.	23-4-17	Wounded (Dd. of Wds. 24-4-17)
110068 Cannings, Gnr. S.,	D/147 Bty. R.F.A.	21-10-16	Wounded
55511 Cannon, Gnr. G.,	97 Bty. R.F.A.	16-4-15	Drowned
20971 Cant, Sgt. H.,	13 Bty. R.F.A.	8-5-15	Wounded
32588 Canter, R.S.M. C.,	HQ. 15 Bde. R.H.A.	28-9-18	Wounded
745086 Capel, Dvr. J.,	460 Bty. R.F.A.	20-9-17	Wounded (Dd. of Wds. 16-10-17)
59686 Capstick, Gnr. E.,	"B" Bty. R.H.A.	8-6-17	Dd of Wds
51537 Carcary, Gnr. R.,	460 Bty. R.F.A.	20-6-15	Wounded
282352 Carefull, Gnr. S.,	13 Bty. R.F.A.	25-9-17	Wounded
671242 Carey, Gnr. C.,	460 Bty. R.F.A.	20-9-17	Wounded
20660 Carey, Dvr. W.,	460 Bty. R.F.A.	27-6-15	Wounded
43579 Carmichael, Sgt. G.,	460 Bty. R.F.A.	19-8-17	Killed
1709 Carnall, Bdr. A. E.,	Y/29 T.M .Bty.	15-6-18	Wounded
72337 Carpmail, Gnr. W.,	26 Bty. R.F.A.	6-7-16	Wounded
116536 Carr, Gnr. F.,	D/147 Bty. R.F.A.	28-7-16	Wounded (Gas)
58209 Carr, Gnr. W.,	10 Bty. R.F.A.	4-9-16	Wounded
116470 Carroll, Gnr. P. C.,	13 Bty. R.F.A.	23-11-17	Wounded
15019 Carter, Dvr. A.,	26 Bty. R.F.A.	30-7-17	Wounded
45872 Carter, Gnr. F.,	29 D.A.C.	11-7-15	Wounded
62158 Carter, Bdr. H.,	HQ.15 Bde. R.H.A.	30-8-17	Killed
98124 Carter, Gnr. S. F.,	V/29 T.M. Bty.	28-2-17	Wounded
40927 Case, Dvr. A.,	"B" Bty. R.H.A.	4-4-17	Wounded
120007 Casey, Dvr. J.,	29 D.A.C.	8-10-17	Wounded
240468 Cass, Dvr. T.,	"B" Bty. R.H.A.	12-4-18	Wounded
66560 Casson, Gnr. B. S.,	"L" Bty. R.H.A.	4-8-17	Killed
78017 Casson, Gnr. C.,	10 Bty. R.F.A.	4-6-15	Wounded
26297 Castle, Gnr. A.,	14 S.B. R.G.A.	22-12-15	Wounded
109418 Cathcart, Gnr. W.,	26 Bty. R.F.A.	30-7-17	Wounded (Gas)

Name & Rank.	Unit.	Date.	Casualty.
48558 Catherall, Gnr. C. J.,	"B" Bty. R.H.A.	12-7-15	Wounded
72114 Catterall, Gnr. F.,	92 Bty. R.F.A.	24-4-17	Wounded
60858 Cato, Bdr. W. H.,	460 Bty. R.F.A.	7-1-16	Wounded
222017 Cawthorne, Gnr. L.,	13 Bty. R.F.A.	25-9-17	Wounded
4419 Cavanagh, Gnr. J.,	14 S.B. R.G.A.	{ 29-6-15	Wounded
		11-7-15	,,
608287 Caves, Gnr. T.,	War. Bty. R.H.A.	5-9-18	Wounded
4619 Chadwick, Dvr. J.,	147 B.A.C.	16-4-15	Drowned
L/47328 Chadwick, Gnr. R.,	"Y" Bty. R.H.A.	22-10-16	Killed
42957 Challinor, Gnr. G.,	132 Bde. R.F.A.	18-5-16	Wounded
,, ,, ,,	Z/29 T.M. Bty.	25-7-17	Wounded
7614 Chalmers, a/Bdr. E.,	D/132 Bty. R.F.A.	19-8-16	Wounded
			Dd of Wds
35375 Chambers, Sgt. L.,	26 Bty. R.F.A.	5-7-15	Wounded
616390 Champ, Gnr. H.,	War. Bty. R.H.A.	15-10-18	Wounded
87578 Champness, Dvr. F. C.,	HQ. 29 D.A.	30-11-17	Killed
45780 Chaplin, Gnr. W.,	26 Bty. R.F.A.	23-9-17	Killed
108406 Chaplin, Gnr. W. D.,	"B" Bty. R.H.A.	9-10-17	Wounded
12602 Chaplin, Gnr. W. J.,	92 Bty. R.F.A.	11-4-17	Wounded
45389 Chapman, Dvr. G. E.,	26 Bty. R.F.A.	15-10-17	Wounded
68443 Chapman, Gnr. H.,	13 Bty. R.F.A.	1-6-15	Wounded
,, ,, a/S.S.		13-7-15	Wounded
98457 Chapman, Gnr. W. J.,	D/147 Bty. R.F.A.	22-6-16	Wounded
			(Dd. of Wds. 24-6-16)
54305 Chappell, Gnr. H.,	"B" Bty. R.H.A.	22-8-17	Wounded
244341 Charnley, Gnr. E.,	460 Bty. R.F.A.	7-10-18	Wounded
59578 Chatwin, Gnr.,	14 S.B. R.G.A.	7-1-16	Wounded
614352 Checkley, Bdr. C. R.,	War. Bty. R.H.A.	9-10-17	Wounded
63149 Cheras, Gnr. R.,	"Y" Bty. R.H.A.	14-8-15	Wounded
48501 Chester, Gnr. A. F.,	14 S.B. R.G.A.	12-7-15	Wounded
118059 Chicken, Gnr. F.,	92 Bty. R.F.A.	23-4-17	Wounded
7865 Child, Gnr. C.,	92 Bty. R.F.A.	4-2-17	Wounded
129029 Child, Gnr. S. B.,	"L" Bty. R.H.A.	22-7-17	Wounded (Gas)
86647 Childs, Gnr. H.,	29 D.A.C.	11-7-15	Killed
88073 Childs, Dvr. S. G.,	"Y" Bty. R.H.A.	2-6-15	Dd of Wds
67681 Chittenden, Bdr. L. H.,	D/17 Bty. R.F.A.	22-10-16	Killed
154796 Choat, Dvr. C. E.,	29 D.A.C.	19-9-17	Dd of Wds
177006 Chote, Gnr. A. J.,	"L" Bty. R.H.A.	24-4-17	Wounded
51750 Chown, Gnr. W.,	14 S.B. R.G.A.	7-1-16	Wounded
77910 Churchill, Gnr. H.,	"B" Bty. R.H.A.	16-6-15	Wounded
			(Dd. of Wds. 18-6-15)
135664 Churchward, Bdr. E.,	29 D.A.C.	31-5-18	Wounded
69897 Clair, Sgt. S.,	13 Bty. R.F.A.	16-4-17	Wounded
2375 Clamp, Dvr. L.,	HQ. 17 Bde. R.F.A.	12-8-17	Wounded
6737 Clark, Dvr. D.,	13 Bty. R.F.A.	28-9-18	Killed
17238 Clark, Gnr. G.,	13 Bty. R.F.A.	21-10-18	Wounded
113255 Clark, Gnr. G. H.,	"B" Bty. R.H.A.	22-8-17	Wounded
82758 Clark, Dvr. J. O.,	460 Bty. R.F.A.	25-12-15	Wounded
77378 Clark, Dvr. N.,	"B" Bty. R.H.A.	21-11-17	Wounded (Gas)
147003 Clark, Gnr. N. C.,	26 Bty. R.F.A.	23-9-17	Killed
831669 Clark, Gnr. W.,	War. Bty. R.H.A.	30-8-17	Wounded
38117 Clarke, Gnr. A. E.,	460 Bty. R.F.A.	24-7-17	Wounded (Gas)
51848 Clarke, Ftr. S/Sgt.,	17 Bde. R.F.A.	22-6-15	Wounded
			(Dd. of Wds. 22-7-15)
66729 Clarke, S/S. D.,	13 Bty. R.F.A.	13-7-15	Wounded
69697 Clarke, Bdr. E. H.,	"L" Bty. R.H.A.	12-7-15	Wounded
80821 Clarke, Dvr. J.,	147 B.A.C.	16-4-15	Drowned
57859 Clarke, Gnr. J. T.,	D/132 Bty. R.F.A.	19-8-16	Wounded
51923 Clarke, Gnr. J. W.,	"B" Bty. R.H.A.	7-5-15	Wounded
127536 Clarke, Gnr. R. W.	HQ. 17 Bde. R.F.A.	17-8-17	Wounded
46177 Clarke, Dvr. W.,	29 D.A.C.	23-4-17	Wounded
38330 Clarke, Gnr. W.,	10 Bty. R.F.A.	23-5-15	Wounded
133771 Clarkson, Cpl. T.,	13 Bty. R.F.A.	19-7-18	Wounded
			(Dd. of Wds. 21-7-18)
63117 Claydon, a/Sgt. A.,	"L" Bty. R.H.A.	26-4-17	Wounded
17965 Clayton, Gnr. P.,	D/17 Bty. R.F.A.	{ 23-6-17	Wounded
		20-9-17	,,
245591 Clegg, Dvr. G. N.,	92 Bty. R.F.A.	30-9-18	Wounded
11991 Cleland, Sgt. J.,	"B" Bty. R.H.A.	12-7-15	Wounded
73687 Clements, Gnr. A.,	92 Bty. R.F.A.	7-8-15	Wounded
			(Dd. of Wds. 13-8-15)
88258 Clements, Dvr. J.,	"B" Bty. R.H.A.	14-2-17	Wounded
51937 Clements, Dvr. J.,	HQ. 15 Bde. R.H.A.	7-10-18	Wounded

	Name & Rank.	Unit.	Date.	Casualty.
35996	Cleminson, Gnr. W.,	147 B.A.C.	16-4-15	Drowned
L/34319	Clinton, Gnr. A.,	Y/29 T.M. Bty.	18-6-18	Wounded (Gas)
50995	Clist, Gnr. A. B.,	"B" Bty. R.H.A.	26-6-16	Wounded
44837	Clohesy, Gnr. S. T.,	14 S.B. R.G.A.	17-5-15	Wounded
122716	Coaley, Gnr. W. J.,	26 Bty. R.F.A.	23-7-17	Wounded (Gas)
11958	Cocklin, Gnr. C. H.,	13 Bty. R.F.A.	18-8-17	Wounded (Gas)
46335	Cocksedge, Dvr. S.,	"L" Bty. R.H.A.	22-3-18	Wounded (Gas)
45288	Coe, Gnr. W.,	26 Bty. R.F.A.	17-4-17	Wounded
87960	Cole, Gnr. F. H.,	"B" Bty. R.H.A. att'd. HQ. 29 D.A.)	21-7-17	Wounded
121205	Cole, S/S., J. E.,	92 Bty. R.F.A.	26-4-16	Wounded
31699	Coleman, Gnr. G. H.,	D/147 Bty. R.F.A.	13-11-16	Killed
70035	Coles, Gnr. W. H.,	13 Bty. R.F.A.	4-5-15	Wounded
56197	Coll, Gnr. J.,	D/147 Bty. R.F.A.	21-10-16	Wounded
98555	Colley, Gnr. W. G.,	D/147 Bty. R.F.A.	24-8-16	Wounded
77967	Collier, Gnr. H.,	13 Bty. R.F.A.	13-8-15	Wounded
81021	Collings, Gnr. F.,	460 Bty. R.F.A.	2-5-15	Wounded
75180	Collins, Gnr. F.,	"B" Bty. R.H.A.	8-10-17	Wounded
86223	Collins, Dvr. J.,	97 Bty. R.F.A.	1-5-15	Wounded
52209	Collins, Gnr. W.,	"L" Bty. R.H.A.	2-5-15	Wounded (Dd. of Wds. 23-7-15)
215901	Collinson, a/Bdr. G.,	26 Bty. R.F.A.	28-11-17	Wounded (Dd of Wds 30-11-17)
221974	Collinson, Gnr. H.,	13 Bty. R.F.A.	7-8-17	Wounded
176921	Colyer, Gnr. A.,	"B" Bty. R.H.A.	8-10-17	Wounded
614038	Comley, Bdr. A. R.,	War. Bty. R.H.A.	12-10-18	Wounded
71893	Commerford, Gnr. B.,	26 Bty. R.F.A.	2-5-17	Wounded (Gas)
45789	Compsty, Gnr. R.,	14 S.B. R.G.A.	6-5-15	Wounded
52958	Condon, Gnr. E.,	26 Bty. R.F.A.	18-5-15	Wounded
22871	Connor, Gnr. J.,	460 Bty. R.F.A.	9-10-17	Killed
205602	Connor, Gnr. P.,	26 Bty. R.F.A.	17-11-17	Missing
91275	Conway, Gnr. E. J.,	D/17 Bty. R.F.A.	11-3-18	Wounded
12234	Cook, Gnr. H.,	26 Bty. R.F.A.	{14-8-17 / 5-10-17	Wounded "
42247	Cook, a/Bdr. J. B.,	13 Bty. R.F.A.	19-4-17	Killed
29713	Cook, B.S.M., T. G.,	460 Bty. R.F.A.	23-4-17	Killed
205594	Cook, Dvr. T. J.,	92 Bty. R.F.A.	17-10-18	Wounded
68428	Coombes, a/Bdr. A.,	"B" Bty. R.H.A.	2-7-16	Wounded
614129	Coomes, Gnr. J.,	War. Bty. R.H.A.	30-11-17	Wded & Missing Dd of Wds 2-12-17 as a P.O.W.
86526	Coomes, Dvr. N. J.,	460 Bty. R.F.A.	22-11-17	Wounded
122703	Cooper, Gnr. A. A.,	13 Bty. R.F.A.	18-4-17	Wounded
10637	Cooper, a/B.Q.M.S., E.,	10 Bty. R.F.A.	16-4-15	Drowned
44525	Cooper, Sgt. E. T.,	26 Bty. R.F.A.	14-6-15	Wounded
138823	Cooper, Gnr. G. A.,	13 Bty. R.F.A.	24-4-17	Wounded (Dd. of Wds. 4-5-17)
99823	Cooper, B.Q.M.S. J. H.,	14 S.B. R.G.A.	7-6-15	Wounded
75824	Cooper, Dvr. W.,	460 Bty. R.F.A.	15-10-16	Wounded
24099	Cooper, B.S.M.,W. J.,	"L" Bty. R.H.A.	7-1-16	Wounded
61290	Cope, Gnr. E. L. N.,	"L" Bty. R.H.A.	27-6-18	Wounded Dd of Wds
614035	Cope, a/Bdr. F. A.,	War. Bty. R.H.A.	9-4-17	Killed
84321	Copsey, Gnr. E.,	X/29 T.M. Bty.	12-7-17	Killed
59686	Copstick, Gnr. E.,	460 Bty. R.F.A.	8-6-17	Wounded
119959	Corcoran, Dvr. J. T.,	29 D.A.C.	19-7-17	Killed
24711	Cordner, Dvr. H.,	147 B.A.C.	27-10-15	Wounded
55302	Cork, Dvr. T. J.,	460 Bty. R.F.A.	7-5-15	Wounded
128774	Corp, Dvr. J.,	"B" Bty. R.H.A.	25-11-17	Wounded
12993	Cotsford, Gnr. A.,	Y/29 T.M. Bty.	25-4-17	Killed
5740	Cotton, Gnr. W.,	13 Bty. R.F.A.	24-11-17	Wounded
745107	Cottrell, Gnr. A.,	13 Bty. R.F.A.	15-10-18	Killed
74754	Coulling, Cpl. H. J.,	"L" Bty. R.H.A.	{9-5-17 / 5-6-17	Wounded "
L/46939	Coulson, Dvr. E.,	"B" Bty. R.H.A.	18-10-16	Killed
112880	Coulthard, Gnr. H. C.,	13 Bty. R.F.A.	19-7-18	Killed
51586	Coulton, Gnr. A.,	90 H.B. R.G.A.	30-6-15	Wounded
49569	Coupe, Gnr. R.,	14 S.B. R.G.A.	4-6-15	Killed
32860	Coupland, Gnr. J. J.,	10 Bty. R.F.A.	21-10-16	Wounded
76479	Court, Dvr. A.,	17 B.A.C.	5-9-15	Wounded
69482	Courtney, Cpl. J.,	X/29 T.M. Bty.	1-12-17	Wounded
30135	Courtney, Gnr. P.,	13 Bty. R.F.A.	16-6-15	Killed
23324	Cowan, Gnr. C.,	13 Bty. R.F.A.	{24-4-17 / 18-8-17	Wounded " (Gas)
72059	Cowley, Dvr. S.,	460 Bty. R.F.A.	23-10-17	Wounded

Name & Rank.	Unit.	Date.	Casualty.
81068 Cox, a/Bdr. G.,	460 Bty. R.F.A.	6-6-15	Dd of Wds
11700 Cox, B.Q.M.S.,	460 Bty. R.F.A.	2-8-15	Wounded
15239 Cox, Gnr. G.,	14 S.B. R.G.A.	2-8-15	Wounded
53499 Cox, Cpl. G.,	"L" Bty. R.H.A.	11-5-15	Wounded
177198 Cox, Gnr. G.,	"B" Bty. R.H.A.	14-7-17	Wounded
42767 Cox, Sgt. G. H.,	97 Bty. R.F.A.	16-4-15	Drowned
53492 Cox, Bdr. G. W. H.,	"B" Bty. R.H.A.	10-8-15	Dd of Wds
608346 Cox, Gnr. H.,	War. Bty. R.H.A.	27-8-17	Killed
67586 Cox, Dvr. H. J.,	92 Bty. R.F.A.	23-4-17	Wounded
60128 Cox, Gnr. P.,	368 Bty. R.F.A.	16-4-15	Died from effects of attack on H.M.T. Manitou
745143 Crabbe, Dvr. J.,	"L" Bty. R.H.A.	8-10-17	Wounded
72947 Crafts, Sgt. W. R.,	26 Bty. R.F.A	23-7-17	Wounded (Gas)
84431 Craig, Dvr. J.,	29 D.A.C.	17-3-18	Wounded
99963 Cramer, Gnr. T. H.,	97 Bty. R.F.A.	16-4-15	Drowned
127829 Cramp, Gnr. G. T.,	92 Bty. R.F.A.	25-8-17	Killed
149418 Crawford, Gnr. R.,	13 Bty. R.F.A.	24-4-17	Wounded
50716 Creasey, Cpl. L.,	26 Bty. R.F.A.	14-8-17	Wounded
86232 Creer, Dvr. A.,	10 Bty. R.F.A.	16-4-15	Drowned
229909 Crewer, Gnr. J. E.,	92 Bty. R.F.A.	25-4-18	Wounded
745093 Criddle, Dvr. J., Z/29 T.M. Bty. R.F.A.		5-11-17	Wounded
79053 Crisp, Dvr. A.,	10 Bty. R.F.A.	31-7-15	Wounded
73254 Crisp, Dvr. S.,	147 B.A.C.	23-12-15	Wounded
74821 Crittenden, Bdr. S.,	X/29 T.M. Bty.	9-4-17	Wounded
152009 Crofts, Gnr. G. E.,	13 Bty. R.F.A.	19-4-17	Killed
172037 Croper, Gnr. P. J.,	26 Bty. R.F.A.	3-12-17	Wounded
114991 Cross, Gnr. G.,	13 Bty. R.F.A.	24-11-17	Wounded
47129 Cross, Dvr. W.,	26 Bty. R.F.A.	14-10-18	Killed
206120 Crouch, Sig. E. C.,	D/17 Bty. R.F.A.	15-10-18	Killed
34314 Crouch, Gnr. J. H.,	"B" Bty. R.H.A.	31-3-18	Wounded
82918 Croucher, Gnr. J.,	26 Bty. R.F.A.	21-6-15	Wounded
50183 Croucher, Gnr. W. R., 90 H.B. R.G.A.		7-8-15	Killed
191897 Crown, Pnr. C. R. N. (R.E.), 15 Bde. R.H.A.		31-5-18	Killed
614089 Crowther, Bdr. G.,	War. Bty. R.H.A.	30-8-17	Killed
54338 Croxford, Bdr. W.,	"B" Bty. R.H.A.	19-12-15	Killed
46709 Cryan, Cpl. J. H.,	14 S.B. R.G.A.	7-1-16	Wounded
84805 Cudd, Cpl. H.,	92 Bty. R.F.A.	3-12-17	Wounded
139496 Cuin, Gnr. A. M.,	War. Bty. R.H.A.	21-4-17	Wounded
108662 Cummings, Gnr. R.,	10 Bty. R.F.A.	6-11-16	Wounded
55597 Curley, Gnr. G. V.,	"B" Bty. R.H.A.	{9-5-15 / 1-1-16	Wounded / Killed
96694 Curtis, Gnr. C. J.,	460 Bty. R.F.A.	9-4-17	Wounded
59166 Curtis, Bdr. E. W.,	13 Bty., R.F.A.	17-8-16	Wounded
2223 Cuthbertson, Gnr. G.,	4th H.M. Bde. R.G.A.	28-6-15	Killed
40697 Cutler, Gnr. G.,	14 S.B. R.G.A.	12-7-15	Wounded
68728 Dadd, Gnr. R. C., D.C.M.,	"L" Bty. R.H.A.	30-11-17	Wounded
65300 Dadson, Gnr. G. C., "L" Bty. R.H.A.		{15-5-15 / 26-12-15	Wounded / „
45699 Dale, a/B.S.M., F. C., 368 Bty. R.F.A.		9-8-15	Wounded
86975 Dale, Dvr. W.,	26 Bty. R.F.A.	24-4-17	Wounded
481 Dalley, Dvr. F.,	29 D.A.C.	17-11-16	Wounded
113841 Dalley, Gnr. R.,	26 Bty. R.F.A.	22-4-18	Wounded (Gas)
65300 Dallson, Cpl. C.,	"L" Bty. R.H.A.	?-5-15	Wounded
40206 Dalton, Bdr. T. A. G., "B" Bty. R.H.A.		30-6-15	Wounded
936014 Dalziel, Gnr. J.,	92 Bty. R.F.A.	10-8-17	Wounded
106056 Daniel, Sgt. H. E.,	Y/29 T.M. Bty.	7-5-16	Killed
971152 Daniels, Dvr. P.,	13 Bty. R.F.A.	25-9-17	Wounded
53537 Darbyshie, Bdr. H. G.,	"L" Bty. R.H.A.	12-7-15	Wounded / Dd of Wds
15235 D'Arcy, Gnr. J.,	"B" Bty. R.H.A.	21-7-17	Killed
34032 Dare, Sgt. W. R.,	368 Bty. R.F.A.	6-7-15	Wounded
42491 Darrington, Gnr. E.,	"B" Bty. R.H.A.	18-10-16	Wounded
49147 Daters, Gnr. G. W.,	"L" Bty. R.H.A.	25-3-18	Wounded
54311 Dauncey, Gnr. E.,	"B" Bty. R.H.A.	20-6-15	Wounded
81251 Davey, Dvr. B.,	13 Bty. R.F.A.	15-10-18	Wounded
7641 Davey, Gnr. W.,	V/29 T.M. Bty.	30-6-16	Wounded / Dd of Wds
65812 Davidson, Gnr. D.,	"L" Bty. R.H.A.	19-8-15	Wounded
314041 Davies, a/Bdr. F. E., War. Bty. R.H.A.		9-4-17	Wounded
77560 Davies, Gnr. J.,	10 Bty. R.F.A.	21-10-16	Wounded (Dd. of Wds. 22-10-16)

Name & Rank.	Unit.	Date.	Casualty.
L/46982 Davies, Dvr. J.,	29 D.A.C.	1-12-17	Wounded
140094 Davies, Gnr. J. L.,	"L" Bty. R.H.A.	18-1-17	Wounded
131635 Davies, Dvr. J. R.,	26 Bty. R.F.A.	8-10-17	Wounded
786156 Davies, Gnr. W.,	HQ. 17 Bde. R.F.A.	29-9-17	Wounded (Gas)
13437 Davies, a/Bdr. W.,	13 Bty. R.F.A.	15-5-17	Wounded
„ „ Bdr.	„ „	21-10-17	Wounded (Gas)
		15-10-18	Wounded
67089 Davis, Sgt. A. J., M.M.,	92 Bty. R.F.A.	{ 16-9-17	Wounded
		12-10-17	„
77454 Davis, Dvr. D. P.,	29 D.A.C.	1-12-17	Wounded
51271 Davis, Gnr. F.,	14 S.B. R.G.A.	19-6-15	Wounded
53308 Davis, Gnr. J.,	368 Bty. R.F.A.	10-6-15	Wounded
74621 Davis, Gnr. J.,	13 Btv. R.F.A.	16-4-17	Wounded
951624 Davis, Gnr. O. L. A.,	26 Bty. R.F.A.	3-4-18	Wounded
73208 Dawe, Gnr. J. H.,	92 Bty. R.F.A.	30-11-17	Wounded
68944 Dawes, Gnr. H.,	14 S.B. R.G.A.	29-6-15	Wounded
127508 Dawson, Gnr. C.,	D/132 Bty. R.F.A.	31-7-16	Wounded
37637 Dawson, Bdr. F. A.,	92 Bty. R.F.A.	28-5-15	Wounded
700580 Dawson, Gnr. N.,	26 Bty. R.F.A.	23-7-17	Wounded (Gas)
45752 Day, Gnr. J.,	V/29 T.M. Bty.	30-6-16	Wounded
825926 Day, Gnr. L.,	460 Bty. R.F.A.	2-10-17	Wounded (Gas)
or 247944			
68564 Deag, Dvr. A. J.,	"L" Bty. R.H.A.	{ 11-6-15	Wounded
		25-3-18	„
139204 Dean, Gnr. A. G.,	"L" Bty. R.H.A.	30-8-17	Wounded
30967 Dean, Gnr. F. W.,	147 B.A.C.	16-4-15	Drowned
89800 Dean, Gnr. H. L.,	460 Bty. R.F.A.	23-4-17	Wounded
221912 Dean, Gnr. J.,	26 Bty. R.F.A.	6-8-17	Wounded
61389 Dean, Gnr. R. H.,	HQ. 17 Bde. R.F.A.	25-4-17	Wounded
42085 Dean, Gnr. W.,	V/29 T.M. Bty.	15-8-16	Wounded
21014 Deans, Dvr. A.,	26 Bty. R.F.A.	{ 28-4-15	Wounded
„ „ Cpl.	„ „	20-7-17	Wounded
			(Dd. of Wds. 21-7-17)
4671 Dearden, Bdr. J.,	460 Bty. R.F.A.	9-4-17	Wounded
			(Dd. of Wds. 13-4-17)
172250 Dearling, Gnr. E.,	War. Bty. R.H.A.	30-11-17	Wounded (Gas)
			Dd of Wds 8-12-17
614094 Dee, Gnr. G.,	War. Bty. R.H.A.	{ 21-5-17	Wounded
		21-9-17	„
614439 De Heriz, Gnr. C. E.,	War. Bty. R.H.A.	9-4-17	Killed
14883 Delaney, Gnr. L. F.,	14 S.B. R.G.A.	6-8-15	Wounded
83086. Denham, Gnr. R.,	V/29 T.M. Bty.	3-2-18	Killed
68552 Dennis, a/Cpl. G.,	13 Bty. R.F.A.	19-4-17	Killed
32964 Denny, Gnr. H.,	29 D.A.C.	13-9-17	Wounded (Gas)
68867 Denton, Gnr. R. R.,	"B" Bty. R.H.A.	{ 20-5-15	Wounded
		14-8-15	Wounded
		21-11-17	Wounded & Gas
14459 Devere, Sgt. W. G.,	V/29 T.M. Bty.	1-8-16	Wounded
57721 Devey, Gnr. S.,	13 Bty. R.F.A.	7-8-17	Wounded
45892 Devine, Dvr. J.,	26 Bty. R.F.A.	24-7-17	Wounded (Gas)
70765 Devonport, Gnr. T.,	368 Bty. R.F.A.	26-7-15	Wounded
98575 Dibben, a/Bdr. A.,	D/17 Bty. R.F.A.	1-8-17	Wounded
87723 Dickens, Gnr. L.,	"L" Bty. R.H.A.	25-12-15	Wounded
810609 Dickinson, Gnr. C.,	29 D.A.C.	5-9-17	Wounded
775370 Dickinson, Gnr. C. A.,	92 Btv. R.F.A.	24-6-17	Wounded
776280 Dickinson, Bdr. J.,	26 Bty. R.F.A.	29-11-17	Wounded
196574 Dicks, Gnr. C. H.,	War. Bty. R.H.A.	14-6-17	Killed
7176 Dickson, Bdr. W.,	D/147 Bty. R.F.A.	23-6-16	Wounded
			(Dd. of Wds. 25-6-16)
8032 Dight, Gnr. W. G.,	92 Bty. R.F.A.	10-8-15	Killed
178558 Dighton, Gnr. H.,	D/17 Bty. R.F.A.	12-5-17	Wounded
614443 Dilger, Gnr. J. G.,	War. Bty. R.H.A.	30-11-17	Wounded (Gas)
37423 Dingley, Cpl. A. E.,	26 Bty. R.F.A.	30-12-15	Wounded
	Y/29 T.M. Bty.	26-7-16	Wounded (Gas)
221913 Dinsdale, Gnr. W.,	92 Bty. R.F.A.	24-9-17	Wounded (Gas)
137683 Dixon, Gnr. J.,	26 Bty. R.F.A.	23-7-17	Wounded (Gas)
162974 Dobbins, Gnr. T.	Y/29 T.M. Bty.	8-5-18	Wounded & Gas
185952 Dobson, Bdr. W.,	26 Bty. R.F.A.	30-9-17	Wounded
159309 Doherty, Gnr. S.,	D/17 Bty. R.F.A.	25-4-17	Wounded
5689 Dohney, Gnr. P.,	26 Bty. R.F.A.	22-10-17	Wounded
205997 Donald, Dvr. J. C.,	"B" Bty. R.H.A.	21-11-17	Wounded (Gas)
36623 Doney, a/Bdr. E. J.,	14 S.B. R.G.A.	16-5-15	Wounded
			(Dd. of Wds. 17-5-15)
66410 Doody, Gnr. T.,	"L" Bty. R.H.A.	25-3-18	Wounded

	Name & Rank.	Unit.	Date.	Casualty.
78623	Doran, Dvr. G.,	26 Bty. R.F.A.	20-2-17	Wounded
50263	Doran, Gnr. H.,	10 Bty. R.F.A.	16-4-15	Drowned
66059	Doughtery, Cpl. J.,	13 Bty. R.F.A.	23-7-17	Wounded (Gas)
614338	Dowling, Gnr. A. B.,	War. Bty. R.H.A.	23-4-17	Wounded
50976	Dowling, Cpl. C. G.,	92 Bty. R.F.A.	11-5-15	Wounded
				(Dd. of Wds. 12-5-15)
51696	Downes, Gnr. W.,	97 Bty. R.F.A.	{ 4-6-15	Wounded
			{ 16-12-15	Wounded
				(Dd. of Wds. 10-1-16)
12076	Downing, Gnr. W.,	26 Bty. R.F.A.	21-3-18	Wounded (Gas)
46836	Downs, Sgt. S. G., D.C.M.,	13 Bty. R.F.A.	{ 19-4-17	Wounded
			{ 5-12-17	,,
35676	Doyle, Dvr. T.,	"L" Bty. R.H.A.	16-4-18	Wounded (Gas)
26621	Drake, a/Bdr. C. W.,	"B " Bty. R.H.A.	17-8-17	Wounded
	.Bdr. ,,	,,	9-10-15	Wounded
33565	Drake, Sgt. W.,	"B "Bty. R.H.A.	7-6-15	Wounded
48505	Draper, a/Bdr. H. E.,	"Y" Bty. R.H.A.	7-8-15	Wounded
66823	Draper, Gnr. W. T.,	"L" Bty. R.H.A.	17-12-16	Wounded
25312	Drew, Gnr. A. L.,	92 Bty. R.F.A.	5-6-17	Wounded
3934	Drew, B.S.M., J. E.,	D/17 Bty. R.F.A.	19-5-17	Wounded
101742	Drinkall, Dvr. A.,	"B " Bty. R.H.A.	2-9-15	Wounded
73533	Dryden, Gnr. H.,	Y/29 T.M. Bty.	29-8-16	Wounded
78293	Dubois, Bdr. O. C., D.C.M.,	460 Bty. R.F.A.	{ 2-1-17	Wounded
			{ 9-4-17	Dd of Wds
75052	Duck, Dvr. J.,	10 Bty. R.F.A.	18-11-15	Wounded
86079	Duckett, Gnr. A. F.,	"L" Bty. R.H.A.	22-7-17	Wounded (Gas)
L/34382	Duckworth, Gnr. T. V.,	92 Bty. R.F.A.	23-4-17	Wounded
4716	Dudley, Gnr. F.,	29 D.A.C.	?-8-15	Wounded
87801	Duffill, Cpl. W.,	"L" Bty. R.H.A.	13-4-18	Wounded
42796	Dunham, Gnr. G.,	29 D.A.C.	25-5-17	Wounded
L/39959	Dunkerley, Gnr. F.,	369 Bty. R.F.A.	30-8-16	Wounded
173950	Dunnill, Gnr. R.,	26 Bty. R.F.A.	19-10-18	Wounded
44787	Dunton, Gnr. C.,	14 S.B. R.G.A.	20-6-15	Wounded
3157	Durham, Dvr. H.,	92 Bty. R.F.A.	24-4-17	Wounded
614023	Durran, Whlr. J. T.,	"L" Bty. R.H.A.	30-8-17	Killed
L/16114	Dutton, Gnr. S.,	29 D.A.C.	16-8-17	Killed
82121	Dwyer, Gnr. C.,	460 Bty. R.F.A.	17-12-16	Wounded
33651	Dyson, Gnr. A.,	97 Bty. R.F.A.	16-10-16	Wounded
177454	Eames, Gnr. J.,	92 Bty. R.F.A.	18-6-17	Wounded (Gas)
616244	Eames, Gnr. J.,	War. Bty. R.H.A.	9-10-17	Wounded
155141	Earlam, Gnr. J. T.,	D/17 Bty. R.F.A.	1-6-18	Killed
97770	Earp, Gnr. E.,	D/147 Bty. R.F.A.		
		(att'd. Z/29 T.M. Bty.)	29-6-16	Killed
L/35030	East, Gnr. E.,	92 Bty. R.F.A.	2-5-17	Killed
40268	East, Dvr. J.,	26 Bty. R.F.A.	4-6-15	Wounded
901067	Eastwood, Dvr. A.,	26 Bty. R.F.A.	16-10-17	Wounded
745032	Eastwood, Dvr. A.,	29 D.A.C.	28-9-18	Killed
38093	Eastwood, Gnr. B.,	92 Bty. R.F.A.	7-8-15	Killed
15182	Eastwood, Dvr. S.,	26 Bty. R.F.A.	5-7-16	Wounded
614045	Eaton, Bdr. C.,	War. Bty. R.H.A.	11-4-17	Wounded
614046	Eaton, Sgt. H. C.,	War. Bty. R.H.A.	{ 7-5-17	Wounded
			{ 30-11-17	,,
614325	Eaton, Bdr. J.,	War. Bty. R.H.A.	9-4-17	Killed
98614	Ebel, Dvr. F. W.,	460 Bty. R.F.A.	10-4-18	Wounded
75437	Eckworth, Gnr. F.,	92 Bty. R.F.A.	7-8-15	Dd of Wds
133699	Edgar, Gnr. J.,	92 Bty. R.F.A.	23-7-17	Wounded (Gas)
178277	Edge, Gnr. A.,	Y/29 T.M. Bty.	16-3-18	Wounded (acc.)
130012	Edge, Gnr. W.,	92 Bty. R.F.A.	23-7-17	Wounded (Gas)
16534	Edgeworth, Gnr. W.,	29 D.A.C.	30-7-17	Dd of Wds
153613	Edgington, Gnr. A.,	"L" Bty. R.H.A.	20-4-17	Wounded
25378	Edmonds, Sgt. C. W.,	"Y" Bty. R.H.A.	4-6-15	Wounded
510	Edmonds, Dvr. W.,	29 D.A.C.	30-6-16	Wounded
121173	Edmondson, S/S., E.,	460 Bty. R.F.A.	8-10-18	Wounded
614044	Edmunds, Cpl. G. E.,	War. Bty. R.H.A.	9-4-17	Killed
23591	Edmunds, Bdr. P. W.,	460 Bty. R.F.A.	4-8-18	Wounded
3040	Edwards, Gnr. A. H.,	D/147 Bty R.F.A.	22-10-16	Wounded
91160	Edwards, Gnr. E.,	HQ. 132 Bde. R.F.A.	12-7-16	Wounded
27980	Edwards, Cpl. E. J. (R.A.M.C.),	17 Bde. R.F.A.	31-10-16	Wounded
1797	Edwards, a/Bdr. G. T.,	92 Bty. R.F.A.	27-7-17	Killed
98792	Edwards, Cpl. S/S J.,	D/17 Bty. R.F.A.	26-4-17	Wounded
610452	Edwards, Dvr. J.,	29 D.A.C.	30-9-18	Wounded
77579	Edwards, Gnr. M.,	368 Bty. R.F.A.	18-5-15	Wounded
58348	Edwards, Gnr. W. W.,	97 Bty. R.F.A.	14-11-16	Wounded

G.

Name & Rank.	Unit.	Date.	Casualty.
159358 Edwards, Gnr. W.,	29 D.A.C.	11-9-17	Wounded
91033 Edwards, Gnr. W. T.,	D/17 Bty. R.F.A.	12-8-18	Wounded
32898 Egan, Bdr. G.,	26 Bty. R.F.A.	11-5-15	Wounded
			(Dd. of Wds. 12-5-15)
42563 Eke, Gnr. W. D.,	D/17 Bty. R.F.A.	12-8-18	Dd of Wds
97864 Eldridge, a/Bdr. J.,	460 Bty. R.F.A.	23-4-17	Wounded
79921 Eldridge, Gnr. J. L.,	"Y" Bty. R.H.A.	19-6-15	Killed
95649 Elgar, Dvr. A. J.,	"B" Bty. R.H.A.	4-4-17	Wounded
38013 Elliott, Gnr. E.,	HQ. 17 Bde. R.F.A.	2-5-15	Wounded
224404 Elliott, Gnr. H.,	26 Bty. R.F.A.	14-8-17	Wounded
199920 Elliott, Gnr. J.,	460 Bty. R.F.A.	7-10-18	Killed
192919 Elliott, a/Bdr. R.,	X/29 T.M. Bty.	8-3-18	Wounded
48532 Elliott, Gnr. S. J.,	14 S.B. R.G.A.	17-5-15	Killed
745220 Ellis, Dvr. A.,	29 D.A.C.	15-8-17	Wounded
24273 Ellis, Bdr. J.,	26 Bty. R.F.A.	28-6-16	Wounded
50965 Ellis, Farr. Sgt. T. E.,	13 Bty. R.F.A.	12-7-15	Wounded
88319 Ellis, Dvr. W. C.,	"B" Bty. R.H.A.	4-4-17	Wounded
117487 Elswood, Gnr. T.,	29 D.A.C.	18-7-17	Wounded
" " "	460 Bty. R.F.A.	7-10-18	Killed
362244 Elton, Pnr. H. J.(R.E.),	15 Bde. R.H.A.	31-5-18	Wounded
237400 Eltringham, Gnr.W. H.,	460 Bty R.H.A.	4-10-18	Wounded
			Dd of Wds
22436 Elwood, Gnr. W.,	92 Bty. R.F.A.	31-7-17	Wounded (Gas)
61665 Emerson, Dvr. A. V.,	26 Bty. R.F.A.	6-10-17	Wounded
			(Dd. of Wds. 12-10-17)
4955 Emerton, Gnr.W.,	4th H.M.Bde. R.G.A.	19-7-15	Dd of Wds
1305 Emery, Gnr. A.,	4th H.M.Bde. R.G.A.	?-5-15	Wounded
199957 Emery, Gnr. C. S.,	460 Bty. R.F.A.	30-11-17	Wounded
38088 Emery, Gnr. G.,	HQ. 17 Bde. R.F.A.	5-6-15	Wounded
42217 Emms, Gnr. C. F.,	370 Bty. R.F.A.	23-6-16	Wounded
177678 Emsden, Gnr. J.,	29 D.A.C.	11-9-17	Wounded
233003 Ensor, Gnr. T.,	"L" Bty. R.H.A.	24-9-18	Wounded
52736 Enticknap, S/S., W.,	460 Bty. R.F.A.	?-5-15	Wounded
120400 Evans, Dvr E.,	13 Bty. R.F.A.	15-10-18	Wounded
69686 *Evans, Gnr. G. F.,	HQ. 15 Bde. R.H.A.	21-6-15	Wounded
12247 Evans, Dvr. H.,	97 Bty. R.H.A.	16-10-16	Wounded
72425 Evans, Gnr. H.,	29 D.A.C.	5-5-17	Wounded
113005 Evans, Gnr. J.,	92 Bty. R.F.A.	23-4-17	Wounded
5625 Evans, Dvr. J.,	460 Bty. R.F.A.	1-4-18	Wounded
56007 Evans, Dvr. R.,	147 B.A.C.	16-4-15	Drowned
213072 Evans, Gnr. R. J.,	29 D.A.C. (att'd. 460 Bty. R.F.A.)	7-8-17	Wounded
			(Dd. of Wds. 15-8-17)
213679 Evans, Gnr. T. G.,	460 Bty. R.F.A.	4-10-18	Wounded
38116 Evans, Gnr. W.,	10 Bty. R.F.A.	31-8-15	Wounded
27109 Evatt, a/Bdr. W. H.,	460 Bty. R.F.A.	19-8-17	Killed
185337 Everett, Gnr. J. H.,	92 Bty. R.F.A.	21-8-17	Wounded
117204 Everett, Dvr. R.,	"B" Bty. R.H.A.	23-8-17	Wounded
614364 Facer, Gnr. H. A.,	War. Bty. R.H.A.	11-4-17	Killed
56812 Fackney, Gnr. G. W.,	"B" Bty. R.H.A.	12-7-15	Wounded
" a/Bdr. "	V/29 T.M. Bty.	3-9-16	Wounded
3149 Fagg, Gnr. W.,	V/29 T.M. Bty.	5-10-17	Wounded
2374 Fairclough, Gnr. J.,	Z/29 T.M. Bty.	28-2-17	Wounded
(afterwards 680767)			
88082 Fairman, Gnr. J.,	"Y" Bty. R.H.A.	23-10-16	Wounded
129466 Fanson, Dvr. C. J.,	"L" Bty. R.H.A.	1-9-18	Wounded
88082 Farman, Gnr. J.,	"Y" Bty. R.H.A.	10-6-15	Wounded
4732 Farquhar, Gnr. J.,	26 Bty. R.F.A.	29-11-17	Wounded
82366 Farrar, Gnr. W.,	26 Bty. R.F.A.	29-5-17	Wounded
179695 Farrow, Gnr. A. W.,	92 Bty. R.F.A.	27-7-17	Wounded
48534 Farrow, Gnr. J. P.,	"B" Bty. R.H.A.	12-7-15	Killed
115793 Faulkner, Dvr. H.,	29 D.A.C.	22-8-17	Wounded (Gas)
28964 Feare, Sgt. J. H.,	D/132 Bty. R.F.A.	11-8-16	Wounded
92705 Feinstein, Gnr. M.,	D/17 Bty. R.F.A.	{31-3-17 3-5-17	Wounded
213993 Fell, Gnr. J.,	26 Bty. R.F.A.	19-8-17	"
56860 Fellows, Dvr. F.,	"B" Bty. R.H.A.	21-10-17	Wounded
? Fellows, Gnr. H.,	War. Bty. R.H.A.	11-4-17	Wounded
224417 Fennings, Gnr. H. G.,	29 D.A.C.	26-3-18	Killed
192677 Ferguson, Gnr. J.,	92 Bty. R.F.A.	9-10-17	Wounded
55311 Fern, Bdr. W. H.,	"L" Bty. R.H.A.	12-8-17	Wounded

* Changed name to Dixon Clements 28-11-16.

Name & Rank.	Unit.	Date.	Casualty.
48098 Few, Gnr. H.,	13 Bty. R.F.A.	25-12-15	Wounded
604249 Fewtrill, Dvr. G. W.,	460 Bty. R.F.A.	8-10-18	Wounded
			Dd of Wds
801945 Field, Dvr. A. E.,	92 Bty. R.F.A.	19-10-18	Wounded
			(Dd. of Wds. 20-10-18)
4393 Field, Sgt. W.,	3rd Hussars (att'd.	21-5-17	Killed
	13 Bty. R.F.A.)		
681187 Fielden, a/Bdr. S. W.,	26 Bty. R.F.A.	20-7-17	Wounded
30414 Filbey, Gnr. G. N.,	92 Bty. R.F.A.	20-9-17	Wounded
26112 Fillingham, Gnr. W.,	"B" Bty. R.H.A.	1-8-17	Wounded
50169 Finch, a/Ftr. O.,	13 Bty. R.F.A.	1-7-15	Wounded
39372 Findlay, Sgt. A.,	10 Bty. R.F.A.	21-5-17	Killed
22118 Findlay, Gnr. W. J.,	D/17 Bty. R.F.A.	15-10-18	Dd of Wds
178227 Fink, Gnr.W.,	T.M. Bty.	4-5-17	Wounded
42592 Finney, Gnr. J.,	Y/29 T.M. Bty.	18-6-18	Wounded (Gas)
222720 Firth, Gnr. A.,	92 Bty. R.F.A.	3-12-17	Wounded
194832 Firth, Gnr. J. W.,	"L" Bty. R.H.A.	18-8-17	Wounded
68889 Fisher, a/Sgt. B., M.M.,	"B" Bty R.H.A.	9-4-17	Wounded
128947 Fisher, Dvr. F. C.,	"B" Bty. R.H.A.	28-3-18	Wounded (Gas)
192595 Fisher, Gnr. R.,	13 Bty. R.F.A.	31-7-17	Wounded
195067 Fisher, Gnr. W.,	29 D.A.C.	19-9-17	Wounded
53812 Fitch, Gnr. F. S.,	460 Bty. R.F.A.	{ 6-6-15	Wounded
		27-6-16	"
50496 Fitzgerald, Gnr. C. F.,	"Y" Bty R.H.A.	25-6-15	Wounded
614049 Fitzgerald, Gnr. P.,	War. Bty. R.H.A.	5-5-17	Killed
72795 Fitzmaurice, Gnr. S.,	460 Bty. R.F.A.	7-7-15	Wounded
44927 Fitzpatrick, Bdr. E.,	26 Bty. R.F.A.	31-12-15	Wounded
159394 Fitzpatrick, Dvr. F. A.,	29 D.A.C.	19-9-17	Wounded
91963 Fitzpatrick, Dvr. J.,	10 Bty. R.F.A.	13-5-15	Wounded
91563 Fitzpatrick, Dvr. P.,	10 Bty. R.F.A.	?-5-15	Wounded
L/33431 Flanagan, Gnr. J.,	26 Bty. R.F.A.	30-7-17	Wounded (Gas)
L/12294 Flanagan, Gnr. L.,	92 Bty. R.F.A.	1-12-17	Wounded
179761 Flatt, Gnr. A. G.,	92 Bty. R.F.A.	24-7-17	Wounded (Gas)
52316 Fletcher, Gnr. C. W.,	"B" Bty. R.F.A.	{ 20-7-15	Wounded
		9-4-17	"
116797 Fletcher, L/Bdr. W.,	26 Bty. R.F.A.	6-10-18	Wounded
110793 Fluck, Gnr. A. S., HQ.	17 Bde. R.F.A.	23-6-16	Killed
36252 Flynn, Gnr. J.,	26 Bty. R.F.A.	18-8-17	Wounded
43857 Foley, Gnr. D. J.,	"B" Bty. R.H.A.	{ 16-5-15	Wounded
		13-7-15	"
47492 Folly, Gnr. F. T.,	14 S.B. R.G.A.	?-7-15	Wounded
38102 Foot, Gnr. R. C.,	26 Bty. R.F.A.	4-6-15	Wounded
614240 Forbes, Gnr. G. E.,	D/17 Bty. R.F.A.	17-7-18	Wounded
128846 Ford, Gnr. J. S.,	"B" Bty. R.H.A.	{ 27-5-17	Wounded
		3-2-18	"
408 Ford, Ftr/Cpl. N. F.,	"B" Bty. R.H.A.	30-11-17	Missing
			(P. of W.)
44519 Fordham, Gnr. C.,	26 Bty. R.F.A.	28-9-17	Wounded
640239 Forson, Dvr. A.,	92 D.A.C.	30-11-17	Wounded
4784 Forster, a/Bdr. R.,	B/132 Bty. R.F.A.	30-4-16	Wounded
53575 Fossett, Gnr. W.,	90 H.B. R.G.A.	7-8-15	Wounded
139579 Foster, Gnr. T.,	D/17 Bty. R.F.A.	19-5-17	Wounded
82138 Fowle, Gnr. S. H.,	92 Bty. R.F.A.	15-2-17	Wounded
200225 Fowler, Gnr. A. E.,	29 D.A.C.	27-5-17	Killed
194861 Fowler, Gnr. C.,	"L" Bty. R.H.A.	19-8-17	Wounded
4410 Fox, Dvr. G.,	"Y" Bty. R.H.A.	31-8-15	Wounded
179091 Fox, Gnr. H. E.,	92 Bty. R.H.A.	20-9-17	Killed
222770 Fox, Gnr. W.,	13 Bty. R.F.A.	10-10-17	Wounded
193938 Foylan, Gnr. J.,	92 Bty. R.F.A.	2-12-17	Dd of Wds
2648 Frailing, Gnr. J.,	HQ. 29 D.A.	30-11-17	Wounded
90178 France, Gnr. C.,	460 Bty. R.F.A.	7-10-15	Wounded
" Cpl.	92 Bty. R.F.A.	8-10-17	Wounded
51314 France, Cpl. F. L.,	"L" Bty. R.H.A.	15-6-17	Wounded
32516 France, Dvr. G. E.,	460 Bty. R.F.A.	23-10-17	Wounded
			(Dd of Wds 26-10-17)
6109 Francey, Cpl. J.,	460 Bty. R.F.A.	23-10-17	Wounded
W/2591 Francis, Gnr. E.,	13 Bty. R.F.A.	28-9-18	Wounded
206063 Francis, Gnr. J. H.,	"B" Bty. R.H.A.	17-8-17	Wounded (Gas)
L/17086 Frankland, Gnr. W.,	460 Bty. R.F.A.	2-10-17	Wounded
79560 Franklin, Gnr. A.,	"L" Bty. R.H.A.	5-4-17	Wounded
614048 Franklin, Cpl. F.W., War. Bty. R.H.A.		23-4-17	Wounded
" Sgt.	"	28-3-18	" (Gas)
87494 Franklin, Gnr. H.,	D/17 Bty. R.F.A.	19-9-17	Wounded
" " "	"B" Bty. R.H.A.	25-9-17	" (Gas)

Name & Rank.	Unit.	Date.	Casualty.
97121 Fraser, Gnr. A.,	26 Bty. R.F.A.	23-7-17	Wounded (Gas)
192581 Fraser, Gnr. D.,	92 Bty. R.F.A.	2-12-17	Wounded
192577 Fraser, Gnr. J.,	26 Bty. R.F.A.	4-5-17	Killed
195014 Fraser, Gnr. J.,	"B" Bty. R.H.A.	2-12-17	Wounded
29808 Fraser, Tptr. J.,	"Y" Bty. R.H.A.	13-8-16	Wounded
83464 Freeman, Cpl. A.,	460 Bty. R.F.A.	24-4-17	Wounded (Gas)
148672 Freeman, Gnr. H. G.,	D/17 Bty. R.F.A.	17-4-17	Wounded
558205 French, Dvr. S. A. (R.E.),	HQ. 29 D.A.	29-9-18	Wounded
59000 Freshwater, Gnr. W.,	368 Bty. R.F.A.	27-7-16	Wounded
14651 Fricker, Cpl. A.,	X/29 T.M. Bty.	17-7-16	Killed
223959 Friend, Gnr. H. W.,	"B" Bty. R.H.A.	8-5-18	Wounded
19530 Fritter, Sgt. W.,	26 Bty. R.F.A.	4-8-17	Wounded
2742 Froud, Sgt. A. G.,	92 Bty. R.F.A.	{21-5-15	Wounded
		13-10-15	„
51002 Froude, Sgt. W. F.,	97 Bty. R.F.A.	{24-5-15	Wounded
		7-8-15	„
179797 Fuller, Gnr. C. R.,	29 D.A.C.	7-9-17	Killed
640197 Fulton, Gnr. S.,	460 Bty. R.F.A.	20-10-17	Wounded
			Dd of Wds
162378 Furnham, Gnr. F.,	D/17 Bty. R.F.A.	28-4-18	Wounded
189232 Gadd, Dvr. E.,	26 Bty. R.F.A.	14-8-17	Wounded
169330 Gadsby, Gnr. W.,	D/17 Bty. R.F.A.	31-3-17	Wounded
770372 Gaffing, Dvr. D.,	D/17 Bty. R.F.A.	14-10-17	Killed
45873 Gage, Cpl. H.,	26 Bty. R.F.A.	24-4-17	Wounded
6791 Gallacher, Bdr. W.,	13 Bty. R.F.A.	15-10-18	Wounded
140318 Gannon, Gnr. A.,	"L" Bty. R.H.A.	2-11-16	Wounded
83093 Garbutt, Gnr. G. S.,	26 Bty. R.F.A.	16-10-18	Wounded
112335 Gardiner, Gnr. H.,	460 Bty. R.F.A.	28-3-18	Wounded (Gas)
181729 Gardiner, Dvr. O.,	HQ. 15 Bde. R.H.A.	31-5-18	Wounded
78041 Gardner, Dvr. A. G.,	92 Bty. R.F.A.	18-6-15	Wounded
38081 Gardner, Gnr. A. W.,	92 Bty. R.F.A.	10-5-15	Wounded
„ „ Sgt.		20-9-17	Killed
170173 Gardner, Gnr. G.,	D/17 Bty. R.F.A.	4-5-17	Wounded
Gatsford, Gnr.,	"B" Bty. R.H.A.	25-4-17	Killed
30745 Gaudion, Dvr. L.,	10 Bty. R.F.A.	18-9-15	Wounded
55550 Gauntlett, a/Bdr. W.,	"B" Bty. R.H.A.	27-5-17	Wounded
49051 Gaylor, Gnr. C.,	97 Bty. R.F.A.	{6-8-15	Wounded
		14-9-15	Killed
128677 Geach, Gnr. P.,	"B" Bty. R.H.A.	27-5-17	Wounded
636 Geary, Dvr. D.,	29 D.A.C.	24-11-16	Dd of Wds
32686 Gelder, Dvr. G. W.,	"Y" Bty. R.H.A.	2-7-16	Wounded
942 Gemmell, Sgt. R.,	460 Bty. R.F.A.	24-7-17	Wounded (Gas)
614414 Gerrish, Gnr. W.,	HQ. 17 Bde. R.F.A.	4-6-18	Wounded
			Dd of Wds
63149 Gheras, Gnr. R.,	"Y" Bty. R.H.A.	{7-8-15	Wounded
		13-8-15	„
87941 Gibbon, Cpl. J.,	15 B.A.C.	16-7-15	Wounded
845223 Gibbs, a/Bdr. G.,	13 Bty. R.F.A.	18-4-17	Wounded
66637 Gibbs, Gnr. G. T.,	"B" Bty. R.H.A.	26-1-17	Wounded
49201 Giblin, Gnr. T.,	90 H.B. R.G.A.	13-7-15	Killed
40635 Gibson, Gnr. A.,	10 Bty. R.F.A.	6-11-16	Dd of Wds
L/1614 Gibson, Gnr. W. O.,	460 Bty. R.F.A.	24-4-17	Wounded (Gas)
82749 Gight, Gnr. W.,	92 Bty. R.F.A.	5-7-15	Wounded
181064 Gilbert, Gnr. F. W.,	92 Bty. R.F.A.	31-7-17	Wounded
? Gilchrist, Gnr. J.,	26 Bty. R.F.A.	21-5-15	Wounded
12976 Gill, Bdr. J.,	D/17 Bty. R.F.A.	5-4-17	Killed
43944 Gill, Gnr. S.,	"L" Bty. R.H.A.	16-11-16	Wounded
116040 Gillespie, a/Bdr. R.,	92 Bty. R.F.A.	11-10-17	Wounded
169330 Gladsby, Gnr. W.,	D/17 Bty. R.F.A.	31-3-17	Wounded
27814 Gladstone, Bdr. P.,	D/147 Bty. R.F.A.	24-8-16	Wounded
195018 Glass, Gnr. J.,	"L" Bty. R.H.A.	22-7-17	Wounded (Gas)
47232 Glaysher, Ftr. W. F., M.M.,	10 Bty. R.F.A.	{28-6-15	Wounded
		21-9-15	„
49503 Glover, Far/Sgt. W.,	13 Bty. R.F.A.	15-10-18	Wounded
12194 Glumbley, Dvr. J.,	147 B.A.C.	3-6-15	Wounded
2778 Goatley, Ftr. E.,	92 Bty. R.F.A.	6-4-18	Wounded
50331 Goddard, Gnr. F.,	14 S.B. R.G.A.	7-1-16	Wounded
51887 Goddard, a/Cpl. H.,	10 Bty. R.F.A.	25-9-15	Wounded
622532 Godfrey, Dvr. W.,	HQ. 15 Bde. R.H.A.	7-10-18	Killed
102961 Godwin, Gnr. C.,	"L" Bty. R.H.A.	30-9-18	Wounded
88169 Goldie, Gnr. W.,	"L" Bty. R.H.A.	22-7-17	Wounded (Gas)
176580 Goldspink, Gnr. A.,	460 Bty. R.F.A.	30-7-17	Wounded (Gas)
53290 Golledge, Dvr. J.,	460 Bty. R.F.A.	2-5-15	Wounded
54992 Good, a/Bdr. E.,	92 Bty. R.F.A.	6-6-15	Wounded
97394 Goode, Cpl. A.,	13 Bty. R.F.A.	23-7-17	Wounded

Name & Rank.		Unit.	Date.	Casualty.
72449	Gooding, Gnr. H. H.,	460 Bty. R.F.A.	{ 7-5-15 { 12-7-16	Wounded Wounded (Dd of Wds 14-7-16)
93933	Goodman, Gnr. A. E.,	26 Bty. R.F.A.	3-10-15	Killed
614488	Goodman, Gnr. A. T.,	War. Bty. R.H.A.	30-8-17	Killed
614448	Goodman, Gnr. E. L.	War. Bty. R.H.A.	22-7-17	Wounded
71542	Goodwin, Gnr. A.,	B/132 Bty. R.F.A.	3-6-16	Wounded
65548	Goodwin, Gnr. H.,	D/17 Bty. R.F.A.	27-6-17	Wounded (Dd of Wds 28-7-17)
85570	Goodwin, Dvr. R.,	10 Bty. R.F.A.	3-9-16	Wounded (Gas)
79128	Goodwin, Dvr. R.,	"L" Bty. R.H.A.	7-9-18	Wounded (Gas)
2416	Goodwin, Gnr. T.,	13 Bty. R.F.A.	16-4-17	Dd of Wds
80989	Goodwright, Gnr. S.,	460 Bty. R.F.A.	{ 9-7-15 { 27-6-16	Wounded "
65827	Goold, a/Bdr. H. E.,	"L" Bty. R.H.A.	2-5-15	Wounded
650131	Gordon, Dvr. B.,	26 Bty. R.F.A.	5-10-17	Killed
53629	Gore, Gnr. T.,	92 Bty. R.F.A.	22-8-17	Wounded (Gas)
212461	Gouge, Gnr. W. H. G.,	460 Bty. R.F.A.	20-9-17	Killed
4972	Gough, Dvr. D.,	D/17 Bty. R.F.A.	23-3-18	Wounded
61279	Gough, Bdr. W. F. H.,	"Y" Bty. R.H.A.	8-8-15	Wounded
88303	Gould, Dvr. A.,	"L" Bty. R.H.A.	{ 22-4-17 { 1-8-17	Wounded "
	Grady, Dvr.,	368 Bty. R.F.A.	8-6-15	Wounded
46876	Grainger, Gnr. J.,	10 Bty. R.F.A.	28-7-15	Wounded
84178	Gralton, Gnr. P.,	Z/29 T.M. Bty.	20-7-17	Wounded
73536	Granby, Dvr. A.,	13 Bty. R.F.A.	28-9-18	Wounded
10019	Granados, B.Q.M.S., F. A.,	368 Bty. R.F.A.	6-6-15	Wounded
253216	Grant, Dvr. F. J.,	26 Bty. R.F.A.	28-9-18	Wounded
57564	Grantham, a/Bdr. W. G.,	D/147 Bty. R.F.A.	9-8-16	Wounded
27670	Grantham, Sgt. W. J.,	17 B.A.C.	26-4-16	Wounded
65161	Gratton, Gnr. G.,	26 Bty. R.F.A.	{ 11-8-17 { 31-10-17	Wounded "
92227	Graves, Bdr. J.,	92 Bty. R.F.A.	19-12-15	Wounded
65721	Graves, Gnr. J.,	V/29 T.M. Bty.	14-9-17	Wounded (Gas)
15304	Gravett, Gnr. W. C.,	"L" Bty. R.H.A.	{ 6-6-15 { 12-7-15	Wounded "
162797	Gray, Gnr. E. A.,	460 Bty. R.F.A.	27-1-18	Wounded
64371	Gray, Gnr. F.,	10 Bty. R.F.A.	6-6-15	Killed
71730	Gray, Dvr. H. D.,	13 Bty. R.F.A.	3-3-17	Wounded
92142	Greatrix, Gnr. W.,	10 Bty. R.F.A.	5-7-16	Wounded
26162	Greaves, Gnr. T.,	29 D.A.C.	11-7-15	Killed
87719	Green, Gnr. A.,	"L" Bty. R.H.A.	23-5-18	Wounded (Gas)
29816	Green, Bdr. G. N.,	"B" Bty. R.H.A.	18-10-16	Wounded
51029	Green, Tptr. J.,	HQ. 17 Bde. R.F.A.	31-7-17	Wounded
178080	Greenaway, Dvr. G.,	29 D.A.C.	8-10-17	Wounded
43552	Greengrass, a/Sgt. J. T.,	"L" Bty. R.H.A.	2-10-15	Wounded
88307	Greenhalgh, Dvr. A.,	"L" Bty. R.H.A.	6-8-17	Wounded
47785	Greenway, Dvr. H. C. H.,	92 Bty. R.F.A.	10-10-17	Wounded
4079	Greenwood, Cpl. A.,	460 Bty. R.F.A.	27-5-17	Wounded
116066	Greenwood, Dvr. J.,	29 D.A.C.	31-5-18	Wounded
38080	Greenwood, Gnr. J. A.,	92 Bty. R.F.A.	18-6-15	Wounded
128795	Greep, Gnr. W. J.,	"B" Bty. R.H.A.	17-8-17	Wounded
88630	Gregg, a/Bdr. F.,	"L" Bty. R.H.A.	9-4-17	Wounded
24918	Gregory, Cpl. G.,	"B" Bty. R.H.A.	{ 3-5-17 { 7-6-17	Wounded "
189123	a/Sgt. Gregory, Dvr. J.,	13 Bty. R.F.A.	25-9-17	Wounded
801835	Gregory, Dvr. J. C.,	26 Bty. R.F.A.	6-12-17	Wounded
44535	Griffen, Gnr. J.,	26 Bty. R.F.A.	8-6-17	Wounded
610	Griffiths, Bdr. J.,	29 D.A.C.	23-11-16	Killed
13438	Griffiths, Gnr. O.,	13 Bty. R.F.A.	20-3-18	Wounded
195021	Griffiths, Gnr. W.,	"L" Bty. R.H.A.	22-7-17	Wounded (Gas)
745125	Griffiths, Bdr. W. G.,	X/29 T.M. Bty. (att'd 13 Bty. R.F.A.)	21-10-18	Wounded
616869	Grigsby, Gnr. W. T.,	460 Bty. R.F.A.	15-10-17	Killed
47493	Grimwood, Gnr. W. R.,	14 S.B. R.G.A.	?-7-15	Wounded
51650	Griswood, Bdr. T.,	"B" Bty. R.H.A.	30-11-17	Wounded and Missing (P. of W.)
614361	Grose, Cpl. H.,	War. Bty. R.H.A.	3-12-17	Wounded (Gas)
72976	Grover, a/Bdr. A.,	HQ. 17 Bde. R.F.A.	23-8-16	Wounded
970391	Grover, Dvr. S. J.,	460 Bty. R.F.A.	7-10-18	Wounded

Name & Rank.		Unit.	Date.	Casualty.
38086	Groves, Gnr. J. G.,	13 Bty. R.F.A.	{ 3-8-17 { 23-10-17	Wounded ,,
614288	Groves, Dvr. W.,	War. Bty. R.H.A.	13-5-18	Wounded (Gas)
790044	Grunwell, Bdr. W.,	460 Bty. R.F.A.	9-10-17	Wounded (Dd of Wds 12-10-17)
17080	Gunn, Gnr. F.,	92 Bty. R.F.A.	12-8-17	Wounded
110010	Guy, Dvr. B.,	13 Bty. R.F.A.	21-10-18	Wounded
25731	Gwilym, Dvr. D.,	29 D.A.C.	1-12-17	Wounded
161097	Hackett, Dvr. G.,	29 D.A.C.	25-9-17	Wounded
751388	Hadaway, Gnr. E.,	460 Bty. R.F.A.	22-8-17	Wounded (Gas)
181035	Hadden, Gnr. W. W.,	13 Bty. R.F.A.	{ 20-9-17 { 22-10-17	Wounded ,,
206556	Haffield, Gnr. L. R.,	29 D.A.C.	25-9-17	Wounded
62047	Haggerty, Dvr. A.,	"L" Bty. R.H.A	21-10-16	Wounded
73583	Hainsworth, Gnr. H.,	26 Bty. R.F.A.	18-4-17	Dd of Wds
614368	Hake, Gnr. F..	War. Bty. R.H.A.	30-11-17	Wounded (Gas)
37292	Hale, Sgt. A.,	26 Bty. R.F.A.	6-12-17	Wounded
62568	Hall, Gnr. B.,	460 Bty. R.F.A.	17-8-16	Wounded
40094	Hall, Gnr. C.,	92 Bty. R.F.A.	23-4-17	Wounded
237154	Hall, Gnr. E. G.,	26 Bty. R.F.A.	18-10-18	Wounded
71954	Hall, Gnr. F. G.,	"L" Bty. R.H.A.	{ 11-5-15 { ?-11-15	Wounded ,,
614056	Hall, Gnr. F. W.,	War. Bty. R.H.A.	9-4-17	Wounded
177011	Hall, Gnr. G.,	War. Bty. R.H.A.	15-7-17	Wounded
51844	Hall, Ftr. S/Sgt. J.,	"Y" Bty. R.H.A.	22-5-15	Wounded
49201	Hall, Gnr. S., ,, Bdr.	"B" Bty. R.H.A.	9-5-15 2-4-17	Wounded ,,
L/34440	Hall, Gnr. W.,	"Y" Bty. R.H.A.	24-10-16	Killed
558252	Hall, Spr. W. G. (R.E.),	15 Bde. R.H.A.	6-10-18	Wounded
32501	Hall, Gnr. W. H.,	D/147 Bty. R.F.A.	3-5-17	,,
	,, ,,	D/17 Bty. R.F.A.	3-9-16	Wounded
L/39936	Hallatt, Bdr. A.,	"Y" Bty. R.H.A.	24-10-16	Wounded
61526	Hallett, Gnr. H. R.,	"B" Bty. R.H.A.	3-5-17	Dd of Wds
45743	Halliday, Gnr. E.,	13 Bty. R.F.A.	19-4-17	Killed
38101	Hambley, Sgt. P., D.C.M.,	26 Bty. R.F.A.	9-7-16	Wounded
7636	Hambling, Dvr. J.,	92 Bty. R.F.A.	18-6-15	Wounded (Dd of Wds 19-6-15)
174322	Hamer, Gnr. E.,	D/17 Bty. R.F.A.	26-6-18	Wounded
326	Hamilton, Gnr. J.,	4th H.M.Bde. R.G.A.	29-6-15	Killed
102432 (afterwards 253209,	Hammerman, Dvr. H., R.E.),	HQ. 15 Bde. R.H.A.	{ 25-4-17 { 5-9-18	Wounded ,,
614100	Hammond, Bdr. A.,	War. Bty. R.H.A.	8-10-18	Wounded
128898	Hammond, Gnr. H. S.,	"L" Bty. R.H.A.	3-5-17	Wounded
895446	Hammond, Gnr. R. A.,	26 Bty. R.F.A.	28-9-18	Wounded
51719	Hammond, Sgt. T.,	"B" Bty. R.H.A.	23-4-17	Wounded
351	Hammond, Gnr. W. H.,	S/29 T.M. Bty.	28-6-16	Wounded
196596	Handley, Gnr. H.,	War. Bty. R.H.A.	23-4-17	Wounded
14605	Hankin, Gnr. J.,	13 Bty. R.F.A.	16-4-17	Dd of Wds
2814	Hanlon, Cpl. W.,	Y/29 T.M. Bty.	15-6-18	Killed
57135	Hannabus, Cpl. C. H.,	10 Bty. R.F.A.	4-2-15	Killed
102490	Hansell, Dvr. J. D.,	"Y" Bty. R.H.A.	23-10-16	Wounded (Dd of Wds 23-10-16)
91530	Hanson, Dvr. W.,	13 Bty. R.F.A.	{ 21-5-15 { 28-9-18	Wounded ,,
244992	Hanson, Gnr. W. H.,	92 Bty. R.F.A.	20-4-18	Wounded
48034	Hansted, Gnr. W.,	147 Bde. R.F.A.	1-11-16	Wounded
82724	Harbourne, Gnr. S. R.,	26 Bty. R.F.A.	18-6-15	Wounded
711803	Hardiman, Dvr. M.,	X/29 T.M. Bty.	9-6-18	Wounded
86182	Harding, Dvr. W.,	368 Bty. R.F.A.	16-4-15	Drowned
11444	Hardingham, Gnr. S.,	HQ. 17 Bde. R.F.A.	9-4-17	Killed
72469	Hardley, Gnr. W.,	26 Bty. R.F.A.	6-8-15	Wounded
86688	Hardy, Bdr. A. J., M.M.,	Z/29 T.M. Bty.	13-7-17	Wounded
75051	Hardy, Gnr. W.,	17 B.A.C.	?-5-15	Wounded
77351	Harman, Gnr. J.,	10 Bty. R.F.A.	15-10-16	Killed
103415	Harmes, Bdr. J.,	D/17 Bty. R.F.A.	22-9-17	Wounded
52859	Harper, Gnr. A.,	"L" Bty. R.H.A.	25-3-18	Killed
32797	Harper, Gnr. T. H.,	29 D.A.C.	?-12-15	Wounded
51540	Harris, Gnr. A. F.,	90 H.B. R.G.A.	7-8-15	Killed
93767	Harris, Gnr. A. J.,	460 Bty. R.F.A.	7-12-15	Wounded
62730	Harris, Dvr. C. E.,	92 Bty. R.F.A.	21-6-15	Wounded
1297	Harris, Gnr. G. F.,	14 S.B. R.G.A.	21-6-15	Wounded
38100	Harris, Gnr. H.,	26 Bty. R.F.A.	10-6-15	Wounded
830263	Harris, Gnr. J. W.,	92 Bty. R.F.A.	19-10-17	Wounded

Name & Rank.		Unit.	Date.	Casualty.
8084	Harris, Dvr. W.,	460 Bty. R.F.A.	{ 2-5-15 { 2-7-15	Wounded "
63162	Harrison, Dvr. J.,	"Y" Bty. R.H.A.	9-8-16	Wounded
78453	Harrison, Cpl. S. J.,	26 Bty. R.F.A.	27-4-17	Killed
47051	Harrop, Dvr. L. W.,	29 D.A.C.	19-9-17	Wounded
L/34350	Harrop, S/S. R.,	26 Bty. R.F.A.	11-4-17	Dd of Wds
831390	Hart, Dvr. A.,	92 Bty. R.F.A.	30-9-18	Wounded
78560	Hart, Gnr. W., M.M.,	"L" Bty. R.H.A.	10-2-17	Wounded
20916	Hartley, Sgt. E. J.,	92 Bty. R.F.A.	7-8-15	Dd of Wds
26759	Hartshore, Cpl. H.,	"L" Bty. R.H.A.	4-9-18	Wounded
195065	Harvey, Gnr. E.,	"L" Bty. R.H.A.	30-11-17	Wounded (Dd of Wds 2-12-17)
43955	Harvey, Gnr. E.,	90 H.B. R.G.A.	17-11-15	Wounded
21648	Harvey, Gnr. H.,	17 B.A.C.	26-6-15	Wounded
588009	Harvey, Sgt. W. (R.E.),	HQ. 29 D.A.	21-8-17	Killed
52759	Harwood, Gnr. A.,	460 Bty. R.F.A.	27-5-15	Wounded (Dd of Wds 30-5-15)
48533	Hatch, Dvr. F. J.,	"B" Bty. R.H.A.	5-6-15	Wounded Dd of Wds
35255	Hattemore, Cpl. F.,	HQ. 15 Bde. R.H.A.	27-5-15	Wounded
"	" Sgt.	"L" Bty. R.H.A.	24-4-17	Killed
56903	Hatton, Cpl. A.,	HQ. 17 Bde. R.F.A.	7-5-15	Wounded
206068	Hawkes, Gnr. A.,	460 Bty. R.F.A.	7-8-17	Wounded
71462	Hawkins, Gnr. A.,	"B" Bty. R.H.A.	27-9-18	Wounded (Gas)
91183	Haycock, Gnr. A.,	B/132 Bty. R.F.A.	30-4-16	Wounded
137874	Hayes, Dvr. M.,	29 D.A.C.	13-7-17	Wounded
L/8624	Hayes, Gnr. T.,	92 Bty. R.F.A.	26-4-18	Dd of Wds
17234	Hayter, Sgt. S. J.,	90 H.B. R.G.A.	7-8-15	Wounded
55194	Hayward, Dvr. W., HQ. 15 Bde. R.H.A.		30-11-17	Missing (P. of W.)
26	Head, Cpl. F. W. J.,	460 Bty. R.F.A.	17-8-16	Wounded
216767	Healey, Gnr. (a/Cpl.) H.,	29 D.A.C.	6-12-17	Dd of Wds
196571	Heard, Gnr. A. E.,	War. Bty. R.H.A.	25-7-17	Wounded (Gas)
92379	Heath, Bdr. F. A.	460 Bty. R.F.A.	30-11-17	Wounded
52554 ?	Hedges, Bdr. W.,	"L" Bty. R.H.A.	11-8-17	Wounded
149893	Hedley, Gnr. G.,	D/17 Bty. R.F.A.	27-4-18	Wounded
78800	Heilbron, a/Bdr. V.,	"B" Bty. R.H.A.	26-4-17	Wounded (Dd of Wds 27-4-17)
419	Helme, Gnr. J.,	S/29 T.M. Bty.	28-6-16	Killed
153872	Hely, Gnr. W. N.,	"B" Bty. R.H.A.	26-4-17	Wounded
26085	Hemmingway, Dvr..W.,	D/17 Bty. R.F.A.	21-7-17	Wounded
59629	Henderson, Dvr. A.,	"B" Bty. R.H.A.	3-10-18	Wounded
59482	Henderson, Dvr. W.,	15 B.A.C.	?-5-15	Wounded
614469	Henn, Dvr. A.,	War. Bty. R.H.A	10-11-18	Wounded
91351	Hennell, B.S.M., J.,	"B" Bty. R.H.A.	13-4-17	Wounded
45660	Hennery, Gnr. W. T.,	90 H.B. R.G.A.	12-7-15	Wounded
7058	Heron, Ftr. J. A.,	D/17 Bty. R.F.A.	22-10-16	Killed
940475	Heryet, Gnr. R. G.,	92 Bty. R.F.A.	23-4-18	Wounded (Gas)
859	Heryet, Cpl. W. A.,	29 D.A.C.	20-6-15	Wounded
31265	Hetherington, Gnr. W.,	13 Bty. R.F.A.	30-9-18	Wounded
153880	Hewins, Gnr. H. J.,	"L" Bty. R.H.A.	16-5-17	Wounded
26536	Hewitt, Sgt. H.,	D/17 Bty. R.F.A.	5-4-17	Wounded
876143	Hewitt, Gnr. J. B.,	460 Bty. R.F.A.	14-10-18	Wounded
108356	Hewitt, L/Bdr. W. B.,	"L" Bty. R.H.A.	30-6-18	Wounded
67654	Heyes, Gnr. W. R.,	13 Bty. R.F.A.	6-11-16	Killed
77262	Hibberd, a/Bdr. J.,	"B" Bty. R.H.A.	20-9-17	Wounded
79925	Hickson, Gnr. J. E.,	"L" Bty. R.H.A.	12-8-17	Wounded (Dd of Wds 12-8-17)
53530	Higgins, Cpl. S.,	"L" Bty. R.H.A.	2-5-17	Killed
140079	Higgins, Gnr. W. M.,	"L" Bty. R.H.A.	30-5-17	Killed
24592	Higham, a/Bdr. A.,	D/132 Bty. R.F.A.	19-8-16	Killed
86182	Higham, Dvr. J.,	368 Bty. R.F.A.	16-4-15	Drowned
19799	Hill, Gnr. F. J.,	92 Bty. R.F.A.	14-6-15	Wounded
90717	Hill, a/Bdr. J.,	10 Bty. R.F.A.	22-12-15	Killed (acc. by landslide)
23196	Hill, a/Bdr. N.,	26 Bty. R.F.A.	18-4-17	Killed
194848	Hill, Gnr. R. H.,	"L" Bty. R.H.A.	14-3-18	Wounded
L/44290	Hill, Sgt. R. W., D.C.M.,	92 Bty. R.F.A.	6-10-18	Wounded
614054	Hill, Bdr. T. J.,	War. Bty. R.H.A.	{ 15-7-17 { 30-8-17	Wounded Killed
24100	Hill, Gnr. W.,	368 Bty. R.F.A.	13-5-15	Wounded
41474	Hill, Gnr. W.,	"Y" Bty. R.H.A.	23-9-16	Wounded (Gas)

Name & Rank.		Unit.	Date.	Casualty.
48927	Hillier, Gnr. R. G. W.,	368 Bty. R.F.A.	14-5-15	Killed
50590	Hills, Gnr. F. C.,	29 D.A.C.	18-7-17	Wounded
67000	Hinchcliffe, a/Sgt. J.,	26 Bty. R.F.A.	12-4-17	Killed
50698	Hindle, Gnr. F.,	97 Bty. R.F.A.	5-7-15	Wounded
50151	Hirschfield, Gnr. E.,	26 Bty. R.F.A.	{ 6-8-15	Wounded
			25-5-17	,,
8666	Hitchin, Gnr. G.,	460 Bty. R.F.A.	7-8-17	Wounded
207608	Hobbs, Gnr. H. J.,	D/17 Bty. R.F.A.	11-8-17	Wounded
128823	Hobdell, Dvr. F. J., M.M.,	"B" Bty. R.H.A.	8-5-18	Wounded
?	Hobley, Sgt.,	War. Bty. R.H.A.	9-4-17	Wounded
38682	Hodges, Bdr. F.,	14 S.B. R.G.A.	6-5-15	Wounded
74756	Hodges, Ftr. F. J.,	"Y" Bty. R.H.A.	25-10-16	Wounded
614320	Hodgkins, Gnr. W.,	War. Bty. R.H.A.	{ 11-4-17	Wounded
			14-4-17	,,
96392	Hodgkinson, Gnr. J.,	460 Bty. R.F.A.	3-10-17	Wounded
85054	Hodgson, Gnr. W.,	10 Bty. R.F.A.	4-12-16	Wounded
				(Dd of Wds 7-12-16)
47316	Hodgson, Bdr. W.,	92 Bty. R.F.A.	17-10-17	Wounded
134435	Holbrook, Gnr. E.,	369 Bty. R.F.A.	19-6-16	Wounded
70706	Holden, Dvr. A.,	29 D.A.C.	8-10-17	Wounded
34872	Holden, Gnr. F. C.,	29 D.A.C.	5-12-17	Dd of Wds
177227	Holden, Dvr. H.,	"B" Bty. R.H.A.	15-10-17	Wounded
				(Dd of Wds 8-11-17)
36242	Holden, Gnr. R.,	90 H.B. R.G.A.	28-5-15	Killed
10601	Holdsworth, Bdr.W.,	D/147 Bty. R.F.A.	20-10-16	Wounded
83528	Holland, Dvr. C.,	147 B.A.C.	23-8-15	Wounded
4846	Holland, Gnr. F.,	D/147 Bty. R.F.A.	9-8-16	Wounded
3102	Holland. Gnr. S.,	D/17 Bty. R.F.A.	2-4-18	Wounded (Gas)
50682	Hollands, Sgt. F.,	10 Bty. R.F.A.	13-8-16	Wounded
43691	Hollick, Gnr. P. W.,	14 S.B. R.G.A.	20-6-15	Killed
163607	Hollingdale, Gnr. S. T.,	26 Bty. R.F.A.	30-11-17	Wounded
79857	Hollyoak, Dvr. A.,	"B" Bty. R.H.A.	16-11-16	Wounded
65981	Holloway, Gnr. J.,	"Y" Bty. R.H.A.	22-10-16	Wounded
49937	Holman, Gnr. A. C.,	"L" Bty. R.H.A.	22-7-17	Wounded (Gas)
33568	Holmes, Cpl. A. C.,	13 Bty. R.F.A.	21-10-17	Wounded
				(Dd-of-Wds 31-10-17)
26020	Holmes, Cpl. G.,	90 H. B. R.G.A.	28-5-15	Killed
48138	Holmes, Dvr. J.,	29 D.A.C.	20-10-17	Wounded
48218	Holroyd, Bdr. W.,	13 Bty. R.F.A.	2-9-17	Killed
76760	Holt, Gnr. J.,	10 Bty. R.F.A.	16-12-15	Wounded
126647	Holyoak, Gnr. E. T.,	HQ. 15 Bde. R.H.A.	30-11-17	Wounded
87127	Honeybun, Dvr. T.,	460 Bty. R.F.A.	7-10-18	Wounded
246006	Hooper, Gnr. E.,	War. Bty. R.H.A.	14-10-18	Wounded
38635	Hopgood, Dvr. J.,	10 Bty. R.F.A.	26-5-15	Wounded
3363	Hopkins, Gnr. F.,	V/29 T.M. Bty.	{ 4-4-17	Wounded
			11-9-17	Wounded (Gas)
97578	Hopkins, Gnr. O. R.,	X/29 T. M. Bty.	6-6-18	Wounded
35166	Hopkinson, Gnr. C.,	10 Bty. R.F.A.	20-10-16	Wounded
86573	Hopper, Dvr. S. A.,	13 Bty. R.F.A.	24-10-16	Killed
215396	Hopwood, Gnr. J. K.,	29 D.A.C.	22-5-18	Wounded
1210	Hornbuckle, Gnr. J.,	13 Bty. R.F.A.	4-5-17	Wounded
845905	Horobin, Dvr. G. V.,	29 Bty. R.F.A.	23-9-17	Wounded
				(Dd 30-9-17)
216543	Horton, Gnr. W. G.,	"B" Bty. R.H.A.	29-4-18	Killed
614137	Hoswell, Sgt. T. A.,	War. Bty. R.H.A.	3-5-17	Wounded (Gas)
614127	Hotchin, Cpl. J. G.,	War. Bty. R.H.A.	25-7-17	Killed
51083	Houghton, Gnr. D. W.,	97 Bty. R.F.A.	3-12-15	Wounded
27477	Howard, Gnr. B. W.,	90 H.B. R.G.A.	7-10-15	Wounded
12023	Howard, Gnr. S.,	13 Bty. R.F.A.	16-5-15	Wounded
29843	Howarth, Gnr. S.,	29 D.A.C.	14-7-15	Killed
L/39898	Howarth, Gnr. S.,	460 Bty. R.F.A.	24-7-17	Wounded (Gas)
1573	Howden, Gnr. P.,	V/29 T.M. Bty.	?-1-16	Wounded
5212	Howe, Bdr. F.,	D/147 Bty. R.F.A.	29-6-16	Killed
		(att'd Z/29 T.M. Bty.)		
14611	Howe, Gnr. J.,	V/29 T.M. Bty.	30-6-17	Wounded
101793	Howell, Sig. G.,	"L" Bty. R.H.A.	23-10-18	Killed
69418	Howells, Gnr. A. L.,	10 Bty. R.F.A.	{ 30-4-15	Wounded
			27-5-15	Killed
614097	Howkins, Dvr. S.,	War. Bty. R.H.A.	25-7-17	Wounded (Gas)
24226	Hoyland, Dvr. G.,	13 Bty. R.F.A.	5-7-15	Wounded
62100	Hudson, Gnr. H. W.,	"Y" Bty. R.H.A.	11-12-15	Wounded
				(Dd of Wds 12-12-15)

Name & Rank.	Unit.	Date.	Casualty.
29740 Hughes, Dvr. A.,	15 B.A.C.	26-5-15	Wounded (Dd of Wds 5-7-15)
745274 Hughes, Dvr. D. L., M.M.,	26 Bty. R.F.A.	25-10-18	Wounded (Dd of Wds 29-10-18)
9576 Hughes, Dvr. D. W.,	29 D.A.C.	15-7-17	Wounded
242905 Hughes, Gnr. H.,	"Y" 29 T.M. Bty.	30-6-18	Wounded
604363 Hughes, Gnr. I. N.,	War. Bty. R.H.A.	20-11-17	Killed
1184 Hughes, Dvr. J. T.,	13 Bty. R.F.A.	25-9-17	Wounded
42259 Hughes, Gnr. L. H.,	13 Bty. R.F.A.	19-4-17	Killed
51478 Hulbert, Bdr. F.,	10 Bty. R.F.A.	25-5-15	Wounded (Dd of Wds 9-6-15)
14146 Humphrey, Gnr. F.,	D/17 Bty. R.F.A.	17-8-17	Wounded
14202 Humphries, Gnr. H.,	26 Bty. R.F.A.	9-6-15	Wounded
14480 Hunt, Gnr.,	460 Bty. R.F.A.	6-8-15	Wounded
76355 Hunt, Gnr. A. G.,	13 Bty. R.F.A.	⎰17-8-16 ⎱21-4-17	Wounded Wounded (Dd of Wds 24-4-17)
15758 Hunt, R.S.M., A. J.,	HQ. 15 Bde R.H.A.	27-5-15	Killed
4951 Hunt, Gnr. A. P.,	4th H.M. Bde. R.G.A.	25-10-15	Wounded
53363 Hunt, Dvr. J.,	368 Bty. R.F.A.	27-5-15	Wounded
59588 Hunt, Gnr. J.,	"B" Bty. R.H.A.	30-11-17	Wounded and Missing
153958 Hunt, Gnr. S. H.,	War. Bty. R.H.A.	12-8-17	Wounded
51572 Hunt, Gnr. W. H.,	370 Bty. R.F.A.	31-8-16	Wounded
14480 Hunt, Gnr. W. T.,	460 Bty. R.F.A.	17-8-16	Wounded
81249 Hunter, Gnr. G.,	"B" Bty. R.H.A.	30-11-17	Wounded
32953 Hurst, Gnr. H.,	460 Bty. R.F.A.	⎰18-6-15 ⎱27-6-16	Wounded ,,
51752 Hurst, Gnr. J. W.,	370 Bty. R.F.A.	31-8-16	Wounded
205952 Hussey, Gnr. W. H.,	"B" Bty. R.H.A.	30-11-17	Missing (P. of W.)
78788 Husson, Gnr. C., (or Musson)	"B" Bty. R.H.A.	9-4-17	Wounded
221187 Hutchings, Dvr. G.,	"B" Bty. R.H.A.	19-9-17	Wounded
128632 Hutchings, Gnr. S. G.,	D/17 Bty. R.F.A.	26-7-17	Wounded
37195 Hutchinson, Gnr. A.,	147 B.A.C.	16-5-15	Wounded
27279 Hutson, Gnr. O.,	D/17 Bty. R.F.A.	12-10-18	Wounded
40052 Hutton, Gnr. E. G.,	"L" Bty. R.H.A.	20-11-16	Wounded
4288 Huxtable, Gnr. F.,	"B" Bty. R.H.A.	14-7-17	Wounded
4625 Hyde, Gnr. A. G.,	13 Bty. R.F.A.	⎰21-6-15 ⎱30-12-15	Wounded ,,
38079 Hyde, Gnr. J.,	92 Bty. R.F.A.	2-12-17	Wounded
31891 Ideson, Sgt. A.,	"B" Bty. R.H.A.	8-5-15	Wounded (See also under officers)
77257 Ilett, Gnr. A. W.,	"Y" Bty. R.H.A.	20-5-15	Wounded
127313 Illingworth, L/Bdr. R.,	D/17 Bty. R.F.A.	12-8-18	Wounded
52590 Indge, Dvr. S. J.,	"B" Bty. R.H.A.	1-7-16	Killed
4762 Inns, Cpl. W. J.,	"Y" Bty. R.H.A.	22-10-16	Killed
79009 Inseal, Dvr. H.,	147 B.A.C.	3-8-15	Wounded
157 Ireton, Gnr. W. H.,	29 D.A.C.	24-1-17	Wounded
614058 Irving, Cpl. G.,	War. Bty. R.H.A.	15-10-16	Wounded
99984 Irving, Gnr. G.,	460 Bty. R.F.A.	24-7-17	Wounded (Gas)
38077 Irving, Gnr. J.,	92 Bty. R.F.A.	15-7-15	Wounded
82746 Ives, Gnr. A.,	460 Bty. R.F.A.	18-6-15	Wounded
111930 Jackson, Gnr. F.,	HQ. 15 Bde. R.H.A.	3-4-17	Wounded
140173 Jackson, Sig. F. A., D.C.M.,	"L" Bty. R.H.A.	⎰13-5-18 ⎱19-10-18	Wounded (Gas) ,,
77265 Jackson, Gnr. G.,	97 Bty. R.F.A.	30-6-15	Wounded
614059 Jackson, Cpl. P.,	War. Bty. R.H.A.	⎰6-4-17 ⎱11-4-17	Wounded Killed
4263 Jackson, a/Bdr. R.,	"L" Bty. R.H.A.	2-11-16	Wounded
26636 Jackson, S/S. W. J.,	"Y" Bty. R.H.A.	20-5-15	Wounded
26385 James, Gnr. C.,	"B" Bty. R.H.A.	9-4-17	Wounded
89157 James, Dvr. F. A.,	460 Bty. R.F.A.	11-4-17	Killed
42313 James, Gnr. P.,	147 B.A.C.	⎰30-4-15 ⎱2-7-15	Wounded Wounded Dd of Wds
91910 James, Dvr. J. H.,	92 Bty. R.F.A.	23-4-17	Wounded
184270 Jary, Gnr. P. N.,	"B" Bty. R.H.A.	1-12-17	Wounded (Dd of Wds 28-12-17)
11909 Jefferson, Gnr. J.,	D/17 Bty. R.F.A.	4-5-17	Wounded
81741 Jefferson, Gnr. W.,	460 Bty. R.F.A.	17-8-17	Wounded (Dd of Wds 18-8-17)

	Name & Rank.	Unit.	Date.	Casualty.
125339	Jeffery, Gnr. T.,	HQ. 17 Bde. R.F.A.	28-9-17	Wounded
49124	Jefford, Cpl. J. W., M.M.,	"B" Bty. R.H.A.	22-8-17	Wounded
93567	Jeffrey, Gnr. J. H.,	26 Bty. R.F.A.	17-8-17	Wounded
102494	Jelly, Dvr. W. J.,	"L" Bty. R.H.A.	20-11-16	Wounded
17656	Jempson, Sgt. W.,	"L" Bty. R.H.A.	10-5-15	Wounded
133335	Jenkins, Dvr. E. G.,	92 Bty. R.F.A.	23-4-17	Wounded
6801	Jenkins, Gnr. R.,	10 Bty. R.F.A.	20-11-16	Killed (acc.)
42297	Jenkins, Gnr. W.,	92 Bty. R.F.A.	21-7-17	Wounded
67003	Jetty, Gnr. H.,	13 Bty. R.F.A.	21-10-18	Wounded
106960	Jewitt, Gnr. W.,	370 Bty. R.F.A.	5-9-16	Wounded
	"	13 Bty. R.F.A.	25-9-17	"
8447	Joel, Bdr. C.,	Y/29 T.M. Bty.	28-3-18	Wounded
67378	John, Bdr. E. T.,	D/17 Bty. R.F.A.	26-8-17	Wounded
117787	John, Gnr. J.,	460 Bty. R.F.A.	9-4-17	Wounded
61394	Johnson, S/S. A. E.,	26 Bty. R.F.A.	21-6-15	Wounded
40414	Johnson, Sdlr. C.,	92 Bty. R.F.A.	18-6-15	Wounded
469	Johnson, Cpl. F. H. E., (alias Dooling)	29 D.A.C.	19-4-17	Wounded
62553	Johnson, Dvr. G.,	368 Bty. R.F.A.	3-6-15	Wounded
48760	Johnson, Gnr. W.,	"B" Bty. R.H.A.	3-5-17	Killed
54113	Johnson, Sgt. W.,	371 Bty. R.F.A.	19-8-16	Wounded (Gas)
57790	Johnson, Gnr. W. W.,	"L" Bty. R.H.A.	30-11-17	Wounded
332	Johnston, Cpl. A.,	4th H.M.Bde. R.F.A.	12-7-15	Killed
178	Johnstone, Sgt. A.,	4th H.M.Bde R.G.A.	P-8-15	Wounded
153814	Johnstone, Gnr. H.,	War. Bty. R.H.A.	16-8-17	Wounded
L/6560	Johnstone. B.S.M., W.,	370 Bty. R.F.A.	31-8-16	Wounded
42887	Jolly, a/Bdr. C., M.M.,	"Y" Bty. R.H.A.	26-6-15	Wounded
858	Jones, Dvr. A.,	92 Bty. R.F.A.	23-4-17	Killed
2640	Jones, Sgt. B. S.,	97 Bty. R.F.A.	4-6-15	Killed
604136	Jones, a/Bdr. C.,	War. Bty. R.H.A	3-10-17	Wounded
32478	Jones, Dvr. C. H.,	97 Bty. R.F.A.	16-4-15	Drowned
177119	Jones, Bdr. C. H.,	War. Bty. R.H.A.	30-11-17	Wounded
108230	Jones, Gnr. C. P.,	15 B.A.C.	14-4-16	Wounded
"	" "	29 D.A.C.	26-9-17	Wounded (Dd of Wds 2-10-17)
45751	Jones, Dvr. E.,	10 Bty. R.F.A.	26-5-15	Wounded
4888	Jones, Gnr. E.,	D/147 Bty. R.F.A.	9-8-16	Wounded
60142	Jones, Sgt. E. G.,	97 Bty. R.F.A.	23-10-16	Wounded
614473	Jones, Gnr. F.,	War. Bty. R.H.A.	26-4-17	Wounded
153666	Jones, Gnr. G.,	"B" Bty. R.H.A.	20-9-17	Wounded
66441	Jones, Gnr. J.,	26 Bty. R.F.A.	18-8-15	Wounded
21885	Jones, Dvr. J.,	13 Bty. R.F.A.	30-12-15	Killed
5246	Jones, Gnr. J.,	369 Bty. R.F.A.	30-8-16	Wounded
24448	Jones, Dvr. J.,	D/17 Bty. R.F.A.	23-7-17	Wounded
118747	Jones, Gnr. J.,	460 Bty. R.F.A.	10-4-17	Wounded (acc.)
4617	Jones, Dvr. J. E.,	26 Bty. R.F.A.	25-10-18	Wounded
82565	Jones, Gnr. L.,	92 Bty. R.F.A.	3-8-17	Wounded
177279	Jones, Gnr. R. J.,	"B" Bty. R.H.A.	30-11-17	Killed
19861	Jones, Bdr. S. A.,	92 Bty. R.F.A.	28-9-17	Wounded
68021	Jones, Gnr. W.,	92 Bty. R.F.A.	9-6-15	Wounded
14211	Jones, Bdr. W.,	D/17 Bty. R.F.A.	15-7-16	Wounded
	Sgt.	460 Bty. R.F.A.	30-11-17	Dd of Wds
117822	Jones, Gnr. W.,	460 Bty. R.F.A.	17-8-17	Killed
42157	Jones, Gnr. W.,	X/29 T.M. Bty. (att'd 13 Bty. R.F.A.)	21-10-18	Killed
89913	Jones, Dvr. W. H.,	460 Bty. R.F.A.	15-7-17	Wounded
178922	Jones, Dvr. W. J.,	13 Bty. R.F.A.	2-10-18	Wounded
29190	Jones, Dvr. W. R.,	HQ. 15 Bde. R.H.A.	10-6-15	Wounded
676074	Jones, Gnr. W. R.,	26 Bty. R.F.A.	12-5-17	Killed
113105	Jones, Gnr. W. S.,	"Y" Bty. R.H.A.	22-10-16	Dd of Wds
226368	Jordan, Gnr. W.,	D/17 Bty. R.F.A.	26-8-17	Killed
48546	Joynson, Dvr. F. H.,	90 H.B. R.G.A.	7-8-15	Dd of Wds
65810	Judd, Cpl. H.,	"L" Bty. R.H.A.	3-5-17	Wounded
98554	Judd, a/Bdr. R. F.,	D/17 Bty. R.F.A.	17-12-16	Wounded
126609	Judge, Gnr. W. D.,	"L" Bty. R.H.A.	{ 3-4-17 / 3-5-17	Wounded "
153830	Jupp, Gnr. T.,	"L" Bty. R.H.A.	2-5-17	Killed
62138	Kail, Sgt. H. R.,	460 Bty. R.F.A.	19-8-17	Wounded
69704	Kairis, Gnr. A.,	10 Bty. R.F.A.	4-6-15	Wounded
	" "	X/29 T.M. Bty.	23-1-17	Killed
74711	Kane, Gnr. A.,	92 Bty. R.F.A.	27-4-17	Wounded
68396	Kane, Gnr. H. W.,	D/147 Bty. R.F.A.	3-7-16	Wounded
618173	Kaveny, Gnr. W.,	War. Bty. R.H.A.	28-3-18	Wounded (Gas)
796325	Kay, Gnr. G.,	Y/29 T.M. Bty.	18-6-18	Wounded (Gas)

Name & Rank.		Unit.	Date.	Casualty.
91868	Kay, Dvr. J.,	17 B.A.C.	26-5-15	Dd of Wds
67781	Kay, Sdlr. W.,	10 Bty. R.F.A.	16-4-15	Drowned
4839	Keam, Gnr. W.,	D/147 Bty. R.F.A.	21-10-16	Wounded
				(Dd of Wds 22-10-16)
195035	Kearton, Gnr. J. W.,	"B" Bty. R.H.A.	20-11-17	Dd of Wds
87265	Keefe, Gnr. H.,	92 Bty. R.F.A.	20-9-17	Killed
614336	Keen, Cpl. F.,	War. Bty. R.H.A.	9-10-17	Killed
614060	Keen, Sgt. G. H. M., M.M.,	War. Bty. R.H.A.	29-3-18	Wounded (Gas)
885380	Keen, Gnr. S.,	V/29 T.M. Bty.	1-12-17	Wounded
72772	Keene, Bdr. A.,	460 Bty. R.F.A.	8-6-15	Wounded
92086	Kelley, Gnr. E.,	X/29 T.M. Bty.	1-12-17	Wounded
38076	Kelly, Gnr. R.,	92 Bty. R.F.A.	28-6-15	Wounded
87158	Kelly, Gnr. T.,	Z/29 T.M. Bty.	1-12-17	Wounded
153865	Kelvey, Gnr. W. G.,	"L" Bty. R.H.A.	19-8-17	Wounded
32043	Kemp. Sgt. E. W.,	92 Bty. R.F.A.	22-5-15	Wounded
77308	Kemp, a/Bdr. R. C.,	26 Bty. R.F.A.	22-12-15	Killed
73508	Kemptom, Gnr. H.,	29 D.A.C.	?-10-15	Wounded
103481	Kench, Gnr. F. C.,	10 Bty. R.F.A.	20-10-16	Wounded
1676	Kennedy, Gnr. J. C.,	Z/29 T.M. Bty.	30-4-16	Wounded
4212	Kennedy, Sgt. M., 4th H.M.Bde. R.G.A.		?-9-15	Wounded
40012	Kennelly, Gnr.,	460 Bty. R.F.A.	17-8-17	Wounded (Gas)
2408	Kennett, Gnr. S. E.,	14 S.B. R.G.A.	11-6-15	Wounded
23522	Kent, Sgt. G. F.,	97 Bty. R.F.A.	16-4-15	Drowned
65108	Kent, Gnr. J.,	13 Bty. R.F.A.	23-7-17	Dd of Wds (Gas)
715812	Kenyon, Gnr. J.,	460 Bty. R.F.A.	30-8-17	Wounded
10961	Kerr, B.S.M. W.,	460 Bty. R.F.A.	12-7-15	Dd of Wds
189042	Kershaw, Gnr. W. T.,	92 Bty. R.F.A.	20-4-18	Dd of Wds
217290	Kerswell, Dvr. W.,	92 Bty. R.F.A.	5-5-17	Wounded
				(Dd of Wds 6-5-17)
92377	Kewin, Bdr. T. S.,	D/132 Bty. R.F.A.	29-7-16	Killed
70512	Kiddie, Gnr. D.,	92 Bty. R.F.A.	6-10-18	Wounded
57699	Kiff Gnr. J.,	26 Bty.R.F.A.	14-8-17	Wounded
79669	Kilbride, Sgt. J. T.,	D/17 Bty. R.F.A.	25-9-17	Wounded
112152	Kilburn, Bdr. W.,	460 Bty. R.F.A.	22-8-17	Wounded
224005	Kilby, Gnr. P. C.,	"L" Bty. R.H.A.	14-10-18	Wounded
43919	Kilcourse, a/Bdr. J.,	97 Bty. R.F.A.	4-6-15	Wounded
122198	Kime, Gnr. C.,	D/132 Bty. R.F.A.	24-6-16	Wounded Dd of Wds
49932	Kimpton, Cpl. E.,	Z/29 T.M. Bty.	30-4-16	Wounded
16834	Kinally, Gnr. F.,	460 Bty. R.F.A.	17-8-17	Wounded (Gas)
115774	King, Dvr. E.,	13 Bty. R.F.A.	15-10-18	Wounded
42928	King a/Sgt. G.,	"L" Bty. R.H.A.	20-4-17	Dd of Wds
52092	King, Gnr. H. R.,	"B" Bty. R.H.A.	7-8-15	Wounded
65173	King, a/Cpl. J. W.,	370 Bty. R.F.A.	22-8-16	Wounded
176078	King, Dvr. T. P.,	13 Bty. R.F.A.	15-10-18	Wounded
62647	King, Gnr. W.,	92 Bty. R.F.A.	15-7-16	Killed
79254	King, Gnr. W.,	D/147 Bty. R.F.A. (att'd Z/29 T.M. Bty.)	29-6-16	Wounded
103263	King, Bdr. W.,	Z/29 T.M. Bty.	16-4-17	Killed
201495	Kingcombe, Gnr. A. H.,	D/17 Bty. R.F.A.	7-8-17	Wounded
28726	Kingdom, Gnr. H.,	29 D.A.C.	23-6-15	Wounded
38112	Kingstone, a/Bdr. D.,	368 Bty. R.F.A.	10-6-15	Wounded
88768	Kinley, Cpl. W.,	D/17 Bty. R.F.A.	28-4-18	Wounded Dd of Wds
614376	Kinman, Sgt. W. N., M.M.,	War. Bty. R.H.A.	30-11-17	Wounded (Gas)
84360	Kinnear, Gnr. J.,	13 Bty. R.F.A.	29-4-18	Wounded
31191	Kinner, Dvr. D.,	92 Bty. R.F.A.	18-7-17	Killed
663130	Kinniburgh, Gnr. D.,	460 Bty. R.F.A.	23-7-17	Wounded (Gas)
63392	Kirkhope, Gnr. H.,	92 Bty. R.F.A.	20-10-17	Wounded
78292	Kirton, Gnr. T.,	D/17 Bty. R.F.A.	28-7-16	Wounded
48854	Kitchen, Dvr. J.,	17 B.A.C.	15-5-15	Wounded
19983	Kitchen, Cpl. J.,	10 Bty. R.F.A.	1-11-16	Wounded
123576	Kitney, Gnr. L.,	D/17 Bty. R.F.A.	15-10-18	Wounded
76828	Knapper, Gnr. C. W.,	D/17 Bty. R.F.A.	22-10-16	Killed
88195	Knight, a/Bdr. C. J., M.M.,	X/29 T.M. Bty.	19-7-16	Wounded
"	"	"B" Bty. R.H.A.	13-7-17	"
"	Bdr.	"	22-7-17	" (Gas)
101812	Knight, Gnr. J.,	"B" Bty. R.H.A.	{ 9-4-17 3-5-17	Wounded "
47807	Knight, Gnr. R.,	"Y" Bty. R.H.A.	16-6-15	Wounded

Name & Rank.	Unit.	Date.	Casualty.
91473 Knock, Gnr. W.,	92 Bty. R.F.A.	31-10-16	Killed
56035 Knowles, Dvr. A. E.,	97 Bty. R.F.A.	13-7-15	Wounded
			(Dd of Wds 14-7-15)
63066 Knowles, Gnr. J.,	26 Bty. R.F.A.	11-8-17	Killed
600227 Laing, Bdr. W.,	"B" Bty. R.H.A.	9-10-17	Wounded
8790 Lakin, Gnr. W.,	D/147 Bty. R.F.A.	30-6-16	Wounded
14443 Lamb, Dvr. J.,	460 Bty. R.F.A.	15-6-15	Wounded
840027 Lambe, Gnr. W.,	D/17 Bty. R.F.A.	1-12-17	Wounded
40581 Lambert, Gnr. W.,	26 Bty. R.F.A.	22-10-17	Wounded (Gas)
125679 Lambie, Gnr. J.,	460 Bty. R.F.A.	20-10-17	Wounded
			Dd of Wds
56271 Laming, Gnr. W. W.,	"B" Bty. R.H.A.	13-7-15	Dd of Wds
153861 Lamkin, Dvr. J.,	"B". Bty. R.H.A.	1-8-17	Wounded
55713 Lane, Bdr. F., D.C.M.,	97 Bty. R.F.A.	2-7-16	Wounded
227109 Lane, Gnr. J.,	"Y" Bty. R.H.A.	23-10-18	Wounded
	(att'd. 460 Bty. R.F.A.)		(Dd of Wds 25-10-18)
56576 Lane, Bdr. R. J.,	97 Bty. R.F.A.	3-7-15	Wounded
„ Gnr.	„	23-10-16	„
98385 Lane, S/S. W.,"	26 Bty. R.F.A.	14-7-15	Wounded
60513 Langford, Gnr. A.,	"Y" Bty. R.H.A.	22-10-16	Killed
40374 Langford, a/Bdr. R.,	92 Bty. R.F.A.	9-10-17	Wounded
88283 Langlands, Dvr. W.,	"B" Bty. R.H.A.	22-8-17	Wounded
81036 Langley, Gnr. A.,	460 Bty. R.F.A.	28-6-15	Wounded
14864 Langridge, Dvr. J.,	460 Bty. R.F.A.	27-6-15	Wounded
62907 Lathbury, Gnr. A.,	97 Bty. R.F.A.	20-12-16	Wounded
227595 Lauder, Gnr. R.,	26 Bty. R.F.A.	28-11-17	Wounded
21054 Lavel, a/Bdr. A.,	26 Bty. R.F.A.	9-8-17	Wounded
60300 Law, Dvr. E.,	97 Bty. R.F.A.	16-4-15	Drowned
127154 Lawn, Gnr. E. C.,	13 Bty. R.F.A.	2-9-17	Wounded
93907 Lawrence, Dvr. A. H.,	29 D.A.C.	12-10-17	Killed
82329 Lawrence, Dvr. B.,	97 Bty. R.F.A.	16-4-15	Drowned
155490 Lawrence, Gnr. C.,	460 Bty. R.F.A.	3-10-17	Wounded
68305 Lawrence, a/Bdr. S.,	460 Bty. R.F.A.	7-4-17	Wounded
620259 Lawrie, Gnr. A. R.,	460 Bty. R.F.A.	9-10-17	Wounded
23434 Lawrie, Gnr. P.,	13 Bty. R.F.A.	24-10-16	Wounded
88403 Lawson, Dvr. J.,	"L" Bty. R.H.A.	12-8-17	Wounded
222822 Lawson, Gnr. J. H.,	92 Bty. R.F.A.	19-10-17	Wounded (Gas)
			Dd of Wds 26-10-17
68386 Lay, Gnr. W.,	"Y" Bty. R.H.A.	26-5-15	Wounded
44441 Lazell, Gnr. R. J.,	26 Bty. R.F.A.	29-10-16	Wounded
89589 Leaming, Gnr. S. W.,	D/17 Bty. R.F.A.	8-5-18	Wounded
102425 Leaning, Cpl. W.,	"L" Bty. R.H.A.	30-11-17	Wounded
10091 Leary, Gnr. F.,	29 D.A.C.	1-12-17	Wounded
64232 Leary, Gnr. P.,	"Y" Bty. R.H.A.	4-6-15	Wounded
67902 Lee, Gnr. A. E.,	"Y" Bty. R.H.A.	3-1-16	Wounded
4883 Lee, Gnr. E., 4th H.M. Bde. R.G.A.		2-10-15	Wounded
21529 Lee, Gnr. T. W.,	"Y" Bty. R.H.A.	11-6-15	Wounded
		7-8-15	
50126 Lee, Gnr. W.,	368 Bty. R.H.A.	4-6-15	Wounded
„ a/Bdr.	„	24-8-16	„
104034 Lee, Dvr. W. (or J.),	460 Bty. R.F.A.	25-8-17	Wounded
614422 Leeder, Gnr. R. R.,	War. Bty. R.H.A.	30-11-17	Wounded (Gas)
82359 Leek, a/Bdr. G. W.,	460 Bty. R.G.A.	25-8-17	Wounded
154372 Leese, Gnr. C.,	26 Bty. R.F.A.	20-9-17	Wounded
14940 Lefevre, Gnr. A.,	460 Bty. R.F.A.	8-5-15	Killed
79045 Legge, Dvr. T.,	17 B.A.C.	27-5-15	Wounded
34358 Leigh, Gnr. J.,	V/29 T.M. Bty.	30-6-16	Killed
7341 Leishman, Bdr. P.,	460 Bty. R.F.A.	7-10-17	Wounded
86271 Lemmon, Dvr. J. W.,	HQ. 15 Bde.	30-11-17	Missing
	R.H.A.		(P.O.W.)
67549 Le Pla Gnr. H. A.,	D/147 Bty. R.F.A.	24-8-16	Wounded
21840 Leslie, Gnr. F. C.,	Y/29 T.M. Bty.	4-5-18	Wounded (Gas)
2596 Leslie, Dvr. E. R.,	460 Bty. R.F.A.	15-10-18	Wounded
50365 Levett, Bdr. A. J.,	"B" Bty. R.H.A.	19-7-15	Wounded
97303 Lewin, Dvr. J. H.,	17 B.A.C.	?-5-15	Wounded
226718 Lewis, L/Bdr. C.,	26 Bty. R.F.A.	30-3-18	Wounded (Gas)
35113 Lewis, Dvr. H.,	"B" Bty. R.H.A.	2-1-16	Wounded
25357 Lewis, Dvr T.,	92 Bty. R.F.A.	18-6-15	Wounded
35398 Lewis, Gnr. W., HQ. 15 Bde. R.H.A.		3-4-17	Dd of Wds
1319 Liddell, Gnr. A., 4th H.M. Bde. R.G.A.		12-7-15	Wounded
13642 Lightfoot, Gnr. W.,	97 Bty. R.F.A.	1-7-15	Wounded
157841 Lincoln, Gnr. W.,	War. Bty. R.H.A.	30-11-17	Missing
			(P.O.W.)
253198 Lindop, Spr. J. A.,	(R.E.) 17 Bde.	8-12-17	Wounded
	R.F.A.	14-10-18	„

Name & Rank.	Unit.	Date.	Casualty.
216363 Linsley, Dvr. W.,	13th Bty. R.F.A.	25-9-17	Wounded
143631 Linton, Gnr. J.,	460 Bty. R.F.A.	30-11-17	Wounded
69073 Livingstone, Gnr. D.,	26 Bty. R.F.A.	6-5-17	Wounded (Gas)
73267 Livisey, Dvr. A.,	26 Bty. R.F.A.	6-10-17	Wounded
			(Dd of Wds 7-10-17)
68870 Llewellyn, Gnr. C.,	"L" Bty. R.H.A.	26-7-15	Wounded
30757 Lock, Dvr. W.,	147 B.A.C.	16-4-15	Drowned
39630 Lockwood, Ftr. J. N.,	13 Bty. R.F.A.	2-10-18	Killed
98821 Logan, Gnr. T.,	92 Bty. R.F.A.	12-10-17	Wounded
44477 Lomax, Gnr. J. R.,	26 Bty. R.F.A.	23-7-17	Wounded (Gas)
76727 Lonergan, Gnr. J.,	26 Bty. R.F.A.	5-6-15	Wounded
			(Dd of Wds 28-6-15)
122343 Long, Gnr. R. J.,	460 Bty. R.F.A.	30-11-17	Wounded
66744 Long Dvr. S.,	10 Bty. R.F.A.	6-6-15	Wounded
„ „ Bdr.	HQ. 29 D.A.	2-12-17	Wounded
206335 Long, Sig. W. J. E.,	"L" Bty. R.H.A.	23-10-18	Wounded
			Dd of Wds
40374 Longfoot, Dvr. G. W.,	92 Bty. R.F.A.	18-6-15	Wounded
„ „ a/Bdr.	„ „	9-10-17	„
„ „ Bdr.	„ „	30-9-18	„
105228 Longmire, Gnr. H.,	D/17 Bty. R.F.A.	24-9-17	Wounded
26742 Lord, Gnr. J. R.,	V/29 T.M. Bty.	13-5-17	Wounded
74271 Lough, Gnr. T. E.,	"L" Bty. R.H.A.	28-2-17	Dd of Wds
52805 Love, Cpl. L. N.,	"B" Bty. R.H.A.	6-1-16	Killed
425 Lovell, Gnr. H. le M.,	"Y" Bty. R.H.A.	25-10-16	Wounded
	(late Notts R.H.A.)		(Dd of Wds 11-11-16)
82940 Lovett, Gnr. W.,	D/147 Bty. R.F.A.	9-8-16	Wounded
70559 Low, Gnr. M.,	13Bty. R.F.A.	6-12-17	Wounded (Gas)
31584 Lowe, Sgt. F. E.,	10 Bty. R.F.A.	9-8-15	Dd of Wds
80375 Lowe, a/Bdr. J. H.,	"L" Bty. R.H.A.	{9-5-17 / 6-9-17	Wounded / „
244708 Lowe, Gnr. W. E.,	26 Bty. R.F.A.	14-10-18	Killed
111738 Lowell, Gnr. W.,	D/147 Bty. R.F.A.	29-6-16	Wounded
80677 Lowther, Gnr. T.,	13 Bty. R.F.A.	24-11-15	Wounded
77389 Lowther, Gnr. W.,	368 Bty. R.F.A.	27-6-15	Wounded
55612 Luck,, a/Bdr. J.,	15 B.A.C.	6-1-16	Wounded
63210 Luck, Gnr. R.,	"L" Bty. R.H.A.	18-1-17	Wounded
2261 Lund, Gnr. E.,	90 H.B. R.G.A.	6-8-15	Wounded
			Dd of Wds 17-8-15)
266816 Lunn, Gnr. E.,	460 Bty. R.F.A.	17-8-18	Wounded
53346 Lyddall, Gnr. G.,	14 S.B. R.G.A.	20-5-15	Wounded
745343 Lynbeck, Gnr. A.,	460 Bty. R.F.A.	7-10-18	Wounded
82637 Lynch, Dvr. A.,	15 B.A.C.	26-5-15	Wounded
„ „ Bdr.	"L" Bty. R.H.A.	23-4-17	Killed
49449 Lynch, Gnr. E. P.,	13 Bty. R.F.A.	4-5-15	Wounded
44952 Lynch, Gnr. J.,	26 Bty. R.F.A.	18-4-17	Wounded
142959 Lynch, Gnr. W. S.,	29 D.A.C.	23-7-17	Wounded
346 Lyons, Gnr. P.,	90 H.B. R.G.A.	10-5-15	Wounded
52988 Mabey, Bdr. C.,	368 Bty. R.F.A.	16-4-15	Drowned
4401 MacAulay, Gnr. M. 4th H.M.Bde.R.G.A.		15-7-15	Dd of Wds
362 MacCullum, Gnr. J.,	„ „	?-6-15	Wounded
4403 Macdonald, Gnr. J.,	„ „	15-5-15	Dd of Wds
4318 Macdonald, Gnr. K.,	„ „	15-5-15	Dd of Wds
1015 MacDougall, Gnr. D. C.,	„ „	29-4-15	Wounded
20969 Mace, a/Bdr. J.,	"B" Bty. R.H.A.	2-6-17	Wounded
51665 Macey, Gnr. E. G., HQ. 15 Bde. R.H.A.		3-12-15	Wounded
11975 MacFarlane, Dvr. J.,	„ „	3-4-17	Dd of Wds
4913 MacKay, Gnr. D., 4th H.M.Bde. R.G.A.		?-8-15	Wounded
4175 MacKay, Gnr. D. J.,	„ „	?-9-15	Wounded
4361 MacKay, Gnr. J.,	„ „	6-5-15	Wounded
5056 MacKay, Gnr. R.,	„ „	12-7-15	Wounded
320 MacKay, a/Bdr. R.,	„ „	?-7-15	Wounded
4319 MacKenzie, Bdr. A. A.,	„ „	2-5-15	Killed
4185 MacKenzie, Gnr. D.,	„ „	14-5-15	Dd of Wds
4169 MacKenzie, Gnr. H.,	„ „	?-8-15	Wounded
4086 Mackenzie, Sgt. M.,	„ „	?-8-15	Wounded
4379 Mackenzie, Gnr. M.,	„ „	5-6-15	Dd of Wds
12873 Mackie, Gnr. A.,	29 D.A.C.	23-11-15	Killed (acc.)
4135 MacKinnon, Bdr. A.,	4th H.M. Bde. R.G.A.	?-7-15	Wounded
317 Maclean, Bdr J.,	„ „	12-7-15	Killed
4208 Macleod, Cpl. D.,	„ „	12-7-15	Wounded
4374 Macleod, a/Bdr. D.,	„ „	?-9-15	Wounded
4330 Macleod, Gnr. D.,	„ „	?-9-15	Wounded
4316 Macleod, Gnr. J.,	„ „	9-8-15	Dd of Wds

Name & Rank.	Unit.	Date.	Casualty.
1078 MacMillan, Gnr. Don,	„ „	18-8-15	Killed
339 MacNeill, Gnr. A.,	„ „	9-5-15	Wounded
356 MacPherson, Whlr. T.,	„ „	?-7-15	Wounded
4053 Macrae, Gnr. J.,	„ „	16-5-15	Dd of Wds
4353 Macritchie, Gnr. D.,		2-5-15	Wounded
55326 Mahoney, Gnr. C. E.,	13 Bty. R.F.A.	28-9-18	Wounded
140063 Malcher, Gnr. H. J.,	"B" Bty. R.H.A.	{ 3-5-17 / 9-10-17	Wounded (Gas) / Killed
26429 Mallison, Dvr. D.,	368 Bty. R.F.A.	3-6-15	Wounded
706072 Mallinson, Cpl. L.,	13 Bty. R.F.A.	15-10-18	Wounded (Dd of Wds 17-10-18)
745196 Manifold, Dvr. R.,	92 Bty. R.F.A.	7-8-17	Wounded
147890 Manlove, Gnr. F. H.,	92 Bty. R.F.A.	8-9-17	Wounded
56548 Mann, Gnr. H. B.,	"L" Bty. R.H.A.	30-11-17	Missing
138928 Manning, Gnr. J.,	26 Bty. R.F.A.	2-5-17	Wounded (Gas)
L/34369 Marland, Gnr. A.,	X/29 T.M. Bty.	23-11-16	Killed (acc.)
17264 Marlow, Gnr. F.,	"B" Bty. R.H.A.	12-7-15	Wounded
120113 Marner, Gnr. T.,	26 Bty. R.F.A.	2-11-17	Wounded (Gas)
26117 Marriman, Sgt. J. J.,	14 S.B. R.G.A.	20-5-15	Wounded
L/5249 Marriner, Gnr. G.,	26 Bty. R.F.A.	6-8-17	Wounded
94230 Marsden, L/Bdr. J. F.,	War.Bty.R.H.A.	{ 25-4-18 / 5-5-18	Wounded / „
L/8609 Marsden, Gnr. J. T.,	D/17 Bty. R.F.A.	18-5-17	Dd of Wds
118086 Marsden, Gnr. R. S.,	X/29 T.M. Bty.	{ 27-7-17 / 20-1-18 / 3-6-18	Wounded / „ / „
196555 Marsh, Dvr. E.,	War. Bty. R.H.A.	15-5-18	Wounded
5771 Marsh, Bdr. G. T.,	HQ. 17 Bde. R.F.A.	20-6-15	Killed
512 Marsh, Gnr. H ,	- 29 D.A.C.	14-8-16	Wounded
88491 Marsh, Dvr. J.,	29 D.A.C.	24-8-16	Wounded (acc.)
51692 Marsh, Gnr. J. H. A.,	92 Bty. R.F.A.	28-6-15	Wounded (Dd of Wds 29-6-15)
50405 Marsh, Bdr. N. E., M.M.,	"Y" Bty. R.H.A.	22-10-16	Wounded
5458 Marsh, Gnr. W.,	92 Bty. R.F.A.	19-10-17	Wounded (Gas)
L/34264 Marsh, Cpl. W.,	D/17 Bty. R.F.A.	21-1-18	Killed
1302 Marshall, Gnr. H.,	4th H.M. Bde. R.G.A.	?-6-15	Wounded
836667 Marson, Gnr. G.,	26 Bty. R.F.A.	14-8-17	Wounded
159001 Martin, Gnr. A. F.,	"L" Bty. R.H.A.	27-4-17	Wounded
68851 Martin, Bdr. D. R.,	"L" Bty. R.H.A.	13-4-18	Wounded
4295 Martin, Bdr. J., 4th H.M. Bde. R.G.A.		?-6-15	Wounded
48497 Martin, a/Bdr. W. H.,	368 Bty. R.F.A.	16-4-15	Drowned
Maskell, Gnr.,	92 Bty. R.F.A.	2-12-15	Wounded
13322 Mason, Gnr. R. H.,	92 Bty. R.F.A.	4-6-15	Wounded
848 Mason, Gnr. W.,	90 H.B. R.G.A.	18-5-15	Wounded
845888 Mason, Gnr. W.,	92 Bty. R.F.A.	11-8-17	Wounded (Gas)
65873 Mason, Cpl. W. T.,	"L" Bty. R.H.A.	31-7-17	Wounded (Gas)
54958 Masters, Gnr. A.,	460 Bty. R.F.A.	17-8-17	Wounded
52767 Masters, a/Bdr. F. E.,	460 Bty. R.F.A.	14-11-16	Wounded
79066 Masterson, Gnr. D.,	26 Bty. R.F.A.	24-4-17	Killed
6756 Matchett, Dvr J.,	HQ. 147 Bde. R.F.A.	16-4-15	Drowned
961100 Mathews, Dvr. S. S.,	29 D.A.C.	22-4-17	Wounded
17496 Maton, Sgt. A. J.,	29 D.A.C.	19-8-17	Wounded
140067 Matthews, Gnr. F.,	"B" Bty. R.H.A.	16-8-17	Wounded
845601 Matthews, Dvr. J.,	D/17 Bty. R.F.A.	21-7-17	Wounded
169671 Mavor, Gnr. D.,	D/17 Bty. R.F.A.	{ 22-9-17 / 5-9-18	Wounded / „
42487 Maxted, a/Bdr. A.,	371 Bty. R.F.A.	26-7-16	Wounded
89135 May, Gnr. F.,	13 Bty. R.F.A.	20-10-17	Wounded (Gas)
220851 May, Dvr. R. G ,	29 D.A.C.	19-9-17	Wounded
796909 Mayers, Dvr. J. G.,	460 Btv. R.F.A.	7-10-18	Wounded
614063 Maynard, a/Bdr. A. J.,	War.Bty.R.H.A.	9-10-17	Wounded
15010 Mayo, Bdr. S. J.,	13 Bty. R.F.A.	22-4-17	Killed
40323 McCafferty, Gnr. A.,	"B" Btv. R.H.A.	12-7-15	Wounded
26032 McCamley, Sgt. J.,	26 Btv. R.F.A.	27-5-15	Wounded
614587 McCarthy, Gnr. E.,	War. Bty. R.H.A.	{ 21-5-17 / 2-10-17 / 14-10-18	Wounded / „ / „
6461 McCarthy, Gnr. P.,	14 S B. R.G.A.	12-7-15	Wounded
54673 McCarthy, Gnr. J.,	"Y" Bty. R.H.A.	5-8-15	Wounded
52533 McCartney, Gnr. A.,	"B" Bty. R.H.A.	2-6-15	Killed
9341 McCauley, Dvr. G.,	"B" Bty. R.H.A.	21-10-17	Wounded
100905 McClatchey, Bdr. S.,	92 Bty. R.F.A.	10-8-17	Killed
126223 McClellan, Gnr. A.,	26 Bty. R.F.A.	10-5-18	Killed

Name & Rank.	Unit.	Date.	Casualty.
56949 McClure, Gnr. H.,	97 Bty. R.F.A.	28-6-15	Killed
50287 McConaghy, Gnr. H.,	10 Bty. R.F.A.	6-6-15	Wounded
4866 McCully, B.S.M. W.,	4th H.M. Bde. R.G.A.	5-9-15	Dd of Wds
36207 McDonald, Gnr. D.,	V/29 T.M. Bty.	20-8-16	Killed
440 McDonald, Dvr. L.,	26 Bty. R.F.A.	10-6-15	Wounded
35747 McDonald, Dvr. R.,	17 Bde. R.F.A.	24-6-16	Wounded
31105 McDonald, Gnr. W.,	368 Bty. R.F.A.	16-4-15	Drowned
59725 McDonald, a/Sgt. W.,	"B" Bty. R.H.A.	15-5-17	Wounded
41761 McDonald, Gnr. W. D.,	"B" Bty R.H.A.	12-7-15	Wounded
82193 McDonough, Gnr. T.,	V/29 T.M. Bty.	24-7-17	Wounded
26363 McEntree, Dvr. D.,	368 Bty. R.F.A.	8-6-15	Wounded
88177 McFarlane, Dvr. T.,	"L" Bty. R.H.A.	28-7-17	Wounded
103794 McGilvory, Gnr. R.,	26 Bty. R.F.A.	18-3-18	Wounded
34103 McGilvray, Bdr. A.,	"L" Bty. R.H.A.	30-8-17	Wounded
40882 McGonigal, Gnr. W. J. T.,	15 B.A.C.	26-5-15	Wounded
2255 McGowan, Gnr. G.,	4th H.M. Bde. R.G.A.	12-7-15	Killed
51525 McGowan, Gnr. M.,	97 Bty. R.F.A.	14-11-16	Wounded
63184 McGowan, Dvr. W.,	10 Bty. R.F.A.	22-5-15	Wounded
614545 McGregor, Bdr. T.,	War. Bty. R.H.A.	11-3-18	Wounded
14206 McGuire, Gnr. W.,	14 S.B. R.G.A.	20-6-15	Wounded
43675 McHard, Cpl. W.,	"Y" Bty. R.H.A.	22-10-16	Killed
192757 McIlwraith, Gnr.,	13 Bty. R.F.A.	10-8-17	Killed
96666 McInnis, Gnr. G.,	460 Bty. R.F.A.	10-8-17	Wounded (Gas)
4180 McIntosh, Dvr. W.,	92 Bty. R.F.A.	23-4-17	Wounded
253189 McIntyre, 2/Cpl. J.,	(R.E.) 15 Bde. R.H.A.	30-11-17	Wounded
77868 McKay, Gnr. G.,	26 Bty. R.F.A.	1-9-16	Killed
1304 McKeith, Gnr. A.,	4th H.M. Bde. R.G.A.	9-5-15	Dd of Wds
1323 McKenna, Gnr. R.,	4th H.M. Bde. R.G.A.	4-5-15	Wounded
57155 McKenzie, Bdr. A.,	368 Bty. R.F.A.	?-5-15	Wounded
59347 McKenzie, Dvr. G. M.,	15 B.A.C.	8-5-15	Wounded
48332 McKenzie, Sgt. H., M.M.,	97 Bty. R.F.A.	21-10-16	Wounded
1323 McKenna, Gnr. R.,	4th H.M. Bde. R.G.A.	4-5-15	Wounded
82939 McKillop, Dvr. R.,	460 Bty. R.F.A.	23-4-17	Wounded
7671 McLean, a/Bdr. J.,	D/17 Bty. R.F.A.	22-10-16	Wounded
176078 McLeish, Dvr. W.,	13 Bty. R.F.A.	15-10-18	Wounded
5842 McManus, Gnr. R.,	14 S.B. R.G.A.	7-1-16	Wounded
2766 McMichael, Dvr. W.,	92 Bty. R.F.A.	?-5-15	Wounded
72936 McMorrow, Gnr. J.,	26 Bty. R.F.A.	21-4-17	Wounded
1325 McNab, Gnr. G., 4th H.M. Bde.	R.G.A.	5-5-15	Wounded
68576 McNicoll, Gnr. A.,	14 S.B. R.G.A.	19-7-15	Woundedl
10928 McNulty, Gnr. F.,	29 D.A.C.	?-8-15	Wounded
51693 McPheat, Gnr. A.,	97 Bty. R.F.A.	4-6-15	Wounded (Dd of Wds 6-6-15)
217172 McQueen, Dvr. J. G.,	92 Bty. R.F.A.	11-4-17	Wounded (Dd of Wds 27-4-17)
538 McSweeney, Gnr. B.,	15 B.A.C.	26-5-15	Wounded
51582 McWilliams, Gnr. J.,	90 H.B. R.G.A.	3-8-15	Wounded
81796 McWilliams, Gnr. T.,	10 Bty. R.F.A.	?-5-15	Wounded
45553 Meadows, Sgt. C. H.,	460 Bty. R.F.A.	25-12-15	Wounded
128873 Meadows, Dvr. W.W.,	"Y" Bty R.H.A.	23-10-16	Wounded
41807 Meadth, Dvr. J.,	10 Bty. R.F.A.	16-4-15	Drowned
217361 Mears, Dvr. J.,	92 Bty. R.F.A.	24-4-17	Wounded
1520 Measures, Gnr. G.,	29 D.A.C.	27-12-15	Wounded (Dd of Wds 28-12-15)
208262 Medhurst, Gnr. H.,	Y/29 T.M. Bty.	30-6-18	Wounded
42493 Mellish, Dvr. T.,	"L" Bty. R.H.A.	1-8-17	Wounded
42287 Melrose, Gnr. J.,	460 Bty. R.F.A.	9-4-17	Wounded
68087 Melville, S/S. D.,	26 Bty. R.F.A.	?-5-15	Wounded
117495 Merrifield, Dvr. T.,	29 D.A.C.	19-9-17	Wounded
52270 Merrill, Gnr. E.,	13 Bty. R.F.A.	8-5-15	Wounded
55583 Messenger, Cpl. L. W., M.M.,	"L" Bty. R.H.A.	20-8-16	Wounded
55554 Metcalf, Dvr. T.,	92 Bty. R.F.A.	17-10-18	Wounded
51900 Meyer, Gnr. J. H.,	10 Bty. R.F.A.	8-5-15	Wounded
79826 Meyrick, L/Bdr. G.,	13 Bty. R.F.A.	15-10-18	Wounded
11495 Michael, Sgt. S.,	460 Bty. R.F.A.	10-8-17	Wounded
224145 Mickerson, Gnr. H. S.,	"L" Bty. R.H.A.	2-10-18	Wounded
50540 Micklam, a/Bdr. E. C.,	26 Bty. R.F.A.	28-4-15	Wounded
99601 Middleton, Dvr. J.,	"B" Bty. R.H.A.	3-6-17	Wounded

Name & Rank.	Unit.	Date.	Casualty.
37202 Milburn, Gnr. J.,	29 D.A.C.	29-5-16	Wounded
197399 Millard, Dvr. E.,	29 D.A.C.	8-10-17	Wounded
29613 Miller, Gnr. A. R.,	10 Bty. R.F.A.	12-5-15	Wounded
73489 Mills, Sgt. H. A.,	13 Bty. R.F.A.	{ 3-5-17	Wounded
		{ 20-8-17	,, (Gas)
31740 Mills, Gnr. T.,	92 Bty. R.F.A.	3-4-18	Wounded
25235 Mills, Gnr. W.,	97 Bty. R.F.A.	23-10-16	Wounded
53588 Mills, Sgt. W.,	D/17 Bty. R.F.A.	25-4-17	Wounded
427 Milroy, Dvr. J.,	17 B.A.C.	20-5-15	Dd of Wds
73462 Milward, Gnr. J. W.,	92 Bty. R.F.A.	5-10-15	Wounded
99404 Minor, Gnr. G. H.,	"L" Bty. R.H.A.	6-6-16	Wounded
59935 Mitchell, Dvr. A.,	13 Bty. R.F.A.	{ ?-5-15	Wounded
		{ 7-8-15	Wounded
635227 Mitchell, Dvr. A.,	460 Bty. R.F.A.	7-10-18	Wounded
77946 Mitchell, Cpl. A. C.,	26 Bty. R.F.A.	14-8-17	Dd of Wds
59935 Mitchell, Dvr. E. A.,	13 Bty. R.F.A.	{ 17-5-15	Wounded
		{ 7-8-15	,,
69976 Mitchell, Tptr. G.,	460 Bty. R.F.A.	6-6-15	Wounded
,, ,, Bdr.		10-8-17	,,
227596 Mitchell, Gnr. G.,	92 Bty. R.F.A.	20-10-17	Wounded (Gas)
79260 Mitchell, Gnr. W.,	X/29 T.M. Bty.	13-7-16	Wounded
99649 Mock, Gnr. A.,	"Y" Bty. R.H.A.	22-12-15	Wounded
33674 Moffat, Sgt. R. M.,	97 Bty. R.F.A.	16-4-15	Drowned
367 Molloy, Dvr. P.,	92 Bty. R.F.A.	23-7-17	Wounded (Gas)
740665 Monaghan, S/S. D.,	13 Bty. R.F.A.	15-10-18	Wounded
134294 Moncaster, Dvr. W.	13 Bty. R.F.A.	15-10-18	Wounded
45841 Montague, a/Bdr. A. E.,	"Y" Bty. R.H.A.	22-10-16	Wounded
93975 Montague, Gnr. J.,	97 Bty. R.F.A.	18-12-15	Wounded
61527 Moody, Cpl. H.,	"L" Bty. R.H.A.	23-4-17	Wounded
13054 Moody, a/Bdr. W.,	14 S.B. R.G.A.	11-6-15	Wounded
,, ,, Bdr.		18-8-15	Killed
26122 Mooney, Dvr. H.,	147 B.A.C.	16-4-15	Drowned
620345 Moore, a/Bdr. A.,	War. Bty. R.H.A.	6-10-17	Wounded
26270 Moore, Cpl. C.,	92 Bty. R.F.A.	{ 4-6-15	Wounded
		{ 7-8-15	,,
44006 Moore, Gnr. G.,	D/147 Bty. R.F.A.	24-8-16	Wounded
34450 Moore, Gnr. J.,	10 Bty. R.F.A.	28-6-15	Wounded
38111 Moore, Gnr. J.,	10 Bty. R.F.A.	18-8-15	Dd of Wds
79262 Moores, S/S. H.,	368 Bty. R.F.A.	15-9-15	Wounded
96688 Moorhouse, Gnr. H. R.,	HQ. 29 D.A.	21-7-17	Wounded
32565 Morgan, Dvr. A.,	"B" Bty. R.H.A.	20-4-17	Wounded
Morgan, Gnr. E. H.,	War. Bty. R.H.A.	11-4-17	Wounded
32334 Morgan, Cpl. E. J.,	"B" Bty. R.H.A.	8-10-17	Wounded
139628 Morgan, Gnr. F.,	"B" Bty. R.H.A.	9-10-17	Wounded
201513 Morgan, Gnr. T. L.,	13 Bty. R.F.A.	19-4-17	Killed
73194 Morgan, Dvr. W.,	26 Bty. R.F.A.	13-4-17	Wounded
93877 Morgan, Dvr W. J.,	368 Bty. R.F.A.	9-5-15	Wounded
			(Dd of Wds 11-5-15)
38443 Morissey, Sgt. T., M.M.,	371 Bty. R.F.A.	22-8-16	Wounded
34863 Morraghan, Sgt. F. B., M.M.,	"B" Bty. R.H.A.	1-7-16	Wounded
66196 Morris, Sgt. A. E.,	"B" Bty. R.H.A.	8-10-17	Wounded
			Dd of Wds
73239 Morris, Gnr. B. C.,	HQ. 17 Bde. R.F.A.	25-4-18	Wounded
87709 Morris, Bdr. C.,	HQ. 15 Bde. R.H.A.	12-4-17	Wounded
71384 Morris, Bdr. G. S.,	92 Bty. R.F.A.	2-5-15	Wounded
,, ,, Sgt.	13 Bty. R.F.A.	7-8-17	Wounded
2829 Morrison, Gnr.,	14 S.B. R.G.A.	6-8-15	Wounded
51995 Morrison, Dvr. F.,	HQ. 15 Bde. R.H.A.	20-6-15	Wounded
166910 Morrison, Dvr. J.,	13 Bty. R.F.A.	20-5-17	Wounded
175522 Morrison, Gnr. J. W.,	92 Bty. R.F.A.	5-5-17	Wounded (Gas)
4244 Morrison, a/Bdr. M.,	4th H.M. Bde. R.G.A.	?-8-15	Wounded
82380 Morse, Dvr. T.,	368 Bty. R.F.A.	16-4-15	Drowned
19223 Mort, Dvr. T.,	26 Bty. R.F.A.	6-10-18	Wounded
172970 Mortimore, Sgt. R. C.,	460 Bty. R.F.A.	23-4-17	Wounded
99700 Morten, Gnr. A.,	26 Bty. R.F.A.	2-10-18	Wounded
255321 Morton, Ftr. G. A., M.M.,	26 Bty. R.F.A.	18-10-18	Wounded
159550 Morton, Gnr. H.,	92 Bty. R.F.A.	25-7-17	Wounded (Gas)
160114 Morton, Dvr. W.,	D/17 Bty. R.F.A.	23-7-17	Wounded
47954 Moseley, Sgt. W.,	"B" Bty. R.H.A.	22-7-17	Wounded
107721 Moss, Dvr. A.,	460 Bty. R.F.A.	23-4-17	Wounded
154283 Moss, Gnr. J.,	13 Bty. R.F.A.	2-2-17	Wounded
43064 Mosson, Gnr. J. W. F.,	13 Bty. R.F.A.	4-6-15	Wounded

Name & Rank.	Unit.	Date.	Casualty.
4148 Mower, Gnr. A. C.,	90 H.B. R.G.A.	14-5-15	Wounded
129015 Moyse, Gnr. W. E.,	"L" Bty. R.H.A.	30-11-17	Killed
58293 Mudd, Bdr. H.,	368 Bty. R.F.A.	1-7-16	Wounded
55348 Mulkerns, Gnr. P.,	368 Bty. R.F.A.	16-4-15	Drowned
971320 Mullins, Cpl. A. J., M.M.,	D/17 Bty. R.F.A.	11-3-18	Wounded
102708 Mullins, Gnr. J.,	"B" Bty. R.H.A.	{ 4-3-17 { 30-11-17	Wounded ,,
91673 Mullis, Gnr. T.,	460 Bty. R.F.A.	22-8-17	Wounded (Gas)
66790 Mullis, Sgt. W. H.,	460 Bty. R.F.A.	19-8-17	Killed
614554 Munday, a/Bdr. E.,	War. Bty. R.H.A.	21-9-17	Wounded
32461 Munday, Sgt. T.,	"Y" Bty. R.H.A.	22-10-16	Wounded (Dd of Wds 23-10-16)
L/37021 Mundy, Gnr. E.,	460 Bty. R.F.A.	25-8-17	Wounded (Dd of Wds 27-8-17)
134861 Murgatroyd, Gnr. E.,	92 Bty. R.F.A.	22-8-17	Killed
L/8682 Murphy, Gnr. E.,	26 Bty. R.F.A.	11-8-17	Wounded
196609 Murphy, Gnr. F. M.,	War. Bty. R.H.A.	11-3-18	Wounded (Gas)
42938 Murphy, Dvr. J. E.,	29 D.A.C.	16-9-17	Wounded
4206 Murray, Sgt. A., 4th H.M. Bde. R.G.A.		?-12-15	Wounded
7067 Murray, a/Bdr. J.,	D/17 Bty. R.F.A.	{ 22-10-16 { 8-1-17	Wounded ,,
4297 Murray, Gnr. M., 4th H.M. Bde. R.G.A.		?-8-15	Wounded
218282 Murray, Gnr. N.,	V/29 T.M. Bty.	1-12-17	Missing
92792 Murray, Dvr. R.,	29 D.A.C.	22-4-17	Wounded (Dd of Wds 25-4-17)
35956 Musgrave, Dvr. J.,	97 Bty. R.F.A.	16-4-15	Drowned
72751 Muskett, Gnr. W. H. R.,	460 Bty. R.F.A.	10-10-15	Wounded
26077 Myers, Gnr. G. D., M.M.,	"B" Bty. R.F.A.	3-5-17	Wounded
,, L/Bdr. ,,	,,	31-5-18	Wounded
207776 Nadonnick, Gnr. H.,	26 Bty. R.F.A.	23-7-17	Wounded (Gas)
5771 Naish, Bdr. A. T.,	HQ. 17 Bde. R.F.A.	20-6-15	Killed
86682 Naish, Gnr W.,	"B" Bty. R.H.A.	30-6-16	Wounded
865563 Nankerville, Dvr. J.,	D/17 Bty. R.F.A.	21-7-17	Wounded
5051 Napier, Gnr. T., 4th H.M. Bde. R.G.A.		2-5-15	Wounded
690182 Narburgh, Gnr. L. M.,	X/29 T.M. Bty.	12-10-18	Wounded
51807 Nash, Gnr. F.,	13 Bty. R.F.A.	17-8-16	Wounded (Dd of Wds 24-8-16)
L/44283 Nash, Dvr. F.,	29 D.A.C.	21-4-17	Wounded
44492 Nash, a/Bdr. W.,	26 Bty. R.F.A.	23-7-17	Wounded (Gas) (Dd of Wds 28-7-17)
34532 Needham, Cpl. H.,	26 Bty. R.F.A.	22-10-17	Wounded
4888 Nelson, Bdr. J., 4th H.M. Bde. R.G.A.		?-9-15	Wounded
21408 Nesbit, Gnr. W. A.,	97 Bty. R.F.A.	1-7-16	Wounded
40092 Nesbitt, Bdr. H. T.,	"B" Bty. R.H.A.	9-4-17	Wounded
36208 Nettle, Gnr. F.,	90 H.B. R.G.A.	9-6-15	Wounded
L/42824 Newcombe, a/Bdr. E.,	371 Bty. R.F.A.	22-8-16	Wounded
172223 Newcombe, Gnr. S. J.,	War. Bty. R.H.A.	13-8-17	Wounded
65321 Newell, a/Bdr. W.,	"L" Bty. R.H.A.	30-11-17	Wounded and Missing
116353 Newiss, Gnr. F.,	26 Bty. R.F.A.	6-8-17	Wounded
81490 Newman, Sgt. F.,	HQ. 17 Bde. R.F.A.	26-7-15	Wounded
58046 Newman, Sgt. F.,	460 Bty. R.F.A.	7-10-17	Wounded (Dd of Wds 8-10-17)
Newman, Gnr. H.,	War. Bty. R.H.A.	30-11-17	Missing
142034 Newman, Gnr. M. J. R.,	26 Bty. R.F.A.	12-5-17	Wounded
174391 Nichol, Gnr. J.,	13 Bty. R.F.A.	23-5-17	Wounded (Dd of Wds 12-6-17)
60179 Nichol, Gnr. J.,	368 Bty. R.F.A.	20-8-15	Wounded
4770 Nicholls, Cpl. A.,	460 Bty. R.F.A.	2-4-17	Wounded
614334 Nicholls, Gnr. G.,	War. Bty. R.H.A.	11-4-17	Killed
614064 Nichols, Gnr. W. H.,	War. Bty. R.H.A.	{ 30-8-17 { 9-10-17	Wounded Killed
173540 Nightingale, Dvr. B.	X/29 T.M. Bty.	9-6-18	Wounded
93818 Nixon, Dvr. A.,	460 Bty. R.F.A.	{ 2-7-15 { 7-10-18	Wounded Killed
614337 Nixon, Gnr. S.,	War. Bty. R.H.A.	25-7-17	Wounded
32443 Noble, Cpl. H., M.M.,	13 Bty. R.H.A.	5-10-17	Wounded
99649 Nock, Gnr. A.,	"Y" Bty. R.H.A.	22-12-15	Wounded
Nodolheck, Gnr.,	26 Bty. R.F.A.	23-7-17	Wounded

H

Name & Rank.		Unit.	Date.	Casualty.
15199	Nolan, Gnr. J. J.	14 S.B. R.G.A.	6-5-15	Wounded
				(Dd of Wds 24-5-15)
78224	Norris, a/Bdr. C.,	460 Bty. R.F.A.	4-10-17	Wounded
46354	Norris, B.Q.M.S. F.,	10 Bty. R.F.A.	28-6-15	Wounded
81551	North, Gnr. G. W.,	92 Bty. R.F.A.	12-10-17	Wounded
614145	North, Gnr. H.,	War. Bty. R.H.A.	25-5-17	Wounded
88604	North, Gnr. J. W.,	War. Bty. R.H.A.	30-3-18	Wounded (Gas)
915281	Norwood, Dvr. W.,	D/17 Bty. R.F.A.	21-7-17	Wounded
50381	Nunn, Gnr. H.,	"L" Bty. R.H.A.	10-5-15	Wounded
54332	Oak, Gnr. G.,	"L" Bty. R.H.A.	28-7-17	Wounded
345	O'Brien, Gnr. C.,	90 H.B. R.G.A.	14-5-15	Wounded
606014	O'Brien, Gnr. H.,	26 Bty. R.F.A.	8-5-18	Wounded
70836	O'Brien, Sgt. J. W.,	92 Bty. R.F.A.	3-5-17	Wounded
4973	O'Brien, Gnr. T.,	D/17 Bty. R.F.A.	22-10-16	Killed
40842	O'Callaghan, Gnr. D.,	14 S.B. R.G.A.	19-7-15	Wounded
87026	O'Connell, Gnr. P. J.,	"Y" Bty. R.H.A.	22-10-16	Wounded
98101	O'Donnell, Gnr. J.,	460 Bty. R.F.A.	23-4-17	Killed
44858	O'Donnell, Gnr. M.,	14 S.B. R.G.A.	4-5-15	Wounded
L/34358	Ogden, Dvr F.,	369 Bty. R.F.A.	4-9-16	Wounded
"	„ a/Bdr.	26 Bty. R.F.A.	12-4-17	Killed
25259	Ogden, Cpl. S. J. B., м.м.,	"Y" Bty. R.H.A.	22-7-15	Wounded
134441	Ogilvie, Gnr. C. O.,	13 Bty. R.F.A.	7-5-18	Wounded
49323	O'Hara, Gnr. F.,	92 Bty. R.F.A.	15-8-15	Wounded
44857	Oldfield, Gnr. S.,	90 H.B. R.G.A.	31-12-15	Dd of Wds
91483	Oliver, Gnr. G.,	D/17 Bty. R.F.A.	16-4-17	Wounded
160019	Oliver, Gnr J. L.,	X/29 T.M. Bty.	9-12-16	Dd of Wds
169385	O'Neil, Gnr. M.,	13 Bty. R.F.A.	23-4-17	Killed
58806	O'Neill, Gnr. S.,	29 D.A.C.	31-5-18	Killed
45367	Onslow, Gnr. A. W.,	26 Bty. R.F.A.	8-10-17	Killed
614450	Opperman, Bdr. W.,	War. Bty. R.H.A.	23-4-17	Wounded
76202	Oram, Gnr. G. J.,	92 Bty. R.F.A.	19-10-17	Wounded (Gas)
89879	Ord, Gnr. G. J.,	13 Bty. R.F.A.	7-8-15 / 17-8-16 / 16-4-17	Wounded / Wounded „ / Dd of Wds
38091	O'Regan, Gnr. J.,	13 Bty. R.F.A.	6-8-15	Wounded
76686	Orr, Gnr. D.,	97 Bty. R.F.A.	16-10-16	Wounded
54005	Osborne, Sgt. A. T.,	"L" Bty. R.H.A.	18-8-17	Wounded
177154	Osborne, Gnr. J.,	War. Bty. R.H.A.	30-8-17	Wounded
44853	Osbourne, Gnr. E. D.,	14 S.B. R.G.A.	8-6-15	Wounded
57329	O'Shea, a/Bdr. M.,	97 Bty. R.F.A.	28-6-15	Wounded
				(Dd of Wds 29-6-15)
53582	Otto, Dvr. W. A.	29 D.A.C.	30-9-18	Wounded
70932	Ottoway, Gnr. C. B.,	29 D.A.C.	11-7-15	Wounded
745263	Owen, Ftr. S.,	26 Bty. R.F.A.	10-4-17	Wounded
140320	Owen, Gnr. W. E.,	"B" Bty. R.H.A.	12-8-17	Wounded
12634	Owens, Gnr. P.,	368 Bty. R.F.A.	27-6-15 / 28-10-15	Wounded / Killed
138843	Owens, Gnr. W. R.,	Y/29 T.M. Bty.	28-3-18	Killed
24175	Oyitch, a/Bdr. T.,	10 Bty. R.F.A.	15-10-16	Wounded
"	„ Bdr.	D/17 Bty. R.F.A.	21-7-17	Wounded
121001	Packham, Dvr. G.,	"B" Bty. R.H.A.	21-10-17	Wounded
				(Dd of Wds)
80089	Page, Dvr. F.,	V/29 T.M. Bty.	27-4-17	Wounded
121880	Page, Gnr. G.,	10 Bty. R.F.A.	2-11-16	Wounded
30088	Paice, Bdr. F. G.,	14 S.B. R.G.A.	8-5-15	Wounded
136395	Palfreyman, Dvr. F.,	460 Bty. R.F.A.	6-6-17	Wounded
(or 136394)				
82006	Palmer, Bdr. A. R.,	92 Bty. R.F.A.	2-5-17	Wounded
91141	Pardoe, Gnr. F.,	10 Bty. R.F.A.	28-6-15	Killed
124234	Pardoe, Gnr. H. A.,	460 Bty. R.F.A.	17-8-16	Wounded
79287	Parker, Cpl. A.,	147 B.A.C.	25-7-15	Wounded
79297	Parker, Cpl. J.,	10 Bty. R.F.A.	31-7-15	Wounded
66652	Parker, a/Bdr. J. H.,	460 Bty. R.F.A.	17-8-16	Wounded
55162	Parker, Sgt. T.,	370 Bty. R.F.A.	30-8-16	Wounded
1056	Parker, Dvr. W.,	368 Bty. R.F.A.	7-6-15	Wounded
736677	Parker, Gnr. W.,	War. Bty. R.H.A.	14-10-18	Wounded
87939	Parker, Dvr. W. H.,	"Y" Bty. R.H.A.	23-10-16	Wounded
231570	Parnell, Gnr. G.	92 Bty. R.F.A.	30-4-18	Wounded
614068	Parsons, Gnr. E. H.,	War. Bty. R.H.A.	11-4-17	Wounded
76753	Parton, Gnr. J.,	368 Bty. R.F.A.	13-8-15	Wounded
47840	Pask, L/Bdr. J. W.,	X/29 T.M. Bty.	21-10-18	Killed
		(att'd 13 Bty. R.F.A.)		
56507	Passmore, Gnr. L. T.,	92 Bty. R.F.A.	4-2-17	Wounded

	Name & Rank.	Unit.	Date.	Casualty.
93035	Paterson, Gnr. W.,	460 Bty. R.F.A.	28-3-19	Wounded (Dd of Wds)
49793	Patrick, Gnr. A.,	368 Bty. R.F.A.	16-4-15	Drowned
6453	Patrick, Gnr. R. .G,	Z/29 T.M. Bty.	24-10-16	Wounded
78393	Pavey, Sgt. R. G., D.C.M.,	Y/29 T.M. Bty.	5-7-17	Wounded (Dd of Wds 6-7-17)
52839	Pawley, Bdr. C. E.,	"B" Bty. R.F.A.	{ 2-5-15	Wounded
			7-8-15	Killed
202424	Paxton, Dvr. J.,	29 D.A.C.	28-9-18	Killed
7873	Paxton, Dvr. W.,	13 Bty. R.F.A.	8-7-15	Wounded
87965	Payne, Gnr. C.,	"Y" Bty. R.H.A.	11-12-15	Wounded
L/14081	Payne, Ftr. M.,	D/17 Bty. R.F.A.	6-10-18	Wounded
67026	Payne, Gnr. R.,	13 Bty. R.F.A.	13-7-15	Wounded
44528	Payne, Dvr. W.,	13 Bty. R.F.A.	15-10-18	Wounded
67106	Payne, Gnr. W. G.,	HQ. 17 Bde. R.F.A.	2-5-15	Killed
94163	Payton, Gnr. S. G.,	26 Bty. R.F.A.	7-8-15	Wounded (Dd of Wds 8-8-15)
78828	Peach, Cpl. W.,	Y/29 T.M. Bty.	1-12-17	Wounded
40969	Peachment, Gnr. G.,	14 S.B. R.G.A.	16-7-15	Wounded
20738	Pearce, Cpl. A.,	X/29 T.M. Bty.	19-7-16	Wounded
35657	Pearce, Gnr. G.,	D/17 Bty. R.F.A.	18-6-17	Wounded
944576	Pearce, Sgt. H.,	460 Bty. R.F.A.	6-6-18	Killed
49031	Pearce, Cpl. J. C.,	26 Bty. R.F.A.	5-7-15	Wounded
L/22423	Pearmain, Gnr. W. F.,	371 Bty. R.F.A,	22-8-16	Wounded (Dd of Wds 24-8-16)
70016	Peel, Dvr. F.,	10 Bty. R.F.A.	26-5-15	Killed
44453	Pegram, Gnr. G. S.,	26 Bty. R.F.A.	25-5-17	Killed
96801	Pelan, Gnr. J.,	13 Bty. R.F.A.	24-10-16	Wounded
612547	Pell, Dvr. T.,	War. Bty. R.H.A.	6-9-18	Wounded (Gas)
80500	Pennell, Gnr. O.,	92 Bty. R.F.A.	16-5-15	Wounded
47556	Pepper, Gnr. B.,	"B" Bty. R.H.A.	19-9-17	Killed
725888	Percival, Sig. J.,	460 Bty. R.F.A.	7-10-18	Wounded
202805	Perham, Dvr. F.,	13 Bty. R.F.A.	28-9-18	Wounded (Dd of Wds 29-9-18)
86057	Perkins, Gnr. A.,	"L" Bty. R.H.A.	12-9-17	Wounded
	Perkes, Gnr. C.,	War. Bty. R.H.A.	11-4-17	Wounded
614069	Perks, Bdr. J. C., M.M.,	War Bty. R.H.A.	14-10-18	Wounded
5785	Perrin, Dvr.	D/147 Bty. R.F.A.	31-12-16	Wounded
2637	Perry, Sgt. F.,	460 Bty. R.F.A.	15-5-17	Wounded
24541	Perryman, Cpl. W.,	26 Bty. R.F.A.	7-3-17	Wounded
26844	Perryment, Dvr. T. (A.S.C.),	90 H.B. R.G.A.	7-8-15	Wounded
614457	Peterkin, Gnr. J. W.,	War Bty. R.H.A.	9-4-17	Killed
77232	Pettifer, Gnr. C. H.,	"B" Bty. R.H.A.	22-7-17	Wounded (Gas) (Dd of Wds 27-7-17)
78135	Pettitt, Dvr. H.,	97 Bty. R.F.A.	16-4-15	Drowned
177158	Petty, Gnr. W.,	"B" Bty. R.H.A.	14-7-17	Wounded
51101	Phillips, Dvr. E.,	14 S.B., R.G.A.	11-6-15	Wounded
222375	Phillips, Gnr. F. E.,	460 Bty. R.F.A.	19-6-18	Killed
2227	Phillips, Gnr. W.,	D/17 Bty. R.F.A.	31-3-17	Wounded
L/39078	Phinn, Dvr. M. J.,	460 Bty. R.F.A.	31-5-18	Wounded (Dd of Wds)
42638	Phipps, Gnr. W.,	"L" Bty. R.H.A.	2-5-18	Wounded (Gas)
239950	Pickarchick, Gnr. J.,	26 Bty. R.F.A.	14-10-18	Wounded
96756	Picken, Gnr. A. E.,	13 Bty. R.F.A.	5-6-17	Wounded
42925	Pickerill, Gnr. H.,	29 D.A.C.	7-9-17	Killed
34471	Piddington, Dvr.,	10 Bty. R.F.A.	16-4-15	Drowned
72732	Piggott, Cpl. W. H.,	"L" Bty. R.H.A.	16-2-17	Wounded
195190	Pilbrow, Dvr. A.,	"B" Bty. R.H.A.	21-11-17	Wounded (Gas)
153638	Pilbrow, Gnr. F.,	"L" Bty. R.H.A.	22-7-17	Wounded (Gas)
76898	Pinchen, Gnr. J. T.,	92 Bty. R.F.A.	16-11-16	Wounded
59043	Pink, Gnr. A.,	29 D.A.C.	?-7-15	Wounded
78960	Pitcher, Gnr. G.,	97 Bty. R.F.A.	7-6-15	Wounded
		D/17 Bty. R.F.A.	20-4-17	Wounded
86077	Pitt, Dvr. O.,	"B" Bty. R.H.A.	22-8-17	Wounded (Gas)
11643	Pittman, S/S., W.,	147 B.A.C.	16-4-15	Drowned
745298	Platt, Gnr. N.,	29 D.A.C.	19-8-17	Killed
12194	Plumbley, Dvr. J.,	147 B.A.C.	4-6-15	Wounded
180372	Poate, Bdr. G.,	13 Bty. R.F.A.	2-10-18	Killed
34228	Poll, Gnr. R.,	10 Bty. R.F.A.	31-5-15	Wounded
54994	Pollendine, Gnr. C.,	D/147 Bty. R.F.A.	9-8-16	Wounded
36611	Pollick, Gnr. W.,	460 Bty. R.F.A.	20-10-17	Wounded
L/29667	Pollidor, Gnr. H.,	92 Bty. R.F.A.	12-4-17	Wounded

	Name & Rank.	Unit.	Date.	Casualty.
79283	Pond, Bdr. A. C.,	13 Bty. R.F.A.	23-7-17	Wounded (Gas)
19723	Poole, Dvr. F.,	147 B.A.C.	7-8-15	Killed
745322	Pooley, Gnr. G. A.,	13 Bty. R.F.A.	20-10-17	Wounded
673	Pope, Gnr. S.,	13 Bty. R.F.A.	24-11-17	Wounded
71947	Port, Bdr. A. J.,	"B" Bty. R.H.A.	1-7-16 ·	Wounded
4373	Porter, Gnr. J.,	13 Bty. R.F.A.	22-10-18	Wounded
67025	Portlock, Gnr. E.,	92 Bty. R.F.A.	7-8-15	Killed
98778	Posnett, Gnr. J.,	460 Bty. R.F.A.	10-5-16	Killed
81193	Potter, Dvr. G.,	17 B.A.C.	2-6-15	Wounded
212692	Pout, Gnr. W. A.,	92 Bty. R.F.A.	17-10-17	Wounded
58737	Povey, Gnr J. C.,	D/17 Bty. R.F.A.	17-8-17	Wounded (Gas)
159347	Powell, Gnr. J.,	92 Bty. R.F.A.	29-4-17	Killed
745065	Powell, Dvr. V. K.,	13 Bty. R.F.A.	{25-9-17	Wounded
			15-10-18	Killed
81086	Powell, S/S., W.,	"L" Bty. R.H.A.	7-9-18	Wounded (Gas)
44209	Powrie, Sgt. H., M.M.,	92 Bty. R.F.A.	{13-11-16	Wounded
			17-10-17	"
77873	Poxton, Dvr. W.,	13 Bty. R.F.A.	8-7-15	Wounded
46852	Poyser, Gnr. F.,	13 Bty. R.F.A	15-10-18	Wounded
212009	Preston, Gnr. J.,	26 Bty. R.F.A.	18-10-18	Wounded
58949	Pretlove, Gnr. J. W.,	13 Bty. R.F.A.	23-4-17	Wounded
30475	Price, Bdr. C.,	92 Bty. R.F.A.	29-9-18	Wounded
				(Dd of Wds 7-10-18)
188536	Price, Dvr. H.,	"L" Bty. R.H.A.	9-10-17	Wounded
79892	Price, Gnr. H.,	Y/29 T.M. Bty.	26-7-16	Wounded (Gas)
68337	Price, Gnr. S. P.,	97 Bty. R.F.A.	12-12-15	Wounded
13136	Price, Bdr. W. C.,	92 Bty. R.F.A.	17-8-18	Wounded
				(Dd of Wds ?)
154332	Pridmore, Gnr. W. G.,	92 Bty. R.F.A.	12-4-17	Wounded
				(Dd of Wds 18-4-17)
49199	Priest, Gnr. J. W.,	29 D.A.C.	20-4-17	Wounded
614431	Priest, Dvr. W.,	War. Bty. R.H.A.	21-4-17	Killed
82264	Priestly, Dvr. W.,	368 Bty. R.F.A.	12-7-15	Wounded
67539	Prior, Gnr. W.,	10 Bty. R.F.A.	23-7-15	Wounded
32543	Proctor, Sgt. M. W.,	92 Bty. R.F.A.	12-8-17	Wounded
				(Dd of Wds)
199519	Prout, Gnr. F.,	26 Bty. R.F.A.	6-12-17	Wounded
54304	Prosser, Gnr. S. G.,	"B" Bty. R.H.A.	4-5-15	Wounded
614102	Pugh, a/Bdr. L. R.,	War. Bty. R.H.A.	9-10-17	Wounded
745384	Pulford, Gnr. A.,	13 Bty. R.F.A.	28-9-18	Wounded
92837	Pullen, Gnr. G.,	HQ. 15 Bde. R.H.A.	30-11-17	Missing
154393	Pyett, Gnr. P. E.,	D/17 Bty. R.F.A.	16-4-17	Wounded
52588	Pyke, Gnr. H. E.,	"B" Bty. R.H.A.	8-5-15	Wounded
	" Bdr. "		8-10-17	Wounded
40671	Pyper, a/Bdr. G.,	"B" Bty. R.H.A	22-7-17	Wounded (Gas)
14479	Quelch, Cpl. W.,	X/29 T.M. Bty.	4-6-18	Wounded
930743	Quillian, Gnr. A.,	29 D.A.C.	8-10-17	Wounded
				(Dd of Wds 25-10-17)
61449	Quinn, Dvr. C.,	29 D.A.C.	16-4-17	Wounded
50506	Quinn, 2/A.M., H. (R.F.C.),	HQ. 29 D.A.	30-11-17	Missing
42051	Quirk, Cpl. J. W..	"B" Bty. R.H.A.	28-4-15	Wounded
16210	Raby, Sgt. J.,	D/147 Bty. R.F.A.	22-10-16	Wounded
79056	Rackham, Gnr. W.,	10 Bty. R.F.A.	9-6-15	Wounded
L/42680	Radford, Dvr. A.,	29 D.A.C.	25-9-17	Wounded
508	Radford, Gnr. E.,	460 Bty. R.F.A.	30-1-17	Wounded
83724	Radford, Gnr. T.,	26 Bty. R.F.A.	14-4-17	Wounded
955161	Raishbrook, Gnr. F.,	15 Bde. R.H.A.	12-5-17	Wounded
	" "	Z/29 T.M. Bty.	1-12-17	"
1563	Ralph, Bdr. N. B.,	29 D.A.C.	27-12-15	Wounded
16873	Randall, Sgt. H., D.C.M.,	X/29 T.M. Bty.	1-12-17	Wounded
84322	Randall, Dvr. W.,	147 B.A.C.	16-4-15	Drowned
614073	Randall, Gnr. W. J.,	War. Bty. R.H.A.	22-7-17	Wounded
145825	Ransome, Gnr. E. A.,	92 Bty. R.F.A.	12-5-17	Wounded
				(Dd of Wds 13-5-17)
60442	Ratcliff, Cpl. W. J.,	17 B.A.C.	16-6-15	Wounded
53093	Rathbone, Gnr. A.,	97 Bty. R.F.A.	16-4-15	Drowned
66711	Rawlings, Gnr. T.,	460 Bty. R.F.A.	5-6-16	Wounded
				(Dd of Wds 15-6-16)
82708	Rayburn, Dvr. G.,	10 Bty. R.F.A.	15-10-16	Wounded
L/1704	Rayment, Gnr. G.,	371 Bty. R.F.A.	22-8-16	Killed
15474	Raymond, Cpl. F. A.,	460 Bty. R.F.A.	2-7-15	Wounded
112896	Raynor, Gnr. J. B.,	92 Bty. R.F.A.	7-10-17	Wounded
61772	Rea, Gnr. A. E.,	"L" Bty. R.H.A.	20-4-18	Wounded
27540	Read, Sgt. T. A.,	"B" Bty. R.H.A.	23-7-17	Wounded
20613	Redding, Gnr. A.,	92 Bty. R.F.A.	24-4-17	Wounded

	Name & Rank.	Unit.	Date.	Casualty.
115293	Redhead, Gnr. R.,	26 Bty. R.F.A.	6-12-17	Wounded
51978	Reed, a/Bdr. E. G.,	"Y" Bty. R.H.A.	{ 11-6-15 / 6-7-15	Wounded / ..
2253	Reed, Sgt. A. G.,	369 Bty. R.F.A.	30-8-16	Wounded
54310	Reed, Gnr. E. F.,	"Y" Bty. R.H.A.	23-7-15	Wounded
59655	Reed, Gnr. R.,	"Y" Bty. R.H.A.	{ 28-12-15 / 5-7-16	Wounded / „
126667	Reed, Gnr. W.,	"L" Bty. R.H.A.	22-7-17	Wounded (Gas)
57508	Reeks, Gnr. E.,	26 Bty. R.F.A.	24-4-17	Dd of Wds
42395	Rees, Dvr. E.,	17 B.A.C.	16-12-15	Wounded
88151	Reeve, Gnr. B.,	13 Bty. R.F.A.	25-12-15	Wounded
140021	Reeve, Gnr. E. F.,	War. Bty. R.H.A.	27-5-17	Killed
77660	Reeves, Gnr. G.,	15 B.A.C.	25-5-15	Wounded
86033	Reeves, Gnr. W.,	"B" Bty. R.H.A.	9-4-17	Wounded
38091	Regan, Gnr.,	17 Bde. R.F.A.	4-11-16	Wounded
103238	Reid, Ftr. S.-Sgt. D. B.,	HQ. 15 Bde. R.H.A.	29-9-18	Wounded (Dd of Wds)
166922	Reid, Gnr. J.,	92 Bty. R.F.A.	25-4-17	Wounded
113194	Reid, Gnr. W.,	"B" Bty. R.H.A.	8-8-16	Wounded
27625	Remment, Gnr. F.,	14 S.B. R.G.A.	31-5-15	Wounded
106130	Rendell, Gnr. J. C.,	29 D.A.C.	16-9-17	Wounded
42410	Rennocks, Dvr. J.,	29 D.A.C.	8-10-17	Wounded
46628	Restorick, Sdlr./Cpl. E.,	92 Bty. R.F.A.	29-9-17	Wounded (Gas)
62980	Revely, Dvr. A.,	10 Bty. R.F.A.	15-10-16	Wounded
72597	Rewin, Bdr. I. S.,	D/132 Bty. R.F.A.	29-7-16	Killed
60933	Reynolds, Gnr. G.,	97 Bty. R.F.A.	28-6-15	Killed
128929	Reynolds, Gnr. W.,	"L" Bty. R.H.A.	4-8-17	Wounded (Dd of Wds 14-8-17)
229850	Reynolds, Gnr. W. J.,	26 Bty. R.F.A.	28-11-17	Wounded
745091	Rich, Dvr. W.,	29 D.A.C.	9-7-17	Wounded
63845	Richards, Gnr. E.,	460 Bty. R.F.A.	24-7-17	Wounded (Gas)
74956	Richards, Gnr. J.,	D/132 Bty. R.F.A.	3-6-16	Wounded
50648	Richards, Sgt. W.,	92 Bty. R.F.A.	26-4-16	Wounded
94381	Richardson, Gnr. E., a/Bdr.	26 Bty. R.F.A.	25-5-17 / 21-9-17	Wounded / Killed
96711	Richardson, Gnr. T.,	"17 B.A.C.	27-7-15	Wounded
85963	Richardson, Gnr. W.,	92 Bty. R.F.A.	30-12-15	Wounded
23296	Richardson, Cpl. W.,	"B" Bty. R.H.A.	9-4-17	Wounded
76176	Richardson, Sgt. W. J., M.M.,	"B" Bty. R.H.A.	30-11-17	Wounded (Dd of Wds 5-12-17)
895	Richmond, Gnr. G.,	92 Bty. R.F.A.	4-6-15	Wounded
17755	Rickman, Dvr. H. W.,	147 B.A.C.	18-11-15	Wounded
31613	Ridding, Gnr. A.,	92 Bty. R.F.A.	24-4-17	Wounded
745040	Ridgway, Dvr. J.,	29 D.A.C.	29-9-18	Killed
745050	Ridley, Gnr. J.,	29 D.A.C.	28-9-18	Wounded
51961	Rigler, Gnr. C.,	"B" Bty. R.H.A.	13-6-15	Wounded
63398 or 68988	Riley, a/Bdr. F. W., M.M.,	"B" Bty. R.H.A.	15-10-18	Wounded
66848	Riley, Gnr. G.,	92 Bty. R.F.A.	5-6-15	Wounded
„	„ a/Bdr.	„ „	28-9-15	„
„	„ Cpl.	„ „	10-8-17	„
75833	Riley, Dvr. H.,	10 Bty. R.F.A.	26-5-15	Killed
15423	Riley, Dvr. H.,	26 Bty. R.F.A.	23-7-17	Wounded (Gas)
30464	Ringwood, Gnr. T.,	D/147 Bty. R.F.A.	29-6-16	Wounded
84484	Risk, Bdr. T.,	"B" Bty. R.H.A.	17-10-18	Killed
150432	Roberts, Gnr. H. J.,	26 Bty. R.F.A.	21-9-17	Wounded
70482	Roberts, a/Bdr. L. J.,	"L" Bty. R.H.A.	31-3-18	Wounded
62544	Roberts, a/Bdr. W.,	97 Bty. R.F.A.	21-10-16	Wounded
84906	Roberts, Gnr. W.,	460 Bty. R.F.A.	2-5-15	Wounded (Dd of Wds 27-5-15)
195193	Robertson, Gnr. A.,	"B" Bty. R.H.A.	25-11-17	Wounded
358	Robertson, Gnr. J.,	4th H.M. Bde. R.G.A.	?-8-15	Wounded
4896	Robertson, Gnr. J.,	4th H.M. Bde. R.G.A.	?-9-15	Wounded
139468	Robertson, Gnr. J. J.,	460 Bty. R.F.A.	6-6-17	Wounded
42383	Robinson, Gnr. A.,	460 Bty. R.F.A.	26-6-16	Wounded
820155	Robinson, Ftr. A. H.,	13 Bty. R.F.A.	28-9-18	Wounded
56809	Robinson, Dvr. F.,	368 Bty. R.F.A.	11-6-15	Wounded
106156	Robinson, Gnr. F. A.,	92 Bty. R.F.A.	1-12-17	Wounded
77093	Robinson, Gnr. H.,	368 Bty. R.F.A.	1-8-15	Wounded
L/8788	Robinson, Dvr. J.,	26 Bty. R.F.A.	28-9-18	Wounded
614078	Robinson, Gnr. R. E.,	War. Bty. R.H.A.	11-4-17	Wounded
196911	Robinson, Gnr. S.,	26 Bty. R.F.A.	{ 25-4-17 / 8-6-17	Wounded / „

Name & Rank.	Unit.	Date.	Casualty.
65458 Robson, Bdr. R.,	13 Bty. R.F.A.	24-11-17	Dd of Wds
761347 Robson, Gnr. W.,	V/29 T.M. Bty.	25-4-17	Wounded
	(att'd 92 Bty. R.F.A.)		
30108 Roche, Gnr. M.,	13 Bty. R.F.A.	5-6-15	Killed
91210 Roche, Sdlr. J.,	D/147 Bty. R.F.A.	1-7-16	Wounded
87673 Rodber, Dvr. A. W. G.,	HQ. 15 Bde. R.H.A.	30-11-17	Wounded
175385 Roddom, Gnr. J.,	13 Bty. R.F.A.	24-4-17	Wounded
645573 Rodgers, Ftr. R. A.,	D/17 Bty. R.F.A.	18-4-17	Wounded
98595 Rogers, Dvr. A. G.,	29 D.A.C.	8-11-16	Killed
140045 Rogers, Gnr. G. W.,	"L" Bty. R.H.A.	24-4-17	Killed
78866 Rogers, a/Bdr. H.,	10 Bty. R.F.A.	5-7-16	Killed
21405 Rogers, Gnr. J.,	10 Bty. R.F.A.	13-8-16	Wounded
614105 Rollason, Bdr. H. E.,	War. Bty. R.H.A.	11-4-17	Killed
120126 Rolls, Gnr. F.,	HQ. 17 Bde. R.F.A.	17-8-17	Wounded
62338 Rose, Dvr. A.,	10 Bty. R.F.A.	5-7-16	Wounded
147949 Rose, Gnr. H. H.,	Y/29 T.M. Bty.	22-10-18	Killed
	(att'd "L" Bty. R.H.A.)		
147494 Rose, Gnr. H. J.,	Y/29 T.M. Bty.	18-6-18	Wounded (Gas)
139942 Rose, Gnr. T.,	"B" Bty. R.H.A.	17-7-17	Wounded
109724 Rose, Gnr. W.,	371 Bty. R.F.A.	22-8-16	Wounded
745329 Rothwell, Gnr. W.,	26 Bty. R.F.A.	2-10-17	Wounded (Gas)
223910 Routley, Gnr. S.,	"B" Bty. R.H.A.	10-4-18	Wounded
116782 Rowberry, Gnr. H.,	26 Bty. R.F.A.	30-7-17	Wounded (Gas)
113306 Rowe, Gnr. J.,	"L" Bty. R.H.A.	11-6-18	Wounded
30357 Rowe, Gnr. R.,	92 Bty. R.F.A.	12-10-17	Wounded
95515 Rowlands, Gnr. N. T.,	"L" Bty. R.H.A.	16-2-17	Wounded
33925 Rozier, Sgt. A.,	26 Bty. R.F.A.	24-7-17	Wounded (Gas)
165365 Rudler, Gnr. J.,	26 Bty. R.F.A.	4-10-17	Wounded
57940 Rudman, Gnr. F.,	92 Bty. R.F.A.	23-7-17	Wounded
14979 Ruemens, Bdr. A.,	460 Bty. R.F.A.	3-10-17	Wounded
,, ,, Sgt.	,, ,,	14-10-18	,, Dd of Wds
223866 Rumbelow, Dvr. J.,	"B" Bty. R.F.A.	21-10-17	Killed
53368 Rushbrook, Sgt. G. W.,	92 Bty. R.F.A.	3-12-17	Wounded
32313 Rushton, Dvr. A.,	D/17 Bty. R.F.A.	22-7-17	Wounded
72193 Rusling, Dvr. W. F.,	13 Bty. R.F.A.	15-10-18	Wounded
L/44529 Russell, Bdr. A. H. S.,	370 Bty. R.F.A.	1-7-16	Wounded
22065 Russell, Gnr. D.,	D/17 Bty. R.F.A.	30-11-17	Wounded
72145 Russell, Dvr. G.,	29 D.A.C.	12-10-17	Wounded (Gas)
50602 Russell, Gnr. H.,	92 Bty. R.F.A.	10-6-15	Wounded
50869 Russell, Bdr. W. H.,	92 Bty. R.F.A.	4-5-15	Wounded
,, ,, Sgt.	D/17 Bty. R.F.A.	5-4-17	Wounded (Dd of Wds 10-4-17)
37785 Rust, Bdr. E.,	"Y" Bty. R.H.A.	3-5-15	(Dd of Wds 19-5-15)
82539 Ryan, Dvr. B.,	147 B.A.C.	16-4-15	Drowned
51182 Ryan, Gnr. T.,	"Y" Bty. R.H.A.	28-5-15	Wounded (Dd of Wds 30-5-15)
44486 Sabey, Gnr. H. V.,	370 Bty. R.F.A.	30-8-16	Wounded
614314 Sadler, Bdr. A.,	War. Bty. R.H.A.	30-8-17	Killed
99371 Sadler, Gnr. H.,	"B" Bty. R.H.A.	23-4-17	Killed
20426 Salmon, Gnr. B.,	Y/29 T.M. Bty.	27-3-18	Wounded (Gas)
635918 Salmond, Gnr. J.,	Y/29 T.M. Bty.	28-3-18	Wounded
196573 Salter, Gnr. J. E.,	War. Bty. R.H.A.	4-8-17	Killed
54003 Samson, Bdr. W. H.	"L" Bty. R.H.A.	28-2-17	Wounded
75301 Sandell, Gnr. W. B.,	26 Bty. R.F.A.	22-5-15	Killed
30502 Sanders, Gnr. S. W.,	92 Bty. R.F.A.	9-7-15	Wounded
101240 Sankey, Dvr. E.,	460 Bty. R.F.A.	17-5-18	Wounded (Gas)
194956 Sansom, Dvr. E.,	"L" Bty. R.H.A.	7-9-18	Wounded (Gas)
60342 Sansum, Bdr. W., D.C.M.,	97 Bty. R.F.A.	1-7-16	Wounded
2118 Sargeant, Cpl. S.,	D/147 Bty. R.F.A.	22-10-16	Wounded
53016 Sargent, Dvr. C.,	10 Bty. R.F.A.	11-6-15	Wounded
45421 Sargent, Dvr. T. H.,	29 D.A.C.	5-12-17	Wounded
78046 Saunders, Dvr. E.,	17 B.A.C.	16-12-15	Wounded
91038 Saunders, Gnr. H.,	D/132 Bty. R.F.A.	11-8-16	Wounded
52182 Saunders, Sgt. J., M.M.,	"B" Bty. R.H.A.	8-10-17	Wounded (Dd of Wds 24-10-17)
4099 Saunders, Bdr. R.,	26 Bty. R.F.A.	5-5-17	Wounded (Gas)
4116 Saunders, Bdr. W. C.,	10 Bty. R.F.A.	13-8-16	Wounded
51186 Saunders, Bdr. W. G.,	D/17 Bty. R.F.A.	7-4-17	Wounded (Dd of Wds 14-4-17)
163453 Saunders, Gnr. W. J.,	13 Bty. R.F.A.	10-5-18	Wounded (Dd of Wds)

Name & Rank.		Unit.	Date.	Casualty.
9819	Savage, Dvr. B. P.,	460 Bty. R.F.A.	30-12-15	Wounded
16288	Savage, Gnr. E. A.,	"L" Bty. R.H.A.	30-8-17	Killed
"	" L/Bdr. " M.M.,		25-3-18	Wounded
53484	Savage, Bdr. J.,	460 Bty. R.F.A.	27-6-15	Wounded
"	" Cpl.	"	9-4-17	Dd of Wds
88268	Savage, Dvr. S.,	15 B.A.C.	18-5-15	Wounded
88538	Sawtell, Gnr. W.,	D/132 Bty. R.F.A.	11-8-16	Wounded
97552	Sayers, L/Bdr. Sig. F., M.S.M.,	26 Bty. R.F.A.	18-10-18	Wounded
129274	Sayers, Bdr. W.,	460 Bty. R.F.A.	14-10-18	Wounded
87857	Scalley, a/Bdr. A.,	"B" Bty. R.H.A.	22-7-17	Wounded (Gas)
614044	Scampton, Sgt. C.,	War. Bty. R.H.A.	5-4-17	Wounded
48478	Scarsbrook, Sgt. J.,	"L" Bty. R.H.A.	12-7-15	Killed
195091	Schibl, Gnr. V. C. J.,	"L" Bty. R.H.A.	30-11-17	Missing (P.O.W.)
711504	Schofield, a/Bdr. H.,	26 Bty. R.F.A.	28-11-17	Wounded ?
W/4001	Scholes, Gnr. J.,	460 Bty. R.F.A.	17-8-17	Dd of Wds
1312	Schroder, Gnr. A.,	4th H.M. Bde. R.G.A.	?-8-15	Wounded
81133	Scott, Dvr. E.,	460 Bty. R.F.A.	19-6-15	Wounded
"	" Cpl.		15-7-17	"
175471	Scott, L/Bdr. J.,	Y/29 T.M. Bty.	23-4-18	Wounded
165116	Scott, Gnr. L.,	V/29 T.M. Bty.	5-10-17	Wounded
77366	Scott, Bdr. R. C.,	368 Bty. R.F.A.	4-6-15	Wounded
223822	Scott, Gnr. W.,	"L" Bty. R.H.A.	30-11-17	Wounded and Missing (P.O.W.)
745505	Scowcroft, Gnr. H.,	26 Bty. R.F.A.	6-10-17	Killed
14210	Seagrave, Gnr. G.,	460 Bty. R.F.A.	{6-4-16	Wounded
	a/Bdr.		{24-7-17	" (Gas)
99347	Seal, Gnr. C.,	"L" Bty. R.H.A.	28-2-17	Wounded
25331	Searle, Cpl. J.,	29 D.A.C.	4-5-17	Wounded (Dd of Wds 5-5-17)
59429	Seeney, Gnr. W.,	"Y" Bty. R.H.A.	23-10-16	Wounded
73182	Selby, Dvr. T. H.,	26 Bty. R.F.A.	1-10-18	Killed
66832	Sellman, Dvr. R.,	29 D.A.C.	14-8-17	Wounded
88479	Semple, Gnr. C.,	"L" Bty. R.H.A.	18-7-17	Wounded
52108	Seston, Bdr. A.,	17 B.A.C.	5-1-16	Wounded
"	" Cpl.	26 Bty. R.F.A.	23-7-17	Wounded (Gas)
L/39989	Settle, Dvr. J. B.,	29 D.A.C.	20-10-17	Wounded
88158	Severn, Sdlr. F.,	13 Bty. R.F.A.	30-12-15	Wounded (Dd of Wds 31-12-15)
38018	Severn, Bdr. W.,	460 Bty. R.F.A.	4-8-18	Wounded (Dd of Wds)
74384	Seymour, a/Bdr. W. J.	13 Bty. R.F.A.	16-6-17	Wounded
26402	Shackleton, Dvr. S.,	147 B.A.C.	16-4-15	Drowned
40465	Shadgett, Bdr. J. H.,	29 D.A.C.	18-3-18	Wounded
614136	Sharland, Cpl. R.,	War. Bty. R.H.A.	21-5-17	Killed
36019	Sharman, Gnr. H. J.,	17 B.A.C.	26-5-15	Wounded
76977	Sharp, Dvr. P.,	13 Bty. R.F.A.	15-10-18	Killed
L/42704	Sharpe, a/Bdr. H.,	371 Bty. R.F.A.	3-8-16	Wounded (Dd of Wds)
4872	Sharples, Cpl. J.,	D/147 Bty. R.F.A.	24-8-16	Killed
79967	Sharratt, Gnr. J. T.,	D/132 Bty. R.F.A.	7-7-16	Killed
43332	Shaw, Sgt. G. G. P.,	13 Bty. R.F.A.	6-8-15	Wounded
96725	Shaw, Bdr. H.,	26 Bty. R.F.A.	19-5-16	Wounded
L/17762	Shaw, Gnr. W.,	26 Bty. R.F.A.	14-7-18	Wounded
21075	Shean, Gnr A.,	13 Bty. R.F.A.	7-10-18	Wounded
61622	Shearer, Dvr. J. A.,	13 Bty. R.F.A.	21-5-15	Wounded
145	Sheddan, Cpl. C.,	4th H.M.Bde. R.G.A.	12-6-15	Killed
78640	Sheedy, Gnr. T.,	97 Bty. R.F.A.	28-6-15	Killed
185451	Sheehan, Dvr. P. R.,	29 D.A.C.	22-7-17	Wounded
91637	Sheehy, Dvr. J.,	26 Bty. R.F.A.	14-7-15	Wounded (Dd of Wds 31-8-15)
54744	Sheldon, Bdr. H.,	D/17 Bty. R.F.A.	31-3-17	Wounded
126259	Shelley, Dvr. A.,	"L" Bty. R.H.A.	4-9-18	Killed
614076	Shelley, Gnr. R.,	War. Bty. R.H.A.	23-4-17	Wounded
663212	Shelston, Gnr. C.,	26 Bty. R.F.A.	18-10-18	Wounded (Dd of Wds 19-10-18)
48190	Shepperd, Gnr. H.,	29 D.A.C.	11-7-15	Wounded
94869	Sherborne, Gnr. F.,	97 Bty. R.F.A.	7-8-15	Wounded
86272	Sheridan, Gnr. P.,	26 Bty. R.F.A.	12-5-15	Wounded
194987	Sherman, Gnr. H. F.,	"B" Bty. R.H.A.	30-11-17	Missing (P.O.W.) Died in Germany 7-12-17
59066	Shewring, Sgt. T.,	17 Brigade, R.F.A.	5-6-16	Wounded
614263	Shilcock, Gnr. H.,	War. Bty. R.H.A.	30-11-17	Wounded

Name & Rank.		Unit.	Date.	Casualty.
129217	Shippen, L/Bdr. E. C.,	26 Bty. R.F.A.	14-10-18	Wounded
78100	Shipway, Dvr. C.,	368 Bty. R.F.A.	6-6-15	Wounded
42435	Shore, Gnr. J.,	371 Bty. R.F.A.	{ 6-6-16	Wounded
			{ 4-8-16	,,
185565	Shore, Gnr. R.,	X/29 T.M. Bty.	13-2-18	Wounded (acc.)
4871	Shrewsbury, Cpl. A.,	460 Bty. R.F.A.	11-8-17	Wounded
556607	Shreive, Spr. C. (R.E.),	HQ. 29 D.A.	22-10-17	Wounded
140084	Shrubsole, Gnr. G. L., "L" Bty. R.H.A.		28-2-17	Wounded
49692	Shrubsole, Bdr. P. A.,	HQ. 15 Bde. R.H.A.	23-5-15	Wounded
614534	Sidaway, Gnr. G.,	War. Bty. R.H.A.	{ 11-4-17	Wounded
,,	,, a/Bdr.	,, ,,	{ 30-11-17	,, (Gas) (P.O.W.)
706409	Sidebotham, Gnr. F.,	92 Bty. R.F.A.	9-10-17	Wounded
88925	Sillence, Gnr. W. G., "L" Bty. R.H.A.		10-12-15	Killed
52704	Simmonds, Dvr. W.,	460 Bty. R.F.A.	2-7-15	Wounded (Dd of Wds 3-7-15)
29717	Simpson, Bdr. G.,	460 Bty. R.F.A.	24-7-17	Killed
701179	Simpson, Gnr. R.,	92 Bty. R.F.A.	11-10-17	Killed
19616	Sims, Gnr. W. A.,	92 Bty. R.F.A.	29-6-16	Wounded
78554	Skelton, Dvr. T.,	92 Bty. R.F.A.	4-7-15	Wounded
140291	Skennerton, Gnr. W. G. C., "B" Bty. R.H.A.		17-6-17	Wounded (Dd of Wds 17-6-17)
235286	Skerry, Dvr. H. V.,	26 Bty. R.F.A.	8-10-17	Wounded
96816	Skinner, Gnr. E.,	V/29 T.M. Bty.	20-8-16	Wounded
1573	Skinner, Gnr. V.,	26 Bty. R.F.A.	18-4-17	Wounded
68425	Skinner, Dvr. W. G., "B" Bty. R.H.A.		1-8-17	Wounded
2403	Slater, Gnr. E. D.,	"B" Bty. R.H.A.	12-8-16	Wounded
73511	Slater, Dvr. F.,	13 Bty. R.F.A.	6-12-17	Wounded
99686	Slater, Gnr. H.,	X/29 T.M. Bty.	30-8-16	Wounded
	Slater, a/Bdr. L.,	War. Bty. R.H.A.	11-4-17	Wounded
98507	Slater, Dvr. M.,	29 D.A.C.	5-10-17	Wounded
71340	Sleights, Gnr. H.,	"B" Bty. R.H.A.	3-5-17	Wounded
79414	Slinn, Dvr. W.,	10 Bty. R.F.A.	4-6-15	Wounded
67406	Sloan, Cpl. S. J.,	460 Bty. R.F.A.	9-4-17	Wounded
16563	Smart, Gnr. B.,	"B" Bty. R.H.A.	1-1-16	Wounded (Dd of Wds 13-1-16)
88242	Smart, Dvr. D. R.,	"B" Bty. R.H.A.	9-4-17	Dd of Wds
183675	Smart, Dvr. E.,	"L" Bty. R.H.A.	5-10-18	Wounded
53188	Smart, Bdr. F.,	"L" Bty. R.H.A.	4-9-18	Wounded
L/29811	Smee, a/Bdr. W. E.,	460 Bty. R.F.A.	5-5-17	Dd of Wds
51701	Smith, Gnr. A.,	97 Bty. R.F.A.	4-6-15	Wounded (Dd of Wds 6-6-15)
126791	Smith, Gnr. A.,	92 Bty. R.F.A.	31-10-16	Killed
99348	Smith, Gnr. A.,	"L" Bty. R.H.A.	24-4-17	Wounded
614345	Smith, B.Q.M.S., A. B.,	War. Bty. R.H.A.	12-8-17	Wounded (Dd of Wds)
614015	Smith, Cpl. A. E.,	War. Bty. R.H.A.	{ 11-4-17	Wounded
			{ 22-7-17	,, (Gas)
95062	Smith, Gnr. A. E.,	460 Bty. R.F.A.	17-8-17	Wounded
87144	Smith, Dvr. A. J.,	"L" Bty. R.H.A.	4-9-18	Killed
59121	Smith, Bdr. A. M.,	368 Bty. R.F.A.	31-5-15	Wounded
176957	Smith, Gnr. A. W.,	"L" Bty. R.H.A.	25-11-17	Wounded
5124	Smith, Dvr. C.,	13 Bty. R.F.A.	21-5-15	Wounded
78064	Smith, Gnr. C.,	10 Bty. R.F.A.	6-8-15	Wounded
49069	Smith, Gnr. E. A.,	"Y" Bty. R.H.A.	26-6-15	Wounded
23193	Smith, Sgt. F. G.,	10 Bty. R.F.A.	23-8-16	Wounded (Gas)
50041	Smith, Sgt. F.,	D/17 Bty. R.F.A.	24-4-17	Wounded
203938	Smith, Gnr. F. R.,	92 Bty. R.F.A.	20-9-17	Wounded
77104	Smith, Dvr. G.,	97 Bty. R.F.A.	1-5-15	Wounded
L/4082	Smith, Dvr. G.,	29 D.A.C.	18-7-17	Killed
139162	Smith, Gnr. G. H.,	460 Bty. R.F.A.	9-10-17	Wounded
78019	Smith, a/Bdr. G. W.,	26 Bty. R.F.A.	23-4-17	Wounded
614631	Smith, Dvr. H.,	War. Bty. R.H.A.	22-7-17	Wounded (Gas)
215592	Smith, Gnr. H.,	26 Bty. R.F.A.	14-8-17	Wounded
109993	Smith, Gnr. H. or A.,	460 Bty. R.F.A.	8-10-18	Wounded
614106	Smith, Dvr. H. A.,	War. Bty. R.H.A.	27-4-18	Wounded
54155	Smith, Gnr. H. C.,	26 Bty. R.F.A.	30-12-15	Wounded
42187	Smith, Dvr. H. E.,	29 D.A.C.	21-5-17	Wounded
63928	Smith, Sgt. J.,	26 Bty. R.F.A.	1-9-16	Wounded
L/1703	Smith, Gnr. J.,	"L" Bty. R.H.A.	11-4-17	Wounded
88532	Smith, Dvr. J.,	"L" Bty. R.H.A.	24-4-17	Wounded
786288	Smith, Bdr. J.,	X/29 T.M. Bty.	21-10-18	Wounded (Dd of Wds 26-10-18)

	Name & Rank.	Unit.	Date.	Casualty.
149373	Smith, Gnr. J. C.,	D/17 Bty. R.F.A.	17-9-17	Wounded (Dd of Wds 3-10-17)
55342	Smith, Gnr. J. S.,	"Y" Bty. R.H.A.	26-6-15	Wounded
65305	Smith, Cpl. J. T.,	"L" Bty. R.H.A.	30-11-17	Wounded and Missing
216824	Smith, Gnr. J. W.,	460 Bty. R.F.A.	14-10-18	Wounded
78020	Smith, Dvr. J.W.,	17 B.A.C.	26-4-16	Wounded
20995	Smith, Dvr. J. W.,	14 S.B. R.G.A.	20-6-15	Wounded
106	Smith, Gnr. M.,	4th H.M. Bde. R.G.A.	?-8-15	Wounded
L/34360	Smith, Gnr. N.,	"Y" Bty. R.H.A.	22-10-16	Killed
59431	Smith, Gnr. P. W.,	13 Bty. R.F.A.	3-10-18	Wounded
87722	Smith, Gnr. R.,	"L" Bty. R.H.A.	{ 2-5-15 { 23-8-15	Wounded ,,
87307	Smith, Gnr. R. J.,	"B" Bty. R.H.A.	22-7-17	Wounded (Gas)
204199	Smith, Gnr. S. M.,	26 Bty. R.F.A.	5-10-17	Wounded
65259	Smith, Dvr. T.,	13 Bty. R.F.A.	15-10-18	Wounded
56741	Smith, Dvr. W.,	17 B.A.C.	{ 2-6-15 { 16-6-15	Wounded ,,
38071	Smith, Gnr. W.,	92 Bty. R.F.A.	26-4-15	Wounded
10390	Smith, Gnr. W.,	29 D.A.C.	11-7-15	Wounded
93900	Smith, Gnr. W. H.,	29 D.A.C.	19-7-17	Killed
72882	Smith, Gnr. W. J.,	92 Bty. R.F.A.	21-9-17	Wounded
134934	Smith, Dvr. W. K.	D/17 Bty. R.F.A.	26-4-17	Wounded
114968	Smithers, Dvr. W.,	29 D.A.C.	16-9-17	Wounded
113022	Smitton, Gnr. F.,	D/17 Bty. R.F.A.	11-3-18	Wounded
3672	Smythe, Dvr. C.,	460 Bty. R.F.A.	31-5-18	Wounded
52723	Snelgrove, Gnr. P.,	"L" Bty. R.H.A.	19-6-15	Wounded
80479	Snelson, Gnr. S.,	97 Bty. R.F.A.	16-10-16	Killed
23572	Snow, Gnr. H. E.,	92 Bty. R.F.A.	24-9-17	Wounded (Gas)
111655	Somerville, 2/A.M., W. (R.F.C.),	17 Bde. R.F.A.	25-4-18	Wounded
43758	Sone, Dvr. J.,	10 Bty. R.F.A.	7-6-15	Wounded
134489	Spear, Gnr. G.,	26 Bty. R.F.A.	16-10-17	Wounded (Dd of Wds 29-10-17)
152233	Speight, Gnr. W.,	29 D.A.C.	15-7-17	Wounded (Dd of Wds 16-7-17)
70091	Spence, Gnr. H.,	368 Bty. R.F.A.	27-6-15	Killed
138815	Spence, Gnr. J.,	26 Bty. R.F.A.	16-10-18	Killed
17250	Spencer, Dvr. G.,	29 D.A.C.	29-9-17	Wounded (Dd of Wds 30-9-17)
21827	Spencer, Gnr. P. E.,	26 Bty. R.F.A.	1-8-17	Killed
49346	Spencer, Gnr. T.,	V/29 T.M. Bty.	26-11-17	Wounded
45432	Sperrin, Dvr. J. G.,	370 Bty. R.F.A.	31-8-16	Wounded
614139	Spicer, Gnr. R. A.,	War. Bty. R.H.A.	22-7-17	Wounded (Gas)
83458	Spike, Gnr. H.,	92 Bty. R.F.A.	22-10-16	Wounded
67023	Spinks, Gnr. W.,	HQ. 17 Bde. R.F.A.	2-5-15	Wounded
122349	Spinks, Gnr. H.,	D/132 Bty. R.F.A.	24-6-16	Wounded
59096	Springhall, a/Bdr. J.,	"B" Bty. R.H.A.	17-8-17	Wounded
77359	Spurgeon, Gnr. G. A.,	13 Bty. R.F.A.	16-6-15	Wounded
51661	Stace, Bdr. H. J.,	"B" Bty. R.H.A.	22-7-17	Wounded (Gas)
67001	Stafford, a/Bdr. A. E.,	92 Bty. R.F.A.	23-12-15	Wounded
53316	Stafford, Gnr. C.,	13 Bty. R.F.A.	7-6-15	Wounded
103551	Stanhope. Gnr. P. J.,	D/17 Bty. R.F.A.	16-10-17	Wounded
L/46902	Stanley, Gnr. E. A.,	"L" Bty. R.H.A.	18-1-17	Wounded
614321	Stanley, Gnr. G.,	War. Bty. R.H.A.	11-5-17	Wounded
195152	Starling, Gnr. H. J.,	"L" Bty. R.H.A.	12-8-17	Killed
10845	Stead, Dvr. J. H.,	V/29 T.M. Bty.	7-7-17	Killed
13521	Steeden, Sgt. F.,	"B" Bty. R.H.A.	13-7-15	Wounded
31046	Steer, Sgt. W. H.,	14 S.B. R.G.A.	4-5-15	Killed
217029	Stemp, Dvr. T.,	460 Bty. R.F.A.	7-10-18	Killed
55295	Stent, Dvr. H.,	26 Bty. R.F.A. (att'd HQ. 29 D.A.)	20-7-15	Wounded
62045	Stephenson, Gnr. G.,	13 Bty. R.F.A.	18-4-17	Dd of Wds
55321	Sterr, Dvr. H. D.,	460 Bty. R.F.A.	23-4-17	Wounded
1003	Stewart, Sgt. D.,	4th H.M. Bde. R.G.A.	7-11-15	Killed
23819	Stewart, Gnr. H.,	26 Bty. R.F.A.	28-4-17	Killed
4814	Stewart, Gnr. R.,	4th H.M. Bde. R.G.A.	?-8-15	Wounded
88206	Stewart, Gnr. W.,	"L" Bty. R.H.A.	4-6-15	Wounded
52213	Stiles, Bdr. W. J.,	"Y" Bty. R.H.A.	10-7-15	Wounded
99368	Stock, Gnr. E.,	"L" Bty. R.H.A.	22-7-17	Wounded (Gas)
614458	Stone, Dvr. H. S., m.m.,	War. Bty. R.H.A.	20-11-17	Wounded
101869	Stone, Gnr. J. E.,	"B" Bty. R.H.A	2-7-16	Wounded (Dd of Wds 2-8-16)

Name & Rank.	Unit.	Date.	Casualty.
87660 Stone, Bdr. T.,	D/17 Bty. R.F.A.	13-8-18	Wounded
152900 Stone, Gnr. W.,	13 Bty. R.F.A.	18-4-17	Wounded
18277 Storey, Dvr. N. J.,	460 Bty. R.F.A.	27-6-15	Wounded
204070 Stork, Gnr. A.,	92 Bty. R.F.A.	20-9-17	Killed
4899 Strachan, Gnr. G.,	4th H.M. Bde. R.G.A.	6-6-15	Dd of Wds
67174 Stratford, a/Bdr. A.,	29 D.A.C.	25-5-17	Wounded
51587 Streek, Gnr. F.,	90 H.B. R.G.A.	7-8-15	Wounded
786589 Street, Dvr. H.,	26 Bty. R.F.A.	14-10-18	Killed
68487 Stringer, Bdr. A. E.,	460 Bty. R.F.A.	3-4-18	Wounded
153844 Stringer, Gnr. P.,	War. Bty. R.H.A.	30-8-17	Wounded
41272 Stringer, Dvr. T.,	29 D.A.C.	29-9-17	Wounded (Gas)
66690 Stripp, a/Bdr. A. J.,	26 Bty. R.F.A.	21-6-15	Killed
59355 Strong, Dvr. C. W.,	26 Bty. R.F.A.	23-9-17	Wounded (Dd of Wds 24-9-17)
36943 Stroud, Bdr. A. E., D.C.M., M.M.,	HQ. 15 Bde. R.H.A.	28-6-15	Wounded
„ „ a/Sgt.	"B" Bty. R.H.A.	29-4-18	„
45703 Stroud, Cpl. G.,	370 Bty. R.F.A.	31-8-16	Wounded (Dd of Wds 12-10-16)
68995 Strutton, Dvr. J. B.,	14 S.B. R.G.A.	18-5-17	Wounded
881732 Stubbs, Gnr. F.,	460 Bty. R.F.A.	4-8-18	Wounded
77121 Sturland, Cpl. C.,	13 Bty. R.F.A.	28-9-18	Wounded
92704 Styles, Sgt. F.,	26 Bty. R.F.A.	9-7-16	Killed
168551 Styles, Gnr. F.,	92 Bty. R.F.A.	20-10-17	Wounded
50470 Sugar, S/S. E.,	"B" Bty. R.H.A.	{1-1-16, 21-11-17	Wounded „ (Gas)
745115 Sullivan, Dvr. F.,	26 Bty. R.F.A.	6-12-17	Wounded
74214 Sullivan, Dvr. J.,	29 D.A.C.	2-6-16	Dd of Wds
4875 Summers, Bdr. J. D.,	D/17 Bty. R.F.A.	{11-6-17, 17-8-17	Wounded „
745289 Sumner, Gnr. H.,	92 Bty. R.F.A.	17-9-17	Wounded
745248 Sumner, Cpl. W.,	Y/29 T.M. Bty.	18-3-18	Dd of Wds
45355 Sutcliffe, Dvr. H.,	13 Bty. R.F.A.	18-7-17	Dd of Wds
38945 Sutcliffe, Gnr. J.,	460 Bty. R.F.A.	14-11-17	Wounded
153816 Sutton, Gnr. W.,	War. Bty. R.H.A.	25-7-17	Wounded
36945 Swaffer, Dvr. H.,	"Y" Bty. R.H.A.	9-8-15	Wounded
92743 Swaine, Dvr. C.,	D/17 Bty. R.F.A.	24-4-17	Wounded
656204 Sweeney, Dvr D.,	29 D.A.C.	15-9-17	Wounded
42797 Sweet, Gnr. G. H.,	371 Bty. R.F.A.	3-8-16	Wounded
195001 Sweeting, Gnr. S.,	"L" Bty. R.H.A.	{2-10-17, 23-3-18	Wounded „
614533 Sweetzer, Gnr. J.,	War. Bty. R.H.A.	23-4-17	Wounded
90733 Swinerton, Dvr. B.,	HQ. 17 Bde. R.F.A.	4-5-15	Killed
53346 Syddall, Gnr. G.,	14 S.B. R.G.A.	20-5-15	Wounded
63334 Sydenham, Sgt. G.,	29 D.A.C.	28-9-18	Wounded
253187 Sykes, Cpl. T. (R.E.),	15 Bde. R.H.A.	30-11-17	Missing (P.O.W.)
614335 Symes, Gnr. J.,	War. Bty. R.H.A.	9-4-17	Wounded
195149 Taffander, Sgt. W. H.,	HQ. 29 D.A. (Gas services)	7-10-18	Killed
62475 Tamplin, Cpl. F.,	29 D.A.C.	22-4-17	Missing (Believed Killed)
3037 Tanner, Bdr. H. C.,	D/17 Bty. R.F.A.	26-6-17	Wounded
13778 Taylor, Gnr. A.,	D/17 Bty. R.F.A.	31-3-17	Wounded
50460 Taylor, a/Bdr. A.,	"B" Bty. R.H.A.	21-4-17	Killed.
51720 Taylor, Ftr. A.,	"L" Bty. R.H.A.	15-6-17	Killed
86397 Taylor, a/Bdr. A.,	92 Bty. R.F.A.	22-8-17	Wounded (Gas)
614633 Taylor, Bdr. B. F.,	War. Bty. R.H.A.	9-10-17	Killed
71967 Taylor, Tptr. E. W. G.,	"L" Bty. R.H.A.	11-6-15	Wounded
53209 Taylor, Gnr. F.,	"L" Bty. R.H.A.	6-6-15	Wounded
55392 Taylor, Gnr. F. J.,	"L" Bty. R.H.A.	12-7-15	Wounded
63111 Taylor, a/Bdr. F., D.C.M., M.M.,	"Y" Bty R.H.A.	15-10-15	Wounded
„ „ Bdr. „		15-8-16	Wounded (Gas)
155835 Taylor, Gnr. G. A.,	26 Bty. R.F.A.	3-5-17	Wounded (Gas)
70610 Taylor, Tptr. G. J. S.,	92 Bty. R.F.A.	{12-7-15, 24-4-17	Wounded „
112001 Taylor, Gnr. H.,	Z/29 T.M. Bty.	29-10-16	Killed
49733 Taylor, a/Bdr. H. G.,	26 Bty. R.F.A.	5-7-15	Wounded
192938 Taylor, Gnr. J.,	92 Bty. R.F.A.	2-12-17	Wounded
8138 Taylor, Dvr. J. E.,	"L" Bty. R.H.A.	1-8-17	Wounded

Name & Rank.	Unit.	Date.	Casualty.
50530 Taylor, Cpl. S. J.,	92 Bty. R.F.A.	29-5-15	Wounded (Dd of Wds 30-5-15)
71965 Taylor, Sgt. S. J.,	"L" Bty. R.H.A.	22-7-17	Wounded (Gas)
111111 Taylor, Gnr. S. L.,	"L" Bty. R.H.A.	28-2-17	Killed
207742 Taylor, Gnr. T. W.,	13 Bty. R.F.A.	14-10-18	Wounded
128791 Taylor, Gnr. W.,	X/29 T.M. Bty.	25-4-17	Wounded
198315 Taylor, Gnr. W. C.,	26 Bty. R.F.A.	12-9-17	Killed
110636 Tearle, Gnr. A.,	V/29 T.M. Bty.	27-4-17	Wounded
23604 Teat, Dvr. A. S.,	29 D.A.C.	28-9-18	Wounded
49570 Tempest, Gnr. W.,	14 S.B. R.G.A.	19-12-15	Wounded
79978 Terry, a/Bdr. A. E.,	"L" Bty. R.H.A.	2-10-17	Wounded
20102 Terry, Dvr. W. G.,	D/17 Bty. R.F.A.	24-4-17	Wounded
58913 Tetlow, Cpl. S/S. J.,	147 B.A.C.	16-4-15	Drowned
51826 Thackray, S/Sgt. Ftr. A.,	368 Bty. R.F.A.	3-7-15	Wounded
96336 Thackray, Gnr. J.,	29 D.A.C.	24-12-16	Killed
725582 Thomas, Dvr. E.,	War. Bty. R.H.A.	28-9-18	Wounded
202120 Thomas, Gnr. F. S.,	92 Bty. R.F.A.	19-10-17	Wounded (Gas)
91573 Thomas, Cpl. H. I. P.,	D/17 Bty R.F.A. (att'd. Z/29 T.M. Bty.)	29-6-16	Killed
80008 Thomas, Gnr. J.,	15 B.A.C.	20-10-15	Wounded
745224 Thomas, Cpl. W.,	29 D.A.C.	{29-11-17 27-1-18	Wounded "
8639 Thomas, Gnr. W.,	92 Bty. R.F.A.	29-5-15	Wounded
73835 Thompson, Gnr. J. W.,	26 Bty. R.F.A.	29-6-15	Wounded
125957 Thompson, Gnr. J.,	D/17 Bty. R.F.A.	{23-4-17 8-8-17	Wounded "
770808 Thompson, Dvr. M.,	29 D.A.C.	9-10-17	Wounded
88322 Thornton, Dvr. T.,	15 B.A.C.	9-5-15	Killed
45686 Thorpe, Dvr. G. J.,	92 Bty. R.F.A.	19-10-17	Wounded
146587 Thorpe, Gnr. H. E.,	26 Bty. R.F.A.	25-4-17	Wounded
42914 Thrussell, Bdr. A.,	"Y" Bty. R.H.A.	20-7-15	Killed
243049 Tiley, Dvr. J. A.,	29 D.A.C.	11-8-17	Killed
5125 Tillotson, Gnr. H.,	460 Bty. R.F.A.	25-8-17	Wounded
57496 Timbrell, Dvr. F. J.,	HQ. 15 Bde. R.H.A.	3-4-17	Wounded
68431 Timms, a/Bdr. F. J., M.M.,	"Y" Bty. R.H.A.	22-10-16	Wounded
614146 Timms, Gnr. J.,	War. Bty. R.H.A.	23-4-17	Wounded
3152 Tindale, Gnr. G.,	460 Bty. R.F.A.	25-8-17	Killed
160161 Tipping, Gnr. J.,	13 Bty. R.F.A.	20-3-18	Wounded
55901 Tobin, Sgt. J., M.M.,	460 Bty. R.F.A.	7-4-17	Killed
48443 Todman, Cpl. S/S., F.,	97 Bty. R.F.A.	4-6-15	Wounded
59848 Tolly, Bdr. W.,	92 Bty. R.F.A.	10-10-17	Wounded
42250 Tompkins, Bdr. A. G.,	370 Bty. R.F.A.	1-7-16	Wounded
63598 Tomlinson, Dvr. L.,	29 D.A.C.	20-7-17	Wounded
175777 Tomlinson, Gnr. W.,	HQ. 29 D.A.	30-11-17	Missing
27532 Toomey, Gnr. A.,	"L" Bty. R.H.A.	23-4-17	Wounded
120848 Tooth, a/Bdr. W.,	X/29 T.M. Bty.	20-3-18	Wounded
253193 Topple, Pnr. F. J. (R.E.),	15 Bde. R.H.A.	7-10-18	Wounded
66688 Town, Sgt. J.,	26 Bty. R.F.A.	14-8-17	Wounded
231689 Townend, Gnr. J.,	War. Bty. R.H.A.	9-10-17	Wounded
166638 Travis, Gnr. W.,	13 Bty. R.F.A.	22-4-17	Wounded
Trazes, Pte. T. (R.A.M.C.),	15 Bde. R.H.A.	11-7-15	Wounded
Trench, Armr. S/Sgt. J. (A.O.C.),	"B" Bty. R.H.A.	30-11-17	Missing (P.O.W.)
546 Trengrove, Gnr. G.,	29 D.A.C.	17-5-16	Wounded
91908 Trengrove, Gnr. G. H.,	460 Bty. R.F.A.	22-8-17	Wounded (Gas)
56570 Trevethan, Sgt. J.,	26 Bty. R.F.A.	25-10-18	Wounded (Dd of Wds 30-10-18)
36247 Trice, Dvr. J.,	17 B.A.C.	2-5-15	Wounded
38089 Triggs, Gnr. H., L/Bdr.	13 Bty. R.F.A.	21-10-17 15-10-18	Wounded "
29070 Trippick, Gnr. F.,	10 Bty. R.F.A.	{7-12-15 22-12-15	Wounded Killed (by landslide)
103670 Truckle, Gnr. H. G.,	10 Bty. R.F.A.	10-6-16	Wounded
44463 Tudor, Gnr. G. J.,	13 Bty. R.F.A.	27-10-16	Wounded
61499 Tullett, Gnr. H. W.,	"L" Bty. R.H.A.	2-5-15	Wounded
3588 Touhy, Dvr. S. O.,	29 D.A.C.	20-8-17	Wounded
52855 Turberville, Gnr. P. G.,	"B" Bty. R.H.A.	22-5-15	Wounded (Dd of Wds 25-5-15)

Name & Rank.	Unit.	Date.	Casualty.
750869 Turnbull, Gnr. J.,	92 Bty. R.F.A.	29-4-17	Killed
196880 Turnbull, Gnr. J.,	26 Bty. R.F.A.	12-4-17	Wounded
52579 Turner, Gnr. F. N.,	X/29 T.M. Bty.	2-6-17	Wounded
53757 Turner, Dvr. C. J.,	D/17 Bty. R.F.A.	9-10-17	Killed
4818 Turner, Gnr. J.,	D/132 Bty. R.F.A.	11-8-16	Wounded
614328 Turner, Gnr. R. P.,	War. Bty. R.H.A.	11-5-17	Wounded
		22-7-17	,, (Gas)
47535 Turney, Sgt. G. J.,	"Y" Bty. R.H.A.	22-10-16	Killed
622515 Twaites, Dvr.,	"L" Bty. R.H.A.	7-9-18	Wounded (Gas)
614644 Tweedale, Dvr. H.,	War. Bty. R.H.A.	24-4-17	Wounded
45256 Twohig, Gnr. J.,	"B" Bty. R.H.A.	22-7-17	Wounded (Gas)
891427 Tyers, Gnr. C.,	Y/29 T.M. Bty.	18-6-18	Wounded (Gas)
75471 Tyler, Gnr. F.,	370 Bty. R.F.A.	29-7-16	Killed
42569 Ulyatt, a/Bdr. C.,	371 Bty. R.F.A.	22-8-16	Wounded
			(Dd of Wds)
47584 Uncles, Dvr. J. W.,	13 Bty. R.F.A.	12-7-15	Wounded
32044 Unsworth, Cpl. J.,	26 Bty. R.F.A.	20-9-17	Wounded
68926 Upchurch, Gnr. P.,	"B" Bty. R.H.A.	1-6-18	Killed
154773 Upson, Gnr. P. S.,	92 Bty. R.F.A.	19-8-17	Wounded
130035 Upton, Gnr. G. H.,	460 Bty. R.F.A.	20-10-17	Wounded
8158 Urry, Dvr. J. H.,	147 Bde. R.F.A.	16-6-15	Wounded
			(Dd of Wds 17-6-15)
65292 Vallas, Bdr. A. J.,	"Y" Bty. R.H.A.	15-11-15	Wounded
		24-12-15	,,
155883 Vane, Gnr. A. H.,	92 Bty. R.F.A.	28-4-17	Wounded
64252 Vann, Sgt. H.,	460 Bty. R.F.A.	31-10-16	Wounded
65811 Vanson, Bdr. L.,	"L" Bty. R.H.A.	22-7-17	Wounded (Gas)
37430 Varley, Gnr. T.,	368 Bty. R.F.A.	27-6-15	Wounded
163957 Varney, Gnr. H.,	92 Bty. R.F.A.	12-4-17	Wounded
			(Dd of Wds 3-5-17)
91876 Vaughan, Gnr. A.,	147 B.A.C.	30-7-15	Killed
229775 Vernon, Gnr. P. W.,	29 D.A.C.	3-12-17	Wounded
87713 Vickerstaffe, Bdr. O.,	"L" Bty. R.H.A.	9-10-17	Wounded
54374 Vitty, S/S. W.,	13 Bty. R.F.A.	3-5-15	Wounded
8074 Wade, Dvr. C.,	460 Bty. R.F.A.	2-7-15	Wounded
43992 Waite, Gnr. C. H.,	97 Bty. R.F.A.	17-10-16	Wounded
101793 Waite, Dvr. W.,	"B" Bty. R.H.A.	26-11-17	Wounded
155372 Wakefield, Gnr. H. H.,	92 Bty. R.F.A.	7-8-17	Killed
L/26372 Wakefield, Gnr. W. E. G.,	460 Bty. R.F.A.	31-10-16	Wounded
		30-8-17	Killed
42156 Wakelam, Gnr. J.,	26 Bty. R.F.A.	7-6-15	Dd of Wds
196563 Walburne, Gnr. J.,	460 Bty. R.F.A.	17-8-17	Wounded
86961 Waldron, Gnr. F.,	Z/29 T.M. Bty.	13-7-17	Wounded
45926 Walford, Cpl./Ftr. J. M.,	92 Bty. R.F.A.	23-8-17	Wounded
			(Dd of Wds 24-8-17)
94490 Wall, Gnr. A. S.,	460 Bty. R.F.A.	9-4-17	Wounded
6843 Wallace, Cpl. A.,	13 Bty. R.F.A.	6-12-17	Wounded
60904 Wallace, Gnr. P.,	97 Bty. R.F.A.	16-4-15	Drowned
200069 Waller, Gnr. A. F.,	460 Bty. R.F.A.	9-4-17	Wounded
102422 Walkden, Dvr. J.,	"L" Bty. R.H.A.	18-1-17	Wounded
78180 Walker, Dvr. C.,	15 B.A.C.	26-5-15	Wounded
42246 Walker, Dvr. C.,	370 Bty. R.F.A.	28-7-16	Wounded
111454 Walker, Dvr. C. A.,	370 Bty. R.F.A.	3-8-16	Wounded
123767 Walker, Sdlr. E.,	460 Bty. R.F.A.	7-10-18	Wounded
35999 Walker, Bdr. G. (or P.),	"B" Bty. R.H.A.	19-6-15	Wounded
49205 Walker, Gnr. G.,	13 Bty. R.F.A.	25-7-15	Wounded
Walker, a/Bdr. J.,	368 Bty. R.F.A.	23-5-15	Wounded
218423 Walker, Gnr. J.,	26 Bty. R.F.A.	13-10-17	Wounded and
			Gassed
14478 Walsh, a/Bdr. N. J.,	460 Bty. R.F.A.	6-6-17	Killed (acc.)
40930 Walter, Gnr. E. J.,	90 H.B. R.G.A.	?-5-15	Wounded
176954 Walters, a/Bdr. H. P.,	"L" Bty. R.H.A.	12-8-17	Wounded
			(Dd of Wds 12-8-17)
113272 Walton, Gnr. E.,	"B" Bty. R.H.A.	25-4-17	Wounded
174657 Walton, Gnr. J.,	Z/29 T.M. Bty.	27-2-17	Wounded
42853 Ward, Dvr. E.,	"L" Bty. R.H.A.	24-4-17	Wounded
201234 Ward, Gnr. G. W.,	HQ. 29 D.A.	30-11-17	Missing
			(P.O.W.)
48472 Ward, Bdr. J.,	X/29 T.M. Bty.	22-7-16	Wounded
140088 Ward, Gnr. K. W.,	"L" Bty. R.H.A.	24-7-17	Wounded
158972 Ward, Gnr. W.,	"L" Bty. R.H.A.	29-7-17	Wounded
88413 Ward, a/Bdr. W.,	"B" Bty. P.H.A.	17-8-17	Killed
55563 Warden, Gnr. P.,	"B" Bty. R.H.A.	5-7-15	Killed
263467 Wardhill, Gnr. H.,	D/17 Bty. R.F.A.	5-9-18	Wounded

Name & Rank.		Unit.	Date.	Casualty.	
38299	Wareham, Gnr. C.,	"Y" Bty. R.H.A.	23-10-16	Wounded	
139439	Warne, Gnr. F.,	"L" Bty. R.H.A.	1-12-17	Wounded	
77691	Warner, Gnr. E. S.,	26 Bty. R.F.A.	31-12-15	Wounded	
15144	Warr, Sgt. H. F. D.,	460 Bty. R.F.A.	9-4-17	Wounded	
194960	Warren, Dvr. C. L.,	"L" Bty. R.H.A.	27-7-17	Wounded	
149260	Warwick, Gnr. A. N. B.,	29 D.A.C.	9-10-17	Wounded	
69956	Warwick, Gnr. F.,	10 Bty. R.F.A.	21-8-17	Wounded	
32259	Waterfield, Gnr. C.,	13 Bty. R.F.A.	30-9-17	Wounded	(Gas)
48913	Waterhouse, Bdr. R.,	460 Bty. R.F.A.	3-6-18	Wounded	
614344	Waters, a/B.S.M., G.,	War. Bty. R.H.A.	24-4-17	Wounded	
54625	Waterson, Sgt. F.,	26 Bty. R.F.A.	23-7-17	Wounded	(Gas)
1070	Watkins, Dvr. J. T.,	147 B.A.C.	1-7-15	Wounded	
52211	Watson, a/Bdr. A.,	97 Bty. R.F.A.	4-6-15	Wounded	
	Watson, Gnr. E.,	"B" Bty. R.H.A.	25-4-17	Wounded	
14914	Watson, Gnr. J.,	92 Bty. R.F.A.	5-5-17	Wounded	(Gas)
253194	Watson, Pnr. P. T. (R.E.),	att'd. 15 Bde. R.H.A.	31-5-18	Wounded	
95765	Watson, Dvr. R.,	29 D.A.C.	23-10-15	Drowned	
34964	Watt, Sgt. E.,	10 Bty. R.F.A.	27-5-15	Killed	
34219	Watts, B.Q.M.S., R. H., M.M.,	"L" Bty. R.H.A.	25-3-18	Wounded	
93287	Weatherall, Gnr. J.,	460 Bty. R.F.A.	10-8-17	Wounded	(Gas)
99462	Weatherhog. S/S. T.,	"B" Bty. R.H.A.	4-4-17	Killed	
33633	Webb, Sgt. C. J.,	26 Bty. R.F.A.	7-8-15	Wounded	
148147	Webb, Gnr. H. C.,	26 Bty. R.F.A.	10-12-17	Wounded	(Gas)
177096	Webb, Dvr. H. J.,	92 Bty. R.F.A.	17-10-18	Wounded	
139121	Wedge, Gnr. F. E.,	War. Bty. R.H.A.	15-7-17	Wounded	
102665	Webster, Dvr. F.,	"B" Bty. R.H.A.	21-11-17	Wounded	(Gas)
224036	Weekes, Gnr. A. E. B. V.,	"L" Bty. R.H.A.	1-4-18	Wounded	
614635	Weighall, Gnr. F. A.,	War. Bty. R.H.A.	11-5-18	Wounded	
49196	Weller, Gnr. S. G.,	"Y" Bty. R.H.A.	7-8-15	Wounded	
133922	Wells, Gnr. W.,	29 D.A.C.	26-9-17	Wounded	
213443	Welsby, Gnr. T.,	26 Bty. R.F.A.	14-8-17	Wounded	
93789	Welsh, Gnr. H.,	10 Bty. R.F.A.	16-4-15	Drowned	
96358	Welsh, Dvr. J. W.,	13 Bty. R.F.A.	23-7-17	Wounded	(Gas)
98570	Welsh, Cpl. T. F.,	Z/29 T.M. Bty.	25-7-17	Wounded	
33893	Wesley, Dvr. A.,	D/17 Bty. R.F.A.	24-4-17	Wounded	
79531	Wesson, Dvr. J.,	"B" Bty. R.H.A.	9-4-17	Wounded	
36492	West, Dvr. J.,	10 Bty. R.F.A.	26-5-15	Wounded	
614413	West, Cpl. N. A.,	War. Bty. R.H.A.	28-3-18	Wounded	(Gas)
8225	West, a/Bdr. W. E.,	"L" Bty. R.H.A.	27-7-17	Wounded	
23682	West, Sdlr. W. G.,	"B" Bty. R.H.A.	2-5-15	Wounded	
152703	West, Dvr. W. H.,	92 Bty. R.F.A.	23-7-17	Wounded	
32750	Weston, Gnr. G.,	460 Bty. R.F.A.	8-8-17	Wounded	
615079	Westwood, Gnr. W.,	War. Bty. R.H.A.	22-7-17	Wounded	(Gas)
L/34413	Whalley, Gnr. E.,	369 Bty. R.F.A.	13-8-16	Wounded	
62105	Wheaton, Gnr. E. C. S.,	"B" Bty. R.H.A.	30-7-15	Wounded	
96631	Wheelan, Gnr.W. G.,	D/132 Bty R.F.A.	19-8-16	Wounded	
7446	Wheeldon, Gnr. R. F.,	D/17 Bty. R.F.A.	18-4-17	Wounded	
614532	Wheeler, Gnr.	War. Bty. R.H.A.	5-3-17	Wounded	
43952	Wheeler, a/Bdr. E.,	10 Bty. R.F.A.	13-7-15	Killed	
44483	Wheeler, Bdr. F.,	26 Bty. R.F.A.	3-12-17	Dd of Wds	
80007	Wheeler, Gnr. F. R.,	"B" Bty. R.H.A.	29-8-15	Killed	
925435	Wheeler, Cpl. I.,	13 Bty. R.F.A.	28-9-18	Wounded	
55890	Whelan, Gnr. W.,	368 Bty. R.F.A.	24-5-15	Wounded	
96631	Whelan, Gnr. W. G.,	D/132 Bty. R.F.A.	19-8-16	Wounded	
4762	Wheler, Gnr.,	14 S.B. R.G.A.	7-1-16	Wounded	
L/34557	Whincup, Dvr. A.,	29 D.A.C.	25-9-17	Killed	
21425	Whinery, Dvr. T.,	"L" Bty. R.H.A.	11-7-15	Wounded	
15060	Whitbread, Bdr. J.,	460 Bty. R.F.A.	24-5-15	Wounded	
14297	Whitcombe, Dvr.,	460 Bty. R.F.A.	17-5-15	Wounded	
196693	White, Gnr. A.,	"B" Bty. R.H.A.	22-7-17	Wounded	(Gas)
L/42546	White, Dvr. A. I..	13 Bty. R.F.A.	22-10-16	Wounded	
75192	White. Gnr. C.,	460 Bty. R.F.A.	9-4-17	Wounded	
33960	White, Gnr. C. G.,	460 Bty. R.F.A.	10-4-17	Wounded	(acc.)
1411	White, Gnr. E.,	26 Bty. R.F.A.	3-6-17	Wounded	
73291	White, Dvr. E.,	13 Bty. R.F.A.	15-10-18	Wounded	
63074	White, Gnr. F. R.,	"Y" Bty. R.H.A.	2-5-15	Wounded (Dd of Wds 5-5-15)	
19873	White, Gnr. G.,	13 Bty. R.F.A.	22-10-16	Wounded	
181060	White, Gnr. H. E.,	13 Bty. R.F.A.	23-7-17	Wounded	(Gas)
196564	White, Gnr. H. P..	War. Bty. R.H.A.	9-10-17	Wounded	
177026	Whitehouse, Gnr. W..	"B" Bty. R.H.A.	21-3-18	Wounded	(Gas)

Name & Rank.	Unit.	Date.	Casualty.
47313 Whithead, Gnr. J.,	14 S.B. R.G.A.	19-7-15	Wounded
34462 Whitley, a/Cpl. A.,	Y/29 T.M. Bty.	25-10-18	Wounded
		26-10-18	Wounded
222393 Whittaker, Gnr. W.,	Y/29 T.M. Bty.	18-6-18	Wounded (Gas)
57245 Whittaker, a/Bdr. W. N.,	29 D.A.C.	20-5-17	Wounded
L/2384 Whittle, Gnr. J.,	29 D.A.C.	30-6-16	Wounded
99226 Wibrew, S/S. J.,	460 Bty. R.F.A.	24-11-15	Wounded
830948 Wiggin, Dvr. A.,	Y/29 T.M. Bty.	30-11-17	Wounded
48536 Wiggins, a/Bdr. S.,	"B" Bty. R.H.A.	29-8-17	Wounded
		30-11-17	Missing
32444 Wilbar, Gnr. G.,	"L" Bty. R.F.A.	18-1-17	Wounded
9543 Wilcox, Bdr. C. J.,	13 Bty. R.F.A.	22-7-17	Wounded
			(Dd of Wds 29-7-17)
614492 Wilday, Gnr. F.,	War. Bty. R.H.A.	30-11-17	Killed
L/20872 Wilde, Sgt. G.,	V/29 T.M. Bty.	1-12-17	Missing (presumed kd. auth. W.O. 12-8-18)
137154 Wilding, Gnr. A.,	"B" Bty. R.H.A.	18-10-16	Missing
49688 Wilding, Dvr. R.,	HQ. 15 Bde. R.H.A.	1-9-15	Wounded
Wilkes, Gnr. H.,	War. Bty. R.H.A.	11-4-17	Wounded
24277 Wilkin, Cpl. F.,	368 Bty. R.F.A.	24-5-15	Wounded
126482 Wilkin, Gnr. S. E.,	"L" Bty. R.F.A.	19-10-16	Wounded
		12-9-17	Killed
75216 Wilkins, Gnr. H.,	147 Bde. R.F.A.	21-9-16	Wounded
85143 Wilkins, Gnr. H.,	10 Bty. R.F.A.	20-10-16	Wounded
61948 Wilkins, Sgt. R.,	29 D.A.C.	6-8-17	Wounded
51770 Wilkinson, S.Sgt./Ftr. H. E.,	10 Bty. R.F.A.	6-6-15	Dd of Wds
240660 Wilkinson, Gnr. J. F.,	26 Bty. R.F.A.	13-10-18	Wounded
58289 Willard, Gnr. E. H.,	13 Bty. R.F.A.	17-8-17	Wounded (Gas)
76307 Willey, Gnr. H. J.,	HQ. 29 D.A.	30-11-17	Wounded
63446 Williams, Gnr. H.,	460 Bty. R.F.A.	17-5-15	Wounded
			(Dd of Wds 21-5-15)
214691 Williams, Gnr. E. J.,	War. Bty. R.H.A.	11-3-18	Wounded
			(Dd of Wds)
34964 Williams, Gnr. F. J.,	"B" Bty. R.H.A.	9-4-17	Wounded
26352 Williams, S/S. G.,	90 H.B. R.G.A.	19-6-15	Wounded
68584 Williams, a/Bdr. G.,	29 D.A.C.	13-8-15	Wounded
56535 Williams, Gnr. G.,	29 D.A.C.	27-12-15	Killed
63229 Williams, Gnr. G.,	"L" Bty. R.H.A.	22-4-17	Wounded
53345 Williams, Sgt. G. H.,	371 Bty. R.F.A.	22-8-16	Wounded
75286 Williams, Gnr. H.,	D/147 Bty. R.F.A.	22-9-16	Wounded
38340 Williams, a/Bdr. H.,	97 Bty. R.F.A.	14-11-16	Wounded
614336 Williams, Gnr. H.,	War. Bty. R.H.A.	5-4-17	Wounded
59513 Williams, Bdr. H.,	"B" Bty. R.H.A.	19-9-17	Wounded
71380 Williams, Gnr. H. A.,	HQ. 15 Bde. R.H.A.	15-6-15	Wounded
38070 Williams, Gnr. J.,	13 Bty. R.F.A.	14-5-15	Wounded
64033 Williams, Bdr. J.,	92 Bty. R.F.A.	10-8-17	Wounded
62660 Williams, Gnr. J.,	"B" Bty. R.H.A.	17-8-17	Wounded
			(Dd of Wds 4-9-17)
215726 Williams, Ftr. O.,	92 Bty. R.F.A.	22-8-17	Killed
112298 Williams, L/Bdr. O.,	92 Bty. R.F.A.	13-10-18	Wounded
99511 Williams, Gnr. P.,	X/29 T.M. Bty.	19-6-16	Wounded
96633 Williams, Gnr. R.,	"B" Bty. R.H.A.	12-8-17	Wounded
L/34608 Williamson, Dvr. E.,	"L" Bty. R.H.A.	1-8-17	Wounded
31326 Williamson, Dvr. J.,	97 Bty. R.F.A.	9-1-17	Wounded (Gas)
51480 Willis, Gnr. A.,	V/29 T.M. Bty.	1-12-17	Missing
54881 Willis, Gnr. T. A.,	97 Bty. R.F.A.	16-4-15	Drowned
70199 Wilson, a/Bdr. A. R.,	92 Bty. R.F.A.	13-5-15	Wounded
	Bdr.		30-7-15	Dd of Wds
67468 Wilson, Gnr. C.,	13 Bty. R.F.A.	18-6-15	Wounded
51251 Wilson, Cpl. F.,	371 Bty. R.F.A.	7-5-16	Wounded
			(Dd of Wds)
77926 Wilson, Dvr. F.,	10 Bty. R.F.A.	26-5-15	Wounded
101024 Wilson, Dvr. J.,	D/147 Bty. R.F.A.	25-5-16	Wounded
87053 Wilson, a/Bdr. J.,	460 Bty. R.F.A.	17-8-17	Killed
137260 Wilson, a/Bdr. J.,	92 Bty. R.F.A.	22-8-17	Wounded (Gas)
175312 Wilson, Gnr. J.,	13 Bty. R.F.A.	6-12-17	Wounded
91058 Wilson, S/S. Cpl. J.,	460 Bty. R.F.A.	7-10-18	Killed
98408 Wilson, Gnr. J. F.,	D/17 Bty. R.F.A.	26-8-17	Killed
15780 Wilson, Bdr. J. R.,	14 S.B. R.G.A.	11-12-15	Wounded
93998 Wilson, Dvr. T.,	26 Bty. R.F.A.	4-6-18	Wounded
69115 Wilson, a/Bdr. W.,	460 Bty. R.F.A.	28-6-15	Wounded
			(Dd of Wds 3-7-15)

Name & Rank.	Unit.	Date.	Casualty.
55286 Wilson, Dvr. W. J.,	26 Bty. R.F.A.	12-5-15	Wounded
10842 Windle, Gnr. B.,	460 Bty. R.F.A.	10-4-17	Wounded (acc.)
94732 Windsor, Dvr. J.,	13 Bty. R.F.A.	16-2-17	Wounded
176979 Wingrove, Dvr. L.,	"B" Bty. R.H.A.	22-10-18	Wounded (Gas)
8202 Winter, Gnr. J.,	HQ. 15 Bde. R.H.A.	30-11-17	Missing
614021 Winyard, S.Sgt./Sdlr. H.,	War. Bty. R.H.A.	9-4-17	Wounded (Dd of Wds)
90309 Wishart, Gnr. C.,	26 Bty. R.F.A.	19-5-16	Wounded
80105 Witham, Gnr. C. F.,	13 Bty. R.F.A.	2-5-15	Wounded
44992 Withers, Gnr. G.,	368 Bty. R.F.A.	27-6-15	Wounded
6364 Withers, Gnr. J.,	90 H.B. R.G.A.	3-8-15	Killed
614607 Wood, Dvr. B.,	"L" Bty. R.H.A.	5-10-18	Killed (?)
47046 Wood, Gnr. C.,	14 S.B. R.G.A.	12-7-15	Wounded
19182 Wood, Bdr. G.,	26 Bty. R.F.A.	17-4-17	Wounded
55967 Wood, Gnr. J.,	97 Bty. R.F.A.	3-7-15	Killed
99416 Wood, Gnr. W. L.,	"Y" Bty. R.H.A.	20-10-15	Wounded
160419 Woodall, Gnr. R.,	26 Bty. R.F.A.	13-5-17	Wounded
614365 Woodfield, Gnr. W. C.,	War. Bty. R.H.A.	22-7-17	Wounded (Gas)
L/34403 Woodhead, Gnr. N.,	369 Bty. R.F.A.	30-8-16	Wounded
39590 Woodman, a/Bdr. A., m.m.,	460 Bty. R.F.A.	9-4-17	Wounded
2281 Woodnutt, Gnr. F. H.,	D/147 Bty. R.F.A.	29-1-17	Wounded
56524 Woodroffe, Gnr.,	14 S.B. R.G.A.	7-1-16	Wounded
123662 Woods, Gnr. B.,	D/17 Bty. R.F.A.	25-4-17	Wounded
58360 Woodthorpe, Gnr. A.,	368 Bty. R.F.A.	16-4-15	Drowned
249389 Woollen, Dvr. C.,	13 Bty. R.F.A.	15-10-18	Wounded
68062 Woolley, Gnr. A.,	13 Bty. R.F.A.	15-5-17	Wounded
915678 Woolstone, a/Cpl. S. J.,	D/17 Bty. R.F.A.	20-9-17	Wounded
115320 Wornell, Gnr. J.,	92 Bty. R.F.A.	5-5-17	Wounded
745293 Worsley, Gnr. W. T.,	D/17 Bty. R.F.A.	21-1-18	Wounded (Dd of Wds)
94992 Wright, Sgt. H. W.,	460 Bty. R.F.A.	28-4-15	Wounded
43431 Wright, Gnr. J.,	460 Bty. R.F.A.	12-10-18	Wounded
84781 Wright, L/Bdr. J. H.,	460 Bty. R.F.A.	23-10-18	Killed
38972 Wright, Bdr. W.,	"L" Bty. R.H.A.	7-10-15	Wounded
32008 Wright, Gnr. W.,	26 Bty. R.F.A.	24-4-17	Wounded
99226 Wybrew, S/S. J.,	460 Bty. R.F.A.	24-11-15	Wounded
87260 Wye, Sgt. A. V.,	460 Bty. R.F.A.	9-10-17	Wounded (Dd of Wds 11-10-17)
631523 Wylie, Gnr. D. A.,	26 Bty. R.F.A.	28-6-18	Wounded (Dd of Wds)
47241 Wynne, Pte. J. (R.A.M.C.),	War. Bty. R.H.A.	27-4-18	Wounded
78845 Wyper, Gnr. P.,	460 Bty. R.F.A.	{ 12-6-15 / 12-7-15	Wounded „
1171 Yeoman, Gnr. J.,	4th H.M. Bde. R.G.A.	12-8-15	Dd of Wds
60673 Young, Sgt.,	Y/29 T.M. Bty.	1-7-16	Wounded
46901 Young, Dvr. H.,	29 D.A.C.	16-10-16	Wounded

PART III.

RECORD OF OFFICERS' SERVICES IN THE 29th DIVISIONAL ARTILLERY, BETWEEN THE GALLIPOLI LANDING (25th APRIL, 1915,) AND THE COMMENCEMENT ON THE ARMISTICE, (11th NOVEMBER, 1918.)

EXPLANATORY NOTES.

1. The period covered is from the landing at Cape Helles on the Gallipoli peninsula on the 25th April, 1915, to the commencement of the Armistice on the 11th November, 1918.

2. Services in units of the 29th Divisional Artillery *only* are recorded. Similarly, no mention of wounds received during service elsewhere whilst only those honours which were conferred for services in the 29th Divisional Artillery are mentioned.

3. The rank, placed immediately after the name of an officer, is that held by him on joining the 29th D.A.

4. Two dates shown after the name of a unit show the period during which the officer served in that unit: words in brackets after the second date indicate the cause of termination of such service.

5. The "landing" referred to in this record is that at Cape Helles on 25th April, 1915. The "evacuation" is the evacuation of Cape Helles which terminated on 9th January, 1916.

6. There may be confusion in the reader's mind owing to two different batteries having become D/17 in succession. This confusing element is explained in the history of the D.A. (Part IV).

Adams, Temp. 2nd Lieut. D., (2nd Lieut. 15/6/15), joined the detachment from the 29th D.A.C. at Helles 17/10/15.

Allan, Captain (Temp. Major) B., R.G.A. (T.F.), commanded the Ross Battery, 1/4th Highland Mountain Brigade, R.G.A. (T.F.), at the landing; was attached to 29th D.A. H.Q. from 10/5/15 to 20/8/15 when he was evacuated as a result of a fall from his horse.

Allen, Battery Sergeant-Major F., D.C.M., 13th Battery, R.F.A., on being given a regular commission, was posted to the 31st D.A. 19/3/17.

Allin, Temp. Captain J. R. P., R.A.M.C., came to the D.A. with the H.Q. 57th Brigade, R.F.A., on formation of the 132nd Brigade, R.F.A.; was later attached to the 147th Brigade R.F.A. and D.A.C. between 18/3/16 and 10/12/16.

Anders, Rev. C. G., C.F., served with the 29th D.A. throughout the year 1918.

Anderson, Lieut. (Temp. Capt.) R. W., R.E. (T.F.), (promoted Captain T.F. 1/6/16), was signal officer to the H.Q. D.A. from March, 1916, to 4/9/16, when he rejoined the 29th Divisional Signal Coy., R.E.   (M.C. and mention).

Anderson, Major T. G., R.F.A. (attached Egyptian Army), commanded the 17th B.A.C. 14/6/15 to 1/7/15 (appointed B.M. 126th Inf. Bde.) Served as liaison officer 88th Inf. Bde. and Group I 28/6/15 to   ?

Andrew, 2nd Lieut. B. C., (T.F.), 1/1st Warwickshire Bty., R.H.A. (T.F.), 16/12/16 to 29/12/16 (sick).

Andrew, Temp. Capt. W., A.V.C., was attached to H.Q. 15th Bde., R.H.A., from December 1917 to April 1918 (to No. 15 Veterinary Hospital).

Archdale, Major T. M., D.S.O. (Reg.), commanded 15th Bde., R.H.A., from 8/5/16 to 22/5/16 (to 3rd Bde., R.H.A.); afterwards drowned at sea 10/10/18.

Armstrong, Capt. C., A.V.C., was attached to 17th Bde., R.F.A., in 1916.

Armstrong, Capt. J., A.V.C., was attached to 132nd Bde., R.F.A., from 3/3/16 to 6/9/16 (to hospital with sprained ankle).

Armstrong, Lieut. R. A., R.G.A. (Reg.), 14th S.B., R.G.A., 6/10/15 to 27/10/15 (to 7th Indian Mountain Arty. Bde.).

Aschwanden, Lt.-Col. S. W. L., (T.F.),(Lt.-Col. 1/6/16), commanded 17th Bde., R.F.A., from 17/10/17 to 10/11/17 (hospital—gassed).

Ashmore, Lt.-Col. (Temp. Brig.-Genl.) E. B., C.M.G., M.V.O., (Reg.), commanded the 29th D.A. from 20/12/16 to 28/7/17 (to command of London Aircra Defences).   (Mention).

Austing, Battery Sergeant-Major A., "L" Battery, R.H.A., was sent to a cadets' course in September 1917 and was subsequently given a regular commission.

Bailey, Lieut. G. H. (Reg.), (Temp. Capt. 27/7/16); 460th Bty, R.F.A., landing to 25/9/15; "L" Bty., R.H.A., 26/9/15 to 17/10/15; Adjt. 15th Bde., R.H.A., 18/10/15 to 30/11/15 (hospital); "L" Bty., R.H.A., 28/12/15 to 26/6/16; 371st Bty., R.F.A., 27/6/16 to 12/9/16; "L" Bty., R.H.A., 12/9/16 to 22/10/16; D.T.M.O., 23/10/16 to 30/11/16; "L" Bty., R.H.A., 1/12/16 to 28/2/17 (killed in action).   (M.C. and Mention).

Bain, Temp. 2nd Lieut., F. O., (2nd Lieut. 26/8/14, Lieut. 4/10/16), came to the Division with B/132 in February 1916 and remained with this battery throughout its changes of title to D/147 and D/17, until gassed on 3/5/17 and evacuated to hospital.   (Mention).

Bake, Capt. S. R. G. (Reg.), served in 1/4th Highland Mountain Bde., R.G.A. (T.F.) in Gallipoli 1915.   Was employed as a Flank Observing Officer to the R.N. at the landing and subsequently.   Went to hospital 8/7/15 and was invalided to the U.K.

Baldwin, 2nd Lieut. H. F., R.G.A. (Reg.), was commissioned from, and posted to, the 90th H.B., R.G.A. 14/10/15.

* Ball, 2nd Lieut. C. J. P., (S.R., afterwards Reg.), (2nd Lieut. S.R. 7/10/14; 2nd Lieut. Reg. 7/7/15; Lieut. 1/7/17; Temp. Lieut. 6/12/15; actg. Capt. 3/2/16; actg. Major 24/4/17, 18/6/17 & 1/11/17); Orderly Officer 15th Bde., R.H.A., landing to 11/8/15; Adjt. 15th Bde., R.H.A., 12/8/15 to 17/10/15; "B" Bty., R.H.A., 18/10/15 to 19/5/17 (wounded); "B" Bty., R.H.A., 31/5/17 to 25/6/17 (hospital as a result of wound on 20/8/17); "B" Bty., R.H.A., 7/9/17 to 31/10/17 (wounded a third time on 22/10/17); 460th Bty., R.F.A., 1/11/17 to Armistice.   (M.C., D.S.O. and two Mentions).

Ball, Capt. K. M. (Reg.), (actg. Major 25/9/16), Adjt. 147th Bde., R.F.A., landing to 17/10/15; 97th Bty., R.F.A., 18/10/15 to time of 147th Bde. leaving the D.A.   (Mention).

* Ball, 2nd Lieut. S. G. (S.R.), (2nd Lieut. 15/3/18), "B" Bty., R.H.A., 16/6/18 to 23/6/18 (hospital); "B" Bty., R.H.A., 29/7/18 to armistice.

* Brothers.

Bankes-Williams, Temp. 2nd Lieut. I. M., (2nd Lieut. 1/12/14; Lieut. 25/2/16; actg. Capt. 3/4/18), "B" Bty., R.H.A., 16/6/15 to 16/9/15 (hospital); 26th Bty., R.F.A., 13/10/17 to 2/11/17; Orderly Officer 17th Bde., R.F.A., 3/11/17 to 31/3/18; 26th Bty., R.F.A., 1/4/18 to 19/7/18 (wounded); 26th Bty., R.F.A., 31/8/18 to 1/11/18; Adjt. 17th Bde., R.F.A., 2/11/18 to armistice.

Barber, Temp. 2nd Lieut. S., (2nd Lieut. 1/10/14; Lieut. 1/7/17; actg. Capt. 3/12/17), No. 3 Sec., D.A.C., 20/5/16 to 30/5/16; T.M. Bty., 31/5/16 to 8/8/16; D.A.C., 9/8/16 to ?/3/17; T.M. Bty., ?/3/17 to armistice (commanded V/29 from 1/12/17 until 4/2/18 when the battery was broken up; afterwards X/29 till the armistice).

Barker, Temp. 2nd Lieut. A. G. Clayton, (Temp. Lieut. 6/12/15; Temp. Capt. 6/4/16), served in the ranks of the 10th Bty., at the landing and until commissioned on 18/11/15. Was then posted to the 147th B.A.C. and commanded it from 6/3/16; continued in command of this section when it became No. 3 Section, 29th D.A.C., and when it reverted to its former title on the 147th Bde. leaving the D.A.

Barker, 2nd Lieut. G. H. (S.R.), (2nd Lieut. 24/5/15), 29th D.A.C., 24/5/15 to 1/9/15;* "L" Bty., R.H.A., 2/9/15 to 26/9/15; VIII Corps R.A. Staff, 27/9/15 to 2/11/15; "L" Bty., R.H.A., 3/11/15 to 9/11/15; attached French H.Q., 10/11/15 to 17/11/15; "L" Bty., R.H.A., 18/11/15 to ? He was transferred subsequently to the 15th B.A.C. and was in it when it became No. 1 Section D.A.C. on 13/5/16. He joined "Y" Bty., R.H.A., from the D.A.C. 28/6/16 and was subsequently reposted to the D.A.C.; was eventually invalided home in January 1917.

Barnett, 2nd Lieut. E. J., 29th Divl. Signal Coy., R.E., was signal officer to the 29th D.A. in Gallipoli. (Mention).

Barrs, 2nd Lieut. E. E. (T.F.), (2nd Lieut. 30/10/15; Lieut. 1/6/16; actg. Capt. 24/9/17), joined B/132 Bty., R.F.A., 4/4/16 and served with it through its changes of title to D/147 and D/17 until posted to the 92nd Bty., R.F.A., 8/11/17. He remained in the 92nd Bty. till the armistice, except for a short period from 10/12/17 to 11/1/18, when he was in temporary command of D/17.

Bayley, Major L. S., R.G.A. (Reg.), commanded 14th S.B., R.G.A., from the landing. (Brevet Lt.-Col. and Mention).

Beardsley, Sergt. W. T., "B" Bty., R.H.A., on being given a regular commission was posted to C/158 Bty., R.F.A., 18/8/16.

Beaver, 2nd Lieut. R. H. (Reg.), (Lieut. 1/7/17), came to the D.A. with the 370th Bty. in March 1916 and served with it till it was broken up in Sept. 1916. He was then transferred to the 13th Bty; he was wounded 23/10/16 but remained at duty; wounded again 22/4/17 and evacuated. He rejoined the D.A. in May 1918 and served as under:—92nd Bty., R.F.A., 24/5/18 to 4/8/18; attached D.A. H.Q., 5/8/18 to 22/8/18; 26th Bty., R.F.A., 23/8/18 to 10/9/18; 92nd Bty., R.F.A., 11/9/18 to 30/9/18 (wounded). (Was in temporary command of the 92nd Bty. for the first three days of the advance in Flanders, 28th—30th Sept., 1918). (M.C.).

Beckett, Lieut. C. T. (Reg.), 368th Bty., R.F.A., landing to 4/6/15 (wounded).

Bedford-Pim, 2nd Lieut. E. W. (T.F.), (2nd Lieut. 23/6/15), D.A.C., 19/9/17 to 28/9/17; D/17 Bty., R.F.A., 29/9/17 to 14/10/17 (wounded); X/29 T.M. Bty., 28/3/18 to 18/4/18; D/17 Bty., R.F.A., 19/4/18 to 26/4/18 (wounded) (Died at home after discharge from hospital).

Belcher, Temp. 2nd Lieut. H. B., (2nd Lieut. 27/10/15; Lieut. 1/7/17; actg. Capt. 27/10/18), came to the D.A. in March 1916 with the 371st Bty., R.F.A.; served with this battery till it was broken up on 12th Sept., 1916, when he was transferred with his section to "B" Bty., R.F.A. His subsequent services were:—No. 2 Section, D.A.C., ?/10/16 to ?/7/17; Y/29 T.M. Bty., 15/7/17 to 28/3/18 (wounded); Y/29 T.M. Bty., 6/4/18 to 18/5/18; No. 1 Section, D.A.C., 19/5/18 to 26/10/18; Adjt. D.A.C., 27/10/18 to armistice.

Bell, Bty. Quartermaster-Sergt. J. G., 97th Bty., R.F.A., was given a commission 23/6/16.

---

* Appears to have served in "Y" Bty., R.H.A., from 29/6/15 to ?

Bellamy, Lieut. C. E. (S.R.), (Lieut. 1/7/17), attached H.Q. 29th D.A., 11/1/18 to 9/8/18; attached H.Q. 17th Bde., R.F.A., 11/8/18 to 9/10/18 (hospital).

Bidgood, Lieut., served in the 91st H.B., R.G.A., in Gallipoli and was attached to the 97th Bty., R.F.A., 22/8/15 to ?

Bindloss, Lieut. T. B., A.V.C., served with the 90th H.B., R.G.A., and with H.Q. 17th Bde., R.F.A., in Gallipoli until admitted to hospital 14/12/15.

Binnie, Temp. 2nd Lieut. A., served with the 368th Bty., R.F.A., in Gallipoli, was transferred to the 10th Bty. 8/6/15, and went to hospital 24/10/15.

Birch, 2nd Lieut. W. (Reg.), "B" Battery, R.H.A., landing to 6/9/15 (hospital).

Bird, 2nd Lieut. D., D.C.M. (Reg.), on being commissioned from Bty. Sergt.-Major, 10th Bty., R.F.A., joined the 147th B.A.C. 10/11/15 and was transferred to the 56th Bde., R.F.A., 29/11/15.

Bishop, Corporal F. H., "L" Bty., R.H.A., on being given a regular commission, was posted to the 30th D.A. 19/6/16.

Blandy, Temp. Lieut. C. G. S., R.A.M.C., was attached to the H.Q. 15th Bde., R.H.A., at the landing and up till about Feb. 1916, when he went to hospital. He afterwards became medical officer to the 29th Divl. Engineers and was killed at Monchy in April 1917. (M.C. and Mention).

Blumenthal, Major A. Z. (Reg.), joined the 460th Bty., R.F.A., 5/9/17 but was not in action with the battery and went to hospital 24/9/17.

Blunt, 2nd Lieut. J. S. (Reg.), 1/1st Warwickshire Bty., R.H.A. (T.F.) 3/8/17 to 21/11/17 (wounded).

Booth, Temp. Lieut. P. D., 26th Battery, R.F.A., landing to 28/4/15 (wounded); 26th Battery, R.F.A., 29/5/15 to ?/7/15 (hospital); "L" Bty., R.H.A., 5/10/16 to 21/11/16; Orderly Officer H.Q. 15th Bde., 22/11/16 to 3/12/16; 13th Battery, R.F.A., 4/12/16 to 26/12/17 (hospital); 92nd Battery, R.F.A., 4/4/17 to 25/5/17; D.T.M.O., 26/5/17 to 30/11/17 (killed in action). (M.C., D.S.O. and 3 Mentions).

Borthwick, Lieut. C. H. (S.R.), (Lieut. 29/10/15), joined "Y" Bty., R.H.A., 30/6/16 and was still serving in the battery when it left the Division.

Bosman, 2nd Lieut. J. P. (S.R.), V/29 T.M. Bty., 26/8/16 to 31/1/17; 26th Bty., R.F.A., 1/2/17 to 18/8/17; 92nd Bty., R.F.A., 19/8/17 to 23/9/17 (to R.F.C.).

Bowles, Sergt. P. W., M.M., "L" Bty., R.H.A., on being given a regular commission, was posted to the 32nd D.A. in March 1917. He was subsequently killed in action 10/9/18.

Bowman, 2nd Lieut. D. (Reg.), was Battery Quartermaster-Sergeant of 147th B.A.C. and was posted to that unit on being commissioned 15/6/15. He left sick on 4/11/15.

Boyle, 2nd Lieut. R. (S.R.), (2nd Lieut. 26/5/17), 92nd Battery, R.F.A. 3/8/17 to 11/3/18 (to R.F.C.).

Bradshaw, 2nd Lieut. G. R. (Reg.), (Lieut. 28/8/18), "B" Bty., R.H.A., 3/8/17 to 20/9/17 (wounded); No. 1 Section, D.A.C., 7/8/18 to 30/10/18; 92nd Bty., R.F.A., 31/10/18 to armistice.

Brand, Bty. Sergt.-Major G., "L" Bty., R.H.A., was posted to the 31st D.A. on being given a regular commission in February 1917.

Bray, 2nd Lieut. E. J. (T.F.), "L" Bty., R.H.A., 4/4/16 to ?/9/16; No. 1 Section, D.A.C., ?/9/16 to 18/9/16 (to 41st D.A.).

Braye, Temp. Lieut. C. J., (Lieut. 2/4/15), 15th B.A.C., 22/10/15 to 26/10/15; "L" Bty., R.H.A., 27/10/15 to 15/12/15 (hospital); "L" Bty., R.H.A., 24/12/15 to 5/3/16 (to Base Details); 10th Bty., R.F.A., 14/5/16 to 16/7/16; No. 4 Section, D.A.C., 17/7/16 to 15/9/16; No. 2 Section, D.A.C., 16/9/16 to 22/6/17 (to R.F.C.).

Breeks, Col. (Temp. Brig.-Genl.) R. W. (Reg.), commanded the 29th D.A. at the landing and until 30/5/15 when he went to hospital.

Brekke, Temp. 2nd Lieut. H. W., 17th B.A.C., landing to 23/7/15 (hospital).

Brickett, 2nd Lieut. F. M. (S.R.), (2nd Lieut. 14/10/17), 92nd Bty., R.F.A., 14/3/18 to armistice.

Bright, Temp. Lieut. F. Y., (Lieut. 25/3/15; actg. Capt. 24/9/16), came to the D.A. with the 369th Battery, R.F.A., in March 1916 and served with it until it was broken up in September 1916, when he went to the 92nd Bty. for a few days. He then commanded No. 1 Section of the D.A.C. from 23/9/16 to the armistice. (Mention).

Briscoe, Capt. W. T., R.A.M.C., came to the D.A. with the D.A.C. on 10/4/16

Brokenshaw, Lieut. G. B. (T.F.), (Lieut. 22/6/15; actg. Capt. 23/7/17 to 20/8/17), 1/1st Warwickshire Bty., R.H.A., 7/6/17 to 17/9/17 (hospital); S.A.A. Section, D.A.C., 29/10/17 to 10/3/18 (posted home).

Brooke, Capt. A. C. (Reg.), commanded the 17th B.A.C. at the landing and until 2/5/15, and the 26th Bty., R.F.A., from 3/5/15 to 8/11/15, when he left to become Staff Capt., 11th D.A. (Chevalier, Legion of Honour and Mention).

Brooke, 2nd Lieut. P. A. (Reg.), 26th Bty., R.F.A., landing to 12/5/15 (wounded).

Brooker, 2nd Lieut. J. H. (S.R.), (2nd Lieut. 17/8/17), 92nd Bty., R.F.A., 31/10/17 to 30/9/18 (wounded). (M.C.).

Brooks, Regimental Sergeant-Major W. J., 15th Bde., R.H.A., was posted to the 19th D.A. on being given a regular commission in Feb. 1917 (Serbian Cross of Kara George).

Brown, 2nd Lieut. M. F. (S.R.), (2nd Lieut. 13/1/17), D.A.C., 7/4/17 to 20/4/17 (wounded).

Brown, 2nd Lieut. T. S. W. (S.R.), (2nd Lieut. 16/12/16), 460th Bty., R.F.A., 27/4/17 to 16/8/17 (wounded).

Browne, Temp. 2nd Lieut. J., "B" Bty., R.H.A., 30/8/15* to 5/3/16 (to Base Details).

Browne, 2nd Lieut. V. F. (Reg.), (Lieut. 1/7/17; actg. Capt. 3/8/17), "L" Bty., R.H.A., 4/2/17 to 15/3/17; Orderly Officer 15th Bde., R.H.A., 16/3/17 to 24/5/17; Adjt. 15th Bde., R.H.A., 25/5/17 to armistice. (M.C., Belgian Croix de Guerre, and 2 mentions).

Brownless, Lieut. J. W., A.V.C., was attached to the 1/4th Highland Mountain Bde., R.G.A. (T.F.) in Gallipoli (killed in action).

Brunner, 2nd Lieut. F. J. M. (S.R.), (actg. Lieut. 12/11/16; Lieut. 12/5/18), attached H.Q. 29th D.A., 1/8/17 to 1/10 17; Reconnaissance Officer, H.Q. 29th D.A., 2/10/17 to 11/8/18; 460th Bty., R.F.A., 12/8/18 to armistice.

Bryant, 2nd Lieut. L. A. (S.R.), (2nd Lieut. 26/2/17), 13th Bty., R.F.A., 5/5/17 to 14/10/17 (hospital).

Bunning, 2nd Lieut. A. H., R.G.A. (Reg.), was commissioned from, and posted to, the 90th H.B., R.G.A., 14/10/15; was transferred to the 10th H.B., R.G.A., 23/11/15.

Burne, Lt.-Col. E. R., D.S.O. (Reg.), commanded the 15th Bde., R.H.A., from 17/10/17 to 1/10/18 when he was killed in action. (Mention).

Burney, Capt. A. E. C., R.G.A. (Reg.), was Adjutant of the 1/4th Highland Mountain Bde., R.G.A. (T.F.) at the landing and subsequently commanded the composite "Highland Mountain Battery" formed from this brigade.

Burrowes, Capt. A., R.G.A., joined the 29th D.A. at Helles from Anzac 14/7/15 and was posted to command the R.G.A. detachment manning Naval guns. He was afterwards in the Trench Mortar Group and went to hospital 28/10/15.

Butler, 2nd Lieut. E. A. (Reg.), came to the D.A. with the 370th Bty., R.F.A., in March 1916 and served in that battery until wounded 31/8/16.

---

* From R.N. Division.

134 29TH DIVISIONAL ARTILLERY.

Buzzard, Major C. N., R.G.A. (Reg.), commanded the 90th H.B., R.G.A., at the landing and subsequently. He was detached temporarily for duty with the R.N.A.S. from 28-8-15 to 21/9/15.

Caiger, 2nd Lieut. F. H. S. (S.R.), joined the 369th Bty., R.F.A., 28/4/16 and served with it until it was broken up on 12/9/16, when he was transferred with his section to the 92nd Bty., R.F.A. He served in this battery until killed in action 11/11/16.

Caldwell, 2nd Lieut. L. N. (S.R.), (2nd Lieut. 28/10/17), S.A.A. Section, D.A.C., 20/12/17 to 23/1/18; 92nd Bty., R.F.A., 24/1/18 to 13/2/18; S.A.A. Section, D.A.C., 14/2/18 to 23/3/18 (to Fifth Army).

Callingham, Temp. Capt. L. G. (Capt. 9/2/18), Staff Capt., H.Q., 29 D.A., 10/8/18 to armistice.

Calvert, Temp. 2nd Lieut. C. H., joined the 147th B.A.C. in Gallipoli; was attached for a period to the 3rd New Zealand Bty.; joined the 368th Bty., R.F.A., 15/6/15 but was with Trench Mortars from July 1915 to the evacuation. After arrival of the Division in France he was D.T.M.O. from 18/4/16 to 23/8/16, and then served as Captain of the 10th Bty., R.F.A. He was still serving in that battery when the 147th Brigade, R.F.A., left the D.A. (M.C. and Mention).

Calvert, 2nd Lieut. J. H. (S.R.), (2nd Lieut. 13/1/17), 13th Bty., R.F.A., 29/4/17 to 23/3/18 (to Fifth Army). (Mention).

Cameron, 2nd Lieut. J. M., 368th Bty., R.F.A., landing to 7/5/15 (killed in action).

Campbell, Capt. G. F., R.G.A. (Reg.), 460th Bty., R.F.A., 11/5/17 to 28/7/17 (wounded).

Campbell, Major N. St. C. (Reg.), commanded the 13th Bty., R.F.A., at the landing and until transferred to command the 69th Bde., R.F.A., 24/1/16. (D.S.O. and Mention).

Carey, 2nd Lieut. W. F., joined the 90th H.B., R.G.A., 6/10/15, went to hospital 17/10/15, and rejoined the battery 7/12/15.

Carter, 2nd Lieut. W. B. (Reg.), (Temp. Lieut. 6/12/15), "Y" Bty., R.H.A., landing to 4/6/15 (wounded); rejoined about a month later and was still serving in the battery when it left the D.A.

Cattell, Lieut. E. E. (S.R.), joined the 97th Bty., R.F.A., 28/4/16; was subsequently in Y/29 T.M. Bty. and was wounded 1/8/16.

Cattell, 2nd Lieut. E. M. (S.R.), (2nd Lieut. 10/9/16), 460th Bty., R.F.A., 20/11/16 to 21/8/17 (wounded—also slightly wounded 8/2/17). (Mention).

Cazeaux, 2nd Lieut. R. J. (Reg.), 92nd Bty., R.F.A., 2,/1/17 to 20/9/17; (was attached to 13th Bty. 22/4/17, and to H.Q. 29th D.A. in May/June 1917); 13th Bty., R.F.A., 27/9/17 to 29/9/17 (wounded).

Chadwick, Temp. 2nd Lieut. T., 26th Bty., R.F.A., 11/4/16 to 19/5/16; S/29 T.M. Bty., 20/5/16 to 6/9/16; No. 3 Section, D.A.C., 7/9/16 to 18/9/16 (to 47th D.A.).

Chalkley, Temp. 2nd Lieut., R., (commissioned from the ranks of the R.N. Division and afterwards given a Regular Commission—Temp. 2nd Lieut. 7/9/15; Reg. 2nd Lieut. 24/6/16; Lieut. 4/12/17; actg. Capt. 16/8/17); 26th Bty., R.F.A., 30/8/15 to 8/7/16 (hospital); 26th Bty., R.F.A., 21/11/16 to 20/12/16; A.D.C. to C.R.A., 21/12/16 to 17/1/16; Reconnaissance Officer H.Q. 29th D.A., 18/1/17 to 20/2/17; 92nd Bty., R.F.A., 21/2/17 to 20/3/17; 26th Bty., R.F.A., 21/3/17 to 24/10/17 (hospital); 26th Bty., R.F.A., 7/12/17 to 29/3/18 (to Fifth Army). (Mention).

Chapman, Capt. A. C., Y/29 T.M. Bty. 10/8/16 to 20/8/16 (killed in action).

Chase, 2nd Lieut. C. B. A. C. (S.R.), (2nd Lieut. 27/8/16), No. 3 Section, D.A.C., 5/1/17 to 14/6/17 (to R.F.C.).

Cheetham, Temp. Lieut. F. G. C. B., (Lieut. 2/4/17), served in No. 1 Section, D.A.C., for a short time in September 1917 before going to hospital.

Chisholm-Batten, Temp. Capt. J. de H. (Reg.), 92nd Bty., R.F.A., 23/7/15 to
?/10/15; commanded 10th Bty., R.F.A., 12/10/15 to 13/8/16 (wounded).
(He was subsequently killed in action).

Chislett, Temp. 2nd Lieut. W. A., (2nd Lieut. 5/3/15), served in the 371st Bty.,
R.F.A., in 1916; joined "L" Bty., R.H.A., 21/11/16 and served therein until
he went to hospital about April 1917.

Clare, 2nd Lieut. H. T. (Reg.), (actg. Capt. 1/11/17), 460th Bty., R.F.A., landing
to 15/5/15; 13th Bty., R.F.A., 16/5/15 to 5/3/16; "Y" Bty., R.H.A., 6/3/16
to 7/5/16; Adjt. 15th Bde., R.H.A., 8/5/16 to 23/9/16 (hospital); "L" Bty.,
R.H.A., ?/5/17 to 14/6/17 (wounded); "B" Bty., R.H.A., 19/10/17 to
27/3/18 (to 6th D.A.). He was killed in action 29/4/18. (Mention and
Order of Crown of Italy).

Clark, Major C. H. (Reg.), Brigade Major 29th D.A. 6/9/15 to 20/5/17 (to 18th
Army Bde., R.F.A.). (D.S.O. and 2 Mentions).

Clark, 2nd Lieut. E. W. (S.R.), (2nd Lieut. 10/6/17), D/17 Bty., R.F.A., 13/9/17
to 13/10/17 (hospital); D/17 Bty., R.F.A., 7/8/18 to 11/8/18; 92nd Bty.,
R.F.A., 12/8/18 to 28/8/18 (hospital).

Clarke, 2nd Lieut. C. (Reg.), (Lieut. 8/8/16), 15th B.A.C., landing to 28/4/15;
"Y" Bty., R.H.A., 29/4/15 to time of battery leaving the D.A. (M.C. and
Mention).

Cleall, 2nd Lieut. E. H., R.G.A. (Reg.), was commissioned from, and posted to,
the 14th S.B., R.G.A., in October 1915; was transferred to 17th S.B., R.G.A.,
8/12/15.

Clempson, 2nd Lieut. L., R.G.A. (Reg.), 14th S.B., R.G.A., landing to 3/7/15
(wounded).

Clutterbuck, 2nd Lieut. B. V. (S.R.), (2nd Lieut. 27/3/17), served in 460th Bty.,
R.F.A., for about a month from 11/5/17; was then transferred to Z/29 T.M.
Bty. and was killed in action 13/7/17.

Coates, Battery Sergt.-Major C. H., 460th Bty., R.F.A., on being given a Regular
commission, was posted to "O" Bty., R.H.A., 21/12/16. (Mention).

Cobb, 2nd Lieut. (Temp. Capt.) B. C., (T.F.), came to the D.A. with the D.A.C.
10/4/16; went on leave in May 1916 and did not return for duty.

Coe, 2nd Lieut. E. (S.R.), (2nd Lieut. 8/9/17), D/17 Bty., R.F.A., 27/11/17 to
3/4/18; No. 1 Section, D.A.C., 4/4/18 to 31/8/18; X/29 T.M. Bty., 1/9/18
to 9/10/18 (to R.A.F. on probation).

Colthurst, 2nd Lieut. A. St. G. (S.R.), "B" Bty., R.H.A., 17/7/16 to 20/9/16
(to 47th D.A.).

Cookson, Lieut. (Temp. Capt.) G. H. (T.F.), came as Adjutant with the D.A.C.
10/4/16; reverted to regimental duty 7/6/16; commanded No. 4 Section
8/6/16 to 21/9/16; employed on salvage work XV Corps October 1916;
transferred to L. of C. for draft conducting duties.

Cooper, 2nd Lieut. C. D. (S.R.), D.A.C., 1/9/16 to 26/10/16; D/147 Bty., R.F.A.
(afterwards D/17), 27/10/16 to 16/6/17 (to hospital). (Was wounded on
5/4/17).

Cooper, Rev. J. P., C.F., attached to D.A.C. from 13/5/17 to about October 1917
(hospital).

Corbett, 2nd Lieut. A. (T.F.), C/132 Bty., R.F.A., 3/4/16 to 8/5/16; S/29 T.M.
Bty., 9/5/16 to 5/9/16; D.A.C., 6/9/16 to 21/9/16 (to 4th D.A.).

Corble, Temp. Lieut. A. H., R.G.A., (Lieut. 8/12/14), served in the 90th H.B.
Ammn. Coln. in Gallipoli.

Costello, Temp. Lieut. C. F., (Lieut. 6/12/15), 97th Bty., R.F.A., 19/10/15 to
23/5/16; Orderly Officer 147th Bde., 24/5/16 to ? 97th Bty., R.F.A.,
? to 24/8/16; 10th Bty., R.F.A., 25/8/16 to 4/12/16 (hospital).

Cottrall, Temp. 2nd Lieut. V. W., (2nd Lieut. 3/6/18), Y/29 T.M. Bty., 21/8/18
to armistice.

Courage, Brevet and Temp. Major M. R. F. (formerly Regular) (actg. Lt.-Col. August 1916), came to the D.A. in command of the 370th Bty., R.F.A., in March, 1916, and remained with it until appointed to command the 147th Bde., R.F.A., 23/7/16; was still in command when the Brigade left the 29th D.A. early in 1917.   (Mention).

Cousens, Major R. B. (Reg.), was Brigade Major 52nd D.A. and served as Staff Officer, Section "A," till posted away as D.A.A. and Q.M.G. 52nd Division 7/12/15.

Cowdery, 2nd Lieut. E. D. (S.R.), (2nd Lieut. 18/10/16), "L" Bty., R.H.A., 16/1/17 to ?

Cowley, 2nd Lieut. R. E., R.G.A. (Reg.), was in the 24th S.B., R.G.A., at Anzac; served in the Trench Mortar Group from 24/11/15 until wounded 28/12/15.

Craib, 2nd Lieut. W. H. (S.R.), (2nd Lieut. 6/1/16; Lieut. 6/7/17; actg. Capt. 21/8/16), 10th Bty., R.F.A., 15/7/16 to 8/8/16; V/29 Heavy T.M. Bty., 9/8/16 to 30/11/17; D.T.M.O., 1/12/17 to armistice.   (M.C. and bar).

Crawford, 2nd Lieut. S. W. K. (Reg.), 26th Bty., R.F.A., 5/7/16 to 21/10/16 (wounded).

Crowdy, 2nd Lieut. E. F. (Reg.), 13th Bty., R.F.A., 2/6/15 to 28/7/15 (hospital).

Crowe, Temp. Capt. J. M., A.V.C., attached 147th Bde., R.F.A., 20/11/16 to ?/2/17; attached 17th Bde., R.F.A., ?/2/17 to   ?

Cunliffe, Capt. E. H. (T.F.), (Capt. 22/10/14), 460th Bty., R.F.A., 28/8/18 to 17/9/18; attached H.Q. 15th Bde., R.H.A., 18/9/18 to 19/10/18 (to Divl. Rest Station).

Cunnison, Temp. Lieut. T. J., (Lieut. 30/5/15; actg. Capt. 2/1/17), joined the D.A. as Adjutant 132nd Bde., R.F.A., in February 1916 and remained as such until the Brigade was broken up in Sept. 1916; Adjt. 17th Bde., R.F.A., 12/9/16 to 19/12/16; Staff Capt. 29th D.A., 20/12/16 to 24/2/18; 92nd Bty., R.F.A., 24/2/18 to 20/5/18; 13th Bty. R.F.A., 21/5/18 to armistice. (M.C., Mention, and Belgian Croix de Guerre).

Cutts, Sergeant F. W., "B" Bty., R.H.A., on being given a regular commission, was posted to the 14th Army Brigade, R.F.A., in February 1917.

Dale, Temp. 2nd Lieut. R. M. (2nd Lieut. 5/3/15), 17th B.A.C., 6/10/15 to 23/12/15; "B" Bty., R.H.A., 24/12/15 to ?/2/16; 92nd Bty., R.F.A., ?/2/16 to 21/3/16; 10th Bty., R.F.A., 22/3/16 to   ? ; H.Q. 147th Bde., R.F.A., 23/3/16 to 9/5/16; D.A.C., 10/5/16 to 7/11/16 (to 60th D.A.).

Daly, Capt. D., R.G.A. (Reg.), (actg. Major 25/9/16; Major 16/9/17), i/c Naval 12-Pdrs. Group V (attached 17th B.A.C.) 16/6/15 to 27/6/15; comdg. 15th B.A.C., 28/6/15 to 2/9/15; comdg. Dumezil T.M. Bty., 3/9/15 to 11/11/15; comdg. 26th Bty., R.F.A., 12/11/15 to 29/3/17 (B.M. 41st D.A.); comdg. 26th Bty., R.F.A., 17/7/17 to armistice.   (M.C., D.S.O., and 3 Mentions).

Dalziel, Temp. 2nd Lieut. W., (2nd Lieut. 5/3/15), D.A.C., 9/9/15 to 8/10/15; 17th B.A.C., 9/10/15 to 18/10/15; 92nd Bty., R.F.A., 19/10/15 to 12/11/15; 13th Bty., R.F.A., 13/11/15 to ?/4/16; D.A.C., ?/4/16 to 7/11/16 (to 60th D.A.).

Dannatt, Sergeant A., m.m., "B" Bty., R.H.A., on being given a regular commission, was posted to the 58th D.A. in April 1918.

D'Apice, Capt. J. E. F. (Reg.), Staff Capt. 29th D.A., landing to 6/9/15 (to D.A.A. and Q.M.G., 52nd Division).   (D.S.O. and 2 Mentions).

Darley, Temp. 2nd Lieut. T. B. (afterwards Regular), (T. 2nd Lieut. 7/10/14; Reg. 2nd Lieut. July 1915), came to the D.A. with C/132 Bty., R.F.A., in February, 1916, and remained in that battery during its change of title to D/132 until 20/7/16, when he became Adjutant 17th Bde., R.F.A.   On 6/8/16 he was accidentally injured whilst riding and was sent home.

Daubuz, Capt. C. (Reg.), Adjutant 15th Bde., R.H.A., landing to 20/8/15 (hospital). (Was wounded 2/5/15). (M.C. and Mention).

Davidson, Lieut. F. H. N. (Reg.), "L" Bty., R.H.A., landing to 31/7/15 (hospital); "L" Bty., R.H.A., 14/10/15 to 1/12/15; comdg. "B" Bty., R.H.A., 2/12/15 to 25/12/15; comdg. 368th Bty., R.F.A., 26/12/15 to 2/1/16 (hospital—scarlet fever); (posted to B/58 Bty., R.F.A., 5/3/16).

Davidson, Brevet Lieut.-Col. N. R., D.S.O. (Reg.), commanded "L" Bty., R.H.A., for a few days from the 18th to the 22nd July, 1917, when he was gassed; also commanded the 15th Brigade, R.H.A., temporarily from 26/8/17 to 18/9/17. He was afterwards killed in action.

Davies, 2nd Lieut. T. L. (S.R.), (2nd Lieut. 16/1/17; Lieut. 16/7/18), D.A.C., 30/7/17 to 9/12/17; 26th Bty., R.F.A., 10/12/17 to 22/10/18 (wounded).

Davis, Temp. 2nd Lieut. D. F., (Lieut. 23/6/16), 15th B.A.C., 23/7/15 to 29/7/16; 13th Bty., R.F.A., 30/7/15 to 8/3/16; 26th Bty., R.F.A., 9/3/16 to 1/7/16 (wounded).

Deams, Capt. W. W., R.A.M.C., had only just taken over the duties of medical officer to the 147th Brigade, R.F.A., when he was severely wounded on 3/1/16 and died the same night.

Denison, Capt. H. (Reg.), (Major 17/9/15), comdg. 97th Bty., R.F.A., landing to 16/10/15; comdg. "B" Bty., R.H.A., 18/10/15 to 2/12/15 (hospital); comdg. 368th Bty., R.F.A., 19/1/16 to 11/9/16; (during this period he was wounded 1/7/16; the 368th Bty. was broken up 12/9/16); comdg. 10th Bty., R.F.A., 12/9/16 to ?/2/17 (to "O" Bty., R.H.A.). (D.S.O. and Mention). Note.—This officer was killed in the Autumn of 1917.

Denton, Lieut. (actg. Capt.) J., (T.F.), attached to D.A.C. as horse adviser 2/3/18 to 19/4/18 (hospital).

de Sain, Temp. 2nd Lieut. E. A., was with the detachment of the D.A.C. on the peninsula for 3 days—from 6th to 9th October, 1915.

Dibbs, Lieut., R.A.M.C., was attached to the 147th Brigade, R.F.A., from 11th to 21st December, 1915.

Dickinson, 2nd Lieut. S. (S.R.), (2nd Lieut. 4/2/18), "B" Bty., R.H.A., 8/4/18 to armistice.

Diggle, Major J. N., D.S.O. (Reg.), commanded "B" Bty., R.H.A., 7/9/17 to 27/11/17 (to B.M. 21st D.A.).

Disley, 2nd Lieut. H. (Reg.), (Lieut. 30/10/17), was a Sergeant in the 460th Bty., R.F.A., at the landing and until transferred as Battery Sergeant-Major to the 370th Bty., R.F.A., in March 1916. He was commissioned on 30th April, 1916, and joined D/132 Bty., R.F.A., about the end of July. He remained with this battery during its change of title to D/17 and was transferred with the left section of this battery to the new D/17 (late D/147) on 1/2/17. He joined the 92nd Bty. 13/3/17 and served in it till 4/2/18, when he was appointed Gas Officer to the 29th D.A. ("D.A.G.O."), which appointment he held till the armistice.

Dixon, Lieut. G. H. S. (T.F.), (Lieut. 1/7/16), 1/1st Warwickshire Bty., R.H.A. (T.F.), 28/11/16 to armistice—but was in hospital from April to August 1917. (M.C.).

Dobson, Temp. 2nd Lieut. A. E., (2nd Lieut. 13/10/15), 460th Bty., R.F.A., 8/8/16 to 3/10/16 (hospital).

Dobson, 2nd Lieut. C. F. A. (S.R.), 15th B.A.C., 7/12/15 to 15/3/16 (transferred home).

Dodds, Temp. 2nd Lieut. J. A., 147th B.A.C., landing to 8/5/15; 97th Bty., R.F.A., 9/5/15 to ?/6/15 (hospital); 97th Bty., R.F.A., 10/8/15 to ?

Dolphin, Capt. (actg. Major) V. O. (Reg.), commanded 26th Bty., R.F.A., from 3/4/17* to 7/6/17 (killed in action).

Donnally, Temp. 2nd Lieut. R. C., (2nd Lieut. 5/4/15), 147th B.A.C., 5/7/15 to 19/7/15; 97th Bty., R.F.A., 20/7/15; 368th Bty., R.F.A., 21/7/15 to 3/8/15 (wounded); 97th Bty., R.F.A., 5/9/15 to 31/1/16 (to Alexandra); 97th Bty., R.F.A., 14/5/16 to 13/8/16; comdg. 10th Bty., R.F.A., 14/8/16 to 24/8/16; 97th Bty., R.F.A., 25/8/16 to 21/10/16 (killed in action).

---

* Did not actually assume tactical control of the battery till after the commencement of the Arras Battle.

Douglas, Temp. 2nd Lieut. J. C., A.D.C. to C.R.A., landing to 17/7/15 (hospital).

Downes, Capt., R.A.M.C., was in medical charge of the 147th Brigade, R.F.A., from 21/12/15 to ?

Downs, 2nd Lieut. J. (S.R.), (2nd Lieut. 16/9/17), 460th Bty., R.F.A., 3/12/17 to armistice. (M.C.).

Drake, 2nd Lieut. W. (Reg.), "Y" Bty., R.H.A., 8/5/16 to 26/6/16 (killed in action).

Driver, 2nd Lieut. H., M.S.M. (S.R.), (2nd Lieut. 17/8/17), No. 2 Section, D.A.C., 13/10/17 to 31/10/17; D/17 Bty., R.F.A., 1/11/17 to armistice.

Drummond-Hay, Temp. Lieut. C. L. H., 147th Bde., R.F.A., ?/8/15 to 11/9/15; attached 90th H.B., R.G.A., 12/9/15 to 1/10/15; 97th Bty., R.F.A., 2/10/15 to 30/1/16; (during this period he was Staff Officer, Section "B," from 12/10/15 to ? ,); Orderly Officer 147th Bde., R.F.A., 31/1/16 to ?/3/16 (appointed Divisional Claims Officer).

Duckworth, 2nd Lieut. P. B., "L" Bty., R.H.A., 4/12/16 to ?/3/17; 1/1st Warwickshire Bty., R.H.A., ?/3/17 to 9/4/17 (killed in action).

Duff, Temp. 2nd Lieut. C. P., (2nd Lieut. 23/12/14; Lieut. 4/10/16), 460th Bty. Ammn. Coln., landing to evacuation; 460th Bty., evacuation to 28/12/16; Orderly Officer 15th Bde., R.H.A., 28/12/16 to 27/2/17; Adjt. 15th Bde., R.H.A., 15/3/17 to 23/5/17 (wounded). (Twice mentioned).

Duncan, 2nd Lieut. M. (Reg.), "B" Bty., R.H.A., 5/9/17 to 24/3/18 (to 159th Bde., R.F.A., as Signalling Officer).

Duncan-Wallace, Lieut. T., R.G.A. (T.F.), served in the 1/4th Highland Mountain Brigade, R.G.A. (T.F.) in Gallipoli. (Mention).

*Durell, 2nd Lieut. R. A. V. (S.R.), (2nd Lieut. 28/10/17), 92nd Bty., R.F.A., 19/3/18 to 13/4/18); 13th Bty., R.F.A., 14/4/18 to armistice.

* Durell, 2nd Lieut. T. C. V. (S.R.), (2nd Lieut. 2/2/17; Lieut. 4/9/18), 26th Bty., R.F.A., 5/5/17 to armistice.

East, Temp. 2nd. Lieut. G. D. W., D/132 Bty., R.F.A., 5/7/16 to 23/7/16; Orderly Officer 147th Bde., 24/7/16 to 14/9/16; No. 3 Section, D.A.C., 15/9/16 to 19/9/16; Z/29 T.M. Bty., 20/9/16 to 27/10/16 (hospital).

Eddis, Major L. A. (Reg.), 460th Bty., R.F.A., 20/11/16 to 20/6/17; attached R.A. XIV Corps, 21/6/17 to 30/9/17; 460th Bty., R.F.A., 1/10/17 to 31/10/17 (to B.M. 4th D.A.).

Eden, Lieut. (actg. Capt.) Hon. R. E., R.H.A. (T.F.), (actg. Major 16/5/17 to 10/6/17; 5/7/17 to 23/7/17; 20/8/17 to armistice), was not actually with the 1/1st Warwickshire Bty., R.H.A. (T.F.) when it joined the D.A. in November, 1916, but rejoined it in February 1917 and commanded it almost continuously from May 1917 till the armistice. He was gassed on 22/7/17 and rejoined 20/8/17. (M.C. and Mention).

Edgar, 2nd Lieut. G. H. S. (S.R.), (2nd Lieut. 25/11/16; Lieut. 25/5/18), 1/1st Warwickshire Bty., R.H.A. (T.F.), 17/5/17 to 25/5/17; H.Q. 15th Bde., R.H.A., 26/5/17 to ?/7/17 (hospital); "L" Bty., R.H.A., 4/11/17 to 4/9/18 (wounded).

Edwards, 2nd Lieut. J. E. (Reg.), 15th B.A.C., landing to 24/9/15 (hospital).

Eggleton, Temp. 2nd Lieut. F., (2nd Lieut. 7/11/15; actg. Capt. 14/4/17; actg. Major 22/4/17), "L" Bty., R.H.A., 20/1/16 to 5/3/16; 13th Bty., R.F.A., 6/3/16 to 13/4/17; 26th Bty., R.F.A., 14/4/17 to 21/4/17; 13th Bty., R.F.A., 22/4/17 to 21/10/17 (killed in action). (Twice mentioned).

Eldred, 2nd Lieut. W., 92nd Bty., R.F.A., 15/6/15; Orderly Officer 17th Bde., 16/6/15 to ? (hospital); 17th Bde., R.F.A., 16/7/15 to ? (hospital— to U.K. from Gibraltar 26/8/15).

Eller, Temp. 2nd Lieut. H. J., served in the 90th H.B., R.G.A., in Gallipoli and was invalided home about August 1915.

* Brothers.

Elliot, 2nd Lieut. J., Orderly Officer 17th Bde., landing to 29/4/15; 26th Bty., R.F.A., 30/4/15 to 9/8/15 (wounded).

Ellis, 2nd Lieut. B. (Reg.), D/17 Bty., R.F.A., 17/12/17 to 23/4/18 (to Anti-Aircraft Battery).

Elworthy, Lieut. P. A. (S.R.), 1st Life Guards, attached to 17th Brigade, R.F.A., as horse adviser 22/7/18 to September 1918.

Ely, 2nd Lieut. D. M. (S.R.), (2nd Lieut. 19/5/15; Lieut. 1/7/17), 13th Bty., R.F.A., 26/10/15 to 25/12/15 (wounded); 13th Bty., R.F.A., 13/7/16 to 5/10/17 (wounded); 13th Bty., R.F.A., 20/1/18 to 11/4/18 (to VIII Corps H.Q.—afterwards evacuated to U.K.).

Emery, 2nd Lieut. H. R. (Reg.), 15th B.A.C., 23/7/15 to 28/7/15; attached 26th Bty., R.F.A., 29/7/15 to 17/8/15; 26th Bty., R.F.A., 18/8/15 to ?/12/15; 460th Bty., R.F.A., ?/12/15 to 17/1/16; 17th B.A.C., 18/1/16 to ?/2/16 (to 11th D.A.).

Enright, 2nd Lieut. A. B., D/147 (afterwards D/17) Bty., R.F.A., 21/11/16 to 21/4/17 (wounded—died of wounds 11/5/17).

* Eppenheim, Temp. 2nd Lieut. H. N., (2nd Lieut. 5/12/14; Lieut. 2/5/16; actg. Capt. 23/4/17 to 8/6/17; actg. Major 9/6/17 to 17/7/17; reverted to Lieut. 18/7/17), 370th Bty., R.F.A., 1/9/16 to 11/9/16 (to 38th D.A. but recalled); 26th Bty., R.F.A., 16/10/16 to 14/8/17; No. 2 Section, D.A.C., 15/8/17 to ?/4/18 (hospital).

Espir, 2nd Lieut. L. (S.R.), 460th Bty., R.F.A., 6/10/15 to 21/10/15 (hospital).

Evans, Capt. A. E., R.A.M.C. (T.F.), Medical Officer to 17th Bde., 12/11/17 to 14/2/18 (hospital).

Evans, Rev. D. G., C.F., attached 29th D.A., 20/10/15 to 3/12/15 (hospital from injuries received at football).

Evans, Lieut. H. J. (T.F.), (Lieut. 28/10/14), came to the D.A. with the D.A.C. 10/4/16 and served till 26/10/16 (hospital).

Fairburn, Lieut. E. N. (T.F.), (Lieut. 1/6/16), No. 1 Section, D.A.C., 12/10/18 to armistice.

Fairley, 2nd Lieut. J. H. B. (S.R.), 92nd Bty., R.F.A., 26/10/15 to 26/11/15; 26th Bty., R.F.A., 27/11/15 to 4/3/16 (hospital); 370th Bty., R.F.A., ? to 22/7/16 (to Etaples for draft conducting duties).

Ferdinando, 2nd Lieut. G. H. F. (Reg.), 147th B.A.C., landing to 7/5/15; 368th Bty., R.F.A., 8/5/15 to 4/6/15 (wounded).

Fergus, 2nd Lieut. B. W. H., 147th B.A.C., 23/9/15 to 28/10/15 (hospital).

Field, Sergt. E. F., D/147 Bty., R.F.A., on being given a commission, was posted to the 6th D.A. 31/10/16.

Fielden, 2nd Lieut. L., Trench Mortar Group, 5/12/15 to 11/12/15 (hospital).

Fifield, 2nd Lieut. L. R., 26th Bty., R.F.A., 15/2/17 to 11/4/17 (wounded).

Fisher, Lieut. C. P., A.V.C. (Reg.), attached 15th Bde., R.H.A., landing to May 1917; attached D.A.C., May 1917 to 1/7/17 (to M.V.S. in 4th Cavalry Division).

Forman, Major D. E. (Reg.), commanded "B" Bty., R.H.A., landing to 10/8/15 (wounded); commanded "B" Bty., R.H.A., 9/9/15 to 15/10/15; commanded 147th Bde., R.F.A., 16/10/15 to 22/7/16; commanded 15th Bde., R.H.A., 23/7/16 to 1/8/16 (hospital—synovitis); commanded 15th Bde., R.H.A., 6/6/17 to 10/6/17 (hospital—synovitis). (C.M.G. and 3 Mentions).

Formby, Temp. 2nd Lieut. C. B., served with the 90th H.B., R.G.A., in Gallipoli.

Foster, 2nd Lieut. A., 370th Bty., R.F.A., 23/8/16 to 12/9/16; D.A.C., 12/9/16 to 21/9/16 (to 4th D.A.).

----

* Changed surname to Elton in 1918 after leaving the D.A.

Fox, Capt., R.A.M.C., Medical Officer 147th Bde., R.F.A., ? to 4/12/15 (hospital).

Fraser, 2nd Lieut. (Temp. Capt.) A. A. (Reg.), was commissioned from Regimental Sergeant-Major 15th Brigade, R.H.A., and posted to command No. 4 Section of the D.A.C. He landed on the peninsula about June 1915 and commanded the D.A.C. detachment there till the evacuation (Mention).

Fulford-Brown, 2nd Lieut. C. (S.R.), D/17 Bty., R.F.A., 21/11/16 to 28/1/17 (wounded).

Fullman, 2nd Lieut. G. E. (Reg.), No. 2 Section, D.A.C., 27/2/17 to 3/7/17 (hospital).

Furze-Morrish, 2nd Lieut. L. S. R. B. (Reg.), 13th Bty., R.F.A., 19/12/16 to 2/10/18 (hospital—he was wounded 22/4/17 and 3/5/17).

Gaisford, 2nd Lieut. J. W. (Reg.), 15th B.A.C., landing to 6/5/15 (wounded); "B" Bty., R.H.A., 2/7/15 to 14/7/15 (wounded).

Gammell, Lieut. J. A. H. (Reg.), 460th Bty., R.F.A., landing to 16/7/15 (wounded on 28/4/15); A.D.C. to C.R.A., 17/7/15 to 13/10/15 (to R.N.A.S.). (Mention).

Garvie, 2nd Lieut. P. T., 14th S.B., R.G.A., landing to 16/9/15 (granted three months leave).

Gascoyne-Cecil, 2nd Lieut. R. W. (T.F.), (2nd Lieut. 3/6/15), 1/1st Warwickshire Bty., 10/4/17 to 25/5/17; commanded X/29 T.M. Bty., 26/5/17 to 30/11/17 (killed in action—had also been slightly wounded 15/7/17).

Gaydon, 2nd Lieut. W. T. (T.F.), (2nd Lieut. 10/11/17), 26th Bty., R.F.A., 20/1/18 to 1/2/18; 13th Bty., R.F.A., 2/2/18 to 10/4/18 (hospital).

Gibbon, Major J. H. (Reg.), commanded 460th Bty., landing to 22/9/15; attached R.N.A.S. at G.H.Q. (M.E.F.), 23/9/15 to Dec. 1915; commanded 460th Bty., ?/12/15 to 27/11/16 (to command the Cadet School at Lark Hill). (D.S.O. and Mention).

Gibson, 2nd Lieut. A. (S.R.), (2nd Lieut. 2/1/17), 460th Bty., R.F.A., 28/5/17 to 30/5/17; V/29 T.M. Bty., 31/5/17 to 5/7/17 (wounded—died of wounds a few days later).

Giffard, Lieut. S. (Reg.), 26th Bty., R.F.A., landing to 2/5/15 (mortally wounded).

Gill, Temp. Lieut. G. F., R.A.M.C., Medical Officer to the D.A.C. 13/5/16 to ?

Gilmore, 2nd Lieut. A. M. (S.R.), (2nd Lieut. 13/1/17), Y/29 T.M. Bty., 14/12/17 to 8/1/18 (hospital).

Goddard, 2nd Lieut. F. T., 14th S.B., R.G.A., landing to 21/12/15 (to H.Q. 29th Division).

Godwin, 2nd Lieut. G. (Reg.), 26th Bty., R.F.A., 28/11/17 to 28/9/18 (killed in action).

Goff, Lieut. W. le M. (Reg.), T.M. Bty., 14/8/18 to 29/8/18; 1/1st Warwickshire Bty., 30/8/18 to armistice.

Goldie, 2nd Lieut. C. J. B. (S.R.), (2nd Lieut. 13/10/15), 369th Bty., R.F.A., ? to 23/7/16; A.D.C. to C.R.A., 24/7/16 to 21/12/16 (to H.Q. I Corps).

Goldney, 2nd Lieut. R. M., served in the 14th S.B., R.G.A., from the landing.

Gooch, Lieut. K. T. (Reg.), (actg. Capt. 25/3/18), "L" Bty., R.H.A., 12/2/18 to armistice.

Gordon, 2nd Lieut. K. E. (Reg.), (Lieut. 24/2/17), 10th Bty., R.F.A., landing to 16/9/15 (hospital); 1/1st Warwickshire Bty., 9/7/17 to 25/7/17 (hospital); D.A.C., 6/5/18 to 6/7/18; 26th Bty., R.F.A., 7/7/18 to 29/9/18; attached R.A. Second Army 30/9/18 to armistice.

Gorst, Battery Sergeant-Major J., 92nd Bty., R.F.A., on being given a commission, was posted to the 3rd D.A. 3/8/16.

Gough, 2nd Lieut. J. N. (S.R.), (2nd Lieut. 13/2/17), 26th Bty., R.F.A., 18/5/17 to ?/8/17; Y & Z/29 T.M. Bty., ?/8/7 to 4/2/18; X/29 T.M. Bty., 4/2/18 to 8/3/18 (killed in action).

Graham, Temp. Lieut. C. E. V., came to the D.A. as O.C. 57th B.A.C. when part of that Brigade formed the nucleus of the new 132nd Brigade, R.F.A., in February 1916. He afterwards served in the D.A.C., presumably from 13/5/16 when the B.A.Cs. were all merged into the D.A.C., in 8/29 T.M. Bty. from 5/6/16 to 5/9/16, in Z/29 T.M. Bty. from 6/9/16 to 21/9/16, and was then transferred to the 4th D.A.

Graham, Capt. G. W., Cork R.G.A. (S.R.), 460th Bty., R.F.A., 2/9/15 to 16/9/15 (to R.N.A.S., Mudros).

Grant, Major H. F. L., R.G.A. (Reg.), attached H.Q. 29th D.A., 10/5/15 to 31/5/15; Brigade Major 29th D.A., 1/6/15 to 6/9/15 (to A.A. and Q.M.G. 42nd Division). (Mention).

Grantley-Smith, Lieut. E., served in the Detachment of the D.A.C. at Helles till 9/7/15 (hospital).

Grant-Suttie, 2nd Lieut. A. R. (Reg.), "B" Bty., R.H.A., 30/10/15 to ?/7/16; "L" Bty., R.H.A., ?/7/16 to 9/11/16; X/29 T.M. Bty., 10/11/16 to 22/3/17; "L" Bty., R.H.A., 23/3/17 to 22/7/17 (wounded—died of wounds subsequently).

Gray, 2nd Lieut. C. E. P. (S.R.) (2nd Lieut. 21/8/16), 97th Bty., R.F.A., 9/11/16 to 22/11/16 (hospital); 97th Bty., R.F.A., 10/12/16 to ?/2/17; "L" Bty., R.H.A., ?/2/17 to 9/10/17 (wounded—died of wounds subsequently).

Gray, Temp. 2nd Lieut. T. H., actg. Staff Capt. 29th D.A. 2/2/16 to 22/3/16; 10th Bty., R.F.A., 23/3/16 to 12/7/16; D/132 (afterwards D/17) Bty., R.F.A., 13/7/16 to 31/1/17 (transferred with his section to new D/17); D/17 (late D/147) Bty., R.F.A., 1/2/17 to 17/8/17; No. 2 Section, D.A.C., 18/8/17 to ?/9/17 (hospital).

Green, Bty. Quartermaster-Sergeant C. A. E., 90th H.B., R.G.A., was given a regular commission 19/11/15.

Green, Lieut. (actg. Capt.) E. E., R.E. (T.F.), Signal Officer H.Q., 29th D.A., 8/4/17 to armistice. (M.C. and Mention).

Greenless, 2nd Lieut. R. W., served in the Ross Battery, 1/4th Highland Mountain Brigade, R.G.A. (T.F.), from the landing.

Greenway, Sergt. M. A. J. E., 15th Brigade, R.H.A., on being given a regular commission, was posted to the 35th D.A. in March 1917.

Greenwood, Temp. 2nd Lieut. E. M., (2nd Lieut. 5/3/15; Temp. Lieut. 1/7/17), D/17 Bty., R.F.A., 28/5/17 to 21/9/17 (to R.F.C.).

Grey, 2nd Lieut. W. E. (T.F.), (2nd Lieut. 14/6/15; Lieut. 1/6/16; actg. Capt. 7/2/18), D.A.C., ?/4/16 to 14/8/16; 92nd Bty., R.F.A., 15/8/16 to 9/1/17; X/29 T.M. Bty., 10/1/17 to 3/2/17; V/29 Heavy T.M. Bty., 4/2/17 to 24/4/17; attached 13th Bty., R.F.A., 25/4/17 to ?/5/17; commanded Z/29 T.M. Bty., ?/5/17 to 3/2/18 (battery broken up); commanded Y/29 T.M. Bty., 4/2/18 to 7/2/18 (wounded). He rejoined for a few days 5/4/18 and was then evacuated to the U.K. (Mention).

Griffiths, 2nd Lieut. W. H., R.G.A. (Reg.), was commissioned from, and posted to, the 90th H.B., R.G.A., 14/10/15.

Griffith-Williams, Temp. 2nd Lieut. G. G., Orderly Officer 147th Bde., 20/1/16 to ? ; 97th Bty., R.F.A., ? to 24/7/16 (hospital); 10th Bty., R.F.A., 12/8/16 to 23/8/16; 97th Bty., R.F.A., 24/8/16 to date of brigade leaving the D.A.

Guiver, Sergt. H.S., M.M., "L" Battery, R.H.A., was given a Regular Commission 23/3/18.

Gye, 2nd Lieut. D. A., "L" Battery, R.H.A., 9/11/15 to 28/2/17 (killed in action).

Hagan, Major (Riding Master) J. (Reg.), 17th B.A.C., 22/10/15 to 20/5/16 (to Home Establishment).

Hall, Bty. Sergt.-Major C. W., D.C.M., 97th Bty., R.F.A., on being given a regular commission, was posted to the 69th Brigade, R.F.A., 4/10/15.

Hancocks, Lieut. A. C. (Reg.), 10th Bty., R.F.A., landing to 2/7/15 (wounded).

Hardy, 2nd Lieut. W. J. (S.R.), (2nd Lieut. 21/8/16), "L" Bty., R.H.A., 9/11/16 to 14/5/17 (hospital).

Harris, Lieut. F., R.A.M.C., attached 17th Brigade, R.F.A., landing to 17/8/17 (wounded—also gassed 6/5/17). (Mention and M.C.).

Hart, 2nd Lieut. F. J. A. (Reg.), (Temp. Lieut. 6/12/15), 147th B.A.C., landing to 4/6/15; 368th Bty., R.F.A., 5/6/15 to ?/3/16; Y/29 T.M. Bty., ?/3/16 to 30/4/16; 368th Bty., R.F.A., 1/5/16 to 11/9/16; 97th Bty., R.F.A., 12/9/16 to date of 147th Bde. leaving the D.A.

Hart, 2nd Lieut. W. L. D'A. (S.R.), D/132 (afterwards D/17) Bty., R.F.A., 23/8/16 to 14/10/16; 13th Bty., R.F.A., 15/10/16 to 22/10/16 (wounded); 92nd Bty., R.F.A., 31/10/16 to 28/4/17; 26th Bty., R.F.A., 29/4/17 to 3/5/17 (wounded); 26th Bty., R.F.A., 14/6/17 to 4/10/17 (wounded).

Haskell, 2nd Lieut. M. O. (S.R.), (2nd Lieut. 10/12/15), 368th Bty., R.F.A., 28/4/16 to 12/5/16; 371st Bty., R.F.A., 13/5/16 to   ?   ; "L" Bty., R.H.A.,   ?   to 20/9/16 (to 47th D.A.).

Haswell, 2nd Lieut. G. D. (S.R.), (2nd Lieut. 12/4/17; Lieut. 14/10/18), "L" Bty., R.H.A., 23/7/17 to 19/8/17; 460th Bty., R.F.A., 20/8/17 to 21/8/17 (wounded); "L" Bty., R.H.A., ?/10/17 to armistice.

Hayley, Major W. B. (Reg.), commanded "Y" Bty., R.H.A., 7/8/16 to date of battery leaving the D.A.

Haynes, 2nd Lieut. A. E. (Reg.), (Lieut. 8/8/16), joined the D.A. with C/132 Bty., R.F.A., in February 1916 and remained with it during its changes of title to D/132 and D/17, till the end of October 1916; he then served as under:—26th Bty., R.F.A., 31/10/16 to 8/11/16; Z/29 T.M. Bty., 9/11/16 to 2/12/16; D.T.M.O., 3/12/16 to 25/5/17; "B" Bty., R.H.A., 26/5/17 to ?/6/17 (hospital); D/17 Bty., R.F.A., 17/9/17 to 26/9/17 (wounded). (M.C.).

Hayward, 2nd Lieut. B. R. (Reg.), 17th B.A.C., landing to 1/5/15; 26th Bty., R.F.A., 2/5/15 to 6/6/15 (killed in action).

Hazlerigg, 2nd Lieut. M. G. (T.F.), (2nd Lieut. 14/10/16), No. 3 Section, D.A.C., 25/1/17 to 29/1/17 (hospital); S.A.A. Section, D.A.C., 12/3/17 to armistice.

Heartfield, Sergt. L. J., 26th Bty., R.F.A., on being given a regular commission, was posted to the 49th D.A. 7/6/18.

Heath, Temp. 2nd Lieut. H. N., came to the D.A. with the 371st Battery in March 1916; served in Y/29 T.M. Bty. in April, but rejoined the 371st Bty. on 1st May and remained in that battery till it was broken up on 12/9/16; he was then transferred to "L" Bty., R.H.A., and served therein until wounded 9/4/17.

Heath, 2nd Lieut. W. P. (S.R.), (2nd Lieut. 12/8/17), No. 2 Section, D.A.C., 20/4/18 to armistice (attached 13th Bty., R.F.A., in Oct. 1918).

Henderson, 2nd Lieut. R. E. (S.R.), (2nd Lieut. 23/11/17), 460th Battery, R.F.A., 14/3/18 to 23/3/18 (to Fifth Army).

Hendrie, Temp. Lieut. A. S., R.A.M.C., attached 147th Brigade, R.F.A., 25/1/16 to date of the brigade leaving the D.A.

Henman, Temp. Lieut. R. M. (Lieut. 16/6/15), "Y" Bty., R.H.A., 17/10/15 to 30/11/15; Adjt., 15th Bde., R.H.A., 1/12/15 to 7/5/16; 15th B.A.C. (afterwards No. 1 Section, D.A.C.), 8/5/16 to 21/9/16; No. 4 Section, D.A.C., 22/9/16 to 5/12/16 (hospital).

Henney, 2nd Lieut. H. N., 371st Bty., R.F.A., 15/7/16 to 11/9/16; 26th Bty., R.F.A., 12/9/16 to 23/4/17 (wounded 22/10/16); 13th Bty., R.F.A., 24/4/17 to 25/4/17 (killed in action).

Hetherington, Capt. C. G., R.G.A. (Reg.), joined the D.A. in command of the 371st Battery, R.F.A., in March 1916 and remained in command until wounded 26/6/16.

Hickes, Capt. L. D., R.G.A. (Reg.), No. 1 Section, D.A.C., landing to 1/5/15; Adjt. 17th Bde., R.F.A., 2/5/15 to 27/8/15; Staff Capt., 29th D.A., 28/8/15 to 20/12/16 (to G.H.Q., France). (M.C. and Mention).

Hicks, Capt. G., R.G.A. (T.F.), commanded the Ammunition Column of the 1/4th Highland Mountain Brigade, R.G.A. (T.F.), from the landing to August 1915 (hospital).

Hilary, 2nd Lieut. H. J., 92nd Bty., R.F.A., 26/12/16 to 3/6/17 (wounded—died of wounds).

Hill, Lieut. A. H., R.G.A (T.F.). served in the 1/4th Highland Mountain Brigade, R.G.A. (T.F.) from the landing; was wounded but rejoined on 3/7/15; was eventually evacuated from Malta 6/11/15 with dysentery.

Hill, 2nd Lieut. J. Shirley (S.R.) (2nd Lieut. 13/1/17), "B" Battery, R.H.A., 18/5/17 to 17/6/17 (wounded). (M.C.).

Hillyer, Sergt. R. A. N., D/17 Battery, R.F.A., was sent to a cadet school 10/3/17 and commissioned in the S.R. 9/9/17.

Hindle, Temp. Lieut. A. H. (Lieut. 1/7/17), 26th Battery, R.F.A., 10/12/17 to 12/5/18 (killed in action).

Hinkley, 2nd Lieut. H. R. (S.R.), (2nd Lieut. 7/10/17), S.A.A. Section, D.A.C., 21/12/17 to 13/7/18 (hospital—accident).

Hogarth, 2nd Lieut. W., 1/4th Highland Mountain Brigade, R.G.A. (T.F.), 26/5/15 to 30/9/15 (invalided).

Holmes, Temp. Lieut. H. O., (Temp. Capt. 28/6/16; actg. Major 1/2/17), came to the D.A. with A/57 Battery, R.F.A., which became B/132 on its arrival in February 1916; he remained with this battery through its changes of title to D/147 and D/17 till the armistice, except for a period of three months from 8/7/18 to 6/10/18 when he was acting Brigade Major, 29th D.A.; he was wounded 28/10/16. (M.C. and bar, Mention, Belgian Croix de Guerre).

Hooghwinkel, Temp. Capt. G. H. J., (Capt. 17/8/15), commanded 147th B.A.C. 11/9/15 to 6/3/16 (to 3rd Echelon M.E.F.).

Hook, 2nd Lieut. S. R., M.M. (S.R.), (2nd Lieut. 8/9/17), No. 2 Section, D.A.C., 20/12/17 to 9/3/18; Y/29 T.M. Bty., 10/3/18 to armistice (accidentally wounded 27/9/18).

Houghton, 2nd Lieut. G. A., 14th S.B., R.G.A., 4/9/15 to   ?

Howells, 2nd Lieut. J. H. (S.R.), (2nd Lieut. 10/6/17), "L" Battery, R.H.A., 30/7/17 to 22/8/17; 460th Bty., R.F.A., 23/8/17 to 9/10/17 (killed in action).

Hughes-Hallett, Lieut. W. E., R.G.A., joined the D.A. 4/7/15; left for Anzac 14/7/15.

Hulbert, 2nd Lieut. B. W. (S.R.), (2nd Lieut. 11/2/17; Lieut. 1/12/17), "L" Bty., R.H.A., 18/5/17 to 30/5/17; X/29 T.M. Bty., 31/5/17 to 24/3/18 (to a Heavy T.M. Bty.); X/29 T.M. Bty., 7/4/18 to 30/4/18 (wounded).

Humble, 2nd Lieut. T. R. (S.R.), (2nd Lieut. 28/10/17), No. 1 Section, D.A.C., 19/3/18 to armistice.

Hunkin, Rev. J. W.. C.F.. attached 29th D.A., 23/12/15 to October 1917; then became Senior Chaplain to the Division. (Mention, M.C. and bar).

Huston, Temp. Lieut. C. E., A.V.C., attached 17th Brigade, R.F.A., landing to   ?

Huttenbach, Lieut. N. H. (Reg.), "B" Battery, R.H.A., landing to 24/8/15 (sick). (M.C. and Mention).

Hutton, 2nd Lieut. J. (S.R.), joined the D.A. with B/132 Bty., R.F.A., in February 1916 and remained with the battery through its changes of title to D/147 until wounded 23/10/16; he rejoined the battery, which had meanwhile again changed its title and was now D/17, on 27/6/17 and remained with it till wounded again on 12/8/17.

Hyde, 2nd Lieut. H. A. (S.R.), 97th Bty., R.F.A., 1/9/16 to 11/9/16; 10th Bty., R.F.A., 12/9/16 to date of the brigade leaving the D.A.

Hyde, 2nd Lieut. E. C., R.G.A. (Reg.), was commissioned from acting Regimental Sergt.-Major, 1/4th Highland Mountain Brigade, R.G.A. (T.F.), and posted thereto 14/10/15.   (Resigned his commission 17/4/19).

Ideson, 2nd Lieut. A. (Reg.), (Temp. Lieut. 6/12/16; Reg. Lieut. 1/7/17), was a sergeant in "B" Battery, R.H.A., at the landing and was twice wounded; he was commissioned in October 1915 and subsequently served as under:— 15th B.A.C., 9/10/15 to 12/5/16; Orderly Officer 15th Bde., R.H.A., 13/5/16 to 22/9/16; Adjt. 15th Bde., R.H.A., 23/9/16 to 28/2/17; "L" Bty., R.H.A., 6/3/17 to 23/4/17 (wounded); 26th Bty., R.F.A., 8/6/17 to 14/6/17; "L" Battery, R.H.A., 14/6/17 to 16/7/17 (wounded); "L" Bty., R.H.A., 13/8/17 to 25/8/17; "B" Bty., R.H.A., 26/8/17 to 7/9/17; "L" Bty., R.H.A., 8/9/17 to 29/9/17 (to command B/76 Bty., R.F.A.).   Retired 11/5/19 with rank of Major.   (M.C. and Mention).

James, 2nd Lieut. M. D. (S.R., afterwards Reg.), (2nd Lieut. S.R. 13/2/17; 2nd Lieut. Reg. 13/1/18), "L" Battery, R.H.A., 18/5/17 to armistice.

Jayes, 2nd Lieut. A. L. (S.R.), (2nd Lieut. 27/3/17), 1/1st Warwickshire Bty., R.H.A. (T.F.), 11/5/17 to 12/6/17 (hospital); 1/1st Warwickshire Bty., R.H.A. (T.F.), 10/2/18 to 11/7/18 (hospital).

Jemmett, 2nd Lieut. W. B. (S.R.), 26th Bty., R.F.A., 11/12/17 to 29/1/18 (to First Army H.Q.).

Jennings, 2nd Lieut. A. (2nd Lieut. 28/7/15), 10th Bty., R.F.A., 22/10/15 to 25/11/15 (sick—was wounded 28/10/15).

Johnson, 2nd Lieut. C. E., M.M. (S.R.), (2nd Lieut. 19/8/17), "B" Bty., R.H.A., 15/10/17 to 30/11/17 (wounded).   Rejoined the 29th D.A. after the armistice.

Johnson, Lt.-Col. (Temp. Brig.-Genl.) R. M., D.S.O. (Reg.), commanded the 29th D.A. from 12/12/17 to the armistice.   (C.M.G., Mention, and French Croix de Guerre).

Johnson, Temp. Lieut. S. G., R.A.M.C., attached 17th Bde., R.F.A., 20/8/17 to 10/11/17 (gassed); attached 15th Bde., R.H.A., 26/12/17 to armistice.

Johnstone, Brig.-Genl. F. B., D.S.O., (Reg.), C.R.A. 52nd Division, officiated in command of the 29th D.A. from the 11th to the 15th October 1915.

Johnstone, 2nd Lieut. J. C. (S.R.), 368th Bty., R.F.A., 28/4/16 to 11/9/16; 10th Bty., R.F.A., 12/9/16 to -5/9/16; D.A.C., 15/9/16 to 26/10/16; 10th Bty., R.F.A., 27/10/16 to time of brigade leaving the D.A.

Jordan, 2nd Lieut. H. R. (S.R.), (2nd Lieut. 2/1/17), 92nd Bty., R.F.A., 18/5/17 to 3/1/18 (hospital—wounded 1/10/17).

Jowett, Temp. 2nd Lieut. C. J. (Temp. 2nd Lieut. 3/6/18), Y/29 T.M. Bty., 21/8/18 to armistice.

Joynson, 2nd Lieut. W. O. H. (S.R.), came to the D.A. with C/132 Bty. in February 1916; was a short time in the 460th Bty., but rejoined C/132 (later D/132) and left sick 23/6/16.

Kay, 2nd Lieut. N. R. W. (Reg.), "L" Bty., R.H.A., 28/5/17 to 30/8/18 (wounded —died of wounds 3/7/18).

Keane, Temp. Capt. J. S., A.V.C., attached 15th Bde., R.H.A., July 1917 to 30/11/17 (wounded).

Kelloch, Lieut. H. P. (S.R.), North Irish Horse, (Lieut. 10/7/17), attached 13th Battery, R.F.A., 25/4/18 to 28/9/18 (wounded—died of wounds).

Ker, 2nd Lieut. S. H. (S.R.), (2nd Lieut. 3/11/17), D.A.C., 20/12/17 to 10/5/18; "B" Bty., R.H.A., 11/5/18 to armistice. (M.C.).

Kershaw, 2nd Lieut. A. E. P. (S.R.), (2nd Lieut. 4/2/18), 460th Battery, R.F.A., 25/4/18 to armistice. (M.C.).

Kidd, 2nd Lieut. E. L. (S.R.), 147th B.A.C. 5/12/15 to date of the brigade leaving the D.A. N.B.—The 147th B.A.C. became No. 3 Section, D.A.C., in April 1916 but reverted to its former title when the 147th Brigade left the D.A.

Kilby, 2nd Lieut. A. R., D/147 Battery, R.F.A., 25/12/16 to ?

King, 2nd Lieut. A. J. (Reg.), (Lieut. 23/7/16), served in the 17th B.A.C. at the landing; this B.A.C. became No. 2 Section, D.A.C., in April 1916; he served in it till the armistice with the exception of the period 25/8/17-6/5/16 when he was sick.

King, Temp. 2nd Lieut. R. H., (2nd Lieut. 7/11/15), "B" Bty., R.H.A., 19/1/16 to 5/3/16; Orderly Officer 15th Bde., R.H.A., 6/3/16 to 12/5/16; "B" Bty., R.H.A., 13/5/16 to June 1916 (to Home Establishment).

Kinnersley, 2nd Lieut. F. A. (Reg.), 97th Battery, R.F.A., landing to 18/8/15 (hospital—neuritis). (M.C. and Mention).

Knatchbull-Hugessen, 2nd Lieut. Hon. M. H. R. (Reg.), "B" Battery, R.H.A., landing to May 1915 (attached R.N.A.S.). (M.C. and Mention).

Knight, 2nd Lieut. J. R. (S.R.), 10th Battery, R.F.A., 25/12/16 to date of brigade leaving the D.A.

Knighton, Lieut. J. M., A.V.C. (S.R.), attached 147th Brigade, R.F.A., landing to ?

Lake, 2nd Lieut. A. H. (T.F.), (2nd Lieut. 15/10/15), 92nd Bty., R.F.A., 4/3/16 to 3/4/16; 13th Bty., R.F.A., 4/4/16 to 30/5/16; 26th Bty., R.F.A., 31/5/16 to 21/7/16; 13th Bty., R.F.A., 22/7/16 to 12/11/16; 92nd Bty., R.F.A., 13/11/16 to 7/3/17 (wounded). He rejoined the 17th Brigade, R.F.A., 3/9/17 but was immediately transferred to the 155th Army Brigade, R.F.A.

Lamb, 2nd Lieut. G. C. T. J. (S.R.), (2nd Lieut. 31/12/15), 370th Battery, R.F.A., 15/7/16 to 12/9/16 (to 41st D.A. on break-up of battery).

Lamb, Temp. Lieut. H. V., R.A.M.C., was attached to the 1/4th Highland Mountain Brigade, R.G.A. (T.F.) in Gallipoli.

Lane-Mullins, 2nd Lieut. J. B. (S.R.), (2nd Lieut. 24/9/16), 1/1st Warwickshire Battery, R.H.A. (T.F.), 18/5/17 to 14/6/17 (killed in action).

Lardelli, 2nd Lieut. M. S. (S.R.), (2nd Lieut. 26/5/17), No. 2 Section, D.A.C., 5/7/17 to 12/10/17 (hospital).

Laslett, Sergt. L. W., "B" Battery, R.H.A., on being given a regular commission, was posted to the 12th D.A. in May 1917.

Lawson, Capt. C. G. (Reg.), (Major 26/8/16), came to the D.A. in command of the 369th Bty., R.F.A., in March 1916; on the break-up of the battery on 12/9/16 he went to "Y" Battery, R.H.A., for about a month and was then posted to command "D" Battery of the 14th Brigade, R.H.A.

Leach, Capt. R. S. (Reg.), (actg. Major 25/9/16), was in the 13th Battery, R.F.A., at the landing; was subsequently attached to the H.Q. 17th Brigade, R.F.A, till 15/8/15, when he went to hospital. He rejoined the 17th Brigade 17/9/15; joined the 460th Battery, R.F.A., 22/9/15; was attached to VIII Corps H.Q. 31/12/15; joined the 13th Battery, R.F.A., 25/1/16 and commanded it from that date till 23/4/17 when he was wounded. (M.C. and Mention).

Leadbetter, 2nd Lieut. A. E. G. (Reg.), 92nd Bty., R.F.A., 2/6/15 to 18/7/15; Orderly Officer 17th Bde., R.F.A., 19/7/15 to 27/8/15; Adjt. 17th Bde., R.F.A., 28/8/15 to 26/7/16; 460th Bty., R.F.A., 27/7/16 to 14/11/16 (wounded); 92nd Bty., R.F.A., 1/6/17 to 22/7/17; "L" Bty., R.H.A., 23/7/17 to 4/8/17 (killed in action). (Twice mentioned).

K

Leal, 2nd Lieut. G. (S.R.), D.A.C., 5/7/16 to 8/7/16; 92nd Bty., R.F.A., 9/7/16 to 8/8/16; V/29 T.M. Bty., 9/8/16 to 18/2/17 (to R.F.C.—killed later).

Lee, 2nd Lieut. P. W., 147th B.A.C., landing to 19/7/15; 97th Bty., R.F.A., 20/7/15 to 19/9/15 (hospital).

Lefeaux, 2nd Lieut. J. F. (S.R.), (2nd Lieut. 20/9/17), 1/1st Warwickshire Bty., R.H.A. (T.F.), 3/12/17 to 15/10/18 (wounded—died of wounds).

Leighton, 2nd Lieut. A. F. (S.R.), (2nd Lieut. 3/6/15), 368th Bty., R.F.A., 26/10/15 to 25/8/16; Adjt. 147th Bde., R.F.A., 25/8/16 to date of brigade leaving the D.A.

Leuchars, 2nd Lieut. A. E. (S.R.), 92nd Bty., R.F.A., 30/6/16 to 9/7/16 (hospital).

Levi, Sergt. F. E., "L" Bty., R.H.A., on being given a regular commission, was posted to the 36th D.A. in April 1918.

Lister, 2nd Lieut. A. R. (Reg.), 10th Bty., R.F.A., landing to Sept. 1915 (hospital.)

Lister, 2nd Lieut. E. J. S. (S.R.), (2nd Lieut. 3/2/17; actg. Capt. 31/5/18), "B" Bty., R.H.A., 18/5/17 to 29/5/17 (wounded); "B" Bty., R.H.A., 17/9/17 to armistice. (M.C.).

Lister, Temp. 2nd Lieut. J. C., C/132 Bty., R.F.A., Feb. 1916 to 22/6/16; 369th Bty., R.F.A., 23/6/16 to 12/9/16; 369th Bty., R.F.A., 12/9/16 to 15/1/17; 26th Bty., R.F.A., 16/1/17 to 20/3/17; 92nd Bty., R.F.A., 21/3/17 to 20/5/17 (killed in action).

Littleton, Temp. Capt. (actg. Major) J. W., M.C., commanded "B" Bty., R.H.A., from 9/7/18 to 13/8/18.

Lloyd, Lieut. C. H. (Reg.), (Temp. Capt. 12/9/15), "L" Bty., R.H.A., landing to July 1915 (hospital); "B" Bty., R.H.A., 26/8/15 to 8/9/15; cL" Bty., R.H.A., 9/9/15 to 23/9/15 (to 69th Brigade, R.F.A.).

Lockwood, 2nd Lieut. F. G. (S.R.), joined the D.A. with B/132 Bty., R.F.A., in February 1916; served with this battery through its changes of title to D/147 and D/17 until wounded 21/10/16; rejoined D/17 in March 1917 and was transferred to the 97th Battery, R.F.A., during the same month.

Lodge, Lieut. H. R. (Reg.), (Temp. Capt. 12/9/15), belonged to, but was absent from, the 368th Battery, R.F.A., at the landing; rejoined 23/7/15 and served as under:—368th Bty., R.F.A., 23/7/15 to 25/9/15; "B" Bty., R.H.A., 26/9/15 to 8/11/15; 13th Bty., R.F.A., 9/11/15 to 14/11/15 (to D/60 Bty., R.F.A.).

Lord, 2nd Lieut. F., ? to 12/9/16; "Y" Bty., R.H.A., 12/9/16 to Nov. 1916 (hospital).

Low, 2nd Lieut. J. (T.F.), attached "L" Bty., R.H.A., 25/8/15 to 1/9/15; Detachment D.A.C., 2/9/15 to 18/9/15 (invalided home).

Lowe, 2nd Lieut. W. (S.R.), (2nd Lieut. 7/8/17), No. 1 Section, D.A.C., 20/12/17 to 1/6/18; "B" Bty., R.H.A., 2/6/18 to armistice. (M.C.).

Lowth, 2nd Lieut. R. A. (S.R.), (2nd Lieut. 30/4/17), 26th Bty., R.F.A., 13/9/17 to armistice.

Lunn, 2nd Lieut. R. W. (S.R.), (2nd Lieut. 27/3/17), "B" Bty., R.H.A., 11/5/17 to 17/6/17 (wounded—died of wounds).

Lush-Wilson, Capt. H. G. (Reg.), commanded 15th B.A.C., landing to 1/7/15; commanded "Y" Bty., R.H.A., 2/7/15 to 21/7/16 (killed in action). (Chevalier, Legion of Honour).

Lyte, Capt. W., joined the Ross Battery, 1/4th Highland Mountain Brigade, R.G.A. (T.F.) 2/8/15 and was invalided home from Alexandria 13/9/15.

Lyon, 2nd Lieut. K. (S.R.), (actg. Capt. 3/8/17), 13th Bty., R.F.A., 25/12/16 to 2/1/17; Adjt. 17th Bde., R.F.A., 3/1/17 to 1/10/17; attached D.A.H.Q., 1/10/17 to 9/12/17; D.A.Q.M.G., 10/12/17 to 29/12/17; Staff Capt. 29th D.A., 20/1/18 to 14/3/18 (hospital). (Mention).

MacDonald, Lieut. A. H., R.G.A. (T.F.), Orderly Officer 1/4th Highland Mountain Brigade, R.G.A. (T.F.) at the landing. (M.C. and Mention)

MacDonald, 2nd Lieut. R. O. C. (S.R.), 97th Bty., R.F.A., landing to 23/8/15 (hospital).

MacFarlane, 2nd Lieut. D. A. (S.R.), (2nd Lieut. 7/6/15; Lieut. 1/7/17; actg. Capt. 2/8/17-9/3/18), 15th B.A.C., 26/10/15 to 3/11/15; "Y" Bty., R.H.A., 4/11/15 to 29/1/16; 15th B.A.C., 30/1/16 to 12/5/16; D.A.C., 13/5/16 to 1/8/17; 92nd Bty., R.F.A., 2/8/17 to 30/8/17; commanded No. 2 Section, D.A.C., 31/8/17 to 9/3/18; D/17 Bty., R.F.A., 31/3/18 to 31/7/18; 13th Bty., R.F.A., 1/8/18 to 1/11/18; 26th Bty., R.F.A., 2/11/18 to armistice.

MacKelvie, Major T., R.G.A. (T.F.), served in the 1/4th Highland Mountain Brigade, R.G.A. (T.F.) in Gallipoli; was wounded and rejoined 28/6/15; wounded again and invalided 8/9/15. (C.M.G. and Mention).

MacKenzie, 2nd Lieut. M. J., served in the 1/4th Highland Mountain Brigade, R.G.A. (T.F.) in Gallipoli and was killed in action 28/6/15.

MacLean, 2nd Lieut. W. I. (S.R.), (2nd Lieut. 20/5/17), D/17 Bty., R.F.A., July 1917 to 24/11/17 (wounded).

Madeley, Temp. Capt. D. J., (Capt. 21/1/16), 26th Bty., R.F.A., 9/11/16 to 13/3/17 (hospital—reposted to the 29th D.A. 21/9/17 but never rejoined).

Magill, Capt. J. M., A.V.C. (T.F.), attached 17th Bde., R.F.A., 25/2/16; subsequently attached to the 147th Brigade, R.F.A., until admitted to hospital 22/10/16.

Maitland, Major (actg. Lt.-Col.) R. G. F., D.S.O. (Reg.), (actg. Lt.-Col. 12/10/18), commanded 17th Bde., R.F.A., 12/10/18 to 29/10/18; commanded 15th Bde., R.H.A., 30/10/18 to armistice. (French Croix de Guerre).

Maitland-Edwards, Temp. Lieut. G., attached D.A.H.Q., 23/7/15 to 5/10/15 (to VIII Corps Miners—became Temp. Capt. R.E. 11/10/15).

Malby, 2nd Lieut. H. F. (S.R.), (2nd Lieut. 20/5/17; actg. Capt. 22/5/18), 1/1st Warwickshire Bty., R.H.A. (T.F.), 18/7/17 to 23/8/17; 460th Bty., R.F.A., 24/8/17 to 22/11/17 (hospital); Y/29 T.M. Bty., 10/1/18 to armistice. (M.C.).

Malcolmson, Temp. Capt. T. S., No. 2 Section, D.A.C., landing to 1/7/15; commanded 17th B.A.C., 2/7/15 to 7/12/15 (during this period he was Staff Officer, Section A, for some two months); Orderly Officer 17th Bde., 8/12/15 to 14/2/16 (hospital—rejoined for one day only in May 1916).

Manchester, Capt. L. L. M., A.V.C., attached 17th Bde., R.F.A., ? to the evacuation.

Marsden, Capt. J. W., R.G.A. (Reg.), B/132 Battery, R.F.A., February 1916 to 28/5/16 (to 38th S.B., R.G.A.).

Marshall, Capt. H. S., R.G.A. (Reg.), (Major 16/10/15), 90th H.B., R.G.A., landing to July 1915; 14th S.B., R.G.A., July 1915 to 27/8/15; 90th H.B., R.G.A., 28/8/15 to 21/9/15; 14th S.B., R.G.A., 16/12/15 to the evacuation. (D.S.O. and Mention).

Martin, 2nd Lieut. J. J. B. (S.R.), 368th Bty., R.F.A., 19/10/15 to 20/11/15; 147th B.A.C., 21/11/15 to 30/11/15; 10th Bty., R.F.A., 1/12/15 to 26/5/16 (to 30th D.A.).

Martin, 2nd Lieut. S. G. (S.R.), 13th Bty., R.F.A., 29/4/16 to 18/4/17 (killed in action).

Martyn, 2nd Lieut. F. C. (S.R.), (2nd Lieut. 2/11/15; Lieut. 1/7/17), "Y" Bty., R.H.A., 29/3/16 to Dec. 1916; "B" Bty., R.H.A., Dec. 1916 to 30/6/17; S.A.A. Section, D.A.C., 1/7/17 to 21/5/18; 26th Bty., R.F.A., 22/5/18 to armistice.

Marx, 2nd Lieut. R. (S.R., afterwards Reg.), (2nd Lieut. S.R. 15/8/14; 2nd Lieut. Reg. 15/5/15; Lieut. S.R. 1/6/15; Lieut. Reg. 1/7/17; Temp. Capt. 27/7/16; actg. Major 15/9/16 to 23/7/17 and 31/5/18 to Oct. 1918; actg. Capt. 29/3/18), 13th Bty., R.F.A., landing to 22/5/15 (wounded); 13th Bty., R.F.A., 3/7/15 to 19/7/15; 92nd Bty., R.F.A., 20/7/15 to 25/9/16 (wounded); 1/10/16 to 16/10/16 (hospital, result of wound); 92nd Bty., R.F.A., 3/11/16 to 23/7/17 (wounded—wounded also 29/5/17); "B" Bty., R.H.A., 15/2/18 to 7/7/18 (attached during this period to H.Q. D.A. for one month and to "G" Staff, H.Q. XV Corps, for a month); D/17 Bty., R.F.A., 8/7/18 to 6/11/18 (attached Second Army H.Q.). (M.C. and French Croix de Guerre).

Matthew, 2nd Lieut. P. M. (T.F.), "L" Bty., R.H.A., 5/5/17 to 9/5/17 (wounded); 1/1st Warwickshire Bty., R.H.A. (T.F.), 24/5/17 to 31/5/17 (hospital); No. 1 Section, D.A.C., 3/8/17 to Oct. 1917 (hospital).

McCracken, 2nd Lieut. A. M. (Reg.), 368th Bty., R.F.A., landing to 16/10/15; Adjt. 147th Bde., R.F.A., 17/10/15 to 24/8/16; 368th Bty., R.F.A., 25/8/16 to 12/9/16; 97th Bty., R.F.A., 12/9/16 to date of brigade leaving the D.A. (M.C. and Mention).

McCrory, 2nd Lieut. H. (Reg.), was commissioned from Battery Quartermaster-Sergeant of the 17th B.A.C; 13th Bty., R.F.A., 14/6/15 to 1/10/15 (hospital); 92nd Bty., R.F.A., 21/6/16 to 1/7/16 (wounded).

McHall, Lieut. H. R., 92nd Battery, R.F.A., 5/7/16 to 21/9/16 (to 41st D.A.).

McInnes, 2nd Lieut. D., Orderly Officer 147th Bde., R.F.A., landing to ?

McKerrow, 2nd Lieut., A. R. C., 13th Bty., R.F.A., landing to August 1915 (hospital—afterwards became Lieut. R.A.M.C., S.R.).

McLachlan, Lieut. E. M., R.E. (Signal Service, T.F.), (Lieut. 1/6/16), attached H.Q. D.A., 23/9/16 to 8/4/17 (to 86th Inf. Bde.). (Mention).

McLeod, Lieut. A. R., "Y" Battery, R.H.A. (killed in action at the landing).

McLeod, Temp. 2nd Lieut. R. (2nd Lieut. 3/6/18), D/17 Bty., R.F.A., 21/8/18 to 30/9/18; 92nd Bty., R.F.A., 1/10/18 to armistice.

McMahon, Temp. Capt. B., A.V.C., attached 17th Bde., R.F.A., 16/3/18 to armistice (died on the Rhine in May 1919).

Medley, Capt. (actg. Major) E. J., M.C. (Reg.), commanded 13th Battery, R.F.A., from 19/11/17 to the armistice.

Meeson, 2nd Lieut. FitzA. R. (S.R.), (2nd Lieut. 6/3/17), 13th Bty., R.F.A., 4/5/17 to 14/10/18 (wounded—died of wounds).

Meldon, Major P. A., D.S.O. (Reg.), commanded C/132 Battery, R.F.A., February 1916 to 5/4/16 (hospital, result of old wound).

Menadue, 2nd Lieut. W. J. (S.R.), (2nd Lieut. 15/12/17), Y/29 T.M. Bty., 11/3/18 to armistice.

Merewether, 2nd Lieut. H. M. (S.R.), 97th Battery, R.F.A., 26/10/15 to date of brigade leaving the D.A. (was attached 147th B.A.C. for the evacuation).

Merritt, Lieut. (Temp. Capt. and actg. Major) F. C. (Reg.), commanded "B" Bty., R.H.A., 8/5/17 to 17/6/17; he was wounded 19/5/17 and killed in action 17/6/17.

Middleton, 2nd Lieut. A. A. (Reg.), 97th Battery, R.F.A. (wounded at the landing whilst serving as F.O.O. to the battleships Albion, Lord Nelson and two cruisers).

Milford, Major K. E. (Reg.), commanded "L" Battery, R.H.A., 15/5/17 to 15/9/18 (to command 110th Bde., R.F.A.); (hospital 21/7/17 to 24/8/17). (D.S.O. and Mention).

Mills, Major J. E., Royal Canadian Artillery, was temporarily attached to the 147th B.A.C. from 27/7/15 to   ?

Mocatta, 2nd Lieut. F. E. (S.R.), 92nd Battery, R.F.A., landing to 7/6/16 (hospital).

Monkhouse, Lt.-Col. W. P., c.m.g., m.v.o. (Reg.), commanded 17th Bde., R.F.A., 31/5/15 to 13/7/16 (to C.R.A. 19th Divn.). (Twice mentioned).

Morden-Wright, 2nd Lieut. H. (T.F.), 369th Bty., R.F.A., 4/4/16 to May 1916; X & Y/29 T.M. Bties., May 1916 to 9/11/16; 10th Bty., R.F.A., 10/11/16 to date of the brigade leaving the D.A. (M.C.).

Morgan, 2nd Lieut. C. S. S. (Reg.), was commissioned from the ranks of the 26th Bty., R.F.A., 25/1/16; 92nd Bty., R.F.A., 30/1/16 to Feb. 1916; 17th B.A.C., Feb. 1916 to 26/4/16 (wounded); 13th Bty., R.F.A., ? to 23/5/16; No. 2 Section, D.A.C., 24/5/16 to 16/7/16; 10th Bty., R.F.A., 17/7/16 to 14/9/16; No. 3 Section, D.A.C., 15/9/16 to ? ; No. 4 Section, D.A.C. ? to 5/1/17 (hospital—died 4/2/18).

Morgan, Lieut. D. P., m.c., joined H.Q. D.A. on probation as Reconnaissance Officer but was transferred away at once.

Morgan, Capt. F. H. L. (Reg.), Adjt. 17th Bde., R.F.A., landing to 2/5/15 (killed in action).

Morgan, 2nd Lieut. W. C. (T.F.), (2nd Lieut. 24/9/15), 17th B.A.C., 22/4/16 to 12/5/16; D.A.C., 13/5/16 to 15/6/16 (hospital).

Morrice, 2nd Lieut. J. (S.R.), (2nd Lieut. 1/6/15; Lieut. 1/7/17; actg. Capt. 1/7/17), joined the D.A. in C/132 Bty., R.F.A., in February 1916 and remained in that battery during its change of title to D/132 until wounded 19/8/16. He rejoined the battery which had meanwhile become D/17 on 27/11/16 but was immediately posted to "B" Battery, R.H.A., his services being then as follows:—"B" Bty., R.H.A., 1/12/16 to 8/9/17; 460th Bty., R.F.A., 9/9/17 to 22/9/17; D/17 Bty., R.F.A., 23/9/17 to 24/7/18; 460th Bty., R.F.A., 25/7/18 to 17/8/18 (granted 6 months leave to Australia).

Morrice, 2nd Lieut. J. S. (S.R.), (2nd Lieut. 1/6/15; Lieut. 1/7/17; actg. Capt. 16/7/17 to 14/8/17 and 25/8/17 to 8/9/17; "L" Bty., R.H.A., 26/10/15 to 23/6/16 (hospital); D.A.C., 26/7/16 to 15/7/17; "L" Bty., R.H.A., 16/7/17 to 17/10/17 (wounded); 460th Bty., R.F.A., 4/6/18 to 19/6/18; "L" Bty., R.H.A., 20/6/18 to armistice.

Morris, 2nd Lieut. R. C. (T.F.), (2nd Lieut. 25/1/16); 460th Bty., R.F.A., 25/1/17 to 16/4/17 (hospital).

Morrison, Lieut. A. D., 1/4th Highland Mountain Brigade R.G.A. (T.F.), landing to 25/7/15 (died of wounds).

Morrison, Temp. Lieut. A. J. McC. C., R.A.M.C., attached 147th Bde., R.F.A., landing to ? (wounded 16/6/15 and 4/7/15).

Morrison, Revd. J. L. C.F., attached D.A.C., 17/4/17 to armistice.

Muir, Temp. Lieut. J. M., R.A.M.C., attached 15th Bde., R.H.A., from 17th to 26th December 1917.

Mulholland, 2nd Lieut. A. E. (Reg.), (Lieut. 12/9/18); No. 1 Section, D.A.C., 12/3/17 to 18/3/17; X/29 T.M. Bty., 19/3/17 to 22/4/17; "B" Bty., R.H.A., 23/4/17 to31/8/17; Orderly Officer and afterwards Signal Officer to the 15th Bde., R.H.A., 1/9/17 to armistice (wounded 30/11/17—resigned commission 2/4/19). (M.C. and French Croix de Guerre).

Munro, 2nd Lieut. A. J. R. (Reg.), 460th Bty., R.F.A., landing to July 1915 (hospital).

Murchison, Lieut. J. K. (S.R.), 1/4th Highland Mountain Brigade R.G.A. (T.F.), landing to evacuation (wounded; rejoined 8/6/15; temp. Capt. 13/10/15 to 7/12/15 whilst commanding the Ross Battery).

Mure, Lieut. G. R. C. (T.F.), (Lieut. 1/6/15; actg. Capt. 21/10/17); came to the D.A. with the 1/1st Warwickshire Battery R.H.A. (T.F.) in Nov. 1916; appointed second in command in Oct. 1917 and remained with the battery till the armistice. N.B.—He commanded "L" Battery, R.H.A., after Lieut. (actg. Major) Leadbetter had been killed, from Aug. 4th to 25th, 1917. (Twice mentioned. M.C., Chevalier, Belgian Ordre de la Couronne and Belgian Croix de Guerre).

Murray, Lieut. J. D'O. (S.R.), No. 2 Section, D.A.C., 7/1/17 to April 1917 (hospital).

Murray, Lieut. J. C. M., R.G.A. (T.F.), Ross Battery, 1/4th Highland Mountain Brigade R.G.A. (T.F.), landing to 18/9/15 (invalided).

Murray, Major W. A. (Reg.), (actg. Lt.-Col. 30/5/17 and 19/7/17), came to the D.A. in command of the 1/1st Warwickshire Battery R.H.A. (T.F.) in Nov. 1916; was wounded 4/12/16; commanded the 17th Bde., R.F.A., in May/June 1917 and from 4/7/17 until gassed 30/9/17; rejoined 21/11/17 and again commanded the 17th Bde. till 10/10/18, except for the period 10/1/18 to 6/3/18 when he was sick; commanded the 15th Bde., R.H.A., for upwards of a fortnight from 10/10/18 and then returned to command the 17th Bde., R.F.A., which command he was still holding at the armistice.   (D.S.O., Bt. Lt.-Col, C.M.G., thrice mentioned, and French Croix de Guerre).

Muspratt, Temp. Capt. P. K., R.A.M.C., attached 17th Bde., R.F.A., 7/5/18 to armistice.

Nelson, Sergt. T. H., D/17 Battery, R.F.A., on being given a regular commission, was posted to the 61st D.A. 7/11/17.

Nicholls, 2nd Lieut. G. A., 1/1st Warwickshire Battery, R.H.A. (T.F.), 5/4/17 to 9/4/17 (killed in action).

Nicoll, 2nd Lieut. D. A. (Reg.), 92nd Battery, R.F.A., landing to 16/5/15 (seriously wounded).

Nicolson, Capt. T., R.G.A. (T.F.), 1/4th Highland Mountain Brigade, R.G.A. (T.F.), landing to 18/7/15 (wounded).

Nowell, 2nd Lieut. W. J. (S.R.), 147th B.A.C., 20/1/16 to   ?   ; 10th Bty., R.F.A., ? to ?; Orderly Officer 147th Brigade, R.F.A., ? to 23/7/16; D/132 (afterwards D/17) Bty., R.F.A., 24/7/16 to 31/1/17; 460th Bty., R.F.A., 1/2/17 to 9/4/17 (killed in action).

Nugent, Capt. W. V., R.G.A. (Reg.), 14th S.B., R.G.A., landing to 30/4/15; attached H.Q. D.A., 1/5/15 to ? (to H.Q. VIII Corps).

Nuttall, 2nd Lieut. H. R. (S.R.), 92nd Bty., R.F.A., 5/7/16 to 20/9/16 (to 41st D.A.).

O'Neill, Temp. Lieut. J. J., (Temp. Capt. 9/2/17), attached 147th Bde., R.F.A., 6/2/17 to ?

Ostler, Temp. 2nd Lieut. A., 15th B.A.C., 16/6/15 to 2/7/15; 26th Bty., R.F.A., 3/7/15 to 15/7/15; 17th B.A.C., 16/7/15 to 22/8/15 (hospital—later killed in the R.F.C.).

Oswald, 2nd Lieut. J. C. (S.R.), (2nd Lieut. 13/2/17); 26th Bty., R.F.A., 18/5/17 to 30/7/17 (gassed).

Painter, 2nd Lieut. L. E. (S.R.), 10th Bty., R.F.A., 9/4/16 to 23/9/16 (to 4th D.A.).

Palethorpe, 2nd Lieut. E. D. (S.R.), "B" Bty., R.H.A., 4/12/16 to 31/12/16; 460th Bty., R.F.A., 1/1/17 to 2/2/17; various T.M. Bties, 3/2/17 to 5/9/17 (actually did duty at times during this period with the Warwickshire Bty.); 1/1st Warwickshire Bty., R.H.A. (T.F.), 6/9/17 to 9/10/17 (killed in action).

Pallin, Capt. J., A.V.C., attached 132nd Bde., R.F.A., March 1916 to   ?

Parcell, 2nd Lieut. R. (S.R.), (2nd Lieut. 23/12/16; Lieut. 23/6/18); No. 2 Section, D.A.C., 18/5/17 to 17/11/17; Signal Officer, 17th Bde., R.F.A., 18/11/17 to armistice.

Park, Temp. 2nd Lieut. K. R. (afterwards Reg.), (Temp. 2nd Lieut. 1/9/15; Reg. 2nd Lieut. May 1916); attached from 2nd New Zealand Bde., R.F.A., to "L" Bty., R.H.A., 5/9/15 to 8/9/15; "Y" Bty., R.H.A., 9/9/15 to 23/9/15; 10th Bty., R.F.A. 24/9/15 to   ?   ; 368th Bty., R.F.A., ? to 11/9/16; 10th Bty., R.F.A., 12/9/16 to 21/10/16 (wounded).

Parker, Temp. Regimental Sergt.-Major A., 15th Bde., R.H.A., was posted home 21/12/17 prior to obtaining a Regular Commission.

Parker, Sergt. J. A., M.M., "B" Bty., R.H.A., on being given a Regular Commission, was posted to the 30th D.A. in April 1918.

Parkinson, 2nd Lieut. F. W. L. (S.R.), (2nd Lieut. 2/4/17; Lieut. 2/10/18); Orderly Officer 15th Bde., R.H.A., 18/6/17 to 20/8/17 (wounded); 460th Bty., R.F.A., 4/9/17 to 20/9/17 (wounded); O.O. 15th Bde., R.H.A., 22/12/17 to 15/3/18 (to 246th Army Bde., R.F.A.); O.O. 15th Bde., R.H.A., 14/9/18 to 10/10/18; "L" Bty., R.H.A., 11/10/18 to armistice.

Parson, 2nd Lieut. C. A. (T.F.), (2nd Lieut. 12/1/18); No. 2 Section, D.A.C., 26/2/18 to 12/5/18 (to R.G.A.).

Parsons, 2nd Lieut. G. V. H. (T.F.), (Lieut. 1/6/16); D.A.C., 10/4/16 to June 1916; X/29 T.M. Bty., June 1916 to 23/9/16; Y/29 T.M. Bty., 24/9/16 to 5/10/16 (hospital); X/29 T.M. Bty., 14/10/16 to 23/11/16 (accidentally wounded); D.A.C., 13/2/17 to Sept. 1917; 1/1st Warwickshire Bty., R.H.A. (T.F.), Sept. 1917 to Oct. 1917; 460th Bty., R.F.A., Oct. 1917 to 15/2/18; Orderly Officer 15th Bde., R.H.A., 16/2/18 to armistice.

Patterson, Temp. 2nd Lieut. J. R. (2nd Lieut. 19/6/15); 460th Bty., R.F.A., 22/10/15 to Jan. 1916 (hospital).

Pattison, Major J. H. (Reg.), commanded 26th Bty., R.F.A., at the landing (killed in action 28/4/15).

Patton, 2nd Lieut. H. W. (S.R.), (2nd Lieut. 17/8/17); S.A.A. Section, D.A.C., 3/11/17 to armistice.

Peake, Colonel (Temp. Brig.-Genl.) M., c.m.g. (Reg.), commanded the 29th D.A. from 22/4/16 to 20/12/16 (to G.O.C. R.A. I Corps—killed in action subsequently). (Mention).

Pearson, Temp. 2nd Lieut. C. H. M., 10th Bty., R.F.A., 30/8/16 to date of the Brigade leaving the D.A.

Peck, Major H. R., (Reg.), was absent from "L" Battery, R.H.A., at the landing; reassumed command 5/5/15 and remained in command till 14/11/15, when he left to command the 55th Bde., R.F.A. (C.M.G. and Mention).

Peel, Lt.-Col. E. J. R., d.s.o. (Reg.), commanded 147th Bde., R.F.A., landing to 15/10/15; commanded 15th Bde., R.H.A. 16/10/15 to 10/1/16 (hospital— rejoined at Suez 7/2/16 but left the next day on leave and never rejoined the brigade). (Mention).

Peppe, 2nd Lieut. W. T. H. (Reg.), 17th B.A.C. (employed as Flank Observing Officer to the Royal Navy) from the landing to 6/6/15; joined the 26th Bty., R.F.A., 7/6/15 and was wounded the same day; rejoined the 26th Bty., 17/10/15 and left on 24/11/15 to command D/55 Bty., R.F.A.

Perceval, Lieut. C. P. W. (Reg.), "L" Bty., R.H.A., landing to 16/8/15 (hospital—actually commanded the battery at the landing and until the return of Major Peck on 5/5/15); "L" Bty., R.H.A. 6/10/15 to 15/10/15; 15th B.A.C., 16/10/15 to 23/10/15 (hospital).

Peto, Lieut. R. A. (T.F.), (Lieut. 1/6/16), came to the D.A. with the 1/1st Warwickshire Bty., R.H.A. (T.F.), in Nov. 1916; was appointed actg. Capt. of the battery 16/5/17 and actg. Major from 23/7/17 to 20/8/17; left for England 17/10/17. (Mention).

Pewtress, Temp. Lieut. A. W., 92nd Bty., R.F.A., 30/8/15 to 24/1/16 (from R.N. Divn.); 17th B.A.C. 25/1/16 to 12/5/16; 92nd Bty., R.F.A., 13/5/16 to 21/9/16 (to 41st D.A.).

Philip, 2nd Lieut. R. T. (S.R.), (2nd Lieut. 23/1/17; Lieut. 23/7/18); 1/1st Warwickshire Bty., R.H.A. (T.F.), 5/5/17 to armistice. (M.C.).

Phillips, Temp. 2nd Lieut. A. S. (2nd Lieut. 28/3/15; Capt. 3/3/16); 460th Bty., R.F.A., 17/10/15 to 2/3/16; 132nd B.A.C., 3/3/16 to 12/5/16; D.A.C., 13/5/16 to 18/7/16; actg. Staff Capt., 19/7/16 to Sept. 1916; 26th Bty., R.F.A., 15/9/16 to 30/10/16 (hospital); 13th Bty., R.F.A., 16/1/17 to 20/2/18; D.A.C. (temp. command), 21/2/18 to 9/3/18; No. 2 Section, D.A.C., 10/3/18 to armistice. (Mention).

Pierson, 2nd Lieut. K. L. M. K. (S.R.), (2nd Lieut. 28/7/15; Lieut. 11/7/17); 368th Bty., R.F.A., 5/12/15 to evacuation; 147th B.A.C., Jan. 1916 to March 1916; 10th Bty., R.F.A., March 1916 to Aug. 1916 (wounded); No. 2 Section, D.A.C., 1/6/17 to July 1917; No. 1 Section, D.A.C., July 1917 to Dec. 1917 (hospital); No. 1 Section, D.A.C., 3/3/18 to 12/7/18; S.A.A. Section, D.A.C., 13/7/18 to armistice.

Pilgrim, 2nd Lieut. H. St. C. (S.R.), (2nd Lieut. 28/1/17); 92nd Bty., R.F.A., 18/5/17 to 30/6/17 (wounded).

Pilling, 2nd Lieut. E., D/132 (afterwards D/17) Bty., R.F.A., 30/8/16 to 31/1/17; 460th Bty., R.F.A., 1/2/17 to 23/4/17 (killed in action).

Pimm, Temp. 2nd Lieut. J. N. H., (2nd Lieut. 7/11/15); "Y" Bty., R.H.A., 19/12/15 to 29/2/16; 15th B.A.C., 29/2/16 to 3/3/16 (to 3rd Echelon, M.E.F.).

Pitcher, 2nd Lieut. M. F. (S.R.), (2nd Lieut. 12/8/16); Y/29 T.M. Bty., 23/8/16 to 26/10/16 (hospital).

Poulett, Capt. the Earl (T.F.), came to the D.A. with the 1/1st Warwickshire Bty., R.H.A. (T.F.) in Nov. 1916; went on a Gunnery Course to England commencing 31/12/17 and never rejoined the battery. (He died in 1918).

Powell, Temp. 2nd Lieut. S. G., 368th Bty., R.F.A., 30/8/15 to 5/3/16 (to base) (from R.N. Divn.).

Pownall, Lieut. (actg. Major) F. H. S., M.C. (Reg.), commanded "L" Bty., R.H.A., 30/10/18 to the armistice.

Price, 2nd Lieut. G. H. (S.R.), (2nd Lieut. 26/5/17); No. 2 Section, D.A.C., 3/8/17 to armistice (att'd. D/17 June to Aug. 1918).

Price-Davies, Major (Temp. and actg. Lt.-Col.) S. D. (T.F.), came to the D.A. in command of the 53rd (Welsh) Divisional Ammn. Col. on 10/4/16, and remained in command of the D.A.C. until invalided home 20/2/18. (Mention).

Prior, 2nd Lieut. G. W. (Reg.), 14th S.B., R.G.A., landing to 20/6/15 (wounded).

Purkis, 2nd Lieut. F. O. L., 147th B.A.C. and 10th Bty., R.F.A., landing to 19/11/15 (wounded).

Pye, Bty. Sergt.-Major, 92nd Bty., R.F.A., on being given a Regular Commission, was posted to the 8th D.A. 15/3/18.

Railton, 2nd Lieut. E. (S.R.), 14th Siege Battery, R.G.A., 20/11/15 to the evacuation.

Ramsey, 2nd Lieut. T. V. (Reg.), 15th B.A.C., 18/6/15 to 24/10/15 (hospital—attached "L" Bty., R.H.A., 21/8/11 to ?).

Ratsey, Temp. 2nd Lieut. T. C., (Lieut. 1/7/17; actg. Capt. 3/8/17 to 2/11/18); 13th Bty., R.F.A., 25/9/15 to 5/3/16 (from R.N. Divn.); Orderly Officer 17th Bde., R.F.A., 6/3/16 to 11/10/17; Adjt. 17th Bde., R.F.A., 12/10/17 to 1/11/18; 13th Bty., R.F.A., 2/11/18 to armistice. (Mention).

Rawson, Temp. 2nd Lieut. E. H., (2nd Lieut. 7/12/16; Lieut. 7/6/18); D/17 Bty., R.F.A., 18/5/17 to 23/7/17 (hospital); D/17 Bty., R.F.A., 16/9/17 to armistice. (M.C.).

Rea, Temp. 2nd Lieut. R. H. T., (2nd Lieut. 12/8/18); D/17 Bty., R.F.A., 18/10/18 to armistice.

Redgate, 2nd Lieut. B. A. (S.R.), (2nd Lieut. 27/3/17); "B" Bty., R.H.A., 11/5/17 to 29/4/18 (killed in action).

Rees, Temp. 2nd Lieut. W. L., "L" Bty., R.H.A., 28/8/15 to 2/9/15 (hospital) (from R.N. Divn.), "L" Bty., R.H.A., 9/9/15 to 27/10/15 (to Cairo).

Reilly, Capt. J. J. (Reserve of Officers), D.A.C., 9/4/18 to 7/5/18 (hospital); D.A.C., 8/11/18 to armistice.

Remington, 2nd Lieut. H. R. (S.R.), 26th Bty., R.F.A., 26/10/15 to 26/4/17 (hospital)—rejoined 14/6/17 but left on transfer to the R.F.C. next day.

Reynolds, Capt. H. (Reg.), "L" Bty., R.H.A., 7/9/17 to 2/11/17; 26th Bty., R.F.A., 3/11/17 to 5/12/17 (wounded).

Rhodes, 2nd Lieut. H. (S.R.), (Lieut. 1/6/16; actg. Capt. 3/8/17); D.A.C., 10/4/16 to 2/10/18 (hospital—was Adjt. D.A.C. from 30/9/16 and attached H.Q. D.A. from 14/2/18 to 7/4/18).

Richardson, 2nd Lieut. S. G. (S.R.), (2nd Lieut. 26/5/17); 26th Bty., R.F.A., 5/8/17 to 5/12/17 (wounded).

Rickett₫, 2nd Lieut. J. S., D.A.C., 10/9/15 to ?

Riddell, 2nd Lieut. W. S. (S.R.), (2nd Lieut. 1/10/17); 1/1st Warwickshire Bty., R.H.A. (T.F.), 3/12/17 to 21/1/18 (hospital).

Robinson, 2nd Lieut. W. C. E. (S.R.), (2nd Lieut. 21/12/15); 97th Bty., R.F.A., 9/4/16 to 4/9/16 (wounded).

Roche, Lieut. C. R., A.V.C., embarked with the 147th Bde., R.F.A., 11/3/16 and went to hospital 27/3/16.

Rowe, Capt. W. B. (Reg.),14th S.B., R.G.A., landing to 11/12/15 (hospital).

Russell, 2nd Lieut. E. A. (S.R.), (2nd Lieut. 19/8/17); No. 1 Section, D.A.C., 2/11/17 to 9/3/18; X/29 T.M. Bty., 10/3/18 to 28/8/18 (to R.A.F.—was in hospital 12/5/18 to 4/6/18).

Russell, 2nd Lieut. G. G., 26th Bty., R.F.A., 4/4/16 to 6/7/16 (hospital).

Russell, 2nd Lieut. W. E., 26th Bty., R.F.A., 20/12/16 to 31/1/17; X & Z/29 T.M. Bties, 1/2/17 to 13/7/16 (killed in action—had been attached to 26th Bty. in May 1917).

Sadler, 2nd Lieut. G. F. (T.F.), "B" Bty., R.H.A., 3/4/16 to ? ; X/29 T.M. Bty., ? to 24/9/16 (to 4th D.A.).

Saggers, 2nd Lieut. W., 92nd Bty., R.F.A., 27/11/17 to 3/12/17 (wounded).

Salberg, 2nd Lieut. E. T., 26th Bty., R.F.A., 15/7/16 to 3/10/16; Z/29 T.M. Bty., 4/10/16 to 20/3/17; 26th Bty., R.F.A., 21/3/17 to 3/5/17 (wounded).

Savours, Capt. D. S. (T.F.), (Capt. 5/8/14); No. 2 Section, D.A.C., 10/4/16 to 12/5/16 (to Home Establishment).

Sayer, Sergt. R. H., D.C.M., 26th Bty., R.F.A., on being given a Regular Commission, was posted to the 40th D.A. 16/3/17.

Scrambker, Temp. Lieut. J. R. I. (afterwards Reg.), (Reg. 2nd Lieut. 3/3/17); D.A.C., 5/1/17 to 11/5/17 (to R.F.C.).

Scott, 2nd Lieut. R. S. (S.R.), No. 3 Section, D.A.C., 31/12/16 to date of leaving the D.A. as 147th B.A.C.

Shaw, 2nd Lieut. V. C., D.A.C., April 1916 to 4/6/16; S/29 T.M. Bty., 5/6/16 to 5/9/16; Z/29 T.M. Bty., 6/9/16 to 15/10/16 (died on admission to hospital).

Shepherd, Temp. 2nd Lieut. J. C., "Y" Bty., R.H.A., 17/6/15 to 24/8/15; "L" Bty., R.H.A., 25/8/15 to 29/9/15 (hospital).

Sherbrooke, Major N. H. C. (Reg.), (actg. Lt.-Col. 13/8/16); commanded C/132 Bty., R.F.A., May 1916 to 12/7/16; commanded 17th Bde., R.F.A., 13/7/16 to 11/9/16; commanded 15th Bde., R.H.A., 12/9/16 to 10/10/17 (wounded 11/5/17; rejoined 14/6/17; in hospital from 25/8/17 to 20/9/17). (D.S.O. and Twice Mentioned).

Shone, Temp. Capt. G. G., M.C., (Capt. 18/9/17); Staff Capt. 29th D.A., 16/4/18 to 31/7/18 (wounded).

Shorney, 2nd Lieut. F. C. (S.R.), (2nd Lieut. 19/8/17); 1/1st Warwickshire Bty., R.H.A. (T.F.), 3/11/17 to 30/11/17 (wounded).

Siggee, Temp. 2nd Lieut. H. N. (2nd Lieut. 27/5/18); "L" Bty., R.H.A., 18/10/18) to armistice.

Simms, 2nd Lieut. H. R. (S.R.), 460th Bty., R.F.A., March 1916 to May 1916; went to a T.M. Bty. in May 1916 and died of cerebro-spinal meingitis the same month.

Simpson-Baikie, Lt.-Col. (Temp. Brig.-Genl.) H. A. D. (Reg.), commanded the 29th D.A. from 30/5/15 to 3/9/15 (sick). (C.B., Mention, Legion of Honour).

Skitt, 2nd Lieut. M. (S.R.), 92nd Bty., R.F.A., landing to Sept. 1916 (wounded 1/5/15; sick for three months from July 1915; rejoined 16/10/15; wounded again 30/11/15; evacuated in Sept. 1916 and transferred to the R.F.C. in Oct. 1916).

Smith, 2nd Lieut. A. C. S. (Reg.), 460th Bty., R.F.A., 27/4/17 to 23/5/18 (hospital); 460th Bty., R.F.A., 6/7/18 to 14/8/18; Reconnaissance Officer, H.Q. D.A., 15/8/18 to armistice.

Smith, Col. Eamund P. (Reg.), commanded 17th Bde., R.F.A., landing to 2/5/15 (killed in action).

Smith, Lt.-Col. H. R. W. M. (Reg.), commanded the 132nd Bde., R.F.A., from its formation in Feb. 1916 until it was broken up on 12/9/16; commanded the 17th Bde., R.F.A., from 12/9/16 to 4/7/17; returned from leave 4/7/17 but went to hospital at once; rejoined 27/7/17 but did not resume command of his brigade and was transferred to England on 25/8/17. He was slightly wounded on 3/9/16.

Smith, Temp. Capt. H. S., R.A.M.C., attached D.A.C., 6/10/16 to armistice.

Smith, Lieut. J. S., R.G.A. (T.F.), served in the 1/4th Highland Mountain Bde. R.G.A. (T.F.) in Gallipoli.

Smith, 2nd Lieut. J. W. (S.R.), (2nd Lieut. 10/6/17); 92nd Bty., R.F.A., 13/9/17 to 23/4/18 (to R.F.C.—was gassed in Oct. 1917 and slightly wounded 11/3/18).

Snowball, 2nd Lieut. W. (T.F.), (2nd Lieut. 27/1/17); D/17 Bty., R.F.A., 5/5/17 to 31/5/17; V/29 T.M. Bty., 31/5/17 to 13/7/17 (wounded).

Spedding, Lt.-Col. E. W., c.m.g. (Reg.), commanded the D.A.C. from 9/3/18 to the armistice. (O.B.E.).

Spencer, Rev. F. W., C.F., attached D.A.C., 19/1/18 to armistice.

Spurling, 2nd Lieut. C. G. (Reg.), was commissioned from Battery Quartermaster Sergt. 92nd Bty., R.F.A.; attached 92nd Bty., R.F.A., 23/7/15 to ? ; 17th B.A.C., 12/9/15 to 5/10/15 (hospital).

Squire, 2nd Lieut. B. B., R.G.A. (Reg.), 90th H.B. R.G.A., landing to 20/11/15; A.D.C. to C.R.A., 21/11/15 to 23/7/16; 370th Bty. ,R.F.A., 24/7/16 to 12/9/16; 92nd Bty., R.F.A., 13/9/16 to 19/9/16; 13th Bty., R.F.A., 20/9/16 to 30/11/16; "L" Bty., R.H.A., 1/12/16 to 31/1/17; 460th Bty., R.F.A., 1/2/17 to 23/4/17 (killed in action).   (Mention).

Stanford, 2nd Lieut. A. W. (S.R.), (2nd Lieut. 18/11/15; Lieut. 1/7/17; actg. Major 24/7/17); came to the D.A. with the 370th Bty., R.F.A., in March, 1916; 370th Bty., R.F.A., March 1916 to 9/7/16; 26th Bty., R.F.A., 10/7/16 to 17/7/16; 370th Bty., R.F.A., 18/7/16 to 11/9/16; 26th Bty., R.F.A., 12/9/16 to 16/9/16; 92nd Bty., R.F.A., 17/9/16 to 29/3/17; 26th Bty., R.F.A., 30/3/17 to 13/4/17; 92nd Bty., R.F.A., 14/4/17 to 27/5/17 (wounded); 92nd Bty., R.F.A., 20/7/17 to armistice (with the exception of a month in hospital immediately prior to the armistice).   (M.C., D.S.O., thrice mentioned, and French Croix de Guerre).

Staveley, Lieut. M. (Reg.), (actg. Capt. 23/7/16); 460th Bty., R.F.A., 23/7/15 to 22/7/16; 370th Bty., R.F.A., 23/7/16 to 11/9/16; "Y" Bty., R.H.A., 12/9/16 to 16/10/16; 92nd Bty., R.F.A., 17/10/16 to 3/11/16; "Y" Bty., R.H.A.. 4/11/16 to date of battery leaving the D.A.; he died of wounds 29/9/18.   (Mention).

St. Clair, Major W. L., d.s.o. (Reg.), commanded "B" Bty., R.H.A., from 10/11/17 to 15/5/18 (gassed).

Steel, 2nd Lieut. G. S., served in the 1/4th Highland Mountain Brigade, R.G.A. (T.F.) in Gallipoli; was wounded and evacuated from Malta 23/12/15.

Stephenson, 2nd Lieut. N. A. (S.R.), 97th Bty., R.F.A.. 21/11/16 to 12/1/17; Z/29 T.M. Bty., 13/1/17 to 14/2/17; V/29 Heavy T.M. Bty., 15/2/17 to May 1917; attached 92nd Bty., May 1917 to 19/5/17 (wounded).

Stevenson, Bt.-Col. (Temp. Brig.-Genl.) E. H., d.s.o. (Reg.), commanded the 29th D.A. from 28/8/17 to 30/11/17 (wounded and captured by the enemy; recaptured by a British counter-attack).   (C.M.G. and thrice mentioned).

Stewart, Temp. 2nd Lieut. J. (afterwards Reg.), (Temp. Lieut. 30/9/14; Reg. 2nd Lieut. 29/7/15; Lieut. 1/1/17; actg. Capt. 28/7/17); 460th Bty., R.F.A., 26/1/16 to 2/2/17; Z/29 T.M. Bty., 3/2/17 to 22/4/17; 460th Bty.. R.F.A.. 23/4/17 to 24/7/18; D/17 Bty.. R.F.A., 25/7/18 to armistice.   (M.C. and mention).

Stewart, Major J. C., Scottish Horse (T.F. Reserve), was horse-adviser to the 15th Bde., R.H.A., from 15/10/17 to 12/8/18.

Stockdale, Lt.-Col. H. E., D.S.O. (Reg.), (Brig.-Genl. 3/9/15); commanded 15th Bde., R.H.A., landing to 2/9/15; commanded 29th D.A., 3/9/15 to 22/4/16 to U.K.). (C.M.G. and thrice mentioned).

Street, Sergt. E. F., X/29 T.M. Bty., on being given a Regular Commission, was posted to the 8th D.A. 10/12/16.

Sullivan, Temp. Lieut. J. L., A.V.C., attached 147th Bde., R.F.A., 31/10/16 to 2/11/16 (hospital).

Sumpter, Capt. (actg. Major) G., D.S.O., M.C. (Reg.), commanded "B" Bty. R.H.A. from 28/8/18 to the armistice.

Swan, 2nd Lieut. D. B., 1/1st Warwickshire Bty., R.H.A. (T.F.), 5/12/16 to 7/3/17 (killed in action).

Syers, Temp. Capt. T. S. (late R.A.—afterwards re-commissioned as Capt. R.F.A.): commanded the 147th B.A.C. at the landing: later commanded the Dumezil Trench Mortar Bty.; was wounded 18/7/15: was evacuated later to the U.K. and did not again serve in the D.A.; he died of wounds 14/11/18. (M.C. and Mention).

Tarrant, 2nd Lieut. S. (S.R.), (2nd Lieut. 2/1/17; Lieut. 2/7/18); D/17 Bty., R.F.A., 18/5/17 to 22/9/17 (wounded); T.M. Bty., Nov. 1917 to 28/4/18; D/17 Bty., R.F.A., 29/4/18 to 9/7/18; D.A.C., 10/7/18 to 12/8/18; Y/29 T.M. Bty., 13/8/18 for a short time; D/17 Bty., R.F.A., Sept. 1918 to armistice.

Tasker, Lieut. (actg. Captain) A. V. B. (T.F.), (Lieut. 1/6/16; actg. Captain 15/11/15); No. 1 Section, D.A.C., 10/4/16 to 7/5/16; No. 4 Section, D.A.C., 8/5/16 to 7/6/16; Adit. D.A.C., 8/6/16 to 29/9/16 (hospital); "Dump" Officer, Jan. 1917 to 5/3/17; S.A.A. Section, D.A.C., 6/3/17 to 14/8/17; D/17 Bty., R.F.A., 15/8/17 to 24/9/17; S.A.A. Section, D.A.C., 25/9/17 to armistice.

Taylor, 2nd Lieut. E. D., "Y" Bty., R.H.A., landing to 28/4/15 (killed in action).

Taylor, Sergt. W. H., D/17 Bty., R.F.A., was sent to a cadet school 14/2/17 and commissioned in the S.R. 17/8/17.

Terrell, 2nd Lieut. C. R. &B. (S.R.), (2nd Lieut. 12/1/16; actg. Capt. 23/4/17): 132nd Bde., R.F.A., 28/4/16 to 7/5/16; 460th Bty., R.F.A., 8/5/16 to 8/6/17 (wounded—died of wounds 10/6/17). (M.C.).

Terry, 2nd Lieut. H. F. (T.F.), D/17 Bty., R.F.A., 25/1/17 to August 1917 (hospital—accident).

Thomas, Lieut. D. G., B/132 Bty., R.F.A., 3/2/16 to March 1916; 132nd B.A.C., March 1916 to April 1916; T.M. Bty., April 1916 to 8/8/16; No. 4 Section, D.A.C., 9/8/16 to 18/9/16 (to 47th D.A.).

Thomas, Revd. E., C.F., attached D.A.C., 30/1/17 to May (?) 1917.

Thomas, 2nd Lieut. E. H., 3/1st N. Somerset Yeomanry, was horse-adviser to the D.A.C. 23/12/16 to 1/4/17 (to 20th D.A.).

Thomas, 2nd Lieut. F. M., 147th B.A.C., 11/8/15 to 22/9/15; 97th Bty., R.F.A., 23/9/15 to 2/10/15. 147th B.A.C., 3/10/15 to ?

Thomas, 2nd Lieut. L. H. (S.R.), (2nd Lieut. 28/4/17); V/29 Heavy T.M. Bty., 2/8/17 to 26/3/18 (to Home Establishment for duty with T.Ms. in Mesopotamia).

Thomas, 2nd Lieut. W. A. V., R.G.A. (Reg.), 90th H.B., R.G.A., Gallipoli.

Thompson, 2nd Lieut. H. B. (S.R.), (2nd Lieut. 11/8/15); joined the D.A. with B/132 Bty. R.F.A., in Feb. 1916; B/132 Bty. R.F.A., Feb. 1916 to March 1916; Orderly Officer 132nd Bde., R.F.A., March 1916 to 11/9/16; Orderly Officer 147th Bde., R.F.A., 12/9/16 to 20/2/17; Reconnaissance Officer, 29th D.A., 21/2/17 to 2/10/17 (killed in action).

Thomson, Major A. F. (Reg.), commanded the 368th Bty., R.F.A., from the landing to 19/2/16 when he left to command the 58th Bde., R.F.A. (D.S.O. and Mention).

Thomson, Capt. J. N., M.C. (Reg.), Bde. Major 29th D.A. 19/5/17 to the armistice, except for the period July to Sept. 1918, when he attended a Junior Staff Course at Cambridge. (D.S.O., Twice Mentioned, French Croix de Guerre).

* Thonemann, 2nd Lieut. E. H., 13th Bty., R.F.A., 31/12/16 to 3(?)-1-17 (hospital).

* Thonemann, 2nd Lieut. H. E., 13th Bty., R.F.A., 31/12/16 to 3/5/17 (missing, believed killed).

Thorneycroft, Capt. G. E. M. (Reg.), (Major 20/5/16); commanded "L" Bty., R.H.A., 25/11/15 to 8/5/17 (appointed Bde. Major 39th D.A.). (Mention).

Tibbs, 2nd Lieut. W. E. (T.F.), 13th Bty., R.F.A., 5/4/16 to 13/7/16 (hospital); 13th Bty., R.F.A., 20/8/16 to 21/8/16; D.A.C., 21/8/16 to 21/9/16 (to 4th D.A.).

Tindal, 2nd Lieut. C. H. (S.R.), (2nd Lieut. 6/5/17); 460th Bty., R.F.A., 9/7/17 to 10/8/17 (wounded). (M.C.).

Tobutt, 2nd Lieut. R. L. W. (S.R.), (2nd Lieut. 11/2/17); S.A.A. Section, D.A.C., 18/5/17 to 1/6/17 (hospital); No. 1 Section, D.A.C., 14/1/18 to 2/2/18 (hospital).

Todd, Capt. W., Argyll Bty., 1/4th Highland Mountain Bde., R.G.A. (T.F.), landing to 29/6/15 (died of wounds).

Toomer, Gunner S. E., 1/4th Highland Mountain Bde., R.G.A. (T.F.), was given a commission 19/7/15.

Touzel, 2nd Lieut. F. G. (S.R.), (2nd Lieut. 5/11/16); 460th Bty., R.F.A., 2/1/17 to 28/2/17; "L" Bty., R.H.A., 1/3/17 to 22/7/17 (gassed); 460th Bty., R.F.A., 15/2/18 to July 1918 (evacuated and subsequently invalided out of the service).

Trappes-Lomax, 2nd Lieut. B. C. (Reg.), "Y" Bty., R.H.A., 26/5/15 to Aug. 1915 (hospital); 92nd Bty., R.F.A., 13/8/15 to ? (M.C. and Mention).

Tulloch, 2nd Lieut. H. T. (S.R.), D.A.C., 1/7/16 to 9/7/16; 26th Bty., R.F.A., 10/7/16 to 3/9/16 (hospital).

Turney, Lieut. A. A. (T.F.), (Lieut. 1/6/16); No. 2 Section, D.A.C., 24/11/17 to 24/2/18 (to Signal Officer 24th Bde., R.F.A.—was O.C. Divl. Signal School Jan./Feb. 1918).

Tyler, 2nd Lieut. L. B., 14th S.B., R.G.A., 18/7/15 to 21/7/15 (to Anzac).

Uniacke, Major C. D. W. (Reg.), commanded "B" Bty., R.H.A., 23/12/15 to 23/4/17 (during this period he commanded the 15th Bde., R.H.A., from 9/1/16 to 8/5/16 and from 4/8/16 to 11/9/16; also commanded the 17th and 147th Brigades for short periods; was slightly wounded 7/8/16 and seriously wounded 23/4/17). (Mention).

Van Cuylenburg, 2nd Lieut. G. W. L. (S.R.), (2nd Lieut. 21/12/17); Y/29 T.M. Bty., 26/2/18 to 16/3/18; X/29 T.M. Bty., 17/3/18 to 11/4/18 (to England).

Veasey, Temp. 2nd Lieut. H. (Temp. 2nd Lieut. 2/8/18); "B" Bty., R.H.A., 22/10/18 to armistice.

Vince, 2nd Lieut. F. H. (S.R.), (2nd Lieut. 6/5/17); "B' Bty., R.H.A., 15/7/17 to 15/10/18 (wounded).

Walford, Capt. G. N. (Reg.), Bde. Major 29th D.A. at the landing; killed on 26/4/15 whilst leading an Infantry attack. (V.C.—posthumous).

Walker, 2nd Lieut. D. S. (T.F.), (2nd Lieut. 13/5/17); 13th Bty., R.F.A., 10/7/17 to 15/10/17 (to 30th D.A.).

Walker, 2nd Lieut. D. S. H. (Reg.), 15th B.A.C., ? to 1/8/15; "L" Bty., R.H.A., 2/8/15 to 16/8/15 (hospital); "L" Bty., R.H.A., 15/9/15 to 16/9/15; "B" Bty., R.H.A., 17/9/15 to 3/12/16 (was in hospital from 5/7/16 to ? with pleurisy); Z/29 T.M. Bty., 4/12/16 to 18/4/17 (wounded).

---

* Brothers.

Walker, Temp. Lieut. F. M., R.A.M.C., attached to 15th Bde., R.H.A., 29/12/15 to 30/11/17 (captured by the enemy; repatriated some months later). (M.C.).

Walker, Bty. Sergt.-Major J. W., D.C.M., "B" Bty., R.H.A., was sent home with a view to obtaining a Regular Commission in the spring of 1918.

Walker, 2nd Lieut. R., 92nd Bty., R.F.A., 27/6/17 to 19/9/17 (wounded).

Walton, 2nd Lieut. G. J. (S.R.), (2nd Lieut. 10/6/17); D.A.C., 30/7/17 to ? ; 92nd Bty., R.F.A., ? to 20/9/17 (hospital).

Warburton, 2nd Lieut. W., R.G.A. (Reg.), was commissioned from and posted to the 14th S.B., R.G.A., 18/10/15.

Watson, 2nd Lieut. F. H. P. (S.R.), (2nd Lieut. 5/8/17; actg. Capt. 25/8/18); 460th Bty., R.F.A., 24/10/17 to armistice (slightly wounded 3/6/18) .

Watson, Capt. J. B. (T.F.), (Capt. 1/2/14); 92nd Bty., R.F.A., 25/12/17 to 19/2/18; 13th Bty., R.F.A., 20/2/18 to 3/4/18; D.A.C., 4/4/18 to 15/6/18 (to Fourth Army).

Waylen, Lieut. A. F. (T.F.), landed with a section of the D.A.C. at Helles in April 1915 but went to hospital a few days later.

Webb, 2nd Lieut. T. C. S. (S.R.), (2nd Lieut. 20/5/17); 460th Bty., R.F.A., 25/7/17 to 21/8/17; "B" Bty., R.H.A., 22/8/17 to 14/10/17; No. 2 Section, D.A.C., 15/10/17 to 21/5/18; D/17 Bty., R.F.A., 22/5/18 to 15/6/18; 460th Bty., R.F.A., 16/6/18 to armistice.

Webster, 2nd Lieut. R. E. R. (S.R.), (2nd Lieut. 28/7/15; Lieut. 1/7/17); came to the D.A. with the 132nd B.A.C. in Feb. 1916 and transferred to No. 2 Section, D.A.C., on reorganisation on 13/5/16; 132nd B.A.C., Feb. 1916 to 12/5/16; No. 2 Section, D.A.C., 13/5/16 to 17/6/16; 92nd Bty., R.F.A., 18/6/16 to 22/6/16; "L" Bty., R.H.A., 23/6/16 to Sept. 1916; "B" Bty., R.H.A., Sept. 1916 to 26/11/16 (hospital); "B" Bty., R.H.A., 13/1/17 to 12/5/17; No. 1 Section D.A.C., 13/5/17 to 3/11/18; No. 2 Section, D.A.C., 3/11/18 to armistice.

Wells, 2nd Lieut. P. (S.R.), (2nd Lieut. 27/3/17); "L" Bty., R.H.A., 11/5/17 to 15/6/17 (wounded); "L" Bty., R.H.A., 28/3/18 to armistice. (M.C.).

Welsh, 2nd Lieut. R. W. H. (S.R.), (2nd Lieut. 16/4/17); 13th Bty., R.F.A., 13/9/17 to armistice.

Wheatley, Major P. (Reg.), commanded "Y" Bty., R.H.A., from landing to 2/7/15; mauled by a mad dog and left for Cairo for Pasteur treatment; rejoined 4/8/15 but did not reassume command; transferred on promotion and left 12/8/15.

White, Bt.-Col. (Temp. Brig.-Genl.) G. H. A., D.S.O. (Reg.), commanded the 29th D.A. 28/7/17 to 28/8/17, when he was transferred to command the 30th D.A.

Whiteford, 2nd Lieut. C. A. B. (T.F.), (Lieut. 1/6/16); Detachment from D.A.C., 23/7/15 to 17/11/15 (invalided to U.K.); Y/29 T.M. Bty., 14/5/16 to 16/8/16; D.A.C., 17/8/16 to 25/8/16; D.T.M.O., 26/8/16 to 30/9/16 (?); No. 4 Section, D.A.C., 5/12/16 to 6/3/17; No. 1 Section, D.A.C., 7/3/17 to 14/8/17; No. 3 Section, D.A.C., 15/8/17 to 25/9/17 (hospital).

Whiteside, 2nd Lieut., W. L. (S.R.), 26th Bty., R.F.A., 16/6/15 to 5/7/15 (killed in action).

Whitley, 2nd Lieut. J. (S.R.), (2nd Lieut. 1/10/17); D.A.C., 20/12/17 to 24/12/17; 92nd Bty., R.F.A., 25/12/17 to 29/9/18 (wounded).

Whitney, 2nd Lieut. W. J., (T.F.), (2nd Lieut. 26/1/18); 1/1st Warwickshire Bty., R.H.A. (T.F.), 26/2/18 to armistice.

Whitworth, Lieut. A. R. (T.F.), (Lieut. 1/6/16); Orderly Officer and Signal Officer 17th Bde., R.F.A., from ? to 26/10/17 (to Signal Officer 286th Bde., R.F.A.).

Wilkinson, 2nd Lieut. C. B., "B" Bty., R.H.A., 27/6/17 to July (?) 1917; V/29 Heavy T.M. Bty., July (?) 1917 to 22/10/17 (to R.F.C.).

Williams, 2nd Lieut. F., 92nd Bty., R.F.A., 31/8/16 to Sept. 1916; No. 4 Section, D.A.C., Sept. 1916 to 26/10/16; D/147 Bty., R.F.A., 27/10/16 to 21/11/16; No. 4 Section, D.A.C., 22/11/16 to Jan. 1917.

Williams, 2nd Lieut. G. G., Orderly Officer, 147th Brigade, R.F.A.,   ?   to 23/5/16; 97th Bty., R.F.A., 24/5/16 to   ?

Williams, Lieut. H. M. Williams, R.A.M.C. (S.R.), attached 90th H.B., R.G.A., in Gallipoli.

Williams, Major R. C. (Reg.), commanded the 92nd Bty., R.F.A., from the landing until wounded 27/6/16; was also wounded 26/6/15.   (D.S.O. and Mention).

Williams, 2nd Lieut. R. W. (S.R.), 92nd Bty., R.F.A., 9/9/15 to 16/10/15; 26th Bty., R.F.A., 17/10/15 to 17/1/16; 17th B.A.C., 18/1/16 to 5/3/16 (to 3rd Echelon, M.E.F.).

Winder, 2nd Lieut. G. M. (S.R.), "B" Bty., R.H.A., 9/9/15 to 15/10/15; A.D.C. to C.R.A., 16/10/15 to 31/10/15 (hospital).

Winter, Major O. de L'E. (Reg.), commanded the 10th Bty., R.F.A., from the landing to 12/10/15 when he was appointed G.S.O.2, 13th Division. (D.S.O. and Mention).

Wolverson, 2nd Lieut. C. E. (S.R.), (2nd Lieut. 9/9/17); 1/1st Warwickshire Bty., R.H.A. (T.F.), 12/12/17 to 27/12/17; "B" Bty., R.H.A., 28/12/17 to 19/4/18 (gassed).

Wood, Bty. Quartermaster-Sergt. E. J. V., 29th D.A.C., was transferred to England 16/2/17 with a view to obtaining a commission.

Wood, Lieut. F. M. A. (S.R.), (Lieut. 1/7/17; actg. Capt. 16/10/17); 26th Bty., R.F.A., 6/10/17 to 9/10/17; 1/1st Warwickshire Bty., R.H.A. (T.F.), 10/10/17 to 11/10/17; "L" Bty., R.H.A., 12/10/17 to 23/3/18 (to Fifth Army—rejoined 3/5/18 and posted to 13th Bty., R.F.A., but transferred on 7/5/18 to command 111th Bty., R.F.A., in the 6th D.A.).

Woodall, 2nd Lieut. J. D., 14th S.B., R.G.A., 3/11/15 to   ?

Woodbridge, 2nd Lieut. C., served in the detachment from the D.A.C. at Helles and was evacuated therefrom 4/8/15.

Wright, 2nd Lieut. J., 368th Bty., R.F.A.,   ?   to 13/12/15 (wounded).   (Mention).

Wylie, Temp. 2nd Lieut. A. L., 97th Bty., R.F.A., 30/8/15 to May 1916 (from R.N. Divn.); Y/29 T.M. Bty., May 1916 to 12/4/17 (to R.F.C.—was killed later).   (Mention and M.C.).

Wynter, Major (Temp. Lt.-Col.) F. A., D.S.O., R.G.A. (Reg.), commanded the 1/4th Highland Mountain Bde., R.G.A. (T.F.) at the landing and subsequently. (Bt. Lt.-Col.).

Zoller, 2nd Lieut. A. (S.R.), (2nd Lieut. 16/9/17); No. 1 Section, D.A.C., 26/11/17 to 24/1/18; 26th Bty., R.F.A., 25/1/18 to 29/1/18; 92nd Bty., R.F.A., 30/1/18 to armistice.

PART IV.

A SHORT HISTORY

of the

29th DIVISIONAL ARTILLERY.

GLOSSARY OF TERMS.

A.M.S.	=	Assistant Military Secretary.
R.H.A.	=	Royal Horse Artillery.
D.A.	=	Divisional Artillery.
R.F.A.	=	Royal Field Artillery.
R.G.A.	=	Royal Garrison Artillery.
H.B.	=	Heavy Battery.
S.B.	=	Siege Battery.
Bde.	=	Brigade.
B.A.C.	=	Brigade Ammunition Column.
D.A.C.	=	Divisional Ammunition Column.
T.M.B.	=	Trench Mortar Battery.
T.M.	=	Trench Mortar.
18 pr.	=	The 18 pr. Quick-firing Field Gun.
Q.F.	=	Quickfirer.
4·5″ How.	=	The 4·5in. Field Howitzer.
B.M.	=	Brigade Major.
S.C.	=	Staff Captain.
Bty.	=	Battery.
H.Q.	=	Headquarters.
S.A.A.	=	Small arm ammunition—i.e., rifle and machine gun cartridges.
I.B.	=	Infantry Brigade.
O.P.	=	Observation Post.
G.H.Q.	=	General Headquarters.
F.O.O.	=	Forward Observation Officer.
H.E.	=	High Explosive Shell.
H.A.	=	Heavy Artillery.
C.B.	=	Counter-battery.
G.O.C.	=	General Officer Commanding.

NOTE :—

The 24 hour timing is used, e.g.,

0001	=	12.1 a.m.
0101	=	1.1 a.m.
1201	=	12.1 p.m.
1801	=	6.1 p.m.
1841	=	6.41 p.m.
2400	=	midnight.

January, 1915.—Mobilization.

The formation of the 29th Divisional Artillery commenced in January 1915 at Leamington at the same time as the remainder of the Division. This artillery consisted at first of the 15th Brigade, R.H.A. ("B" and "Y" Batteries and B.A.C.), the 17th Brigade, R.F.A. (13th, 26th and 92nd Batteries and B.A.C.), 147th Brigade, R.F.A. (10th, 97th and 368th* Batteries and B.A.C.) and 29th Divisional Ammunition Column. All batteries were on a four gun basis only. R.H.A. batteries had the same gun as the R.F.A. batteries, i.e., the 18 pr. Q.F. The composition of this Divisional Artillery at this period was peculiar in that no Brigade of Howitzers formed part of it, but the 460th Howitzer Battery, R.F.A., with a special Ammunition Column of its ówn was allotted to the Division on February 1st, 1915, and remained with the 29th D.A. till the end of the war.

The 15th Brigade, R.H.A., was shortly afterwards completed to a 3 battery basis by the addition of "L" Battery, R.H.A., which was refitting at St. John's Wood after its return from France where it had suffered so severely in its famous action during the retreat in Aug./Sept. 1914. The Brigade was armed with the 18 pr. Q.F. gun, in lieu of the ordinary R.H.A. armament, viz., the 13 pr.

March, 1915.—Addition of R.G.A. Units.

On March 10th the following units were added to the 29th Divisional Artillery :—

> 90th Heavy Battery, R.G.A. (4 60 pr. guns).
> 14th Siege Battery, R.G.A. (4 6" howitzers).
> 1/4th Highland Mountain Brigade, R.G.A. (T.F.).
> (Argyll and Ross Batteries, each having 6 10 pr. mountain guns).

Composition on embarkation for service overseas.

The following units, therefore, embarked at Avonmouth between March 15th, and 21st for service abroad under the command of Brig.-General R. W. Breeks, commanding 29th Divisional Artillery :—

HEADQUARTERS 29TH DIVISIONAL ARTILLERY.

> Brig.-Genl. R. W. Breeks, Commanding.
> Capt. G. N. Walford, Brigade Major.
> Capt. J. E. F. d'Apice, Staff Captain.

15TH BRIGADE, R.H.A. (Lt.-Col. H. E. Stockdale, D.S.O.).

> "B" Bty., R.H A. (Major D. E. Forman).
> "L" „   „   (Major H. R. Peck—absent from bty.).
> "Y" „   „   (Major P. Wheatley).
> Bde. Ammn. Coln. (Capt. H. S. Lush-Wilson).

---

* Formed 3/1/15 from the left sections of the 10th and 97th Batteries.

L

17TH BRIGADE, R.F.A. (Col. E. P. Smith).

    13th Bty., R.F.A. (Major N. St. C. Campbell).
    26th „   „   (Major J. H. Pattison).
    92nd „   „   (Major R. C. Williams).
    Bde. Ammn. Coln. (Capt. A. C. Brooke).

147TH BRIGADE, R.F.A. (Lt.-Col. E. J. R. Peel).

    10th Bty., R.F.A. (Major O. de l'E. Winter).
    97th „   „   (Capt. H. Denison).
    368th „   „   (Major A. F. Thomson).
    Bde. Ammn. Coln. (Capt. T. S. Syers).

460TH HOWITZER BATTERY, R.F.A., and Ammunition Column
    (Major J. H. Gibbon).

90TH HEAVY BATTERY, R.G.A., and Ammunition Column
    (Major C. N. Buzzard).

14TH SIEGE BATTERY, R.G.A. (Major L. S. Bayley).

1/4TH HIGHLAND MOUNTAIN BRIGADE, R.G.A. (T.F.), (Lt.-Col.
    F. A. Wynter, D.S.O.).

    Argyll Battery.
    Ross and Cromarty Battery.

29TH DIVISIONAL AMMUNITION COLUMN (Col. Cleeve).

It may be interesting here to note how many of the units which originally formed part of the 29th D.A. remained with the latter throughout the war.

The following remained only for the Gallipoli Campaign:—

    90th H.B., R.G.A.
    14th S.B., R.G.A.
    1/4th Highland Mountain Brigade, R.G.A.
    29th Divisional Ammunition Column.

The last named was replaced in April 1916, after the Division landed in France, by the 53rd Welsh Divisional Ammunition Column.

The 15th Brigade sent "Y" Battery away to the 2nd Cavalry Division in November 1916 and received the 1/1st Warwickshire Battery in its place. The 15th B.A.C. became No. 1 Section of the (new) D.A.C. in May 1916.

The 17th Brigade remained intact in the D.A. until after the armistice, but its B.A.C. became No. 2 Section of the D.A.C. in May 1916.

The 147th Brigade left the Division in January 1917 to become an Army Brigade, having previously broken up the 368th Battery to make its other two batteries up to six guns apiece.

The 460th Howitzer Battery remained throughout but was amalgamated into three brigades in turn. After the Gallipoli campaign it came to France as part of the then newly formed 132nd Brigade, but was soon afterwards transferred to the 17th Brigade. On the reorganisation which took place in September 1916, it found itself part of the 15th Brigade, R.H.A., and remained therewith till the Divisional Artillery was finally broken up in 1919.

Voyage to Egypt.

The voyage from Avonmouth to Alexandria was uneventful. Malta was called at, and Alexandria reached on or about March 29th —April 2nd.

April, 1915.

All units disembarked and went into camp at Alexandria. The few days spent there were employed in preparing for the Gallipoli landing.

The Headquarters 29th D.A. re-embarked on the 10th April and sailed for Lemnos arriving there on the 12th. The units, who had shed their " Train " wagons and A.S.C. personnel, embarked during the succeeding days and all transports were collected at Lemnos by 20th April. The voyage of the "Manitou," carrying the 147th Brigade, R.F.A., was an eventful one. Soon after 10.00 a torpedo-boat, which had hitherto been believed to be British, came alongside, ran up the Turkish flag, spoke to the Captain of the transport and indicated that three minutes only would be allowed the latter to clear his ship, after which time a torpedo would be fired at her. The troops on the ship were quite helpless, the elaborate arrangements for ensuring celerity and order in the contemplated disembarkation being unsuited to the assumption of an active defence against such an attack as had now presented itself. True there were a couple of 18 prs. on the upper deck but no ammunition, as the wagons and limbers were in the bowels of the ship. There was not even a rifle cartridge available as all the S.A.A. was locked up in the magazine.

There were some 650 soldiers on board, whilst the number of boats available was 8 with a total capacity of 240. Life-belts there were in plenty, so each man was issued with one, and attempts made to lower the boats. Unfortunately the davits of one of the boats broke and several men were killed thereby. The commanding officer gave the order for such men as could not be accommodated in the boats to " shift " for themselves, but it was quite impossible to do anything for the horses in the short time available.

Punctually to the time indicated, the Turkish torpedo-boat fired its first torpedo at the Manitou at a range of 50 yards, but the torpedo managed to miss the ship—one account states definitely that it passed underneath. Another torpedo was fired very soon after, and a third after an interval of some 20 minutes, but neither had greater success than the first.

The torpedo-boat had by this time stayed too long, as its presence had been notified by wireless long since. She was now chased by British destroyers and H.M.S. Dartmouth. She eventually ran ashore on the island of Khios where she was destroyed and her crew interned. This was a most suitable ending to an incident which would have been most humorous were it not for the heavy loss of life due to accidents in lowering the boats and exhaustion of many of those who jumped overboard with lifebelts only. In all, this cost the brigade some 50 valuable lives. The majority of the survivors were picked up by the S.S. Reclaimer, and the Manitou proceeded on her way to Lemnos.

With the exception of the 90th H.B., the 14th S.B. and all but 3 officers and 40 men of the D.A.C., all units of the 29 D.A. were collected in Lemnos Harbour by the 19th.

Artillery observation officers for connecting troops at the landing with H.M. ships covering the advance, and others to go in the battleships, were told off.

The transports escorted by the Fleet sailed from Lemnos on the 24th/25th and the first of them approached Cape Helles on the Gallipoli peninsula at 0430 on 25th. At daybreak the bombardment by the Fleet and the landing of troops commenced on five beaches simultaneously against strong opposition and under heavy rifle fire. The Artillery observation officers, mentioned above, each with a small party of signallers landed at each beach. Of these officers, Lieut. A. R. McLeod of "Y" Battery, R.H.A., was killed at "W" beach and 2nd Lieut. A. A. Middleton, 97th Battery, R.F.A., was wounded at "V" beach.   At 11.50, when Pt. 138 and Sedd-el-Bahr were still held by the enemy, the 26th Battery and one section each of the Argyll and Ross Mountain Batteries were ordered to land and engage those points from "W" beach, but there was much delay in getting boats and it was 15.45 before a start could be made.   Pt. 138 was, however, taken by the infantry in the afternoon with the aid of covering fire from the Fleet.   One section of the 26th Battery landed just before dusk and came into action, the remaining section being landed soon after.   The mountain guns also got ashore, and during the night of the 25th/26th one section each of the 92nd and of the 460th Howitzer Battery were landed.   That night all guns which had been landed were dug in to repel counter-attacks.

April 26th.

At about 11.00 the old fort to the S.E. of Hill 138 was captured with the aid of fire from the 26th Battery and other sections which had been landed.   It was here that the Brigade Major, Capt. G. N. Walford, who had been lent to assist in the organisation of the infantry attack, was killed in the moment of victory and was subsequently awarded the Victoria Cross.

On this day the remaining sections of the 92nd and 460th Batteries were landed, so that the following were in action by the evening:—26th, 92nd, and 460th (How.) Batteries, and a section each from the Argyll and Ross Batteries—the 92nd Battery covering the left from a position on Point 114.

The ponies of the Highland Mountain Brigade were organised into ammunition, water and supply convoys under Major Allen, Ross Battery, and did exceptionally good work in supplying troops in the firing line.

Units of the 15th Brigade, R.H.A., and 147th Brigade, R.F.A., remained on their transports.

On the 27th April, "B" Battery, R.H.A., with all its guns and wagons but only 52 horses was landed.

About 15.00 the H.Q. 29th D.A. moved with H.Q. 29th Division to Pt. 138.

Majors Forman and Gibbon (of "B" and 460th Batteries respectively) did very good work in reconnoitring roads forward and getting the guns along. A working party from their two batteries made a practicable road for the guns between 21.00 and 24.00 that evening. At 22.30 Divisional orders were issued, by which Col. Stockdale with " B," " Y " and 460th was to support the 88th Infantry Brigade attacking on the right, whilst Col. Smith with the 26th and the section of the Argyll Battery was to support the 87th Infantry Brigade on the left. The section of the Ross Bty. was detached to assist the French.

April 28th.

At 01.00, "B," 460th and one section of the 26th advanced and by 06.00 were in action covering the infantry advance. " Y " had not landed in time but was in action by 13.00 this day. This battery had one of its officers, 2nd Lieut. E. D. Taylor, killed. For the night 28th/29th " B " Battery, R.H.A., had one section up in the front infantry trenches.

A good deal of inconvenience and delay was caused by batteries having no transport for rations, stores, etc., other than their mess cart. As, moreover, only a small proportion of horses had been landed, the mobility of the batteries was considerably impaired. The result was that the artillery was unable to give the infantry the full power of its support.

Ammunition was drawn from " W " Beach, but no ammunition column was as yet ashore.

April 29th.

The section of the Ross Battery was withdrawn from the French and joined the section of the Argyll Battery in action on the left.

" L " Battery, R.H.A., continued disembarkation which had commenced at 13.00 on the 28th but was not fully in action until 13.00 the following day.

N.B.—The 10th Battery, R.F.A., appears to have landed this day but this fact is not actually mentioned in any of the war diaries.

The 13th Battery and 17th B.A.C. also commenced their disembarkation.

April 30th.

Early on this morning a section each of the 90th H.B. (60 prs.) and 14th S.B. (6 inch howitzers) was landed.

The left section of the 97th Battery and two boatloads of the 368th Battery came ashore also. The 13th Battery and 17th B.A.C. completed their disembarkation.

The guns were formed into groups, and Lt.-Col. Wynter was given command of the Left Group consisting of the 147th Brigade and the Highland Mountain Brigade.

Great stress was laid on the necessity for economy of gun ammunition which was scarce at this period.

May, 1915.

On the night of the 1st/2nd the Turks made a violent counter-attack against the French and ourselves. Several of our trenches were evacuated.

In Sir Ian Hamilton's Despatch of 20/5/15 the following passage occurs with reference to this Turkish attack:—"The storm next broke in fullest violence against the French left which was held by the Senegalese. Behind them were two British F.A. Bdes. and a howitzer Battery. After several charges and countercharges the Senegalese began to give ground and a company of the Worcester Regt. and some gunners were sent forward to hold the gap."

In a letter from Sir Ian Hamilton's A.M.S. to the G.O.C. 29th Divisional Artillery of 28/7/15 it is stated that the artillery referred to in the passage above quoted were the 15th Brigade R.H.A. and 17th Brigade R.F.A. and the 460th Howitzer Battery and that " Sir Ian Hamilton readily grants permission that a statement to the above effect may be made in the official records of the Brigades and Batteries concerned."

The 17th Brigade war diary, however, states that none of the batteries of this brigade were concerned in this affair which took place in the 15th Brigade R.H.A. zone.

Lt.-Col. Stockdale, commanding the right group, brought the action of the following to the notice of the C.R.A.

Majors Forman ("B") and Gibbon (460) and Lieut. Perceval did good work in preventing the infantry from withdrawing, and Lieut. Blandy, R.A.M.C., in attending to French and British wounded under rifle fire the whole time from 23.00 on 1st May till 12.00 on 2nd.

Capt. Daubuz (Adjutant, 15th Brigade, R.H.A.) displayed valuable initiative in going up to the firing line for information and gallantly helping to organise the men who were retreating past the trenches under heavy rifle and shrapnel fire. He was slightly wounded in this operation.

Bombardiers Pawley, Love and Allpress, all of "B" Battery, R.H.A., are mentioned for gallantry and devotion to duty in maintaining their position in the forward trenches, which had been vacated by the infantry and in maintaining communication with their battery. Bombr. Pawley was wounded here; Bombr. Love was killed in action at a later date.

The withdrawal of the infantry caused a temporary gap in the line. Lt.-Col. Stockdale, on discovering this, sent Major Wheatley of "Y" Battery, R.H.A., and 25 gunners up to co-operate with 2 companies of the Worcestershire Regt. and hold the gap. By this means an effective line of resistance was formed and the advance held in check.

About 23.30 Colonel E. P. Smith, commanding 17th Brigade, R.F.A., and his adjutant, Captain Morgan, left their O.P. to see how matters were faring in the trenches. Both were killed.

The 97th Battery completed its disembarkation this day.

May 2nd.

By 04.30 the Turks were in full retreat and were shelled effectively by "B" and "Y," who covered the advance of the French. Our casualties in telephonists this day were severe. The 15th Brigade lost 9 of theirs and the 460th Battery 3 in the process of laying cables.

With the completion of the landing of the 368th Battery this day, all the field batteries were now ashore, as well as the 90th H.B. and the 14th S.B. Some considerable time was necessary for the construction of platforms for the 6 inch howitzers and for the dragging of the latter into position. Actually the right-half battery of the 14th S.B. was in action on 3rd May, and the left-half battery on 6th.

As mentioned above, the field batteries of the 29th Divisional Artillery were formed into 3 groups, Group I on the right consisting of the 15th Brigade, R.H.A., Group II in the centre being the 17th Brigade, R.F.A., whilst the 147th Brigade with sections of the Highland Mountain Brigade constituted Group III on the left. A further Group was formed consisting of the 460th Battery, 90th H.B. and 14th S.B., under the command of Lt.-Col. Peel.

May 3rd/4th.

At 21.00 a Turkish attack commenced. By daylight on the 4th it had been driven off, all our guns being very active in engaging the retreating enemy. The 90th H.B. did very good work in silencing enemy batteries and assisted the French considerably by cross fire. The 147th B.A.C. completed its disembarkation on 3rd May.

May 4th.

The 1st Australian F.A. Brigade (1st, 2nd and 3rd Batteries), the 6th Australian Battery, and the 3rd New Zealand Battery landed and were attached to the 29th Division.

The field batteries at this period generally had "night" and "day" positions, the guns being withdrawn from the latter at dusk, but from this date it was arranged that one subsection from each battery should be in position at night close to the Headquarters of the Infantry Battalion concerned.

May 5th.

The 1st Australian F.A. Brigade came into action.

Major H. F. L. Grant joined, nominally as an attached General Staff Officer, but actually doing the work of Brigade Major.

May 5th/6th.

This night the 6th Australian Battery and 3rd New Zealand Battery came into action in Group III.

May 6th.—Achi Baba Attack.

In this attack the Groups were reconstituted as follows :—

Group I.   1st Australian Brigade.
Group II. 15th Bde. R.H.A. and 17th Bde. R.F.A.
Group III. 147th Bde. R.F.A., 6th Australian Battery, 3rd New Zealand Battery, and a Mountain Battery organised from the two batteries of the Highland Mountain Brigade.
Group IV. 460th Battery, R.F.A., 90th H.B., R.G.A., and 14th S.B., R.G.A.

In this attack our infantry gained some 600 yards of ground.

May 7th.

The artillery fired in support of the infantry advance which was resumed at 10.00 on the 7th, and again at 16.30 when both flanks made ground.

On the 8th May we again advanced at 17.30 after a heavy bombardment by all the artillery groups.

May 12th.

One section of 6th East Lancashire Battery joined the 29th D.A., and was placed in Group I.

May 13th.

A mountain gun under Lieut. J. T. Wallace was sent forward from the Highland Mountain Brigade to a position close to the Gurkha trenches to engage enemy machine guns at close range. One was reported to have been "knocked out."

May 14th—31st.

The 5th East Lancashire Battery, R.F.A. (T.F.) joined the 29th Divisional Artillery on the 15th. On the 22nd, G.H.Q. ordered a further economy of ammunition and fixed the daily scale as follows :—

18 pdr.	2 rounds per gun.		
10 „	4 „	„	,,
60 „	2 „	„	,,
4·5″	2 „	„	howitzer.
6″	„	„	,,	,,

On the 24th May a composite F.A. Brigade was formed on a temporary arrangement, consisting of 5th East Lancashire Battery, 3rd New Zealand Battery and 6th Australian Battery.

On the 30th, Brig.-Genl. Simpson-Baikie assumed command of the 29th Divisional Artillery vice Brig.-Genl. Breeks invalided to England.

The following were brought to the notice of the C.R.A. for good work during the month, besides those whose names and deeds appear in the Honours portion of this book :—

Lieut. A. C. Hancocks, 10th Battery, R.F.A., for good work as F.O.O. on 1st/2nd and 2nd/3rd May. By good observation he enabled the battery to punish severely the attacking Turks in front of the Inniskillings.

2nd Lieut. A. R. Lister, 10th Battery, R.F.A., for good observation work on several occasions.

Bombr. A. G. Clayton Barker for very useful work at his O.P. on nights 1st/2nd, 2nd/3rd and 3rd/4th. This N.C.O. was recommended for and obtained a temporary commission.

June, 1915.

As the result of a suggestion by the C.R.A. that some naval 12 prs., for which ammunition was plentiful, should be handed over to the R.A. for forward work in the trenches, some of these guns were obtained during this month.

One was handed over to Group II on June 2nd and placed under the command of Lieut. C. P. W. Perceval, "L" Battery, R.H.A. It was manned by 3 men from each of the three R.H.A. batteries. Tangent sights only were available, so the gun was laid by field clinometer. The recoil was checked by drag-shoes. The piece was found very accurate for " range " but not for "line."

June 4th.

Prior to our attack on this date the artillery at Cape Helles was organised as Corps Artillery of the British (afterwards VIIIth) Army Corps under Brig.-Genl. Simpson-Baikie, C.R.A. 29th Division.

The general lines on which the plan of artillery support of the attack was based may be summarised as follows : —

There were 3 main phases.

Phase I consisted of a systematic 4 hours' bombardment of the enemy's front and support trenches with H.E. and shrapnel preparatory to the bayonet assault at noon. At 11.20 a pause of 10 minutes was made to induce the enemy to think the assault would be made at this time. Field batteries were allotted either as " wire-cutting batteries " or "trench batteries " or "approach batteries," whilst the counter-battery work was entrusted to the Royal Navy.

Phase II commenced with the general raising of the fire at noon on to trenches immediately in rear of those which were assaulted at this hour. A proportion of batteries were held in reserve to deal with any hostile batteries which might disclose their position.

Phase III consisted of a general allotment of zones of fire in case of a further advance combined with the allotment of certain batteries

    (a) to particular trenches in rear,
    (b) as counter-batteries,
    (c) to deal with counter-attacks in certain areas.

The wire-cutting by Groups I and II was successful, but a formidable obstacle in front of the trench known as J 10 was not cut by Group III owing to its proximity to our trenches and to the fact that the F.O.O. directing the shoot was put out of action at an early stage in the proceedings.

Red flags and biscuit tin lids carried by the infantry were most useful to the "gunners " who were thus able to locate our men and vary their fire accordingly.

The amount of ammunition fired this day was as follows : —

Group.	Unit.		Shrapnel.	H.E.
I.	1st Aus. F.A. Bde.,	1st Bty.	933	9
	,, ,,	2nd ,,	811	73
	,, ,,	3rd ,,	430	50
	Section 15 prs., 5th E. Lanc. Bty.		317	—
II.	15th Bde., R.H.A.,	"B" Bty.	915	60
	,, ,,	"L" ,,	753	50
	,, ,,	"Y" ,,	444	56
	17th Bde., R.F.A.,	13th ,,	527	60
	,, ,,	26th ,,	700	48
	,, ,,	92nd ,,	796	12
	Section 15 prs., 5th E. Lanc. Bty.		492	—

Group.	Unit.	Shrapnel.	H.E.
III.	147th Bde., R.F.A., 10th Bty.	834	—
	,, ,, 97th ,,	1264	56
	,, ,, 368th ,,	975	—
	Composite Bde., Section 15 prs.,		
	5th E. Lanc. Bty.	500	—
	6th Aus. Bty.	1061	44
	3rd New Zealand Bty.	975	43
	Highland Mountain (composite) Bty.	1156	—
IV.	460th Battery, R.F.A. (4·5″ Hows.)	204	486
	90th Hvy. Bty., R.G.A. (60 prs.)	162	214
	14th Siege Bty., R.G.A. (6″ Hows.)	151*	132
	Naval 12 pounders	134	76

June 6th.

Groups I and II, particularly the latter, were engaged in assisting the 88th Infantry Brigade to repel a Turkish attack.   Both the 15 prs. of the section 5th E. Lanc. Battery in Group I were put out of action owing to bad scoring of the "A" tubes.

June 7th.

Group I assisted the 42nd Division in an attack on the trenches known as "G 11."

June 10th.

The 14th Siege Battery had one of their howitzers "knocked out" by hostile shell fire, and owing to their position having been accurately determined by the enemy, moved into another position on the 12th.

June 14th.

A naval 12 pr. which had been received by Group III was taken up into the support trenches and used for the destruction of a sandbag redoubt in "J 10."

June 18th.

An attack by the East Lancashire Brigade was supported by Groups I and II.

June 21st.

Group I and the howitzers of Group IV fired in support of a successful attack by the French.   A message was received from the French General subsequently, saying that he was extremely pleased with the work done and was grateful for their assistance.

June 23rd.

The 1st Australian Battery was transferred from Group I to Group IV for counter-battery work from 06.00 to 20.00 daily.   A minor attack by the Royal Marine Brigade of the Royal Naval Division was supported by Group II.   The 4th City of Glasgow Battery of the 4th Lowland Howitzer Brigade, armed with four 5″ Howitzers, landed on the 22nd/23rd and moved into action under Group IV on the 23rd.

---

* Common Shell.

June 28th.

The British attack on this day was supported by the whole of the VIII Corps Artillery, many of H.M. ships and the French artillery.   The "Heavy" bombardment started at 09.00—the Field Artillery wire-cutting bombardment at 10.20—and the attack was launched at 11.00.   The first portion of the attack programme was entirely successful but the further advance only partially so.   The 97th Battery came under particularly heavy fire from the Asiatic Shore, and only one of their three guns was in action at noon, though one of those rendered "hors de combat" was in action again the same evening.

Good work was done by the F.O.Os. in maintaining communication between the advanced infantry battalions and the artillery commanders both by day and night.   This greatly facilitated the close and effective support given to the infantry.

The order of battle of the artillery and the ammunition expenditure were:—

Group.	Unit.	Shrapnel.	H.E.
I.	1st Aus. Bde., 1st Bty.*	1280	—
	,, ,, 2nd ,,	236	—
	,, ,, 3rd ,,	817	—
	2 Naval 12 pdrs.	108	35
II.	15th Bde., R.H.A., "B" Bty.	1058	—
	,, ,, "L" ,,*	947	—
	,, ,, "Y" ,,	938	—
	17th Bde., R.F.A., 13th ,,	1173	—
	,, ,, 26th ,,	1250	—
	,, ,, 92nd ,,*	1008	—
	5th E. Lancs. Bty.	533	—
	1 Naval 12 pdr.†	42	—
III.	147th Bde., R.F.A., 10th Bty.	1198	—
	,, ,, 97th ,,	440	—
	,, ,, 368th ,,	1002	—
	Composite Bde., 6th Aus. Bty.	844	—
	3rd N.Z. Bty.	855	—
	6th E. Lancs. Bty.	243	—
	Highland Mountain Bde. (6 guns)	680	—
	1 Naval 12 pdr.	49	21
IV.	90th Heavy Bty., R.G.A. (60 prs.)	118	185
	14th Siege Bty., R.G.A. (6" Hows.)	45‡	371
	460th Bty., R.F.A. (4·5" Hows.)	479	197
	4th City of Glasgow Bty. (5" Hows.)	—	363

* Attached to Group IV. in later stages of the battle.
† In action in a support trench enfilading a fort in the enemy's front line.
‡ Common Shell.

Subsequent to the operations of this date the following message was received from the 29th Divisional Commander:—"General de Lisle wishes to convey to the G.O.C. R.A. and the batteries under his command his high appreciation of the artillery support given in today's fight."

June 30th.

A 12 pr. Naval gun was taken over this day by the 97th Battery and was christened "Marie Lloyd"; whilst one manned by the 10th Battery was named "Harry Tate."

July 2nd.

Major P. Wheatley, commanding "Y" Btattery, R.H.A., was bitten by a mad dog and had to be evacuated temporarily for Pasteur treatment.

Trench mortars are mentioned for the first time on this date in the war diaries. British and French T.Ms. shelled a portion of trench which had not been captured on 28th June. The damage done is described as "disappointing."

July 4th.

The 97th Battery did great execution with shrapnel during a Turkish attack.

July 6th.

The Groups were now as under:—

Group I.	1st Australian F.A. Bde. 1 Section 1/6th E. Lancs. Bty. 1 Naval 12 pdr.
Group II.	15th Brigade, R.H.A. 17th Brigade, R.F.A. 1 Section 1/5th E. Lancs. Bty. 1 Naval 12 pdr.
Group III.	Composite Brigade (6th Aus. Bty.; 3rd N.Z. Bty.; 1/5th E. Lancs. Bty., less one Section.) Highland Mountain Brigade (both batteries). 2 Naval 12 pdrs.
Group IV. (counter-battery).	90th Heavy Battery and such field batteries as were temporarily attached for counter-battery work from other groups.
Group V. (Howitzer).	460th Battery, R.F.A. 4th City of Glasgow Battery, R.F.A. (T.F.). 14th Siege Battery, R.G.A.

July 8th.

The 1st Cumberland Battery of the 4th E. Lancs. Bde., R.F.A., landed. This battery and the H.Q. of the Brigade joined the 29th Divisional Artillery on the 11th.

July 12th.

The guns were all busy this day supporting our infantry in an attack. Turks retiring across the open gave " Y " Battery a grand target for 10 minutes. The battery did great execution. Our bombardment commenced at 06.30 for the infantry advance at 07.35. The two 10 pdrs. and three 15 pdrs. of Group II which were in forward positions enfilading the Turkish trenches were heavily shelled about 08.30 and were temporarily out of action in consequence.

The French bombardment commenced at 16.00, and our second bombardment at 16.20 for a fresh infantry attack at 16.50.

These attacks were carried out by infantry of the 29th and 52nd Divisions.

July 13th.

The Turks counter-attacked at 04.40, and at 16.00 all guns opened fire for our infantry to advance at 16.30. The attack, however, did not actually start till 16.50. The French howitzers which were assisting us did great damage to enemy trenches and killed many Turks.

The ammunition expended during the 12th and 13th totalled upwards of 15,300 rounds.

July 14th.

"Marie Lloyd" was taken into the front line trenches and opened fire at 04.30 on the 15th on the Turkish front line, doing immense damage. The range was 200 yards and the gun was laid by Bombr. Cook laying through the bore. The remainder of the detachment was B.S.M. Hall, Bombrs. Appleby, Archbold and Syratt (?), and Fitter Pearce.

About this date the 13th Division Infantry relieved the 29th Division, and the 29th Divisional Artillery, or properly speaking the VIII Corps Artillery, was covering the 13th and 42nd Divisions.

July 22nd/23rd.

The 91st Heavy Battery, R.G.A. (four 60 pdrs.) landed and came into action.

July 25th.

The daily allowance of ammunition was reduced by one half. The 18th E. Lancs. Battery arrived and was posted to Group III and the whole of the 1/5th E. Lancs. Battery was concentrated in Group II.

July 27th/28th.

H.Q. Lowland (Howitzer) Brigade, 4th City of Glasgow Battery, and B.A.C. embarked for Anzac.

July 28th.

The 66th Brigade, R.F.A., commenced to arrive.

July 30th.

Lieut. Lee took the 12 pdr. Naval gun of the 97th Battery up to the trenches and fired 29 H.E. shell at a Turkish sap at a range of 200 yards doing great execution. Bombr. Cook again laid the gun with success by looking through the bore.

During July a total of 37,740 rounds were fired by guns of all natures, only 1,382 of that number being H.E. shell.

"Except for a few rainstorms in April and in the early part of May and one in June the weather had been uniformly fine. The heat in June and July was considerable. Helmets became a necessity. Flies were a great nuisance and dust was very bad. The prevailing wind was from N. to N.E. and was generally of considerable force. During bombardments the dust raised was so great that no observation was possible and the programme arranged had to be rigidly adhered to. Considerable variation in range and fuze was found according to the time of day and the force of the wind, rendering it most important to register carefully before doing any close shooting. The equipment on the whole had stood well, the 18 pdr. spiral springs alone giving out to any extent. As a general rule guns were dug in with a wagon alongside. Buffers were protected by rope, and wagons by sandbags at the sides and on the top. As a rule positions were not fully covered, either flashes or dust being visible. A severe strain was placed on the telephonists, especially as no trained men came amongst the drafts to replace casualties amongst these signallers, whose work was admirable. Horses were well placed and were all protected from shell fire by parapets but considerable losses occurred. Otherwise the chief trouble amongst the horses was from colic, due apparently to sand and to insufficient exercise. Until the middle of August only 6 lbs. of hay was allowed. This had a marked effect on the condition of the horses, though those of the B.A.C. which had steady work kept big and fit. The remainder were restricted to walking exercise after dark." (Extracts from war diary, 15th Brigade, R.H.A.)

August 6th and 7th.

The artillery was busy supporting attacks by the 29th Division in the first case and by the 42nd Division in the second.

August 6th—12th

All the 60 pdrs. of the 91st Heavy Battery were out of action owing to excessive recoil.

August 13th/14th.

The 97th Battery took the 12 pdr. again up in to the trenches, this time to enfilade a trench. Fire was opened at 05.00 on the 14th—55 out of 64 rounds fired fell in the trench.

August 17th.

The 3rd New Zealand Battery and 6th Australian Battery left Cape Helles for Anzac.

August 18th.

The trench mortars are mentioned as having fired with good effect this day. By this time two British 3·7″ trench mortars had been received and were being used as well as the French Dumezil mortars.

August 19th.

Capt. G. P. Leach of B/66 Battery, attached to 29th Divisional Artillery, was killed.

On August 23rd the Artillery at Cape Helles was reorganised, on the assumption of the command of the VIII Corps Artillery by Brig.-Genl. C. H. de Rougemont.

For tactical purposes two groups were formed as under:—

RIGHT GROUP, under the command of Brig.-Genl. A. d'A. King, consisting of the 1st Australian Field Artillery Brigade, the 1/5th E. Lancashire Battery, R.F.A. (T.F.) and 1 section of the 1/6th E. Lancashire Battery, R.F.A. (T.F.).

LEFT GROUP, under the command of Brig.-Genl. Simpson-Baikie, consisting of the following units of the 29th D.A.:—15th Brigade, R.H.A., 17th Brigade, R.F.A., and 147th Brigade, R.F.A.; two batteries of the 66th Brigade, R.F.A., and the 1/18th E. Lancashire Battery, R.F.A. (T.F.).

The remaining artillery units were grouped as "Counter-batteries," "Howitzers" and "Trench Mortars," and these groups remained directly under the orders of the G.O.C. VIII Corps Artillery.

For administrative purposes units of the 13th and 29th Divisions were administered by the H.Q. 29th Divisional Artillery, those of the 10th and 42nd Divisions by the H.Q. 42nd Divisional Artillery.

The actual distribution of all units at this time is given in Appendix I. (page 179.)

The remainder of this short history is now confined to the doings of the "Left Group," as far as the operations in Gallipoli are concerned.

The Left Group was divided into two Sections, "A" Section being commanded by Col. Stockdale with Major R. B. Cousens as Staff Officer, "B" Section under Lt.-Col. Wynter with Lieut. Drummond Hay as Staff Officer.

September 3rd.

A small operation in conjunction with the T.M. Group was attended with considerable success. 12 pdrs. were effectively used to destroy the parapet of one of the trenches attacked.

September 23rd.

The 1/19th and 1/20th E. Lancashire Batteries of the 1/3rd E. Lancashire Brigade, R.F.A. (T.F.) arrived and were posted to "A" Section of the "Left Group" for tactical purposes.

About this time the batteries of the 66th F.A. Brigade were transferred away.

Sickness was more rife than in previous months, dysentery and Gallipoli fever being the principal complaints. During September in the 15th Brigade, R.H.A. alone, no less than 5 officers and 100 men were admitted to hospital. On the other hand, casualties from enemy causes were few. There was but one heavy rain shower during the month. The days were closing in and observation was possible between 06.00 and 18.30 only. In the middle of the month it became considerably colder and flies became less numerous but a hot S.W. wind was prevalent towards the end. Colic became less prevalent amongst the horses. Units were much reduced in strength, each man in the wagon lines having 6 or 7 horses to attend to.

October.

This month was generally an uneventful one. The weather was good with the exception of the period between the 20th and 25th which was stormy. The percentage of sick was again very high, but fortunately drafts of some 40 men per battery were received about the middle of the month.

On 28th October the young officers who had been given temporary commissions from the ranks of the Royal Naval Division were sent to Cairo for a course.

November.

In the latter half of November upwards of half the number of horses with units were evcuated from the peninsula to Mudros. Thus by the, beginning of December only some 700 remained out of an original total of some 1500 in the 29th Divisional Artillery, and this formation supplied the wants of the other Divisions so far as artillery horses were concerned.

The weather had become very cold and the proportion of sickness was much reduced.

December 11th.

The 1/19th and 1/20th E. Lancashire Batteries were transferred to the Right Group, thus reducing "A" Section of the Left Group to the 17th Brigade, R.F.A.

"A" Section was at this time covering the 87th Infantry Brigade, whilst "B" Section, whose composition was unchanged since 23rd August (vide Appendix I), was covering the 42nd Division.

December 18th.

The Howitzer Group was abolished and the batteries composing it (vide Appendix I) transferred as a Howitzer Section to the Left Group (29th D.A.).

December 25th.

In the final for a football cup presented by Brig.-Genl. Stockdale the 90th Heavy Battery, R.G.A., beat "B" Battery, R.H.A.

There was very little sickness this month. Jaundice, at one time prevalent, had quite died out, and the weather was good.

On the last night of the month, the "dribbling away" of guns, wagons and ammunition to Mudros, prior to the final evacuation was commenced.

1916.

Guns were gradually withdrawn as under:—

	18 Pdrs.	16 Pdrs.	12 Pdrs.	6" How.	5" How.	4.5 How
In action Dec. 31st	36	8	3	4	8	4
night of Dec. 31st/Jan. 1st ...	4	–	–	2	–	2
night of Jan. 1st/2nd	15	–	–	2	4	–
night of Jan. 2nd/3rd	2	–	2	–	–	1
night of Jan. 5th/6th	1	–	1	–	–	–
night of Jan. 6th/7th	3	2*	–	–	–	1
night of Jan. 7th/8th	3	–	–	–	–	–
night of Jan. 8th/9th	8	3	–	–	–	–
night of Jan. 8th/9th	–	3*	–	–	–	–

(withdrawn and evacuated)

* Destroyed.

January 1st to 8th.

The 1st January was called "T" day, "Z" day which was to be the final day of evacuation was to be the 7th January. The evacuation of ammunition commenced on 1st January, orders being given to maintain ammunition as under:—"Y" day. 8—18 pdrs. 3,000 rounds, 8—18 pdrs. 1,800 rounds, 4—5" Hows. 400 rounds. "Z" day. 6—18 pdrs. 1,800 rounds, 2—18 pdrs. 600 rounds, 2—5" Hows. 200 rounds.

All personnel was to be evacuated by "X" day except for Left Group which was allowed to keep 154 for evacuation on "Y" day and 225 for evacuation on "Z" day.

A small detachment accompanied each gun as it was withdrawn for evacuation. Every gun emplacement was left exactly as if in use and where complete batteries were withdrawn men were told off to light the usual fires and give the positions their normal appearance. Hostile artillery fire was moderate from 1st to 6th January except on January 2nd, when it was very active and enemy aeroplanes were active over our lines. On January 5th the weather became bad and necessitated the temporary suspension of the evacuation. The 5th was not called "X" day and the suspension was maintained till the 7th when the weather moderated and the 7th was declared "Y" day. At 14.00 on this day the Turks attacked at Fusilier Bay after a bombardment of unprecedented severity. The Left Group replied effectively to the bombardment and by 16.00 the attack had been repelled—by dusk the situation was normal although the enemy shelled "W" Beach during the night. January 8th was the day of final evacuation. The remaining guns, personnel and horses passed through carefully arranged control posts. All surplus stores and all horses and mules not required for moving the last guns were destroyed. The arrangements were carried out without a hitch

M

according to the detailed programme prepared. As soon as darkness permitted surplus ammunition was buried and the last guns were withdrawn. Positions had been selected for a stand on Hill 138 to cover the retreat but as the enemy did not take alarm the positions were not occupied. All men, horses and guns were checked through the last control post on Hill 138 on their way to the beach, word being received at D.A.H.Q. at 23.00 that all was correct. The G.O.C., R.A. and his staff embarked on the last lighter which left the beach at 01.25 on January 9th.

The following extract from D.A. H.Q. diary is worthy of record:—"During the evacuation one point worthy of special notice was the most excellent work done by the N.C.Os. and Drivers of the D.A. who were working night after night in all weathers and under heavy shell fire removing vehicles to the beach. The orderly and efficient way, in which the arduous task was performed reflects the greatest credit upon all concerned. All artillery and ammunition vehicles on the peninsula were removed by the 29th D.A. The horses and mules that could not be embarked had to be destroyed on the 8th: those kept for withdrawing guns on "Z" night could not be embarked owing to the bad weather and had also to be destroyed. All wagons and vehicles that could not be embarked were parked on the cliff edge for destruction by naval guns. All surplus stores were destroyed."

Egypt.—January 9th to 29th.

The component parts of the 29th D.A. were conveyed in various ships via Mudros to be re-assembled at Suez Camp in Egypt where re-equipping and training proceeded. Training was much handicapped owing to the shortage of horses.

On 30th January 10th and 26th Batteries, R.F.A., proceeded to Ayon Mussa on the east bank of the canal and were attached to 10th Indian Division. 160 horses were lent to these batteries by the Lancashire Territorial D.A.

On February 20th and 21st "L" and "B" Batteries, R.H.A., proceeded to El Shatt on the east bank of the canal, horses being lent to them for the journey. 80 horses were then sent from Ayon Mussa to El Shatt.

On the 25th February D.A.H.Q. moved to El Shatt. On 29th February D.A.H.Q. and all batteries east of the canal moved again to Suez preparatory to embarkation for France.

APPENDIX 1.

ORGANISATION OF THE ARTILLERY AT CAPE HELLES.
23RD AUGUST, 1915.

Group Commander.	Sub-Group Commander.	Brigade.	Battery.	No. of Guns.	Nature.	Division.	Remarks.
Right Group (B.-Genl. King).		56th Brigade R.F.A.	C/56	4	18 Pdr.	} 10th.	Landed 28 Aug.
			D/56	4	,,		
		1st Aus. F.A. Brigade.	1st Ans.	4	,,		
			2nd Ans.	4	,,	} 1st Ans.	
			3rd Ans.	4	,,		
			1/5 E. Lancs.	4	15 Pdr.	} 42 nd.	
			1/6 E. Lancs.	2	,,		
				2	Naval 12 Pdr.		
Left Group (B.-Genl. Simpson-Baikie.)	"A" Section (Lt.-Col. Stockdale.)	17th Brigade R.F.A.	13th	4	18 Pdr.	} 29th	
			26th	4	,,		
			92nd	4	,,		
			A/66	4	,,	} 13th	
			D/66	4	,,		
				1	Naval 12 Pdr.		
	"B" Section (Lt.-Col. Wynter.)	15th Brigade R.F.A.	"B"	4	18 Pdr.	} 29th	
			"L"	4	,,		
			"Y"	4	,,		
		147th Brigade R.F.A.	10th	4	,,	} 29th	
			97th	4	,,		
			368th	4	,,		
			1/18th E. Lancs.	4	15 Pdr.	42nd	
				2	Naval 12 Pdr.		
Counter-Group (Lt.-Col. Peel.)		66th Brigade R.F.A.	B/66	4	18 Pdr.	} 13th	
			C/86	4	,,		
			90th Heavy	4	60 Pdr.	29th	
			91st Heavy	4	,,	13th	
Howitzer Group (Lt.-Col. L. S. Bayley.)		4th E. Lancs. Brigade R.F.A. (T.F.)	460th	4	4.5"How.	} 39 h	
			14th Seige	4	6" How.		
			1st Cumberland	4	5" How.	} 42nd	
			2nd Cumberland	4	,,		
Mortar Group (Capt. T. S. Sayers.)			Trench Mortars	3	French Dumezil		
				2	3.7"		
				1	6"		

APPENDIX 2.

OFFICERS COMMANDING UNITS AT THE EVACUATION.

Brig.-Genl. H. E. Stockdale, D.S.O., Commdg. 29th D.A.
Major C. H. Clark, Brigade Major.
Captain L. D. Hickes, Staff Captain.
2/Lieut. B. B. Squire, A.D.C.

Lt.-Col. E. J. R. Peel, D.S.O., Commdg. 15th Bde., R.H.A.
Major C. D. W. Uniacke, Commdg. "B," R.H.A.
Captain G. E. M. Thorneycroft, Commdg. "L," R.H.A.
Captain H. G. Lush Wilson, Commdg. "Y," R.H.A.
2/Lieut. A. Ideson, Commdg. A.C.
Lieut. R. Henman, Adjutant.

Lt.-Col. W. P. Monkhouse, C.M.G., M.V.O., Commdg. 17th Bde., R.F.A.
2/Lieut. A. E. G. Leadbetter, Adjutant.
Captain A. S. Leach, Commdg. 13th Battery, R.F.A.
Captain D. Daly, Commdg. 26th Battery, R.F.A.
Major R. C. Williams, Commdg. 92nd Battery, R.F.A.
Major J. Hogan, Commdg. A.C.

Lieut.-Colonel D. E. Forman, Commdg. 147th Brigade, R.F.A.
Lieut. A. M. McCracken, Adjutant.
Captain J. de H. C. Batten, Commdg. 10th Battery, R.F.A.
Capt. K. M. Ball, Commdg. 97th & 368th Batteries, R.F.A.
Captain G. Kooghwinlled, Commdg. A.C.

Major J. H. Gibbon, Commdg. 460th Battery, R.F.A.

Lieut.-Col. L. S. Bayley, Commdg. 14th Siege Battery.

Major H. M. Marshall, Commdg. 90th Heavy Battery.

NOTE.—

The original 57th (Howitzer) Brigade, R.F.A., was formed at the Curragh in September 1914 as part of the 10th Division and consisted of the 181st, 182nd, and 183rd four-gun batteries and a B.A.C. About February 1915, it was formed into a four-battery brigade and the battery designations changed. The 181st Battery then became A/57 and also provided the greater portion of the new battery D/57; the 182nd became B/57 and the 183rd C/57. In April 1915 the brigade moved over to Basingstoke with the rest of the 10th Division. In July 1915 the Headquarters with A/57 and D/57 and about half the B.A.C. went to Suvla Bay (Gallipoli Peninsula) via. Havre and Marseilles, leaving their horses and drivers in England, where they were eventually distributed to other batteries. B/57 and C/57 went to France with the 36th Division but eventually went on to Salonika. The Gallipoli portion of the brigade remained at Suvla till the evacuation and then landed at Cape Helles. After the evacuation of this place they went to Egypt, where with the addition of the 460th Battery they formed the 132nd (Howitzer) Brigade, R.F.A. The remnants of the 57th B.A.C. and of the 460th Battery A.C. combined to form the new 132nd B.A.C. The 460th Battery was complete in drivers but had no horses. The full establishment of horses and 100 extra were taken over on the quay at Alexandria prior to embarkation for France, but no drivers. After landing in France two weeks elapsed before any drivers came. The new B.A.C. was drawn by mules whose height ranged from 16 to 18 hands.

FRANCE, 1916—1918.

1916.

March 4th.

Advanced parties left for Alexandria in order to draw G.S. wagons, limbered G.S. wagons, mess carts, water carts, maltese carts.

March 9th—11th.

Units embarked at Alexandria, sailed for Marseilles, arriving 16th—20th, and entrained for Pont Remy (on main 'Nord' line between Abbeville and Amiens).

March 19th—20th.

On arrival in billets about Pont Remy each brigade was (other than the 132nd) made up to 4 batteries by the addition of 369th Battery to the 15th Bde., 370th Battery to the 17th Bde., and the 371st Battery to the 147th Brigade. The new batteries each had four 18-prs. and had recently arrived from England. Units then took over the transport carts and wagons with teams for which parties had been sent on in advance from Egypt.

March 31st.

The whole D.A. marched to Domart en Ponthien.

April 3rd.

D.A. H.Q. moved to Acheux.

April 6th—7th.

The 29th D.A. relieved the 31st D.A. in the Englebelmer Sector of the line, the gun positions being about Mailly Maillet. The new batteries (369th, 370th and 371st) did not go into the line immediately but the personnel was attached to other batteries for instruction. Of the 132nd Bde., the 460th Battery came into action on the 5th/6th, B/132 on 17th and C/132 on the 22nd.

April 10th.

The 53rd (Welsh) Divisional Ammunition Column, a T.F. unit, joined the D.A. and became the 29th D.A.C.

April 22nd.

Brig.-Genl. M. Peake succeeded Brig.-Genl. H. E. Stockdale as C.R.A. 29th Division.

April 23rd.

The 460th Battery assisted in the support of a raid by the 36th Division.

April 30th.

The D.A. supported the 87th and 88th Infantry Brigades in a raid which was unsuccessful. The infantry assaulted 7 minutes before scheduled time on the left and were 20 minutes late on the right—5,500 rounds were expended.

The total expenditure of gun ammunition for the month amounted to some 800 rounds per battery.

May 13th.

Brigade Ammunition Columns were abolished and the D.A.C. reorganised :—

> 15th B.A.C. became No. 1 Section D.A.C.
> 17th B.A.C. became No. 2 Section D.A.C.
> 147th B.A.C. became No. 3 Section D.A.C.
> 132nd B.A.C. ceased to exist, personnel being transferred to the D.A.C.   No. 4 Section, "B" Echelon, D.A.C., was formed from the old Sections of the D.A.C.

May 18th—20th.

Brigades were reorganised so as to give each Brigade 3 18-pr. batteries and (except in the case of the 15th Brigade, R.H.A.) one 4·5″ Howitzer battery.

After this reorganisation, the 29th Divisional Artillery consisted of :—

HEADQUARTERS.

15TH BRIGADE, R.H.A.   Headquarters, "B", "L" and "Y" Batteries (18-pdr.)

17TH BRIGADE, R.F.A.   Headquarters, 13th, 26th and 92nd Batteries (18-pdr.) and 460th Battery (Hows.)

147TH BRIGADE, R.F.A.   Headquarters, 10th, 97th and 368th Batteries (18-pdr.) and D/147 (late B/132 and formerly A/57) (Hows.)

132ND BRIGADE, R.F.A.   Headquarters, 369th, 370th and 371st Batteries (18-pdr.) and D/132 (late C/132, formerly D/57) (Hows.)

29TH D.A.C.

Headquarters.
No. 1 Section (formerly 15th B.A.C.)
No. 2 Section (formerly 17th B.A.C.)
No. 3 Section (formerly 147th B.A.C.)
No. 4 Section "B" Echelon.

N.B.—All batteries were still on a four-gun basis.

NOTE.—The Trench Mortar Batteries must have been formed about this time, but no record appears to have been made in War Diaries as to their formation. The Batteries formed are believed to have been S/29, V/29 (Heavy), X/29, Y/29 and Z/29.

June 4th.

The D.A. fired in support of a successful raid by the 86th Infantry Brigade.

June 8th.

The dumping of ammunition for the great Somme offensive began. Each battery was ordered to have 1,000 rounds per gun.

June 16th.

Registration in preparation for the offensive scheme was commenced.

June 24th—30th.

The preliminary bombardment and wire cutting commenced.

The following extracts from the diary of the 147th Brigade give a good idea of the operations of the month. "Up to this date (24th) all batteries had been hard at work preparing for the bombardment of the enemy's positions in the neighbourhood of Beaumont Hamel. The zone allotted to the 29th Divisional Artillery was sub-divided into two groups—the Right Group, commanded by Lt.-Col. Monkhouse, consisted of the 17th Brigade, the 10th Battery of the 147th Brigade, and the 370th, 371st Batteries of the 132nd Brigade, whilst the Left Group was commanded by Lt.-Col. Forman and consisted of the 15th Brigade, R.H.A., the 147th Brigade (less 10th Battery), and the 369th and D/132 batteries of the 132nd Brigade.

The telephone exchange at (Left) Group Headquarters was connected up to all the batteries of the group, to D.A. H.Q., to various infantry formations, to groups on either flank, etc., by cable laid in trenches six-feet deep. These cables gave complete satisfaction and remained intact throughout the operations. Most batteries had their lines between their guns and their O.P. laid in trenches. Those that had done so suffered no interruption but those that had aerial lines were always having them cut. . . . . It was originally intended to have 5 days of preliminary bombardment but 2 extra days were added. . . . . The ammunition was brought up to batteries by night in trucks on a light railway running from Acheux to Auchonvillers Station and thence across to Mesnil, passing close to all our batteries except the 368th who had to bring up the ammunition in their own wagons. The establishment of ammunition was maintained during the days of bombardment by a convoy consisting of wagons from batteries and the D.A.C. . . . . The rôle of the 18-pdrs. during the preliminary bombardment was to cut wire. For this purpose 160 rounds per gun per diem were allotted. 18-pdrs. also participated in special combined bombardments at specified times each day. By night a section of each battery was on duty, night and night about, and kept up a continuous fire on avenues of approach in the enemy front system. Each section fired 172 rounds nightly. The wire was successfully dealt with along the front allotted. The 4·5″ Howitzers cut 2nd line wire in conjunction with 60-pdrs., and each battery had in addition certain communication trenches to shell systematically. They also fired at night along communications."

July 1st.

The day of the first attack in the great Somme offensive.

The infantry attack was timed to take place at 0730. The rôle of the 29th Divisional Artillery was as follows:—From 06.00 the field howitzers bombarded at various rates and on various targets; at 06.25 the 18-pdrs., with the exception of three in forward positions which were at too close a range to do so, opened fire on the enemy front line; two of the forward batteries fired in enfilade on a trench in front of Beaucourt; at 07.20 all 18-pdrs. quickened to three rounds per gun per minute and at 07.30, the hour of the assault, lifted to the support line; at 07.32 all batteries lifted 100 yards every two minutes till about 07.50 when the fire remained stationary until 08.35 when they lifted again at the same rate till 08.45.

Unfortunately the attack was unsuccessful—the first assaulting wave only entered the enemy trenches, the second being mowed down by machine gun fire. The 4th Division on our left and the 36th Division on our right succeeded in taking the 2nd and 3rd objectives but were then forced to withdraw as their flanks were 'in the air.'

The following extract from the war diary of the 147th Brigade is interesting:—"The infantry assault was timed to take place at 07.30. It was preceded by 65 minutes intense bombardment of the front line trenches by 18-pdrs. All natures of artillery participated and some of the heavy batteries commenced as early as 05.00. But it was obvious that no weight of heavy metal was on the enemy front line. A colossal mine under the "Hawthorn Redoubt" was sprung at 07.20. This turned out a fatal error. It gave away the show all along the line; it afforded an extra obstacle to our infantry (the crater was 130 yards long) and being much nearer to the Huns than to ourselves, it was promptly manned by them with machine guns. The result was that, except in isolated cases, the enemy front line was scarcely entered. The enemy front line trench had not been sufficiently damaged to prevent movement in and out of the dug-outs, and, even before our 18-pdrs. lifted off the enemy front line, many of the enemy machine guns were up on the parapet.

Three other factors militated against the chances of success so far as our division was concerned:—

  (i) Our heavy artillery lifted at 07.25—5 minutes before we did. Although this did not actually affect the enemy front trench it gave the occupants of the dug-outs a signal.

(ii) The breadth of No Man's Land—never less than 200 yards—and our lift off the front line had to synchronise with the advance of our own infantry from our front line. Before our infantry could reach the enemy front line, they had been cut down by machine gun fire.

(iii) *Our own* wire had been insufficiently cut and our dead were soon in bunches in the gaps therein."

As soon as it was known that the attack had been unsuccessful, preparations were made by the artillery to fire a barrage for another attack, which, however, did not materialise. The artillery was then employed in firing at various targets throughout the day and fired a barrage between 21.00 and 22.30 to allow wounded to be brought in.

Each battery supplied a liaison officer and 2 telephonists with an infantry battalion. Casualties amongst these were fortunately few.

The enemy retaliated heavily on our front system of trenches completely blocking many of them. Casualties in the 29th Divisional Artillery were very slight, our gun positions being entirely neglected by the enemy. The only O.P. to be shelled was one within 300 yds. of our front line.

As the end of the day ten 18-pdrs. were out of action through trouble with the buffer springs.

The war diary of the 29th Divisional Artillery Headquarters mentions that the wire cutting was extremely good, all wire visible being cut away.

The only ammunition figures available are those of the 147th Brigade. The expenditure from the commencement of the pre-liminary bombardment to the 1st July, inclusive, in this brigade was as follows :—

Date	10th Bty.	97th Bty.	368th Bty.	D/147 Bty. (Hows.)	Total.
24th June	478	768	643	556	2445
25th ,,	616	800	825	514	2755
26th ,,	818	965	829	635	3247
27th ,,	306	791	815	599	2511
28th ,,	1524	872	1180	632	4208
29th ,,	499	950	926	709	3084
30th ,,	618	1072	1621	841	4152
1st July	601	1141	589	164	2495
			Grand Total (8 days) ...		24,897

NOTE.—The trench mortar batteries expended a total of 5000 rounds during the above period.

July 4th—6th.

The most advanced batteries—"B" R.H.A., 10th, 97th, 13th, 26th, 92nd and D/132 were withdrawn to defensive positions.

July 20th.

The personnel of the Headquarters 15th Brigade, R.H.A.

transplanted 3 trees from the front of "L" Battery's position on the Anchonvillers—Engelbelmer road to a position some 300 yards to the front, as it was believed that these trees drew the enemy's fire. The ruse was quite successful as the trees were regularly shelled afterwards.

July 25th.

The 29th Divisional Artillery was now supporting the 25th Division which had relieved the 29th Division.

July 28th.

The S.A.A. Sub-Sections of Nos. 1, 2, 3 and 4 Sections of the D.A.C. were organized into "A", "B", "C" S.A.A. Sub-Sections and were temporarily detached from the D.A.C. for service with the infantry of the Division.

August 7th.

29th Divisional Artillery took over the task of supporting the 6th Division whilst the 6th Divisional Artillery supported the 25th Division.

August 16th.

A re-organisation into 3 groups took place.

The Right Group, under the command of Lt.-Col. Sherbrooke, consisted of the 13th, 26th, 92nd, 10th and D/147 batteries.

The Centre Group, commanded by Lt.-Col. Marriott Smith, consisted of the 368th Battery and the 132nd Brigade.

The Left Group, under Lt.-Col. Forman, consisted of the 15th Brigade, R.H.A., the 97th Battery and the 460th Battery.

August 25th.

"B", "Y", 10th, 13th, 97th and 369th Batteries moved forward into the Mesnil valley with a view to the coming offensive.

August 27th.

29th Divisional Artillery now covering the 39th Division which relieved the 6th Division.

August 28th.

The 39th Divisional Artillery and 58th F.A. Brigade of the 11th Divisional Artillery (less the Howitzer Battery) came into action under the orders of the C.R.A. 29th Division.

On this day wire cutting commenced and fire was kept up night and day.

September 1st—2nd.

Wire cutting was continued and the 29th Divisional Artillery was also engaged in keeping open blocks made by the Corps Heavy Artillery and in harassing communications.

September 3rd.

The 39th Division attacked the enemy's front system of trenches from the River Ancre to a point 1,500 yards north of it, whilst the 29th Division attacked south of the river.

The 39th Division attack was supported by the following Field Artillery :—

58th F.A. Bde. (Lt.-Col. O. de L'E. Winter) of 11th D.A. acted with one battalion attacking up the river valley.

29th D.A. was supporting the right of the main attack.

39th D.A. was supporting the left of the main attack.

The 11th D.A. (less 58th F.A. Bde.) co-operated on the left with a bombardment.

Zero hour was at 05.10. At this hour all 18-pdrs. opened fire on a line 50 yds. short of the German front line at an intense rate (4 rds. p.g.p.m.) for half a minute, then lifted to German front line till zero + 4 minutes when they lifted 50 yards (sic) to enable the infantry to assault, and the rate was then reduced by one-half . The howitzers opened on the support line and after half-a-minute lifted to the 3rd line of trenches.

After zero + four minutes, the 18-pdrs. lifted 25 yards every round fired, until zero + 11 minutes when the rate was raised to the original rate of 3 minutes whilst the infantry assaulted the support line.

The same process was continued for the attack on the 3rd line.

2-inch and Heavy (9·45″) Trench Mortars supported the attack within the limits of their respective ranges.

Lt.-Col. Courage, commanding 147th Brigade, R.F.A., writes as follows in his brigade war diary:

"From personal observation and reports afterwards received from our own infantry the wire appears to have been sufficiently cut and to have offered no obstacle to our advance. The casualties in No Man's Land at the first advance were very small.

*   *   *   *   *   *

Our barrage was reported to be perfectly satisfactory and our infantry advanced up to it well, but it would have suited them better if it had been kept on the support line for a longer period, the infantry being unable to advance sufficiently fast. Only one machine gun was found in our zone and of the gunners only one was still alive. Their trenches were very much knocked about and in many places they could not pass along without showing themselves.

*   *   *   *   *   *

The G.O.C. 116th Infantry Brigade informed me that he and all his officers were very pleased with the efficiency of the barrage and the effects of subsequent fire."

The Infantry reached the first and second lines with ease, and in some cases the reserve line, but were unable to consolidate. Our barrage was altered from time to time at the request of the infantry but we ceased fire at 14.00 when all our infantry were back in our trenches.

Guns out of action were replaced by those of two 18-pdr. and one Howitzer batteries of the 39th Divisional Artillery, these batteries being specially kept in reserve for the purpose.

The ammunition expenditure in the 29th D.A. was :—

1st September	7540 rounds.
2nd ,,	7252 rounds.
3rd ,,	28,503 rounds.

September 5th—6th.

Batteries of the 29th D.A. came out of action.   S/29 T.M.B. was broken up.

September 7th—12th.

The 29th D.A. concentrated about Amplier and marched on the 8th to about Frevent, on the 9th to about St. Pol, on the 10th to about Lillers, on the 11th to about Cassel, and arrived at Poperinghe on the 12th.

September 12th.

On this date another re-organization of units took place, the main feature of which was the raising of 18-pdr. batteries to a six-gun basis.

In order to carry out this increase (a) the 132nd Brigade ceased to exist, all its batteries sending their sections away to make up other batteries :—

The 369th Battery sent its right section to the 92nd and left section to "Y".

The 370th Battery sent its right section to the 26th and left section to 13th.

The 371st Battery sent its right section to "B" and left section to "L".

(b) D/132 (howitzer) Battery became D/17 Battery and the 460th (How.) Battery was transferred from the 17th F.A. Brigade to the 15th Brigade, R.H.A., but neither of these batteries received any increase to its number of howitzers (4).

(c) In the 147th Brigade, the 368th Battery was broken up, its right section being transferred to complete the 97th Battery and its left section to the 10th Batery. This brigade was therefore now an 18-pdr. battery short of its proper establishment.

The following changes of Brigade Commanders took place at this time.

Lt.-Col. Sherbrooke, from 17th Brigade was transferred to 15th Brigade.

Lt.-Col. Marriott Smith, from 132nd Brigade was transferred to 17th Brigade.

The composition of the 29th Divisional Artillery was now :—

HEADQUARTERS.

15TH BRIGADE, R.H.A.

Headquarters, and "B", "L", "Y", (each six 18-pdrs) and 460th How. Battery (four 4·5″ Hows.)

17TH BRIGADE, R.F.A.

Headquarters, 13th, 26th, 92nd Batteries (each six 18-pdrs.) and D/17 (late D/132, previously C/132 and originally D/57) How. Battery (four 4·5″ Hows.)

147TH BRIGADE, R.F.A.

Headquarters, and 10th and 97th Batteries (each six 18-pdrs.) and D/147 (formerly B/132 and originally A/57) How Battery (four 4·5″ Hows.)

29TH D.A.C.
>   Headquarters.
>   No. 1 Section.
>   No. 2 Section.
>   No. 3 Section.
>   No. 4 Section, "B" Echelon.

September 13th.

The S.A.A. Sub-Sections of Nos. 1, 2, 3, and 4 Sections rejoined their respective sections, on the Divisional Artillery re-uniting with the infantry of the division once more.

September 16th—17th.

The 29th Divisional Artillery relieved the 4th Divisional Artillery in the line at Ypres and Headquarters 29th Divisional Artillery took over command at 08.00 on 17th.

September 20th.

The 29th Divisional Artillery fired in support of an unsuccessful raid by the 86th Infantry Brigade.

September 30th.

The batteries including T.M.Bs. supported successful raids by the 86th and 87th Infantry Brigades.

The raid of the 87th Infantry Brigade was undertaken by Lieut. Robinson and 30 men of the 1st Border Regt. and took place opposite Wieltje. This officer reported that the artillery preparation was most successful in that the wire was well cut, there were no 'shorts' and the enemy was driven to dug-outs by the intensity of the bombardment. The raiders got back with 12 prisoners and had only 2 men slightly wounded. 147th Brigade War Diary states "Lieut. Robinson and his C.O., Colonel Morris, unhesitatingly give the artillery full credit for their great assistance which enabled the raiders to achieve results without molestation."

October 6th.

"L" Battery fired 11 aimed rounds in half a minute in an experiment.

October 8th—9th.

The 29th Divisional Artillery was relieved in the line at Ypres by the 55th D.A.

October 10th—11th.

The 29th Divisional Artillery entrained at Esquelbecq—Proven—Hopoutre, commencing at 00.30 on the 10th, detrained at Saleux and Longueau (on either side of Amiens), and concentrated on the 11th at Camp A near Albert, prior to relieving the 21st D.A. in the XV Corps.

October 13th—14th.

The 29th Divisional Artillery went into the line near Delville Wood and Longueval.

The 147th Brigade and 15th Brigade, R.H.A. (less the 460th Battery) went to the 41st D.A. Group, which consisted of the 30th and 41st Divisional Artilleries and covered the 12th Div. infantry.

The 17th Brigade and 460th Battery became part of the 12th
D.A. Group, which included the 12th and New Zealand D.As. and
covered the 30th Div. infantry on the left.

October 18th.

The artillery took part in the unsuccessful operations of the XV
Corps on this day.

The S.A.A. sub-sections of the D.A.C. were detached and
moved on the 30th to Albert.

October 20th.

The infantry of the 29th Division came into the line in relief of
the 12th Division.

October 22nd.

This was a day of heavy shelling by the enemy of some of our
battery positions. "Y" Battery lost 7 N.C.O's and men killed and
10 wounded by a single shell which dropped amongst the personnel
of the battery as they were clearing away to a flank from the battery
position. D/17 Battery was also unlucky: "A German section of
5·9″ Hows. was very active this fore-noon against the batteries in
S 11 b: they were probably shooting at a 60-pr. battery in the
neighbourhood which had been very active during the night. The
personnel of the batteries was withdrawn but one shell landing on
the road near D/17 killed 4 men and wounded 2 others. One shell
pitched on an ammunition dump and exploded the ammunition with
the result that the whole of the D/17 battery position was wrecked,
three guns being completely destroyed and the fourth very badly
damaged." (17th Brigade War Diary).

October 30th.

The 13th and 92nd Batteries each moved a section forward and
overcame immense difficulties. The 92nd Battery section dismounted
its guns and took them up on a light railway. This movement is
described by the Brigade Commander as "an achievement of great
skill and resource. It was hardly possible to *walk* over much of the
country"

October 31st.

After various changes of divisions and divisional artilleries in the
line, the units of the 29th Divisional Artillery were now as follows :—

2 Brigades grouped with the 30th and 2nd Aus. Div. Arties.
under C.R.A. 30th Division.

Remaining brigade grouped with the 12th and 1st Aus. D.As.
under C.R.A. 12th Division.

"The latter half of October proved wet and rough. The country
on our front, Guedecourt, is waterlogged and transport becomes an
immense difficulty. Ammunition is carried to batteries by pack
horses and mules, improvised as such out of existing material. The
ground round Flers is a swamp of mud and conditions inevitably
cause much hardship to both men and horses. Battery positions are
shelled daily and good cover is impossible. All ground is a series
of shell holes and this combined with the mud and rain renders
digging a great difficulty. A white frost set in from 16th to 20th

but not enough to harden the ground" (29 D.A. H.Q. war diary for October 1916.)

The 10th Battery was very unlucky in October, having most of its guns, and at one time *all*, out of action.

Lt.-Col. Marriott Smith, Comdg. 17th Brigade, writes as follows at the end of the 17th Brigade Headquarters War Diary for October : "The demeanour of all ranks during the past two weeks has been admirable and under conditions of considerable hardship the men have maintained the accustomed cheeriness of the British Soldier."

November 5th.

The 29th Divisional Artillery formed part of the artillery supporting the Australian operations against 'Bayonet' and 'Grid' trenches. A partial success was gained but the attackers were 'bombed out' later in the day.

November 14th.

Operations by the 2nd Australian Division against 'Grid' trench were partially successful, but the infantry were obliged to abandon their gains on the 17th.

Batteries fired night and day, supporting every attack. Mud, rain and cold were excessive. The wastage of horses at this period was abnormal owing to the difficulties of transport over bad ground. The 15th Brigade alone lost 47 animals between 11th and 18th.

November 24th—26th.

The 29th Divisional Artillery was withdrawn from action.

November 27th.

"Y" Battery, R.H.A., was transferred to the 1st Cavalry Division, in exchange for the 1/1st Warwickshire Battery R.H.A. (T.F) which from this date became part of the 15th Brigade, R.H.A.

November 29th.

Headquarters 29th Divisional Artillery moved to Cavalry Camp —15th Brigade R.H.A. to near Carnoy—remaining units about Montauban and Meaulte. "All camps were very muddy and the short rest before again taking over the line was of but little value to horses and men." (29 D.A. H.Q. war diary).

December 5th—6th.

The 15th Brigade R.H.A. and 147th Brigade R.F.A. went into action in the Left Group of the Right D.A., XIV Corps, under the orders of the C.R.A. Guards Division. Batteries took over positions from the French near Combles, and covered the front from north of Sailly Saillisel to opposite Morval. The 17th Brigade remained out of the line.

December 19th—20th.

Brig.-Genl. M. Peake was promoted to command the artillery of the I Corps and left to take up the appointment.

December 28th.

The 17th Brigade relieved the 15th Brigade in action, and the latter came out to rest at Morlancourt.

1917.

January 8th.

The Warwickshire Battery moved into action into their former position.

January 14th.

The 15th Brigade, R.H.A., relieved the 147th Brigade, R.F.A., in the Left Group, Centre Divisional Artillery, less "L" R.H.A. which became part of Left Artillery.

January 18th.

H.Q. 29th D.A. took over command of Left Artillery, XIV Corps, which consisted of the 78th and 79th Brigades of the 17th D.A. and "L" Battery, R.H.A.

January 19th.

The 147th Brigade, R.F.A. (H.Q., 10th and 97th Batteries) severed its connection with the 29th Divisional Artillery on becoming an Army Field Artillery Brigade. It took with it No. 3 Section of the 29th D.A.C., which had originally been the 147th B.A.C. and which now reverted to that rôle. D/147 (Howitzer) Battery remained with its Brigade till the end of the month (see below). The brigade was made up to 3 18 pdr. batteries by the addition of A/81 Battery from the 17th Division on the 21st January, this battery then assuming the title of A/147.

On this date, the 15th Brigade (less "L" and 460th) moved into positions formerly occupied by batteries of the 17th D.A. and became, with "L" Battery, part of Right Group, Left Divisional Artillery, the other batteries of this group being C/78 and D/78. This move was a temporary one only and only held good until the battle of the 27th January was over.

January 21st/24th.

The 76th, 93rd and 147th Army Field Artillery Brigades came into action under the C.R.A., Left Artillery, for the battle.

January 27th.

The Left Artillery Group supported the 29th Division Infantry in their attack on a front of 1,100 yards. This attack was completely successful, and 400 prisoners were taken.

January 28th.

The 15th Brigade (less 460th Battery and "L") returned to their former positions in the Left Group, Centre Artillery.

January 29th.

The A.F.A. Brigades came out of action.

January 31st/February 1st.

On this date there was a considerable change in the organization and allocation of the howitzer batteries, two six-gun batteries being constructed out of the three four-gun batteries, 460th, D/17 and D/147. The battery broken up was D/17 (late D/132, previously C/132 and D/57), which sent its right section to complete the 460th Battery and its left section to D/147 (late B/132 and previously A/57) which now became D/17.   There were no further changes in the batteries now composing the 29th Divisional Artillery till the final break-up in 1919, and it is interesting to note how, more by accident than design, the original 181st Battery, which in February 1915 became A/57 and formed also the basis of D/57, now practically re-assembled again as D/17.   One officer, Temp. Capt. H. O. Holmes, originally joined the 181st Battery, then in the A/57—B/132—D/147 portion, which he had been commanding for some time previous to the final change into D/17, and remained in command of D/17 till after the armistice, when he reverted to his occupation at the Irish Bar.

The composition of the 29th Divisional Artillery was now:—

HEADQUARTERS.

15TH BRIGADE, R.H.A.—H.Q., " B," "L," "Warwickshire" Batteries (each of six 18-pdrs.) and 460th Howitzer Battery (six 4·5″ Hows.).

17TH BRIGADE, R.F.A.—H.Q., 13th, 26th, 92nd Batteries (each of six 18 pdrs.) and D/17 Howitzer Battery (six 4·5″ Hows.).

TRENCH MORTAR BATTERIES.—X/29, Y/29, Z/29 (2″ mortars) and V/29 (Heavy) (9·45″).

29TH DIVISIONAL AMMUNITION COLUMN.—Headquarters, Nos. 1, 2 and 4 Sections.

"The 3 events of the month have been the prolonged hard frost which we have all preferred to unutterable wet and mud—the lamented severance from our old comrades of the 147th Brigade which has become an Army Brigade—and the success of our own gallant infantry on the 27th.   The end of the month finds us still very short of men—much important work being delayed thereby. Batteries have made progress in bomb-proof covers 20′ down for their men. Leave allotment has been more generous and the men who served since the landing in Gallipoli have now been home."   (Lt.-Col. Marriott Smith in 17th Brigade War Diary for January, 1917).

The Trench Mortar Batteries were very busy road making, making gun pits and on multifarious duties during the month but did not take part in any operations.   They were relieved in the line by T.M.Bs. of 20th D.A. on the 20th January.

February 6th.

The 97th Battery (of the 147th Army Brigade) and A/93 came into action under 'Left Artillery.'

February 8th.

The Left Artillery co-operated in an attack by the centre (17th) Division.

February 9th.

C.R.A. 29th Division handed our command of Left Artillery to C.RA. 20th Division.

N

February 18th.

The bombardment for the forthcoming operations of the 28th began.

February 21st.

Brig.-Genl. E. B. Ashmore arrived to assume command of the 29th Divisional Artillery, and relieved the C.R.A. 17th Division in the command of the Centre Artillery, XIV Corps.

The 'Centre Artillery', for the support of the 29th Division in the forthcoming attack consisted of :—

29th D.A. Group (Lt.-Col. Sherbrooke) 15th Brigade, R.H.A. (less " L " Battery*), 17th Brigade, R.F.A., A/76 Battery.

Other Units. 20th Divisional Artillery, 74th, 75th, 76th, 93rd and 147th Brigades, "U" Battery, R.H.A., 4th S.B. R.G.A. (6″ Hows.) 147th S.B. R.G.A. (6″ Hows.) 148th S.B. R.G.A. (9·2″ Hows.) Making a total of 138 18-prs., 6 13-prs., 36 4·5″ Hows., 8 6″ Hows., and 4 9·2″ Hows.

Wire cutting was commenced this day by the Warwickshire and 26th Batteries, the former moving 2 guns forward to within 1,600 yards for the purpose.

February 28th.

The 29th Division carried out a successful attack on a frontage of 1200 yards.

The number of guns available allowed some 16 yards per gun in the creeping barrage and in the standing barrage.

The creeping barrage opened at 4 rds. p.g.p.m. and moved at the rate of 50 yards every 2 minutes up to the objective, remained there an extra 2 minutes and then lifted 100 yards after which it moved at the rate of 25 yds. a minute on to the protective barrage line.

Two howitzers fired a smoke barrage for 45 minutes.

All our telephone wires were cut by the enemy's barrage and messages had to be sent by runners and wireless.

The artillery was afterwards congratulated by the Corps Commander who described the barrage as admirable. No change in the barrage was asked for by the infantry during the attack but many S.O.S. Signals were subsequently reported. Rockets of all colours were, however, freely used by the enemy. "From reports subsequently received from the infantry it appears that a concentration of the enemy on the left was dispersed during the morning by our barrage fire. An attack coming in on our right during the late evening met one of our periodical bursts of barrage fire and came to nothing." (29th D.A. war diary for February, 1919.)

The ammunition expenditure of the 29th Divisional Artillery on 27th and 28th was as under :—

27th   19,365 rounds

28th   18,166 rounds

---

* " L " Battery was detached to the "Left Artillery."

During the month of February the prolonged frost improved health. The ground was dryer than it had been for months. Casualties were few. Nearly all personnel at gun positions were in dugouts 30 feet below ground. Ammunition was brought up to gun positions by light railway. From the 20th February the 17th Brigade supported the infantry of our division for the first time since October; the 15th Brigade, on the other hand, had been more fortunate as they had assisted in the attack of the 29th Division of the 27th January as well as in that of February 28th.

V/29 Heavy T.M.B. handed over 3 T.Ms. to the Third Army on 8th February, but had one gun in action from 11th to the end of the month. All the medium batteries were busy during the month, getting guns into action and firing, but X/29 and Z/29 only took part in the attack on the 28th.

March 1st.

The 'Centre Artillery', XIV Corps, consisting of the 20th D.A. as 'Right Group' and the 29th D.A. as 'Left Group', covered the infantry of the 29th Division in the Sailly-Saillisel sector.

March 5th.

The XIV Corps front was reorganised from a 3 Divisional to a 2 Divisional front. The 29th Division infantry and Headquarters 29th Divisional Artillery were withdrawn, and the 15th Brigade became part of the 'Left Artillery' under the C.R.A. 20th Division, whilst the 17th Brigade went to the 'Right Artillery' under C.R.A. Guards Division. The Trench Mortar Batteries handed over their positions to the Guards Division T.M.Bs.

March 19th—20th.

The 15th and 17th Brigades came out of action and the whole 29th D.A. was assembled on the 21st at Morlancourt.

March 23rd—28th.

The D.A. moved by route march to Gouves, near Arras (except the S.A.A. Section which remained at Morlancourt). Halts for the night were made as under:—

	15th BDE., R.H.A.	17th BDE., R.F.A.	D.A.C. (less S.A.A. Section).
23rd.	Franvillers.	Franvillers.	La Houssoye.
24th.	Flesselles.	Flesselles.	Havernas.
26th.	Heuzecourt.	Beaucourt.	Beauvoir Riviere.
27th.	Rebreuve.	Frevent (Petit Bouret & Honral).	Grand Bouret.
28th.	Gouves·	Gouves.	Gouves.

On arrival at Gouves each brigade sent advance parties of two officers and 25 men or more per battery to Arras to prepare positions under the orders of the C.R.A., 12th Division VI Corps.

March 30th.

The Brigades went into action at Arras under C.R.A. 12th Division, and formed the Left Group under Lt.-Col. Marriott Smith; the 20th D.A. formed the Right Group.

March 31st.

Batteries registered for the attack. All T.M.Bs. took over positions, more or less complete.

April 2nd.

The 17th Brigade prepared their route for advance on the day of attack. A party under 2nd Lieut. Hilary laid artillery bridges over the trenches.

April 4th—8th.

On April 4th ("V" Day) the bombardment commenced. The original day fixed for "Z", i.e. the attack, was the 8th but later it was decided to postpone this to the 9th, so a "Q" day was interposed on the 7th. On the 8th the 17th Brigade brought their wagon lines close to Arras, behind the "Butte de Tir", in anticipation of the advance they were to make as soon as the first stage of the attack was successfully accomplished.

Trench Mortar Batteries were busy, especially V/29 (Heavy) which fired 345 of their heavy bombs in the four days from 5th to 8th.

The D.A.C. (less S.A.A. Section) moved up to Arras on 8th April.

April 9th.

Day of attack by the Third Army of the German front and second line trenches. The VI Corps frontage was from the Cojeul to the Scarpe and their attack was made by three divisions, 15th Division on the right, 12th Division in the Centre, and 17th Division on the left.

The 29th Divisional Artillery supported the attack of the 36th Infantry Brigade of the 12th Division.

Rain was falling heavily at zero hour, 05.30.

At 08.50 the teams to take the 17th Brigade forward about 2000 yds. to positions just in rear of our original front-line arrived at gun positions, and, as previously arranged, at 1100 the brigade moved forward. During the advance the batteries were fired at to a certain extent by enemy batteries but had one man and six horses wounded only, and the enemy soon was forced to leave them alone by their anxiety to get away before our victorious infantry. At 12.00 orders were received by the Brigade that the advance to the second objective—the 'Brown Line'—would take place at 12.10. At this hour about 50% of the guns were in action but the remainder picked up the barrage programme in turn as they came into action.

Most of the batteries of the 15th Brigade, R.H.A. had a very unpleasant time during the opening barrage, as they were consistently shelled and had many casualties. Lt.-Col. Sherbrooke, Commanding 15th Brigade, reported as follows: "The Warwickshire Battery, R.H.A., under command of Captain Hon. R. E. Eden, was in action at St. Sauveur, close to Arras, firing the barrage in support of the attack on that day. Their position was nearly in view, within 1200 yards of our front line. A heavy hostile barrage was put down, and about 7 a.m. two complete detachments were knocked out and two officers killed. The battery continued firing, supporting on three objectives, from 5.30 a.m. till 3.30 p.m., advanced that night in the dark, supported a further attack next morning, and advanced again that afternoon to Feuchy Chapel, where that night it again had a whole detachment knocked out and had to change position again next day, but remained in action. During the same operations the 460th Battery R.F.A., under Major L. A. Eddis, was in action in the railway cutting just north of Arras station. Early in the day two howitzers with their detachments were knocked out by direct hits from a H.V. gun, and one officer was killed. About 11.30 a.m. the battery ammunition dump was exploded blowing up an iron road bridge over the railway, which buried two more howitzers. The remaining two remained in action throughout the day, carrying out all their tasks and advanced with their brigade that evening and again on the 10th."

After capture of the "Brown Line",[1] which was some 4000 yds. from the German front line, the C.R.A. 12th Division went forward to control the forward operations and had the following artillery brigades under his orders, 63rd of 12th Division, 15th of 29th Division, and 71st of 37th Division, to support the infantry of the 37th Division. At the same time 29th Divisional Artillery Headquarters moved to Wagnonlieu and the C.R.A. had under his orders the 17th Brigade, and the 62nd Brigade of the 12th Division, for the support of the 12th Division holding the Brown Line.

The 15th Brigade received orders to advance about 17.00 and came into action again in positions some 3,000 yards in advance of their old ones. This operation was not complete till 03.00 on the 10th.

"A small operation on the night of the 9th and 10th completed the capture of the enemy rearguards in front of the Brown Line." (29th D.A. H.Q. war diary.)

Z/29 T.M.B. followed up the attacking infantry in the morning with 2 Trench Mortars and Y/29 carried up ammunition, but these T.Ms. were not actually used.

April 10th.

The 37th Division attacked and captured Monchy le Preux, supported by the brigades of the 29th D.A. amongst others. Both brigades moved forward again, this time to positions some 3,500 yds. behind Monchy. In the case of the 15th Brigade R.H.A., the occupation of old German battery positions was completed and 1,000 rounds per battery were alongside the guns by 16.00. The two remaining howitzers of the 460th Battery were in pits trail to trail with the German 4·2″ Howitzers which had been abandoned there. In fact, all the positions occupied this evening had been fired on by the brigade up to noon the same morning.

The weather was awful—a snow blizzard raged.

The misfortunes of the Headquarters of the 17th Brigade are described by the Adjutant, Capt. K. Lyon, as follows:—"The possibility of being blown up by a booby trap in a deserted German dug-out decided Brigade Headquarters to spend the night in an old

---

[1] As a matter of fact, the Brown line does not appear to have been captured on the 9th, but the moves described in this paragraph took place that day.

German gun-pit, but their caution was ill rewarded by two tanks during the night who, having lost their way—their wake hotly follow-ed by German 'crumps'—nearly obliterated the Headquarters in their endeavour to find their way to the Cambrai road."

April 11th.

The 17th Brigade moved forward in the afternoon.

April 12th.

Infantry of the 12th Division relieved those of the 37th Division in the front line, and were in turn relieved by the 29th Division the following day.

April 13th.

The C.R.A. 29th Division assumed command of the artillery covering the 29th Division, *vice* the C.R.A. 12th Division. The enemy shelled our gun positions heavily with gas shell.

April 14th.

The 88th Infantry Brigade captured the high ground 1200 yds. east of Monchy, being supported by the 12th and 29th Divisional Artilleries. A strong counter-attack in the evening forced them to evacuate this high ground owing to the divisions on either flank not being in line with them, but Monchy remaied safely in our hands.

April 15th—22nd.

During this period preparations were made for the attack on the 'Red Line' (Bois du Vert and Bois du Sart). Hostile shelling was very severe and there was much loss in personnel and equipment. It was not unusual for 2 or 3 guns of a brigade to be knocked out in the course of 24 hours, whilst on the 17th April the 17th Brigade had one howitzer and six 18-pdrs. put out of action, four of which belonged to the 26th Battery; this battery also had its telephone pit destroyed. The 26th Battery was again unlucky on the 19th when 3 guns were put out of action; on the same day the 13th Battery had six men killed. On the 19th April the 26th and 92nd Batteries were moved to new positions less advanced and somewhat to a flank and the 13th Battery detachments were withdrawn for a rest. Parties were at work on forward positions to which guns would move if the attack proved successful. Considerable difficulty was experienced in getting the ammunition up to these positions, owing to there being no moon, and to the road being crammed with transport and shelled with salvoes of 5·9's. "Men and horses are almost done up—the men make no complaint at all and have 'stuck' it well but continual shelling and no sleep has told on them. 46 horses evacuated to-day for debility." (17th Bde. war diary for 22nd April). The Trench Mortar Batteries were mostly employed at this time in preparing captured guns for firing on the enemy or in re-moving them to the rear. After April 9th, all officers except Capt. Craib (actg. D.T.M.O.) and 2nd Lieut. Mulholland (Z/29 T.M.B.) were attached to gun batteries to replace casualties and in the latter half of the month all other ranks were similarly treated. V/29 T.M.B. parked its heavy T.Ms. at Arras on the 9th April.

April 23rd.

The 29th Division attacked the Bois du Vert and Bois du Sart, with the 15th Division on their right and the 17th Division on their left, all three divisions being in the VI Corps.

The 29th Division attack was carried out by the 88th Infantry Brigade on the right and the 87th Infantry Brigade on the left, and was supported by the following artillery under the command of the C.R.A. 29th Division:—

> Right Group—12th Divisional Artillery.
> Centre Group—155th Army F.A. Brigade.
> Left Group—29th Divisional Artillery.
> Heavy Artillery—25th Heavy Battery, R.G.A.
>   whilst the 72nd Heavy Artillery Group co-operated.

The rate of the barrage was 100 yards every four minutes, and each 18-pdr. battery had a frontage of about 100 yards to cover.

There were two objectives in the attack, it being intended to have a pause of 6½ hours after the first was gained to enable the artillery to move forward for the support of the second. The first objective—the "Blue Line"—was successfully captured, and all artillery brigades, except the 155th which was already within 2000 yards of Monchy, moved up to positions some 1000 yards west of that place. The second phase was not carried out owing to the flank divisions not having advanced sufficiently, so the new line, some 1000 yards east of Monchy, was consolidated.

As a result of this failure to carry out the second phase, the artillery was committed much too far forward. The 15th Brigade war diary states that at one time the enemy was between them and Guemappe and that it seemed likely that the 15th and 17th Brigades would be cut off. Rifles and S.A.A. were issued in the batteries in anticipation of such an eventuality, and an order was actually received by the 15th Brigade to empty their gun limbers, hook in 8-horse teams and withdraw the guns, but this order was subsequently concelled.

Irrespective of the danger of being cut off, the batteries were in a precarious position seeing that they were under machine-gun fire and in full view of the enemy's balloons.

The 13th Battery had experienced a very unlucky week from the 18th to 25th, having one officer (Lt. Henney) killed and four officers, including the Battery Commander, Actg. Major R. S. Leach, wounded.

The 460th Battery was also unfortunate on the 23rd, when a shell landed in a gun pit which had been vacated by the battery and from which ammunition was being taken forward to the new position. This shell exploded the ammunition and as a result two officers and two other ranks were killed and seven other ranks wounded.

April 25th—26th.

The infantry of the 3rd Division relieved that of the 29th Division and the C.R.A. 3rd Division assumed command of the artillery covering their front.

April 26th.

The Headquarters of the 17th Brigade moved into a remarkable cave already occupied by the Headquarters of the 76th Infantry Brigade which the 17th Brigade was supporting. The Adjutant describes this cave as follows:—"The cave reminds me of a witches' haunt in a Drury Lane Pantomine, or a kind of hellish cathedral, gloomy and smoky, with candles burning in the various alcoves as though before some evil shrine."

Wagon lines were moved back to Arras to the great satisfaction of the men.

April 27th—30th.

The artillery was preparing for the attack of 3rd May. The Warwickshire and 460th Batteries prepared new positions further south as their present ones were untenable.

"During the week at their Monchy positions batteries have had a less unpleasant time so far as casualties to men is concerned, but they have been heavily shelled and several guns have been put out of action. At one time the 13th Battery was reduced to 2 guns, and *all* the howitzers were out of action.

This month has seen all the batteries of the (17th) Brigade continuously engaged in hard fighting with varying success. The bearing of officers and men under conditions of great fatigue, hardship and danger has been splendid. The hardest time was in the neighbourhood of Feuchy Chapelle when batteries were engaged day and night by heavy shell. The expenditure of ammunition has been enormous The final advance to the neighbourhood of Monchy was made under shell and machine- gun fire. The brigade has been thanked for its services by the G.Os. C. 36th, 76th and 88th Infantry Brigades, which it supported, and also by the G.O.C. 29th Division and G.O.C. VI Corps. The losses have been two officers killed, seven wounded, 28 other ranks killed, 101 wounded, 44 horses killed and 43 wounded. Most of the losses fell on the 13th Battery." (Lt.-Col. Marriott Smith in 17th Bde. war diary for April).

The casualties in the 15th Brigade R.H.A. during the month were five officers killed, three wounded, 33 other ranks killed, 88 wounded. There is no record in the War Diary of the casualties to animals.

May 1st.

The Warwickshire and 460th Batteries moved into their new positions. The most advanced batteries were now within about 2,200 yards of the front line. The cave, into which the Headquarters 17th Brigade moved on the 26th April, fell in and the Headquarters moved into another cave "less dangerous and considerably less airy."

May 2nd.

Owing to the heavy casualties to howitzers, the 460th and D/17 batteries were organized into a sub-group under the command of Actg. Major H. O. Holmes.

May 3rd.

The 3rd Division attacked with a limited objective about 2000 yards away, but did not achieve success. The enemy shelled both the attackers and the battery areas heavily with lethal and lachrymatory shell. Many gunners succumbed to the effects of the gas, and the infantry were compelled to attack in their gas masks.

May 5th.

The practice of bringing one battery per brigade out of action for a short rest was instituted, "B" and the 92nd being first withdrawn to their wagon lines for this purpose.

May 9th.

Personnel of "B" returned to action and "L" Battery withdrew to wagon lines.

May 11th—12th.

The Warwickshire Battery had three guns knocked out.

May 13th.

Personnel of Warwickshire Battery to rest *vice* "L" back into action.

May 14th—15th.

87th Infantry Brigade relieved the 76th Infantry Brigade in the Monchy defences and the C.R.A. 29th Division took over command of the artillery covering the divisional front from the C.R.A. 3rd Division and established his Headquarters at 35 Rue St. Morrice, Arras.

May 17th.

The 29th Division extended their front northwards to the River Scarpe, taking over the 12th Division front as well as their own. Their new frontage was 3000 yards. The artillery under the C.R.A. 29th Division—i.e. 12th and 29th Divisional Artilleries—was augmented by the addition of the 33rd Divisional Artillery (156th and 162nd Brigades), the 78th Brigade of the 17th Divisional Artillery, and the 48th Army Field Artillery Brigade.

The Warwickshire Battery and 92nd Battery returned into action from their short rest. "L" Battery moved into a new position, their old one being too heavily shelled. This Battery had recently lost four guns in the space of 12 hours.

May 19th.

87th Infantry Brigade carried out an unsuccessful attack. Its failure was due to the severity of the enemy machine gun fire.

The S.A.A. Section rejoined the D.A.C.

Captain J. N. Thomson arrived to take over the duties of Brigade Major from Major C. H. Clark who was appointed to command the 18th Army F.A. Brigade.

May 20th.

"B" Battery was withdrawn to wagon lines for a rest.

May 30th.

An attack was carried out by the 29th Division and the 8th East Lancashire Regt. Three battalions took part on a frontage of

900 yards and the barrage was formed by 90 18-pdrs. Every avail-able gun* was put into action but it was considered advisable to pro-long the flanks of the barrage to cover another 2,500, so that the actual limits of the attack should not be disclosed. The objective was attained but not consolidated, though our infantry slightly improved their original position.

The casualties during May were not nearly so heavy as in the previous month, and conditions, though by no means easy, were not so strenuous as in the first few weeks of the Arras offensive.

Some of the Trench Mortar batteries were reformed this month. Z/29 was reformed on the 16th May and took over 2 mortars in the line from a T.M.B. of the 12th Division on 25th May. X/29 was reformed on 30th May.

June 1st—2nd.

The 3rd Division relieved the 29th Division in the line, and the C.R.A. of the former took over command of the artillery covering the divisional front on the 3rd. 29th D.A.H.Q. remained in the line commanding the Left Group. X/29 relieved Z/29 T.M.B. in the line.

June 3rd.

2nd Lieut. H. J. Hilary, 92nd Battery R.F.A. was wounded and died the same day. He was a great loss to his Brigade. He had been Chairman of the Calcutta Port Trust and though nearly 42 years of age, gave up this important post to enter the ranks as a cadet.

The S.A.A. Section departed this day to join the infantry of the Division.

June 6th.

V/29 Heavy T.M.B. was reformed.

The Headquarters 17th Brigade moved from their stuffy cave to the Bois des Boeufs just east of Tilloy and south of the Cambrai road. "A delightful spot—beautiful green trees and wild flowers. The wood pigeons coo at the same time as a 15-in howitzer fires just behind us. We live in tents—Glorious hot weather: we have our mess in the open." (17th Brigade war diary).

June 14th.

The 3rd Division carried out a completely successful surprise attack on Infantry Hill. The enemy had been 'drilled' into expect-ing a quiet period during the same hours daily. During this period the attack was launched and no artillery barrage was put down by us until 1½ minutes after our infantry had left their trenches. The guns assisted materially in repelling a counter-attack the same evening.

June 16th.

Major W. A. Murray assumed command of the 17th Brigade *vice* Lt.-Col. Marriott Smith (sick).

---

* The total number was 151 18-pdrs. and 50 4.5" Howitzers.

June 21st—22nd.

The 29th Divisional Artillery came out of action and moved to Montenescourt (15th and 17th Brigades) and Gouves (D.A.C. less S.A.A. Section).

June 23rd.

Y/29 T.M.B. was reformed.

June 24th.

The rare opportunity was seized of having a church parade attended by the whole Divisional Artillery. The only thing which marred the ceremony was the piano which was sadly out of tune, even though the Padre preached about 'harmony'.

June 30th.

D.A. Sports were held at Montenescourt—The Warwickshire Battery being particularly successful.

July 1st—8th.

The 29th Divisional Artillery moved from Montenescourt to Houtkerque to join the Fifth Army. Halts were made as under:—

DATE.	15th. BDE., R.H.A.	17th. BDE., R.F.A.	29th. D.A.C. (less S.A.A. Section).
1st.	Rebreuviette.	Rebreuviette.	Etree Wamin
2nd.	Hernicourt.	Gauchin.	Croix.
4th.	Amettes.	Ames.	Nedon & Nedon Chelle.
5th.	Wittes.	Boeseghem.	Neufpré and environs of Aire.
6th.	Staple.	Staple.	Staple.
7th.	Godewærsvelde.	Steenwoorde.	Godewærsvelde.
8th.	Houtkerque.	Houtkerque.	'International Corner' (near Peselhoek).

The trench mortar batteries were sent by motor lorry on 1st July to Herzeele and commenced the following day the construction of emplacements for the bombardment.

The Headquarters 29th Divisional Artillery with small advanced parties from batteries also went ahead and arrived at the Guards Divisional Headquarters at 'J Camp' on the 2nd July. These parties, on arrival of the brigades at Houtkerque, were augmented to 1 officer and 20 men per battery and were employed in preparing positions for the offensive.

X/29 T.M.B. was the first to be in action, and actually commenced firing on the 12th July. Z/29 'registered' two days later. V/29 had its first heavy mortar in action on the 13th.

July 14th—17th.

On the 15th, the 15th Brigade R.H.A. moved into action near Elverdinghe, followed on the 16th and 17th by the 17th Brigade. Forward wagon lines were near Woesten—rear wagon lines remained at Houtkerque.

On the 15th, Headquarters 29th Divisional Artillery took command of the right group of the Left Artillery, XIV Corps. The Left Artillery was commanded by the C.R.A. Guards Division. The Left

Group consisted of the 29th Divisional Artillery and the 84th Army Field Artillery Brigade and its Headquarters was at Marie Jean Farm.

The preliminary bombardment commenced on the 15th and during the next few days the brigades had their first experience of 'mustard' gas. On 23rd, there were 40 casualties in the D.A. as a result of this gas. Batteries at this period were firing 250 rounds by day and 250 by night.

The trench mortar batteries were very busy. 13 emplacements for the medium (2″) mortars and 3 for the heavy (9·45″) were prepared. On July 15th a systematic bombardment of the enemy's wire and strong points commenced, and continued till July 27th, 2,200 rounds of 2″ ammunition being fired. The Heavy T.Ms fired 188 rounds between the 16th and 25th. During this time the casualties in the T.M.Bs. were 3 officers and 3 other ranks killed—2 officers and 11 other ranks wounded.

July 27th.

The Guards Division, which our brigades assisted to cover at this time, pushed out their out-post line about 500 yards beyond the Ypres canal under cover of an 18-pr. and 4·5″ Howitzer standing barrage.

July 28th.

A wireless message of enemy origin was intercepted saying that our troops must be driven back across the canal at all costs. This put everyone much on the alert and the S.O.S. signal was sent up three times. An officer of the Guards is reported to have told the 13th Battery Commander that when the first signal was sent up the first of our shells fell in the German line before the S.O.S. light dropped to the ground!

Brig.-Genl. G. H. A. White assumed command of the 29th Divisional Artillery *vice* Ashmore.

July 31st.

The XIV Corps attacked in conjunction with other corps. Our artillery assisted to cover the attack of the 2nd Guards Brigade, whose right flank was on the Ypres—Staden railway. The Fifth Army gained the whole of its objectives and captured about 3400 prisoners. The Guards spoke in the highest terms of our barrage and said that nothing could live in it. A captured Prussian officer, however, was very disdainful and said that our barrage was 'absolutely rotten'. He could not explain, however, how it was that in these circumstances he surrendered!

August 1st.

The 15th Brigade R.H.A. attempted to advance across the canal. The mud, caused by the heavy rain, and congestion of traffic was, however, too much for them. 2 gun teams of the leading battery, "L", were knocked out by shell fire, and though 4 guns of this battery did manage to cross the canal, in spite of gallant efforts made by Capt. Leadbetter and the detachments under shell fire, they became hopelessly stuck in the mud there. The remainder of the Brigade, therefore, came into action again about Boesinghe.

August 4th—5th.

On the 4th the four guns of "L" which had crossed the canal were got into action. Unfortunately Capt. Leadbetter was killed. Capt. Mure, of the Warwickshire Battery, took over temporary command of "L" and brought the remaining two guns across the canal into action on the 5th.

The 13th Battery had only one gun in action at this time, the remainder having been put out of action from various causes.

The 17th Brigade crossed the canal on the 5th and the remainder of the 15th Brigade the following day.

The C.R.A. handed over command of the Right Group to the O.C. 84th A.F.A. Brigade on the 5th.

August 7th.

The C.R.A. 29th Division took over command of the Left Group of the Left Artillery, XIV Corps. This group consisted of the Guards DA. and 5th Army Brigade R.H.A.

August 8th.

The 29th Division relieved the Guards Division which held a line roughly along the west bank of the Steenbeek.

August 8th—15th.

Preparations for the advance to the Broenbeek. Battery positions were very heavily shelled by the enemy during this period. The replenishment of ammunition was a very difficult matter, as the daily expenditure was considerable (certainly 100 rounds per gun), there was a dearth of roads and the mud was indescribable.

On the 11th there was a minor operation in which our infantry advanced under a creeping barrage to the east bank of the Steenbeek to secure a good 'jumping-off' place. This operation was completely successful.

On the 14th the D.A.C. moved to near Elverdinghe.

August 16th.

The 29th Division attacked, with the rest of the Fifth Army. All objectives were gained, and a new line established on the high ground some 200 yards west of the Broenbeek. As our infantry had been ordered to send patrols out to the Broenbeek, the S.O.S. line for the guns was placed some 200 yards east of it. The enemy took advantage of the large space between the position of our front line and the barrage to mass on our side of the latter. An F.O.O. at Craonne Farm realised the situation and informed D.A.H.Q. The fire of all batteries was at once turned on to the Broenbeek itself and all subsequent reports, both from the infantry and F.O.Os., agreed that this fire was most effective and that it scattered the enemy who were thought to be preparing a counter-attack.

This successful attack included the capture of Langemarck. The barrage was timed at the rate of 100 yards every 5 minutes.

The artillery was accused of short shooting and of not answering S.O.S. calls by one of the infantry units. As a result of this, General de Lisle held an enquiry into the matter the following day and found that all S.O.S. calls had been answered and that the only case of short shooting was one gun which shot short on Cannes Farm for some 10 minutes.

Calls for the S.O.S. barrage were, in fact, rather numerous, the 17th Brigade having recorded that some 3,200 rounds were fired in this manner during the afternoon.

The supply of ammunition was very difficult and arduous work at this period. Even on days when no major operations were taking place, batteries were firing an average of some 600 rounds apiece.

August 17th.

This day was notable for the fact that the 17th Brigade lost the services of their most valuable and universally respected medical officer Captain F. Harris, R.A.M.C. who was badly wounded and had to be evacuated. This officer was with the 17th Brigade at the landing in Gallipoli and had been serving with them ever since. His name had been frequently brought to the notice of the C.R.A. for gallantry. He was mentioned in despatches for his work in Gallipoli and received the M.C. as an immediate award for indefatigable attention to the wounded under heavy shell fire on the 18th/19th July.

August 19th—22nd.

On the night 19th/20th the 26th Battery moved forward to a new position but several guns stuck in the mud en route. The enemy put a very heavy area shoot down and "L" Battery had a very rough time. All its guns and ammunition were buried by 12-inch shells and one gun was blown 30 yards away from its pit. The personnel had to be temporarily withdrawn. On the 20th each battery of the 15th Brigade R.H.A. tried to get a section forward. The Warwickshire section started first and were successful, but a heavy gas bombardment by the enemy put a stop to the movement of the others. On the 21st the other sections reached their forward positions, whilst the 92nd and D/17 batteries also moved forward. The 13th Battery attempted to advance but became stuck in the mud. They managed it all right, however, on the 22nd.

August 26th.

The Guards Division relieved the 29th Division in the line and command of the artillery covering the Divisional front passed to the C.R.A. Guards Division.

August 27th.

The artillery co-operated with an attack by the adjoining (XVIII) Corps.

August 28th.

The daily expenditure of ammunition was raised to :—
            50 rounds per Brigade per hour by day.
            20 rounds per Brigade per hour by night.

August 30th.

The 29th Divisional Artillery came out of action to wagon lines for a rest. The forward sections of the 15th Brigade and the 13th Battery left their guns in action under guards from each battery. The other batteries had their guns taken over in turn by the 11th Army F.A. Brigade.

The trench mortar batteries were nominally resting during the month but actually were employed in preparing positions for the gun batteries and on other equally arduous duties.

September 1st—2nd.

The 15th and 17th Brigades moved to the Proven area on the 1st, and on the 2nd to Munc, Nieurlet, and Polincove (near Audruicq) respectively, leaving the D.A.C. behind for duty with the Left Artillery, XIV Corps. Each battery also left an officer and a party behind to prepare positions on the Steenbeek.

Brig.-Genl. E. H. Stevenson relieved Brig.-Genl. White in command of the 29th D.A on the 1st.

September 2nd—13th.

The Brigades had a good and very well earned rest for these few days, but the 13th Battery had to start on its way back on the 10th to come into action again under the C.R.A. 20th Division in the Right Artillery, XIV Corps. Meanwhile the D.A.C. was unlucky having heavy casualties on the 12th.

September 14th—17th.

The Brigades (less 13th Battery) commenced their return march on the 14th and by the 17th were all in action again near Hey Wood in the 'LeftArtillery', XIV Corps. They had to 'get busy' at once with the ammunition supply, orders having been received that the following had to be at the gun positions by 0900 on the 19th: 875 rounds per 18-pdr., 750 rounds per 4·5″ Howitzer, and an additional 2,500 gas shell per Howitzer Battery.

The enemy shelling was very heavy. On the 19th "B" had two guns knocked out, whilst on the 20th the 92nd received two direct hits which killed five men, and D/17 had a howitzer blown into Hey Wood 50 yards away.

September 21st—22nd.

The 29th Division relieved the Guards Division in the line, and the command of the Left Artillery passed back from the C.R.A. Guards Division to the C.R.A. 29th Division.

The Guards Artillery withdrew from action on the 22nd and the 13th Battery rejoined its brigade the same day, so that the Left Artillery, XIV Corps, was now composed of the 29th D.A. and the 11th Army Field Artillery Brigade. The 15th Brigade R.H.A. moved into positions on the canal bank recently occupied by the 75th Brigade of the Guards Division. The S.A.A. Section rejoined the D.A.C. after having been detached with the infantry of the division.

September 23rd—24th.

This night was remarkable for the very heavy gas shelling of the battery areas, necessitating the wearing of gas masks for some six hours.

September 26th.

The 18-pdrs. fired a creeping and weaving barrage, and the howitzers a weaving barrage and gas bombardment, in support of an attack by troops on our right. Our battery positions were very heavily shelled from 0830 to 1500.

On the previous night the D.A.C. lost 32 animals killed or wounded by aeroplane bombs.

September 27th—30th.

The 15th Brigade was busy dumping 1000 rounds per gun in forward positions in anticipation of the next advance.

The Trench Mortar Batteries during September were, as in the previous month, employed on multifarious duties.

October 1st.

The 15th Brigade moved into the positions of the 11th Army F.A. Brigade. The Guards D.A. came into action again and the artillery under the command of the C.R.A. 29th Division was :—

Right Group.	Left Group.
15th Brigade R.H.A.	
11th Army F.A. Brigade	17th Brigade R.F.A.
(less D/11).	Guards D.A.
A/65 and D/65.	

October 3rd.

29th D.A. H.Q. moved from "J" Camp to Elverdinghe Chateau.

October 4th.

The 29th Division took part in another big attack and was once more completely successful.

October 5th—6th.

The XIV Corps front was re-organised into a 3 Division front-age, the 29th Division being in the centre covered by the "Centre Artillery" composed of :—

Right Group—76th Army F.A. Brigade (less C/76).
A/65 and D/65 Batteries.
29th F.A. Brigade (4th Division).
Left Group—29th D.A.
Total—78 guns, 22 Howitzers.

October 5th—8th.

On the 5th notification was received that it was intended to renew the advance on the 9th. All batteries except A/76 and B/76 were too far back and had to move forward. No positions had been selected or prepared. Continual rain had made the ground very heavy. Roads were very difficult and were heavily shelled by the enemy; tracks were almost impassable. In order to get guns and ammunition forward in time it was necessary to move batteries forward to the Steenbeek in daylight. This meant moving for some 2000 yards down the forward slope of Pilckem ridge within close range of Koekuit slopes which were held by the enemy. It is inconceivable but none the less true that the enemy's artillery took no action, although the movement of guns and ammunition was incessant even when the light was good for observation. Hardly any casualties occurred although all the roads were continually packed with transport of all kinds.

The Centre Artillery was augmented between the 7th and 9th by the addition of C/76 Battery and the 286th F.A. Brigade (less one Battery).

October 9th.

The 29th Division carried out another successful attack, and was relieved by the 17th Division during the following days, the C.R.A. of the latter division taking over command of the centre artillery on the 10th.

October 12th.

The artillery was again busy, supporting an attack by the 17th Division.

October 15th.

Batteries of the 17th Brigade moved forward in front of Langemarck.

October 17th.

The C.R.A. 29th Division took over command of the Right Group, Left Artillery XIV Corps, consisting of :—

> 17th Brigade, R.F.A.
> 150th A.F.A. Brigade, which relieved 15th Brigade, R.H.A. on 17th.
> 152nd and 160th Brigades of the 34th Division.

and preparations were made to support the attack of the 34th Division on the 22nd.

October 19th—20th.

The 15th Brigade R.H.A. relieved the 150th A.F.A. Brigade.

October 22nd.

The 34th Division carried out a partially successful attack.

October 23rd—24th.

Brigades of 29th Divisional Artillery were relieved by the 50th D.A., guns being exchanged, and entrainment commenced at Peselhoek on the evening of the 24th for the movement on transfer to the VI Corps of the Third Army.

October 25th—26th.

Units detrained at Doullens. The 15th Brigade moved into billets at Orville, the 17th Brigade to Authieule, and the D.A.C. to Amplier.

October 28th.

All guns and howitzers were sent into ordnance workshops for overhaul.

October 30th.

The medium T.M.Bs. went to St. Leger for attachment to the 16th Division and were employed in digging gun positions. V/29 Heavy T.M.B. was attached to the 3rd Division.

October 31st.

Parties of 1 officer and 30 men per battery went by train to Achiet-le-Grand to be attached to the 3rd Division and prepare gun positions.

O

November 1st—9th.

Brigades sent their guns to be calibrated on the Fricourt calibration range (near Albert). Plans for future operations were changed and the digging parties of batteries returned.

The 29th Division was now to join the III Corps and take part in the Cambrai operations, all preliminary movements taking place by night and the greatest precautions being taken that the enemy should obtain no inkling of the proposed attack.

The S.A.A. Section moved on the 7th to Braye and on the following day to a camp near Equancourt, where it was joined by the remainder of the D.A.C. on the 14th.

November 12th—19th.

On the 12th/13th the D.A. moved by night to the Treux—Dernancourt area, and on the 13th/14th by night to Hennois Wood, where they came under the orders of the III Corps.

The vehicles were concealed in the wood; horses were tied up to trees in odd groups; no lights were allowed. For real discomfort this camp—or rather bivouac—would be difficult to surpass. The wood was surrounded by a heavy muddy field. The weather was wet for part of the time and bitterly cold all the time. No fires were allowed and the very few tents supplied were worn out, leaked badly and had no floor boards.

On the night of the 16th/17th the 15th Brigade R.H.A. moved into action under the orders of the C.R.A. 6th Division, and on the night of the 18th/19th the 17th Brigade (less 13th Battery which moved into action the previous night) came into action under orders of the C.R.A. 20th Division.

The three medium Trench Mortar batteries were in action and were busy firing at wire and strong points on the 19th.

November 20th.

The III Corps attacked between Banteux and the Canal du Nord with the 20th, 6th and 12th Divisions in front line, and the 29th Division in reserve. The rôle of the last-named was to pass through when the Hindenburg support line on 'Welsh Ridge' had been captured, and seize the line Nine Wood—Marcoing—Masnieres.

The 29th Divisional Artillery was at first allotted to the 20th and 6th Divisions to assist in the advance of those divisions, but was to come under the order of the C.R.A. again as soon as the 29th Division was ordered to advance. The 16th Brigade R.H.A. (less "U" Battery but plus the 111th Battery R.F.A.) was also to come under the orders of the C.R.A.

The attack started at 06.20, was covered by a creeping barrage and was preceded by a dense mass of tanks, which had been brought up into the woods behind our line during the preceding nights from the broad-gauge railway—both road and rail movements having been carried out during the hours of darkness. The three divisions broke clean through the Hindenburg line, the whole of which was captured by 09.30.

At 07.20 2nd Lieut. Vince with an advanced party from the 15th Brigade, consisting of pioneers and gunners with wire cutters and a wagon load of fascines cleared a road for the guns through La Vacquerie. A similar party from the 17th Brigade under Lieut. Calvert did the same for that brigade.

At 09.30 one battery of each brigade was ordered forward, and at 10.12, when the 29th Division had been ordered to advance, all batteries were ordered forward.

No detailed orders for the action of the artillery were issued from D.A. H.Q. but artillery brigades were to work in co-operation with Infantry Brigades as under:—

> 15th Brigade R.H.A. with the 86th Infantry Brigade.
> 17th Brigade R.F.A. with the 87th Infantry Brigade.
> 16th Brigade R.H.A. with the 88th Infantry Brigade.

The leading battery of the 17th Brigade was forced by hostile machine gun fire to halt and come into action between the German front and support systems for $1\frac{1}{2}$ hours.

The 15th Brigade R.H.A. found the sunken road out of La Vacquerie blocked by tanks, no less than four having stuck there, and consequently did not get into action until 16.00.

The 29th Division successfully carried out their task, but was unable to prevent the main bridge over the canal being blown up.

November 21st—29th.

The batteries fired a creeping barrage on the 21st for an unsuccessful attack on Rumilly. On the 23rd, the 29th D.A. was reinforced by the 232nd A.F.A. Brigade, consisting of three 18-pdr. batteries, and, as no further operations were contemplated, all batteries were withdrawn to positions more suitable for defence. On the 26th, the 111th Battery, which had been attached to the 16th Brigade R.H.A. rejoined the 6th D.A., and two days later the 16th Brigade R.H.A. was withdrawn. This left the 15th Brigade R.H.A. in action on the right in Vacquerie valley, the 17th Brigade R.F.A. in the centre and 232nd Army F.A. Brigade on the left, both in the Couillet Wood valley.

Our Trench Mortar Batteries had six 6″ Newton mortars in action in Masneries on the 24th, but of these four were put out of action by enemy shell fire on the 29th.

November 30th.

Was the day of the great German counter-attack. At about 02.00 the enemy opened a heavy destructive and neutralising fire with $77^{m/m}$ guns and 105 (4·2″) and 150 (5·9″) $^{m/m}$ howitzers on all batteries in the Vacquerie valley, using H.E. and gas shell. Our counter-battery efforts in no way affected the severity of this fire.

Between 06.00 and 07.00 the 15th Brigade R.H.A. fired counter-preparatory fire on the approaches north of Rumilly and on likely places of assembly; and at 07.00 at the request of the G.O.C. 86th Infantry Brigade, concentrated its fire on the area opposite Mont Plaisir Farm. An F.O.O. was sent up to this farm who reported no movement visible on the 29th Division front but some in the direction of Revelon Chateau. At 08.00, however, this F.O.O. reported decided movement about Crevecoeur. Numbers of enemy aeroplanes now came flying low and firing at our batteries in the Vacquerie valley and did a good deal of damage. At 08.00 an S.O.S. rocket was seen to be sent up on the front held by the division on our right (20th Division). 10 minutes later all telephone lines from the forward exchange were cut by the hostile shell fire.

The 29th Division held the point of the salient made by our successful attack on the 20th, and successfully held their ground this day against the enemy assault. Divisional Headquarters was situated in Gouzeaucourt Quarry which was more or less in the base of the salient and in the right or southern portion of that base. Consequently when the enemy broke through the front of the divisions on our right his line of advance took him through this Quarry, amongst other places. The first news of this break through received at the Quarry was the opening of machine guns from close range upon it and at 08.40 or thereabouts it had to be abandoned. Unfortunately the C.R.A. (Brig.-Genl. Stevenson) was badly wounded in the knee by shell fire just before and had to be left behind with an orderly. The enemy, however, did not take either of them away and they were rescued by the counter-attack which recaptured the Quarry early the following morning.

To return to the Brigades, it was apparent about 09.00 that the enemy had broken through on the 20th Division front south of the St. Quentin canal. Considerable bodies of infantry of this division were now retiring through the 15th and 17th Brigade gun positions and the enemy infantry was seen advancing over Welsh Ridge, close to the positions of the 17th Brigade.

One battery of the 232nd Army Brigade was forced to abandon its guns, so the personnel was withdrawn, carrying away sights and breech blocks.

The 92nd and D/17 batteries each ran a couple of guns out of their emplacements and engaged bodies of enemy on Welsh Ridge with open sights. Major Stanford, Commanding 92nd Battery, having been wise enough to secure a Lewis gun for his battery, brought this Lewis gun to bear on the advancing enemy himself. Capt. Booth also was busy with another Lewis gun which he commandeered from the retiring infantry.

The fire of the 13th and 26th Batteries and of the two remaining batteries of the 232nd Army Brigade was directed on large numbers of the enemy seen approaching Masnieres from the direction of Crevecoeur. At the same time Lieut.-Col. Burne, Commanding 15th Brigade R.H.A., with the consent of the G.O.C. 86th Infantry Brigade, switched off to cover a gap on our right, and telephoned to the 17th and 232nd Brigades to ask them to cover the whole 29th Division front.

Meanwhile, at the request of the G.O.C. 86th Infantry Brigade, Majors Eden and St. Clair, Commanding the Warwickshire and "B" Batteries respectively, tried to stop the infantry retiring from Bonavis Ridge, whilst the G.O.C. 86th Infantry Brigade made dispositions to cover his flank which was by now completely in the air. The infantry, however, refused to stop saying that they had orders to retire to the Hindenburg support line. On this being reported to the G.O.C. 86th Infantry Brigade, the 15th Brigade was ordered to hold the gap with its guns. Lt.-Col. Burne sent out flank observers and turned intense searching and sweeping fire on to the line of canal crossings from Crevecoeur to the lock east of Mont Plaisir Farm, where enemy cavalry and infantry were crossing.

By 09.15 all the retreating infantry had retired through the guns of the 15th Brigade, and the batteries were left 'high and dry' with no infantry in the vicinity.

About 10.40 the leading lines of the enemy infantry came into full view of the 15th Brigade batteries. These lines were followed by small columns and machine guns. All guns of the 15th Brigade engaged the enemy with direct laying and kept them off till about 11.10 by which time parties had worked round the flanks and were within 40 yards of the guns firing kneeling at the gunners.

Lt.-Col. Burne then ordered the withdrawal of the wounded, and the rest of the personnel with breechblocks and sights, to the Hindenburg support line. "L" Battery remained in action to cover the retirement of the others, inflicted much damage on the enemy and prevented heavy casualties occurring to the withdrawing personnel, who had to move up hill, heavily laden, in full view of the enemy for about 600 yards. The "L" Battery personnel then followed the others.

The infantry holding the Hindenburg Support Line were not enterprising and resisted Col. Burne's efforts to persuade them to advance and recapture the guns, but eventually supplied an officer and 20 men with a Lewis gun to accompany him, 2 other artillery artillery officers and 8 N.C.O's and gunners, to the left flank of the gun positions. This party took up a position covering the former 15th Brigade Headquarters and wireless station, did a lot of execution amongst the enemy and enabled the Headquarters party to burn all maps and secret documents. By 14.00 the enemy had worked round the flanks and the whole party withdrew to the Hindenburg Support Line.

Meanwhile the 92nd and D/17 Batteries assisted to hold the enemy in check between Marcoing and Couillet Wood till about 11.30 when the 29th Division counter-attacked, with the support of the guns of the 17th Brigade, drove the enemy back from Les Rues Vertes and established a line of defence.

The remaining batteries (13th, 26th and 2 Batteries of 232nd A.F.A. Brigade) continued to engage the enemy attacking Masnieres and Les Rues Vertes from the north and east.

Shortly after noon Lt.-Col. Murray, Commanding 17th Brigade R.F.A., took over command of the artillery covering the 29th Division front. The artillery was busy during the afternoon firing on enemy attacks, and on advancing batteries, one of which was put completely out of action, whilst several were silenced. Movement on roads also received attention from the guns.

Replenishment of ammunition to the batteries remaining in action was effected by man-handling trolleys on the broad gauge railway running up the Couillet Wood Valley. By this means the reserve at the battery positions was seldom less than 300 rounds per 18-pdr. and 240 rounds per howitzer throughout the day.

The ammunition expenditure during the day was approximately:

15th Brigade R.H.A. 4000 18-pdr. and 1000 4·5″ Howitzer. other batteries—about 1500 per battery.

The two trench mortars, which were in action, as previously mentioned, in Masnieres, had a busy time. Lieut. Gascoyne-Cecil, Commanding X/29 T.M.B., with one of the mortars fired all the available ammunition at the advancing enemy in the first attack in the early morning, then destroyed the piece and reported to the Infantry Brigadier for orders with his personnel. This officer was, unfortunately, killed the same day.

The other mortar (of Z/29 T.M.B.) was used to fire bursts of 5 rounds every half-hour on such portions of Les Rues Vertes as remained in the hands of the enemy, and on other targets. In this way some 100 rounds were expended, but eventually the mortar succumbed to the strain and was thrown into the canal.

All the remaining personnel (5 officers and 15 O.R.) reported to the O.C. Company holding the canal bank and new support line and remained there until ordered to evacuate at midnight on the 1st/2nd December when all ranks of the T.M.Bs. withdrew to Marcoing carrying wounded on stretchers, and thence proceeded to Equancourt on the 2nd.

December 1st.

The artillery under Col. Murray was busy assisting to repel six attacks by the enemy on Masnieres—firing practically continuous barrage fire.

The gallant actions of Captain Booth, D.T.M.O., who succumbed to his wounds, and of Capt. Craib, Commanding V/29 Heavy T.M.B., this day are described in the Honours section of this record.

On the night of the 1st/2nd. the 92nd and D/17 batteries were withdrawn to positions in front of Ribecourt, and one of the batteries of the 232nd Army Brigade was similarly treated.

The 15th Brigade R.H.A. reformed at their wagon lines on the 1st and moved on the following day to Nurlu to refit.

December 2nd.

The artillery covering the 29th Division was reinforced by the 5th Army Brigade R.H.A. with ten 18-pdrs. and the command passed to the C.R.A. 6th Division.

On the night of the 2nd/3rd, the 29th Division was withdrawn from Masnieres and the 13th and 26th Batteries were brought back to positions alongside those of the 92nd and D/17.

December 3rd—4th.

The 17th Bridage R.F.A. retired to positions behind Ribecourt and the front line was withdrawn to the Hindenburg Support Line.

December 12th.

Brig.-Genl. R. M. Johnson assumed command of the 29th D.A. vice Stevenson evacuated wounded to England.

December 14th.

The 17th Brigade R.F.A. changed positions with the 153rd Brigade R.F.A. and had No. 2 Section of the D.A.C. attached to it. The remainder of the 29th D.A. marched to Treux (D.A. H.Q. and D.A.C.) and Buire (15th Brigade).

The 15th Brigade had received a fresh lot of guns and the major part of the lost stores and equipment. On the 15th December all guns of this brigade were calibrated on the Fricourt range.

December 16th—17th.

The 17th Brigade pulled out of action and moved to Beaulincourt near Bapaume.

December 17th.

The 29th D.A. (less 17th Brigade and No. 2 Section D.A.C.) moved by march route in heavy snow to :—

Acheux—D.A. H.Q.
Acheux and Louvencourt—D.A.C. (less No. 2 Section).
Louvencourt—15th Brigade R.H.A.

The march was very difficult owing to the heavy snow drifts and some vehicles had to be left on the road between Acheux and Louvencourt for the night.

December 18th.

The 17th Brigade and No. 2 Section D.A.C. marched to Dernancourt. The roads by this time were like glass and there were no frost cogs available. The whole day was taken up with the march and the A.S.C. wagons did not get into billets till 21.00. The following day was spent in improvising and fitting frost cogs.

December 20th.

The 17th Brigade and No 2 Section D.A.C. rejoined the 29th D.A., moving by march route to Forceville. Weather still very severe, but large labour gangs on the roads had removed the more serious snow-drifts.

December 21st—24th.

The 29th D.A. moved into G.H.Q. reserve about Maresquel (between Hesdin and Montreuil), halting as follows :—

	15th Bde.	17th Bde.	D.A.C.
21st	Gezaincourt.	Doullens.	Gezaincourt.
23rd	Frevent.	Fillievres.	Aubrometz and Boubers Sur Conche
24th	Aubin St. Vaast.	Beaurainville area.	Offin, Hesmond and Loison.

Units spent Xmas and saw the New Year in at the billets they reached on the 24th. The Headquarters of the D.A. established itself at the mansion of Monsieur Guyot at Maresquel, which was the most comfortable of billets, and where Monsieur Guyot showed the officers princely hospitality.

The weather remained continuously severe but the horses by this time were well supplied with frost cogs.

1918.

January 3rd/4th.

The 29th D.A. moved by march route to the Thiembronne area, halting for one night in intermediate billets. The weather was still severe and the first day's march in particular was very hard on No. 1 Company, 29th Divisional Train, which always accompanied the 29th D.A. on its moves.   Having only two heavy draught animals per vehicle, this unit found the slipperiness of the steep hills very trying.   The second day's march was not quite so long as the first and there were few, if any, steep hills.

January 5th to 10th.

Units remained in the Thiembronne area and were busy training.   A practice ceremonial parade was held in the snow as the Divisional Commander had expressed his intention of inspecting the D.A., but before the date fixed for this inspection the whole Division was whisked off to the Second Army to take over a section of the line in the Ypres salient.

January 11th to 13th.

The D. A. moved by march route to the neighbourhood of Poperinghe to join the VIII Corps, making halts in the Renescure and Steenvoorde areas en route.   The camps near Poperinghe into which the batteries moved baffle description.   Even though the units were well accustomed to mud, they certainly experienced something very near the limit in this respect.

January 15th to 18th.

During the period units remained in their muddy lines and sent a working party of 200 daily by light railway to work on the preparation of battle positions in the " Army Battle Zone," a reserve defence line covering Ypres.   The battery positions which were being prepared were in the neighbourhood of St. Jean and Potijze.

January 19th/20th.

The 29th D.A. relieved the 8th D.A. in the Left Sector of the VIII Corps, the infantry of the 29th Division having taken over from the 8th Division a day or two before.   This sector included the apex of the Passchendaele salient.   The battery positions were for the most part in rear of Abraham's Heights (Gravenstafel ridge), the 15th Brigade, R.H.A., covering the right Infantry Brigade, and the 17th Brigade, R.F.A., the left Infantry Brigade.   The 17th Brigade had its 92nd Battery very much to the left flank, its gun position being actually in the next Corps area.

The T.M.Bs. took over two mortars only in action.   These were placed for the defence of the Bellevue line and were not sited to cover the front line.

The 86th Army F.A. Brigade became part of the artillery under command of the C.R.A. but was in positions covering the Divisional Reserve Line.

The positions occupied by the 15th and 17th Brigades were far from pleasant.   A tunnelling party from a Tunnelling Co. R.E. was working to provide tunnelled dugouts for the personnel of the batteries but only one—for the D/17 position—was ready for occupation.   Other batteries had, as a rule, one small German "pill-box " for accommodation.   The gun positions were about as bad in every respect as could be, but little else could be expected in the country which had been churned up into a morass by our shell fire in the offensive of the latter half of 1917.   O.Ps. were practically non-existent.

January 21st—February 12th.

During the six weeks that the 29th D.A. was in action, there is little to note from the point of view of actual operations. The enemy shelling of the area gradually died down till, at the end of the period, it was not very serious, except in certain well-known spots. Batteries were very busy improving their battery positions. The Trench Mortar Batteries provided a large permanent party for salvage operations and also put two 6″ Newton mortars into action covering the front line. The supply of ammunition to these mortars was no light matter, as every round had to be carried by hand about 1½ miles along a somewhat " dicky " duck-board track which could only be used at night and was usually kept under shell fire by the enemy even then.

The salvage party mentioned above made a great haul. On taking over in this sector we had been told that there were no more guns to be salved, but during the six weeks this party salved fourteen 18 pdrs and six 4·5″ howitzers. The total salvage secured by the 29th Divisional Artillery in the period included 9,327 complete 18 pdr. rounds, 3,507 4·5″ howitzer shells, 177 60 pdr. shells, 227 6″ shells, 38,366 18 pdr. brass cartridge cases and 214 boxes of S.A.A. Yet so great was the amount of derelict ammunition strewn all over the country that the amount salved was a negligeable proportion of the whole.

On the 4th February the Trench Mortar Batteries were reorganized. Heavy T.M.Bs. were henceforth to be Corps Troops and all R.G.A. personnel serving in the old T.M.Bs. was transferred to these new Heavy T.M.Bs., whilst the residue was formed into two Medium T.M.Bs. (X/29 and Y/29). As a matter of fact the new X/29 was made up for the most part from the old V/29 (Heavy), whilst the other three batteries formed the new Y/29.

This was the very last reorganization in the D.A., which now consisted of :—

Headquarters.

15th Brigade, R.H.A. (H.Q., " B," "L," Warwickshire and 460th (How.) Batteries).

17th Brigade, R.F.A. (13th, 26th, 92nd and D/17 (How.) Batteries).

X/29 and Y/29 Medium T.M.Bs. (each with six 6″ Newton Trench Mortars).

29th Divisional Ammunition Column :

Headquarters.
No. 1 Section.
No. 2 Section.
S.A.A. Section.

But little progress was made with the construction of O.Ps. Everyone, from the Corps Commander downwards, was most anxious for the construction of an O.P. in Passchendaele itself, which was the only place from which any view of the country in front of the apex of the salient could be obtained ; but there were many difficulties, and not even by the time that the salient was evacuated in April had any brains devised a practical scheme for the construction of a really satisfactory O.P. there.

On February 5th the 119th Army F.A. Brigade relieved the 86th Army F.A. Brigade. It did not bring any guns into action but provided parties for work on positions, communications and O.Ps. for the defence of the Divisional Reserve Line.

February 13th to March 7th.

The 29th D.A. was relieved by the 8th D.A. on the 12th/13th February and withdrew to wagon lines in the neighbourhood of Poperinghe, the infantry of the Division having been relieved by the 8th Division a day or two previously.

The wagon lines occupied by units were a very great deal better than those occupied in January.

During the whole of this period a daily party of 200 worked on the positions in the Army Battle Zone, but otherwise it was a period of rest. An inter-battery "knock-out" football competition was played for medals presented by the C.R.A. These medals were struck from a special die. The competition evoked the keenest interest and the final between the Warwickshire and "B" batteries had to be replayed before the former was victorious by the odd goal obtained during an "extra ten minutes each way." Subsequently a six-a-side football competition for a 170 kilo pig was won by the D/17 Battery team.

On March 6th the Divisional Commander (Genl. Sir Beauvoir de Lisle) inspected the D.A. in the square at Poperinghe. Each battery in turn formed up on the square, received the inspecting officer with a general salute, and after being inspected moved off to make room for the next. The Divisional band was in attendance and played the R.A. Regimental march during the salute of each battery in turn. The Divisional Commander expressed himself as very pleased with the parade and with the staff arrangements which ensured that there was no pause and that the time table was strictly adhered to. After seeing the last battery file past, General de Lisle rode to a point about half a mile north of the town where the D.A.C. ranked past him. The weather was kind.

March 8th—April 7th.

On March 7th/8th the 29th D.A. again relieved the 8th D.A., the infantry relief, as before, having been completed a day or two previously. The same positions as before were occupied. The trench mortar batteries put another two mortars into the front system.

The Warwickshire battery, less one section which had always been in a forward position close to Bellevue, was moved into a position on the forward slopes of the Gravenstafel ridge. The new position offered great advantages from the point of view of defence as it enabled fire to be brought to bear on a considerable area which would have been dead ground to the other batteries, in case of a break through by the enemy. It was, however, in view from the enemy's lines and the battery therefore had orders only to open fire in the case of an S.O.S. signal being sent up or in any other emergency. The position was thus never discovered by the enemy.

On March 11th 600 of the enemy attacked us at about 6 o'clock in the morning but were easily repulsed.   Both artillery and machine guns did considerable havoc amongst them.

General Sir Beauvoir de Lisle now left the Division on promotion to command an Army Corps and was succeeded by General Cayley who had done most of his service in the war in the Division, both as commanding the Worcestershire Regt. and afterwards as G.O.C. 88th Infantry Brigade.

Between the 11th and 20th March the hostile artillery became very much more active, with the object, no doubt, of distracting attention from the right of the British Army line where his great offensive was shortly to be launched.   It is interesting to note, however, that this outburst deceived none in the Passchendaele salient.

On the night of the 19th/20th March the enemy put a heavy gas concentration on the battery areas, but the "gas discipline" was good, the dugouts, which by this time were more numerous, had been carefully made · gas-proof, and we consequently had no casualties.

On March 15th the Headquarters of the 17th Brigade moved up to Kansas House, whence they were in a much better position than formerly to control the batteries in action.

On March 22nd the 15th Brigade, R.H.A., assisted the 33rd Division on our right in a successful raid.

On April 4th all batteries assisted in a raid by the 87th Infantry Brigade on Teall Cotts.   The raiders reached their objective without difficulty but found no enemy there.

The wagon lines of batteries and the D.A.C. were situated in the neighbourhood of Vlamertinghe.   A great deal of labour was expended on the standings and in the erection of huts.   By the end of March all these lines were quite comfortable.   Lt.-Col. Spedding, commanding the D.A.C., took immense pains with his lines and with the cultivation of the shell-torn ground in and around his camp.   It was most unfortunate that all this labour proved eventually to be wasted as the subsequent withdrawal of our line of defence almost to the ramparts of Ypres brought all this wagon line area much too close to the enemy's lines for it to be kept under cultivation.

April 8th to May 15th.

On April 8th/9th the 29th Division was relieved in the Passchendaele salient by the 41st Division, but left the D.A. behind to cover the infantry of the latter.   On the 10th April the S.A.A. Section went off after the infantry of the Division which moved down by bus to the neighbourhood of Bailleul, where the infantry were heavily engaged in stemming the advance of the enemy who had broken through our line from Armentieres to the south.

Almost immediately after the departure of the infantry of the 29th Division, it was decided to withdraw from the Passchendaele salient.   The general scheme as far as the artillery was concerned was to leave only one gun per battery in action for the night of the final infantry withdrawal, to bring back as much as possible of the ammunition to the Army Battle Zone, and to keep up the normal expenditure of ammunition so as to give as little indication of the impending withdrawal as possible to the enemy. It was found necessary, also, to leave the 15 pdr. "anti-tank" guns in position, owing to the waste of labour which would otherwise have been expended in the saving of these comparatively useless pieces.   There were two of these in our sector, which had been placed in position quite recently. One of these had to be taken up to its position in pieces.   The withdrawal arrangements included the destruction of these guns at the last moment.

In accordance with this plan, the 13th and Warwickshire Batteries (less 1 gun apiece) and 1 section of the 460th Battery were withdrawn after dark on the 10th April to positions covering the Battle Zone.   The remainder were withdrawn to similar positions the following night, the movement being completed by 05.00 on the 12th.   There then remained in action only one gun or howitzer per battery covering the front line and the two anti-tank guns.

On the 12th April, the 119th Army Brigade, which had been covering the right sector of the Corps front with the assistance of two howitzer batteries, A/49 and B/49 newly arrived from England, was withdrawn for service on the battle front to the south of us.   A/49 and B/49 were then attached to the 15th Brigade, R.H.A., which took over from the 119th Brigade the duty of covering the right sector.

On April 14th/15th the main line of resistance was drawn back to about a mile east of Ypres, whilst two lines in advance of this were held as outpost lines, viz:—the original front line, covered by three 18 pdrs. and five 15 pdr. anti-tank guns.   The increase in the number of anti-tank guns was due to our having taken over *both* sectors of the Corps front.   The rear outpost line was on the Army Battle Zone and was covered by the 17th Brigade, R.F.A. and B/49 Howitzer Battery.   The 15th Brigade, R.H.A., and A/49 Howitzer Battery moved back this night to positions west of the canal to cover the main line of resistance.

The following evening (15th April) the 17th Brigade, less the 13th Battery and 1 section of D/17, moved back to positions west of the canal.

During the 14th and 15th the salving of ammunition from the forward area was carried out at high pressure.   The 29th D.A. during these two days brought back 88,000 rounds of 18 pdr. and 4·5″ howitzer ammunition from the area in front of the Steenbeek.

On the night of the 16th/17th the forward outpost line was withdrawn through the rear outpost line.   The three 18 pdrs. and one of the anti-tank guns were withdrawn, the remainder being destroyed. The 3 medium T.Ms. were also destroyed in situ.   Captain T. J. Cunnison was in charge of parties left to destroy dugouts and ammunition, with his headquarters at Kansas House.   These parties all withdrew safely with the outpost line.   D.A.H.Q. moved with the 41st Divisional Headquarters from the Canal Bank to Vlamertinghe Chateau.

On the following days each brigade sent sections forward by day into the Battle Zone to snipe the advancing enemy, and some excellent targets were obtained.

On the 21st April "L" moved forward to a position near St. Jean to cover the outpost line.   On the following day the two howitzer batteries, A/49 and B/49, were transferred to the 66th D.A. on our left. From the 21st to the 23rd, Ypres was heavily shelled by the enemy with Yellow Cross (mustard) gas shell. On the 23rd April the T.M.Bs. commenced digging defensive emplacements, but on the 25th the enemy made a successful advance to the south of us and captured Kemmel Hill the result of which was that we were ordered to draw in our horns still further on the 26th. On this date all guns east of the canal, i.e., "L," 13th and 1 section of D/17, were withdrawn before dusk to positions about Goldfish Chateau—Machine Gun Farm, between Ypres and Vlamertinghe, and that night the remaining batteries joined them in the same area to cover the new main line of resistance. The outpost line was this night withdrawn to the line White Chateau—Potijze, and the main line of resistance became the Canal (north of Ypres) and thence a line within a few hundred yards of the Menin Gate.

D.A.H.Q. moved with the 41st Divisional Headquarters to " Ten Elms " camp.

The wagon lines of batteries had many changes during the month. The D.A.C. on the 15th moved back to lines on the Poperinghe-Elverdinghe road, and on the 25th movel to Hamhoek to make room for the battery wagon lines which then all moved into the area north of Poperinghe.

Much time was now spent in the reconnaissance of positions to cover the various lines of defence in case of a further withdrawal being ordered, but actually the line was never brought any further west. The VIII Corps moved away about the middle of the month and the II Corps took over from them. The II Corps had been for a long time past situated in La Lovie Chateau, but on the 29th April moved back and the H.Q. 41st Division with the H.Q. 29th D.A. moved into the Chateau. On this date the T.M.Bs. were temporarily disbanded and the personnel distributed amongst other units.

For the remainder of this period, things were fairly quiet on our front. On the 12th/13th May the 17th Brigade, R.F.A., was relieved by the 162nd Brigade of the 41st Division and marched down to the XV Corps area to join the 29th Division. On the 15th May the H.Q. D.A. were relieved at La Lovie Chateau by the H.Q. 41st D.A., and on that and the following night the 15th Brigade, R.H.A., was relieved by the 190th Brigade, R.F.A.

It is no exaggeration to say that all ranks of the 29th D.A. were genuinely sorry to part company with the 41st Division. Thanks to the never faily courtesy of the Divisional Commander, Sir Sidney Lawford, and his Brigadiers, staff and commanders, co-operation between the artillery and infantry was made delightfully easy, pleasant and effective.

May 16th to June 30th.

On the morning of the 16th May H.Q. D.A. took over from the H.Q. 38th D.A. which was covering the 29th Division in the La Motte sector of the XV Corps with the 38th, 64th and 119th Army Brigades, R.F.A. The following day the 15th Brigade, R.H.A., and the D.A.C. marched down to the neighbourhood of Lynde.

On the 17th/18th May the 17th Brigade relieved the 38th Army

Brigade in positions west of and close to Nieppe Forest, and on the 20th/21st the 15th Brigade, R.H.A., relieved the 64th Army Brigade in positions more to the north. The 119th Army Brigade remained in action in the centre.

On the 26th May the artillery supported a raid by the 1st Battalion K.O.S.B. on Tern Farm. Lt.-Col. Beatty Pownall, commanding the Battalion, expressed his appreciation of the excellence of this barrage.

On the night of June 2nd/3rd a barrage was fired in support of a most successful attack by the 86th Infantry Brigade on Lug and Ankle Farms. Brig.-Genl. Cheape, commanding the Brigade, sent the most eulogistic letter to the artillery on the subject of the barrage (see Appendix III).

On May 27th the H.Q. 15th Brigade, R.H.A., established its headquarters at Locust Farm, and assumed command of the batteries of its brigade. Up to this time these had been split up under the command of the Os.C. 17th and 119th Brigades.

On June 4th, as Locust Farm had been heavily shelled and the Brigade H.Q. had lost some men thereby, the 15th Brigade H.Q. moved to a cottage near the La Motte-Hazebrouck canal.

On June 14th, whilst the Worcestershire Regiment was carrying out a raid on Tern Farm with artillery support, the enemy managed to recapture Lug and Ankle Farms.

On the night of the 17th/18th June the batteries of the 17th Brigade moved forward to positions north of the forest and the 148th and 149th Brigades of the 30th D.A. came into action for an attack which was to be carried out by the 29th Division and the 5th Division. As the latter Division was in the First Army, it was arranged that the attack should be carried out under the orders of the G.O.C. XI Corps. It was decided, however, that the 31st Division should replace the 29th Division for this attack, which was accordingly postponed. The 148th and 149th Brigades were, therefore, withdrawn from action on the 19th/20th.

Between the 20th and 22nd June the infantry of the 31st Division relieved the 29th Division in the trenches, Lug Farm having been recaptured previously by the 29th Division.

On the 24th/25th the 28th Army F.A. Brigade relieved the 119th Army Brigade, R.F.A.

On the 26th/27th June Ankle Farm was recaptured from the enemy and the Brigades of the 30th D.A. came into action once more for the attack by the 31st and 5th Divisions.

On the 28th June this attack took place and was entirely successful, our line being advanced about a mile at the centre point and the 31st Division alone capturing upwards of 250 prisoners and many machine guns and trench mortars. The artillery covering the 31st Division attack was under the C.R.A. 29th Division and consisted of the 29th and 30th Divisional Artilleries and the 28th Army Brigade, R.F.A. The trench mortar batteries, which had been partially reformed on May 13th, assisted in the initial stages of the attack with the two T.Ms. which could fire on the attack zone.

On June 30th the command of the artillery covering the 31st Division passed to the C.R.A. 31st Division.

July 1st to July 31st.

On July 3rd the Brigades of the 29th D.A. were relieved by the Brigades of the 31st D.A. and marched back with the D.A.C. to the Wardrecques area to rest.   The 17th Brigade, however, had to return on the 8th to take part in the 9th Division attack on Merriss, which took place on the 19th, and the Brigade did not return to rest till the 21st.

On July 11th a Divisional Horse Show was held, in which "B" won the prize for the best gun team and the Warwickshire Battery the N.C.Os. jumping.

On July 22nd the D.A. moved by march route to Coin Perdu, N.E. of the Clairmarais Forest, to join the Xth Corps.   On the 25th a working party of 4 officers and 100 O.R. proceeded to Boeschepe to prepare positions for a proposed attack north of Bailleul, and No. 1 Section of the D.A.C. moved up to the neighbourhood of Caestre. The attack scheme, however, was subsequently abandoned and both working parties and No. 1 Section returned to their units on the 30th.

On the 31st July the D.A. was inspected at a ceremonial parade by the Divisional Commander.   An excellent field was available for the purpose, enabling the walk and trot past and advance in review order to be successfully carried out.   The weather was excellent— in fact the parade was a great success from every point of view.   In the afternoon of the same day a small race meeting was held; this also was most successful.   The Staff Captain, Captain G. G. Shone, was wounded in the afternoon by a rifle bullet whilst driving in the car on Cassel hill.   As no aeroplanes were up at the time it is presumed that the bullet was a ricochet from some rifle range.

August 1st—September 13th.

On the nights of August 1st/2nd and 2nd/3rd the 29th D.A. relieved the 1st Australian D.A. in positions covering the Strazeele sector.   The infantry relief took place at the same time and at 10.00 on the 3rd the D.A.H.Q. moved to St. Sylvestre Cappel with the 29th Divisional Headquarters.   The trench mortar positions taken over were mostly defensive ones.   The 64th Army Brigade, R.F.A., was in action in the sector and came under the orders of the C.R.A. on the latter assuming command of the artillery covering the Divisional front.   Wagon lines of batteries were in the area between Hondeghem and Hazebrouck, except those of the 64th Brigade which shortly afterwards moved to the east of Hazebrouck.

On August 14th most of the battery wagon lines were moved forward and on the 15th/16th the 174th Brigade, R.F.A., of the 39th D.A. came into action in forward positions, whilst the great majority of batteries already in action also went into forward positions in preparation for the impending attack on Hoegenacker Hill and Outtersteene.

On the 18th August the 9th Division captured Hoegenacker Hill. The whole of the artillery covering the 9th and 29th Divisions assisted in this operation; the 15th Brigade, R.H.A., took part in the creeping barrage, the 64th Army Brigade fired an enfilade barrage 100 yards in advance of the creeper, whilst the 17th and 174th Brigades formed a rolling barrage right across the front of attack and afterwards formed part of the protective barrage.

The 87th Infantry Brigade crossed the Meteren Becque and exploited the success of the 9th Division attack, capturing the village and ridge of Outtersteene. Our guns formed a barrage which swept from west to east and a smoke screen was formed by D/64 Howitzer Battery.

A feature of the whole operations was the excellent view obtained of all movements of the infantry from the artillery O.Ps. and the celerity with which, as a result, news of the progress of the infantry was conveyed to the artillery and infantry commanders.

On the 19th August the 86th Infantry Brigade and the 31st Division on their right advanced in order to straighten out the line to conform with the successful advance of the previous day. Our guns fired a creeping barrage and the following message was afterwards received from Brig.-Genl. Cheape.—"My infantry wish to express their admiration for the most perfect barrage which you put up today during our attack. There were no shorts and it was like walking behind a wall."

Our trench mortars helped considerably in both days' operations.

Captures by the 29th Division alone included 450 prisoners, 100 machine guns, 3 field guns and many trench mortars.

The 174th Brigade, R.F.A., withdrew from action on the 22nd/23rd. On the 27th the 64th Army Brigade assisted the 40th Division, which had relieved the 31st Division on our right, in an attack.

On the 29th August D.A.H.Q. moved up with Divisional Headquarters to Borre, and the same evening one battery from each brigade, viz:—460th, 13th and B/64, was withdrawn to wagon lines for a rest.

On the 30th August the enemy started their withdrawal, leaving rear guards only to dispute our advance. "B" and "L" Batteries, under Lt.-Col. Burne, formed part of the advanced guard under Brig.-Genl. Jackson, which by evening had reached the line Gaul Farm—Noote Boom—Mont de Lille. The rest of the D.A. brought teams up to their gun lines in readiness to advance when required.

On the 31st August the enemy continued his retirement, our advanced guard troops keeping touch with his rear guard which attempted to hold up our advance by a screen of machine guns. This local resistance was largely overcome by the bold use of single guns at short range, thus enabling the infantry to rush in without casualties. On one occasion, for instance, a gun of "B" Battery engaged a snipers' house at 50 yards range, blowing the roof off with the first shot. These forward guns were well handled by Major Sumpter on this and succeeding days. The advanced guard artillery was increased by the addition of the Warwickshire Battery, whilst the 119th Army Brigade, which had been operating with the 9th Division on our left and was in action east of Bailleul, also assisted materially.

On September 1st, the 88th Infantry Brigade came into the front line on the left of the 87th and was supported by the 119th Army Brigade. The Division formed an advanced report centre at Travers

Farm, south of Bailleul. By evening the infantry of the two brigades had reached the line De Seule—Steenwerck—Westhof Farm.

On September 2nd the advance was continued. The 460th Battery came up into action, so that the 15th Brigade, R.H.A., was now complete again. In the evening the 87th Infantry Brigade was relieved by the 92nd Infantry Brigade of the 31st Division.

On September 3rd the 86th Infantry Brigade came into the line between the 88th and 92nd Brigades. At 14.00 orders were issued for the 17th Brigade, R.F.A., and both Brigades of the 9th D.A. (50th and 51st) to move into action near Neuve Eglise to support an attack on Hill 63 and Ploegstreet the following morning. By 19.00 all these batteries were in action. D.A.H.Q. moved to Westhof Farm so as to be in close touch with the artillery brigades supporting the attack.

On September 4th the 88th Infantry Brigade commenced their attack on Hill 63 at 08.00, whilst the 86th Infantry Brigade on their right attacked Ploegstreet. The 15th Brigade, R.H.A., was not available to support the attack as it was covering the 92nd Infantry Brigade. Owing to the paucity of guns, all the 18 pdrs. of the available brigades, viz:—17th, 50th, 51st and 119th, formed the creeping barrage for the most important portion of the attack, i.e., that on Hill 63, whilst the 86th Infantry Brigade had D/17 Howitzer Battery only to support them.

Hill 63 was captured without difficulty, but the 86th Infantry Brigade made little progress—not unnaturally seeing that they had little or no artillery support. At 15.00, however, this brigade made a successful advance with the support of the 17th and 119th Brigades, R.F.A.

At dusk the Brigades of the 9th D.A. were withdrawn to the Meteren area and we were informed that the 64th Army Brigade, which had not been allowed to advance with us, had been transferred to the II Corps.

On the 5th September the 29th D.A. and 119th Army Brigade fired a barrage at 15.00 in support of an attack by the 92nd Infantry Brigade which was partially successful, the line Soyer Farm—Oosthove Farm—Pontceau being reached. That night the 31st Division completely relieved the 29th Division, and on the morning of the 6th the C.R.A. 31st Division took over from the C.R.A. 29th Division.

On September 13th, the Brigades of the 29th D.A. withdrew from action to the Strazeele area.

14th to 27th September.

The 29th Division now moved north to join the II Corps prior to taking part in the attack by the Belgian Army and a portion of the Second Army, between Ypres and the sea.

On the 15th/16th September the D.A. moved to the Droglandt area, H.Q.D.A. to Houtkerque. On the 17th the brigades sent working parties to Ypres to prepare positions, the 15th Brigade positions being about the Menin road east of Ypres, whilst those of the 17th Brigade were in Ypres itself, between the Dixmude and Menin Gates.

P

On the 20th September the 29th Division took over the line from the Zillebeke Lake to the Menin Road, D.H.Q. moving to Vogeltje convent.   The artillery defence of the line was entrusted to the 113th Army Brigade, R.F.A., which was already in action and which was preparing battle positions in Ypres between the Menin and Lille Gates.   On the following day the 15th and 17th Brigades moved up to the Peselhoek area.

On the 26th September, an episode unique in the annals of the D.A. occurred.   Two N.C.Os. of the D.A.C., sent out by Lt.-Col. Spedding to reconnoitre roads for the advance, passed through our front line on the Zillebeke road without discovering any of our posts. On seeing a pillbox, one of them, Corporal Shadgett, went inside to enquire the way but found to his surprise that the occupants were Huns!   Luckily, perhaps, for him he happened to stand in front of the rifle rack, in which all the rifles except one were stacked.   That one was being cleaned by its owner at the table in the pillbox. Nothing daunted by the fact that his revolver wasn't even loaded, Corporal Shadgett drew it and covered the eight occupants of the pillbox, and shouted to his companion, Bombr. Almond, to come in.

The Huns surrendered and were marched back to Vlamertinghe by the two N.C.Os., where they were handed over to the prisoners' cage there.   Not even on the way back, however, did these N.C.Os. see a sign of any British troops!   For this action Corporal Shadgett was awarded the D.C.M. whilst Bombr. Almond received the Military Medal.

On the night of the 26th/27th, all batteries of the 17th Brigade (less D/17), the 460th Battery, and one section each of the 18 pdr. batteries of the 15th Brigade, R.H.A., moved into their battle positions.   The following night all remaining guns and howitzers, including those of the 113th Army Brigade, took up their battle positions, whilst Divisional Headquarters moved up to Goldfish Chateau on the 27th.   The D.A.C. moved from Droglandt to Peselhoek and all battery wagon lines to the area between Vlamertinghe and Ypres.

September 28th to October 4th.

The attack by the Belgian Army, with the II Corps (9th and 29th Divisions) on their right, and the 14th Division of the neighbouring Corps on our right, was launched at 05.30 on the 28th September. The Belgian Army had a three hours' preliminary bombardment of the enemy's trenches but our artillery was silent till zero hour.

The attack was a complete success.   Howitzers engaged the enemy's "main line of resistance" with gas and smoke, whilst all the 18 pdrs. and some of the howitzers formed the creeping barrage.   At 08.30 the barrage ceased and batteries commenced to advance.   The difficulties were immense.   The Menin road from Hooge Chateau up to the crest of the hill was absolutely impassable for wheels, and the only possible line of advance was by a very much damaged plank road which skirted round the old demesne of Hooge Chateau.   Even by this road it was not an easy matter to ride a single horse along it, so that it was almost miraculous that all three batteries of the 113th Army Brigade, the 13th and 92nd Batteries of the 17th Brigade, and one section each of "B," "L" and the 460th Batteries, had success-fully negotiated this difficult route by nightfall and were in action on the far side of the crest, covering the infantry which had reached a line well in advance of Gheluveldt.

The personnel of the T.M.Bs. on this and succeeding days was employed in the repair of roads under the R.E.

On the 29th September all batteries which had advanced fired a barrage at 07.00 in support of an attack by the 88th Infantry Brigade against the high ground east of the Kruiseecke cross-roads. The forward batteries all advanced later, except the 113th Brigade which was ordered to stand fast by the II Corps pending transfer else-where. The 13th and 92nd Batteries actually came into action about the Kruiseecke cross-roads but withdrew again after dusk. No more batteries passed across the "morass" this day, as there were already quite as many guns forward as could possibly be kept supplied with ammunition until the routes were improved, but the Menin Road was ·made available for light traffic by the evening. Meanwhile the reserve batteries were concentrated about Birr cross-roads.

On the 30th September the infantry advanced as far as the outskirts of Gheluwe, and all batteries of the 29th D.A. and 113th Army Brigade were in action east of Gheluveldt by the evening. During the day a section of the 92nd Battery under Lieut. Beaver advanced close to Gheluwe under the impression that our infantry had captured the village. These guns had to be withdrawn at dusk as they were too exposed.

The weather of these three days was as vile as it well could be. It scarcely ceased raining and the ammunition supply was carried out under the greatest difficulties. The personnel of the H.Q. of the 17th Brigade turned a captured $10^{c/m}$ gun round and shelled Menin.

On 1st October Lt.-Col. E. R. Burne, commanding the 15th Brigade, R.H.A., was killed whilst on a reconnaissance to ascertain the exact whereabouts of the most advanced infantry, with Brig.-Genl. Jackson. D.A.H.Q., which had moved with Divisional H.Q. to Fort Garry on the 29th ult., now moved up to Gheluveldt.

On 2nd October all batteries fired in support of an attack on Gheluwe, but the attack was not a success.

On the night of the 3rd/4th October the infantry of the 29th Division were relieved by the 41st Division with a view to side-step-ping to the left after a short rest. On the 4th, the 29th D.A. and 113th Army Brigade moved north to positions about Dadizeele, H.Q. D.A. to Becelaere. As these were battle positions for the next big attack, most of the personnel was withdrawn to wagon lines which were in the neighbourhood of Becelaere.

October 5th to 13th.

On the 5th/6th October the 86th Infantry Brigade relieved the 9th and 36th Divisions on the portion of front allotted to the 29th Division for the next attack west of Ledeghem. The rest of this period was spent in preparations for this attack. A considerable number of casualties was caused in the wagon lines by the enemy's harassing fire at night, and the 15th Brigade moved their lines back to Ypres for a few days.

The trench mortar batteries placed 4 mortars in action at Ledeghem station and were also busy placing captured 5·9″ and 4·2″ howitzers into position behind Dadizeele under the direction of Lt.-Col. Spedding, to assist in the forthcoming attack.

On the night of the 13th/14th all batteries were in their battle positions, including A/113 which was to act under the 15th Brigade and A/28 which was to be attached to the 17th Brigade, whilst the D.A.C. moved up to Becelaere.

October 14th to 25th.

On October 14th the general attack was resumed at 05.35 along the whole line. As far as the 29th Division was concerned, the 88th Infantry Brigade was on the right and the 86th on the left. After firing the barrage, the 17th Brigade, R.F.A., worked with the 88th Infantry Brigade, and the 15th Brigade, R.H.A., with the 86th. There was absolutely no wind in the early morning and the smoke used in the barrage impeded the infantry considerably in the initial stages of the advance and interfered with the reconnaissance of forward battery positions. The attack was nevertheless entirely successful and all batteries moved forward during the course of the morning. A/28 and A/113 rejoined their respective brigades after the conclusion of the barrage in the early morning, and these brigades became Corps Reserve.

The Trench Mortars at Ledeghem station fired 100 rounds in the opening stages of the barrage and the T.M. personnel was also busy firing the captured howitzers in advance of the creeping barrage.

On the 15th the attack was resumed by the 87th Infantry Brigade at 09.00 under a barrage fired by the two artillery brigades. Salines was taken and by noon the infantry had reached the line of the Ingelmunstre—Courtrai railway. On the conclusion of the barrage the 92nd Battery moved forward in close support of the K.O.S.B. on the right whilst "B" supported the S.W.B. on the left. By nightfall the infantry had reached the crossings of the Heulebeek at Watermolen and old mill. Two batteries of each artillery brigade covered the front at close range whilst the remainder were close behind but not in action. D.A.H.Q. moved in the afternoon to Muselhoek, and the D.A.C. to Ledeghem, where the ammunition refilling point had been established. That night the infantry pushed on to the River Lys between Courtrai and Cuerne.

In the two days' fighting the 9th and 29th Divisions captured some 2.500 prisoners and 67 guns.

On the 16th October it poured with rain. All batteries were in action to cover the forcing of the passage of the Lys, all bridges over which had been destroyed by the enemy. The 113th Army Brigade was placed under the orders of the C.R.A. once more and came into action early on the 18th. On the 17th D.A.H.Q. moved to Gulleghem. On the 16th the D.A.C. moved to Barakken and on the 18th to Heule.

On the night of the 19th/20th October the infantry forced the passage of the Lys, the only artillery action during the night being the bombardment of the Courtrai—Harlebeke railway for two hours during this operation.

At 06.00 a creeping barrage was fired by all batteries in support of the advance of the infantry from the river in a S.E. direction.

By 08.00 the pontoon bridge over the river was completed and the 113th Army Brigade moved across. The first of its three batteries was in action beyond Staceghem at 10.15 and the other two were in action by noon. The 15th and 17th Brigades followed the 113th Brigade across the river. At 15.00 the 113th Brigade advanced again and assisted in the capture of the St. Louis hill. D.A.H.Q. moved to Staceghem.

On the 21st a creeping barrage was fired at 15.30 for the 86th Infantry Brigade which captured the strong position at Banhout Bosch. All batteries were then ordered forward and were in action ready to fire a barrage for the attack of the 87th Infantry Brigade at 09.00 the following morning. The D.A.C. moved to Staceghem.

On the 22nd the batteries fired what may be described as a "lifting bombardment of selected areas" in support of the attack of the 87th Infantry Brigade, the frontage being too great to admit of an effective creeping barrage being formed. The attack was only partially successful, and "B" R.H.A. and A/113 which advanced after firing this bombardment were left too close to the front line of the infantry, in fact were almost in it, and were withdrawn by order of the C.R.A. after nightfall.

On the 23rd October the 41st Division took over the front. The 15th and 113th Brigades were withdrawn from action in the morning but the 17th Brigade waited till relieved by the 187th Brigade in the evening. The 113th Army Brigade was then taken away and placed under the 36th Division.

On the following day the 15th and 17th Brigades went up into action on the 9th Division front to cover an attack by that Division on the 25th but were withdrawn to their wagon lines again on the conclusion of their barrage tasks that day.

During this period (September 29th to October 25th) the following casualties occurred :—

	OFFICERS.		OTHER RANKS.		ANIMALS.	
	Killed.	Wounded.	Killed.	Wounded.	Killed.	Evacuated.
15th. Bde. R.H.A.	1	2*	12	46	70	56
17th. Bde. R.F.A.	1	6*	13	76	95	60
29th. D.A.C.	-	-	4	7	27	35
TOTAL	2	8	28	129	192	151

* includes 1 Officer who subsequently died of wounds.

October 26th to November 6th.

After one day's rest in their wagon lines the D.A. marched south on the 27th October to the Roncq area where they again came under the XV Corps. A practice ceremonial parade was held and on the 3rd November the D.A. moved into Turcoing. A ceremonial parade for the G.O.C. XV Corps which had been arranged for the 5th November had to be cancelled as it chose to pour with rain all day. On the following day orders were received to go into the line near St. Genois under the X Corps.

November 7th to 11th.

On the 7th/8th November the D.A. moved to the Tromboek area and D.A.H.Q. went with Divisional Headquarters to Polleghem. The 29th Division took over their portion of the line prior to the forcing of the passage of the Scheldt. The front of the division was temporarily covered by the 38th Army Brigade which was already in action, and the 29th D.A. got ammunition up to battle positions. These positions were, however, never used as the enemy did not wait for the attack, and on the 9th our infantry crossed the river in the early morning and advanced some miles on the far side. No artillery was able to cross this day owing to lack of bridges but the 17th Brigade and No. 2 Section of the D.A.C. was moved up to St. Genois preparatory to crossing the next morning. The 38th Army Brigade was transferred to the left (30th) Division of the Corps.

On the 10th November the 17th Brigade crossed the river and billetted that night about Beaureux. The 15th Brigade and H.Q. and No. 1 Section of the D.A.C. moved to St. Genois. D.A.H.Q. moved in the evening with Divisional H.Q. to Celles.

On the 11th November the 17th Brigade was delayed in its further advance by the destruction of the crossings of the small river Rhosnes. Some tools and rope were dropped by arrangement by an aeroplane near the stream so as to allow the gunners to make a bridge but the 13th Battery which actually crossed this bridge only did so a short time before 11.00 when the armistice came into operation. D.A.H.Q. moved to Dergneau, but there were no other movements other than that of the 96th Army Brigade which moved to St. Genois and came under the orders of the C.R.A.

November 12th to 17th.

This period was spent in preparation for the march into Germany. Orders were received that batteries would be reduced to four guns for the march and the odd sections were therefore transferred to the XIX Corps on the 17th. On the 14th the 96th Army Brigade was transferred away and the 38th Army Brigade put under the orders of the C.R.A. for the advance. On the same date D.A. H.Q. moved to Flobecq, where the 38th Brigade was already billetted ,and units of the D.A. moved into the Wodecq area. The two mobile T.Ms. of the T.M.Bs. had been attached to brigades on the 6th November and were now ordered to accompany these brigades into Germany, X/29 being with the 15th Brigade, and Y/29 with the 17th.

The march into Germany.

The 29th Division was fortunate enough to be chosen as one of the leading Divisions in the march and started off on the 18th November. It formed part of the II Corps, having been retransferred to the latter a few days before commencing the march. A Cavalry Division was one day's march ahead until Cologne was reached, and the order of Divisions in the leading line, from left to right was 9th Division, 29th Division—both of the II Corps—and the 1st and 2nd Canadian Divisions of the Canadian Corps.

The 29th Division was split up into four groups for billetting and command purposes, each Infantry Brigadier and the C.R.A. being in command of a group. The 13th Battery was detached from the D.A. Group to the 88th Infantry Brigade, and "B" R.H.A. to the 87th Infantry Brigade. The D.A. Group consisted of :—

> Headquarters 29th Divisional Artillery.
> 15th Brigade, R.H.A. (less "B" Battery).
> > Headquarters.
> > "L," Warwickshire and 460th Batteries.
> > X/29 T.M.B.
> 17th Brigade, R.F.A. (less 13th Battery).
> > Headquarters.
> > 26th, 92nd and D/17 Batteries.
> > Y/29 T.M.B.
> 29th Divisional Ammunition Column.
> > Headquarters.
> > Nos. 1 and 2 Sections.
> > S.A.A. Section.
> 29th Divisional Train.
> > No. 1 Company.

The rate of progress of the march was necessarily slow until the railways had been repaired and were able to function. Luckily the weather was good, as severe weather must have delayed the march considerably through the Ardennes, where some of the gradients were severe.

The D.A. Group marched to the following areas on the dates stated :—

Nov. 18th.	Bois de Lessines area.
Nov. 21st.	Enghien—Saintes area. On the 22nd most of the officers and a few O.R. were sent in by lorry to Brussels to witness the state entry by King Albert.
Nov. 23rd.	Braine le Chateau—Braine l'Alleud. Here our close proximity to the battle-field of Waterloo was taken advantage of on Sunday 24th for a large percentage of the personnel to visit it.
Nov. 25th.	Chestre—Court St. Etienne.
Nov. 27th.	Grand Leez—Tourinnes St. Lambert.
Nov. 28th.	Bierwart—Forville—Seron.
Nov. 29th.	Stree—Tihange.
Nov. 30th.	Mont—Comblain au Pont—Comblain la Tour.
Dec. 4th.	Aywaille.
Dec. 5th.	Francoorscamp—Stavelot.
Dec. 6th.	Crossed the frontier to Malmedy.
Dec. 7th.	Montjoie.
Dec. 8th.	Schmidt—Kommersheidt.
Dec. 9th.	Zulpich—Froitzheim.
Dec. 10th.	Hürth—Gleuel—Berrenrath.
Dec. 13th.	Marched past Lt.-Genl. Sir Claud Jacob, commanding the II Corps, whilst crossing the Rhine in Cologne by the Hohenzollern Bridge. Billeted in the Dellbruck...Gronau area.

On December 21st all units moved into their winter billets. With the exception of " B " Battery, R.H.A., which remained under the orders of the G.O.C. 87th Infantry Brigade, and which was billetted at Witzhelden, the whole D.A. was accommodated in Bergisch Gladbach and the neighbouring village of Paffrath. Bergisch Gladbach civil administrative area became a sub-area under the jurisdiction of the C.R.A. whose headquarters were at the mansion of Frau Olga Zanders in the centre of the town.

1919.

A football league was started for batteries and similar units in the D.A. As there were 21 teams competing, including No. 1 Co. of the Divisional Train, the league was split up into two, the winners of each competing in the final. " B " R.H.A. managed to get through the competition without losing a match and were easily top of their section, whilst D/38 were the winners in the other section. The final between these two batteries left "B " R.H.A. the winners of the silver medals. This battery had been in the final of every football competition organized in the D.A. since the Gallipoli landing, but had never before been fortunate enough to win. The medals were presented to the winners by Lt.-Genl. Sir Claud Jacob, commanding the II Corps.

With the exception of a change of billets between " B " and "L " Batteries in January, units remained in the same places until reduced to cadre shortly before being sent home.

In March, 1919, the 15th Brigade, R.H.A., had a most successful small steeplechase meeting.

On April 1st, 1919, the death knell of the 29th D.A. was sounded, as the 29th Division was then converted into the " Southern" Division of the Army of the Rhine. With the exception of the D.A.C. all the units disappeared in the course of the next few weeks.

APPENDIX III.

Copies of some of the congratulatory messages received by the 29th Divisional Artillery.

1.

From Lieut.-Col. H. T. Beckwith, Commanding 88th Infantry Brigade, 26.4.17.

"I beg to report the splendid gallantry of the Royal Artillery which was in action on April 23rd between Monchy village and the Arras—Cambrai road, about N 12 b. Though continually swept by concentrated enemy's shell fire and shrapnel the guns were served almost continually, which probably had a material effect in enabling our line to be held at various somewhat critical junctures."

The above letter was forwarded to the C.R.A. by the Divisional Commander with the following remarks :—

"This report is most gratifying. Please convey to the units concèrned my appreciation of this fine conduct."

2.

From Major General C. J. Deverell, Commanding 3rd Division, to C.R.A. 3rd Division, 19.6.17.

"Will you please convey to all the artillery under your command the thanks and appreciation of all in the 3rd Division for the splendid co-operation and assistance given during the operations 13th to 19th June 1917.

The large share in our success which is attributable to all our supporting batteries is fully realized. Their constant protection and immediate readiness was invaluable, and we should be glad if every officer and man could be assured how much his individual effort has contributed to the important success gained, and to the severe loss which must have been inflicted on the enemy.

We wish them all good fortune in the future and hope that we may again fight together with the close co-operation which has been so conspicuously marked whilst we have been together.

This letter was forwarded to the 29th Divisional Artillery by Brig.-Genl. Ollivant, C.R.A. 3rd Division, with the following remarks :—

"It is with great pleasure that I forward the attached letter from the G.O.C. 3rd Division. I have already written to you to express my personal thanks to the artillery supporting the division."

3.

From the 35th Division 31st October, 1917.

"Major General Franks wishes me to convey to you his appreciation of the thorough manner in which the 29th Divisional Artillery supported this Division during the recent battle on the borders of the Houthulst Forest.

He would be glad if you will express his thanks to the officers and other ranks whose untiring efforts produced such excellent results."

4.

From Major General Sir Sydney Lawford, Commanding 41st Division, to the C.R.A., May 15th, 1918.

"With the utmost regret at the departure of you and all under your command, I wish you all possible good wishes for the future. Thank you so much for all you have done during the 6 weeks you have been with us. I am sure that liaison and co-operation between artillery and infantry could not have been closer or with better feeling on all occasions. Would you let your people have the enclosed message "*

* No copy of this message is now available, unfortunately.

5.

From Brig.-Genl. A. D. Kirby, Commanding R.A. II Corps, 17th May, 1918.

"I am sorry that opportunity did not permit me to thank personally all your Colonels and Battery Commanders for their good work when with the II Corps. Would you please tell Spedding, Burne and Murray how much I appreciated the work of their units. I also want to say what a pleasure it is to me and my staff to work with you and your staff: always cheery and ready to help the show in every way. I can't say how much my H.A. and C.B. people appreciated your Divisional Artillery Staff and the help you gave and the interest you took in their work. Good luck to you all."

6.

From Brig.-Genl. G. R. M. Cheape, Commanding 86th Infantry Brigade, 4th June, 1918.

"The 2/Royal Fusiliers and 1/Royal Dublin Fusiliers wish to express their admiration on the barrage fired by you on the night of 2nd/3rd June. They state that it was absolutely perfect and that there was not a single short.

Officers and men who have many times advanced under a barrage state that they never saw one like it and hope that when next they "go over" they will be covered by the same brigades."

7.

Extracts from two private letters received on the 27th June 1918 by the C.R.A.

(a)   From Brig.-Genl. S. C. Taylor, Commanding 93rd Infantry Brigade.

"Will you thank your officers and men for their splendid co-operation last night which made the show so successful. The men who went over are loud in their praises of the barrage and the half drowned Boche prisoners who stood up to their necks in the Becque in order to avoid it are equally loud in damning it!"

(b)   From Lieut.-Col. G. D. Wauhope, Commanding 13th Bn. York & Lancaster Regt.

"With the barrage you gave us we had a straight run and all the men were awfully pleased with it, the best they have seen yet."

8.

Two extracts from official letters with reference to the operations of the 31st Division on June 28th, 1918.

(i)   From Lieut.-Genl. Sir Robert Haking, Commanding XI Corps, to the G.OC. 31st Division.

"The action of the Artillery throughout was most carefully planned by Brigadier General Johnson, and all ranks of the Field Artillery of 29th and 30th Divisions and 28th Army Brigade deserve great credit for the manner in which they supported the attack."

(ii)   From Major General J. Campbell, Commanding 31st Division, to the C.R.A. and others.

"I wish to thank you and the officers, N.C.O's and men under your command for the splendid work that has been done during the recent operations, and to congratulate all ranks on the succes obtained.

There were difficulties which had to be contended with in the preparations, owing to the short time available, but they were overcome by the kneenness and goodwill of all ranks.

I particularly wish to thank the Artillery of the 29th Division, 30th Division and 28th Army Brigade R.F.A., for their ever ready and timely support."

9.

From Brig.-Genl. Cheape, Commanding 86th Infantry Brigade 19th August 1918.

"My infantry wish to express their admiration for the most perfect barrage which you put up to-day during our attack.   There were no shorts and it was like walking behind a 'wall'."

10.

Private letter from Brig.-Genl. Godfrey Gillson, G.O.C. R.A. Xth Corps, to the C.R.A. 4th August, 1918.

"Just a line to congratulate you and the 29th Divisional Artillery on the really excellent show they put up at your ceremonial parade the other day. I have seen a good many of them in my time but should not have thought it possible to get such results under our present conditions. To me it was a real treat to see all ranks sitting up and looking so proud of themselves. They have indeed a good right to do so after the last four years. Good luck to you all."

FINIS.